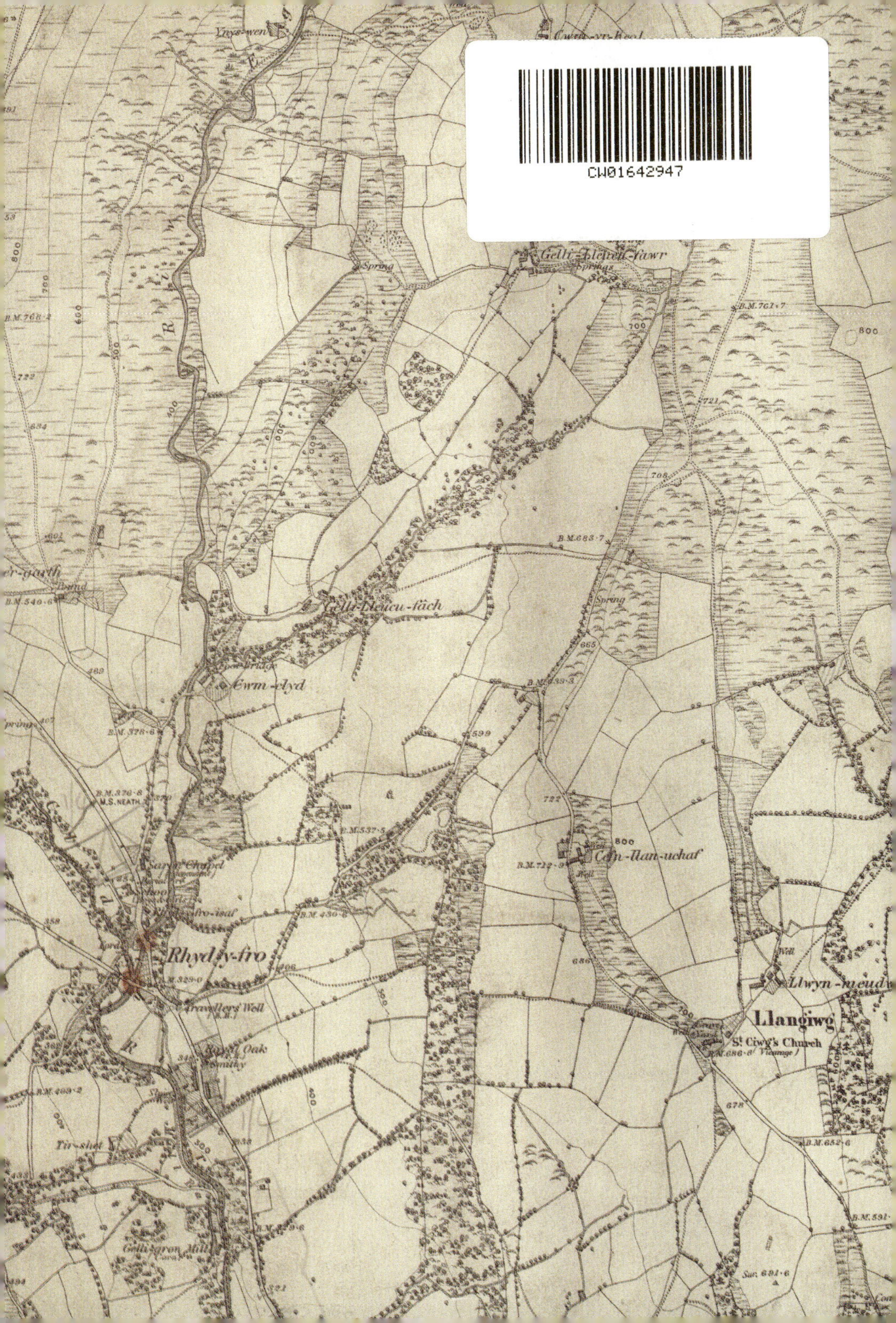

Ynys-wen
Gelli-lleucu-fawr
Gelli-lleucu-fach
Cwm-clyd
Rhyd-y-fro
Travellers' Well
Royal Oak
Cwm-llan-uchaf
Llangiwg
St Ciwg's Church
Gelli-gron Mill

Penrhydd-wen
Coedcae-mawr
Garth
Garth-eithin
Mountain Gate
Coal Levels
Carn Llecharth
(Stone Circle)
Gelli-leiog-uchaf
Cwm-bryn
Coal Level
Coal Levels
Water Wheel
LLECHARTH
G D W Y
D A C H
Acres
7703·947

Publications of the South Wales Record Society

General Editor: Professor Ray Howell

No. 27

THE DIARIES OF
MARGARET PENDEREL JONES OF GARTH
1871 TO 1897

Margaret Penderel Jones (1833-1898)
(Photo: courtesy of Mrs J. Morris)

The Diaries of Margaret Penderel Jones of Garth 1871 to 1897

Edited by

P. W. Jackson

Newport:
South Wales Record Society
2014

Published by the South Wales Record Society
1 Fields Park Avenue, Newport, NP20 5BG

First published 2014

ISBN 978-0-9553387-6-4 (South Wales Record Society)

Printed in Wales by
Dinefwr Press Ltd., Llandybie, Carmarthenshire, SA18 3YD

Dedicated
to the memory of
my beloved wife
Audrey

CONTENTS

LIST OF ILLUSTRATIONS

PREFACE

The diaries of Margaret Penderel Jones provide a personal and unique record of the life of a spinster lady who was born in 1833 to a farming family in south west Wales and later inherited three farms, several cottages and a colliery from her father. Her diaries are reproduced in their entirety and are supplemented by a selection of her correspondence and with data from her various account books. As these documents were private and confidential Margaret wrote with an unaffected candour about her daily activities, the mundane and significant events, her pleasures and problems and her interaction with the many individuals who peopled her days. Central to her life was her young cousin and companion Lizzie who provided the emotional support of a caring family. Margaret was also a landowner with responsibilities for her tenanted farms, rented cottages and a leased colliery, and her frequently problematic financial relationships with these assets were all meticulously noted. From her writings, which span much of the last quarter of the nineteenth century, emerges a dynamic tableau of the rural, commercial and industrial life of her community and its inhabitants during a challenging period of increasing social and occupational mobility.

Transcription

The diaries have been transcribed verbatim, preserving Margaret's variable spelling, punctuation and frequent use of abbreviations and capital letters, but her customary use of the 'long s', as *mifs* for *miss*, has been replaced by its modern equivalent. All prices and costs are expressed in pre-decimal currency and the Imperial system is used for units of length, area, capacity and weight.

ACKNOWLEDGEMENTS

Throughout the process of editing the diaries I have been greatly encouraged by the enthusiasm of Jenny and John Morris who have been generous hosts on my several visits to Garth and to the farms which comprised the nineteenth century estate. I have also valued the expertise and continuing friendship of Professor Emeritus Gwynedd Pierce whose response to my many questions has been immediate and comprehensive. I have benefited too from the help given by Pontardawe historians Jeff Childs, whose wide knowledge of local land ownership has been invaluable, and Keri Thomas, whose processing of the older photographs has been much appreciated. I am also indebted to Kim Collis and his staff at the West Glamorgan Archive Service for their considerable practical help and guidance. The onerous task of word-processing the diaries and of coping with many amendments to layout and presentation was fulfilled with great patience and forbearance by Beth James and I cannot thank her adequately for her care and professionalism. Finally, this project could not have been completed without the unwavering support and encouragement of my daughter Caroline, my grand-daughter Catherine and my son-in-law David who singly and collectively have provided a sustaining and loving environment during an emotionally difficult time. I owe them all a great debt of gratitude. For all errors and misinterpretations I am solely responsible.

PETER JACKSON
1st February 2014

INTRODUCTION

The Garth Estate

The property which provides the location for this study is known locally as Garth and derives its name from its position on the slope of Garth mountain.[1] Garth comprises the main house, a farmhouse, cottage, lodge, outbuildings, orchards and a kitchen garden, and overlooks the Upper Clydach river and the main road from Pontardawe to Gwauncaegurwen. The origin of the house is not documented but surviving wall foundations have suggested the presence of a habitation on the site in the fifteenth century and rent, land tax and tithe records provide a chronology of ownership and occupation from 1584. In 1810 the Garth estate came into the ownership of Richard Jones and on his death in 1823 was transferred to his wife Margaret. Neither was documented in the land tax assessments as 'Occupier' until their son Evan Jones was named as both 'Landowner' and 'Occupier' in the assessment for 1830. Family papers indicate that Evan and his younger brother David inherited a number of properties in Breconshire, Carmarthenshire and Glamorgan from their father, with Evan acquiring Garth House and its farm, Gelliluog Isaf farm in the neighbouring village of Rhyd-y-fro and Cwmllynfell farm with entitlement to the mineral rights of Cwmllynfell colliery. David Jones inherited several farms and small-holdings in Carmarthenshire.

Evan Jones of Garth married Catherine Pendrill of Pontardawe Cottage in Llangiwg [Llanguicke] parish church on 22 March 1831. She was the daughter of Richard Pendrill of Neath who from about 1808 had been the resident agent to the Gough Aubrey family at their Ynyscedwyn estate in Ystradgynlais. Evan and Catherine had one child, Margaret, who was born on 2 September 1833 and, apart from her education in Clifton, Bristol, between 1848 and 1851, she lived all her life in Garth. After her mother's death in 1857 Margaret assumed control of the household and became her father's main support. His death in 1864 was "*indeed an irreparable loss, for never was there a better Father or one more devoted to his child than mine.*"[2]

Margaret was the sole beneficiary of all her father's "*real and personal property, estates and effects . . . absolutely and forever as her own sole and*

The young Margaret dressed in mourning
(Photo: courtesy of Mrs J. Morris)

separate property free from the control, debts, engagements or interference of any Husband with whom she may hereafter intermarry."[3] She thus became the owner of Garth House, several cottages and the three tenanted farms of Garth (141 acres), Gelliluog Isaf (74 acres) and Cwmllynfell (120 acres) with its mineral resources. Whilst her inheritance conferred authority, financial security and social status, Margaret would also have been aware that ownership necessitated her acceptance of personal responsibility for the control and co-ordination of her widespread properties. She had assimilated practical lessons in land management and domestic economy from her parents and had also acquired a deep-seated suspicion of the venality and trustworthiness of the lessees of Cwmllynfell colliery, which occupied several acres of her land. With no husband 'to obey and serve' and no suggestion of marriage and a family to absorb her time and energy, Margaret was now obliged to ensure the optimal profitability of her various fixed assets.

Garth House and its farm were located in the ecclesiastical parish of Llangiwg which experienced considerable growth in its population during the nineteenth century owing to the development and extension of collieries, tinplate, iron and steel works. The decennial census returns for the parish (including parts of Pontardawe, Godre'rgraig and Ystalyfera) showed a population increase from 829 in 1801 to 4229 in 1851, and to 8312 by 1871, by which time Llangiwg was described as "*a very extensive and populous parish, situated on the western side of the valley, and extending to the boundary of the county, where it is joined by Brecon. The distance from Swansea to the first part of the parish is 7 miles, but the extreme limits are 12 miles . . . it is divided into four hamlets – viz. Mawr, Alltgrug, Egel and Caegurwen . . . The church of St. Cuik, or Guick, is an old stone building in the Norman style, and consists of nave and tower, with 2 bells, and, being on the top of a hill, is a very imposing object. The living is a vicarage, yearly value £300, in the gift of the Lord Bishop of St. David's, and held by the Rev. David Jones . . .*"[4] Below the church was Rhyd-y-fro which, according to Margaret's description in 1876, was a village of "*29 Houses, comprising 2 Shops, 2 Public Houses, 1 Smithy, 1 Woollen factory, 2 Flannel Weavers, and a Corn Mill close by . . . situated at a place where 4 Parish roads concentrate, and the Turnpike road from the Borough of Neath Glamorganshire, to Llandeilo, one of the County Towns of Carmarthenshire, passes through thereby indicating its central and accessible position*".

Apart from the industrial communities which were rapidly developing along the Swansea Valley and the close proximity of Pontardawe as a tinplate town, the district around Garth was largely rural in character with many of its farms scattered in the surrounding hills and dating from the sixteenth and seventeenth centuries.[5] Given the largely mountainous nature of the terrain with vast open moorland slopes, pastoral farming predominated. Although not a principal landowner in the district, Margaret Jones was nevertheless regarded as a lady of property and, from her family's long association with the social, religious and economic life of the area, her transmitted status and inherited wealth accorded her considerable respect and deference from all levels of society. As the mistress of Garth, Margaret was aware of her position in local society and proud of her landed heritage and of her Penderel lineage with its heroic royal association (see Appendices 1 and 5).

The Archive of Margaret Penderel Jones

From 1871 to 1897 Margaret Jones kept a record of the daily events and incidents which she saw as significant in annual editions of *Lett's Rough Diary or Scribbling Journal*, with three days allocated to each foolscap page and Sunday being restricted to 3 lines. Eighteen of her diaries for these 27 years have survived and together they evoke an age when social relationships were hierarchically stratified and the ownership of land conferred privilege and responsibility. Her diary entries, written in a clear and unaffected style, refer to the seasonal and daily routines of her household and estate, the maintenance of her property and the physical environment, the dynamics of domestic life, visits to and from her relatives, friends and neighbours, the employment of full-time and occasional staff, purchase of consumable items (particularly of house coal and of beer, fortified wines and spirits), payment of taxes, tithes, rates and rents and her frequent trips to Swansea and the more leisurely excursions to holiday locations. All were noted with a disciplined regularity and, being personal and confidential entries, were expressed with candour and a lack of pretension.

Her diaries were essentially domestic and local records and, whilst not unaware of the many crucial national and international events which occurred during these decades of social and political upheaval, Margaret's diary entries were almost invariably confined to her personal, social and physical environments and rarely referred to any issue which did not directly concern her. More regrettable is the omission from the diaries of information pertaining to the working of Margaret's separate farms. Their location and topography remain unchanged but the physical difficulties of extracting a livelihood from substantial areas of marginal and scrub land, the working of the fields, the crops planted, livestock reared and the productivity of her tenants are not recorded.

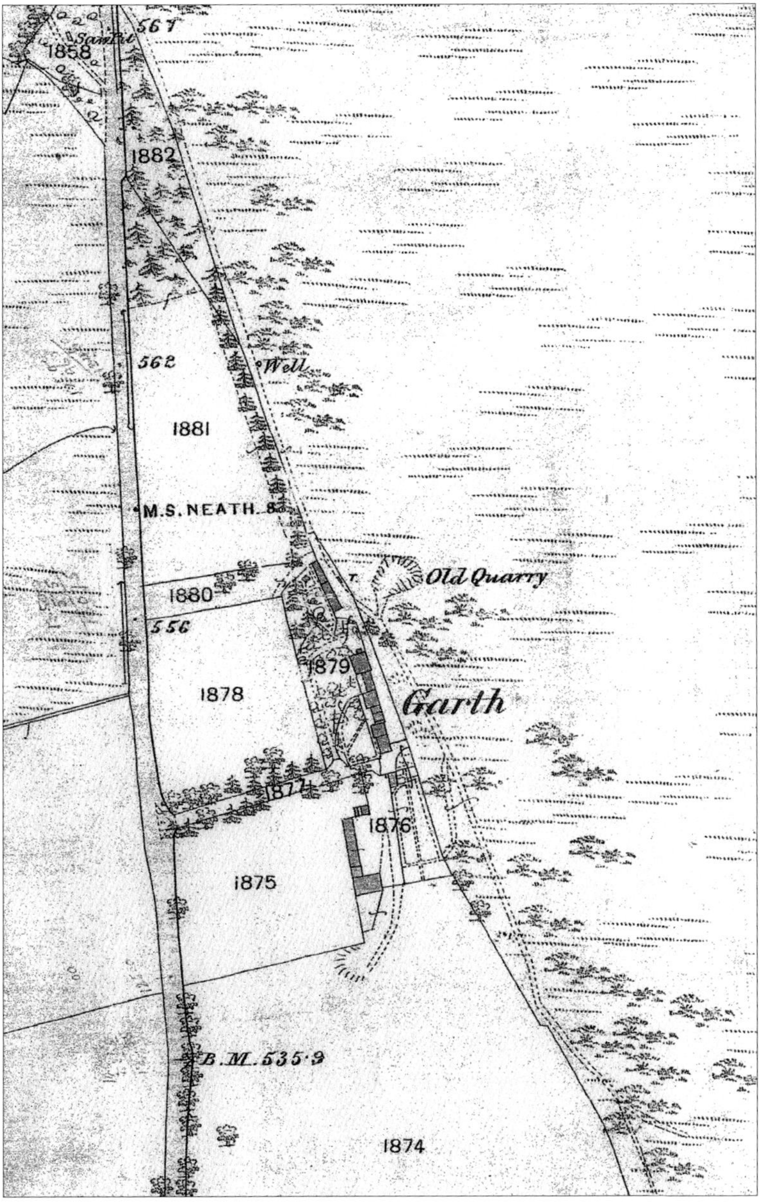

Garth House and Farm as shown on the First Edition 25-inch Ordnance Survey map of circa 1878

Margaret delegated full responsibility for farm management to her tenants and confined herself almost exclusively to her role as rentier, noting only the payment and arrears of rent. In contrast, the proximity of Garth House to Garth Farm permitted frequent references to seasonal work in Garth's fields and around her personal enclave, with diary entries recording when hay was mowed and gathered, trees planted, fields manured and limed, potatoes set, parsnips, turnips, vetches and oats sowed, and garden vegetables, flowers and shrubs planted. There were also regular reports of her output of dairy products and their sale, but details of the farms' livestock and land usage are not described. Replying to a summons served on her by the Pontardawe magistrates on 20 April 1883 Margaret revealed that her stock was restricted to two cows, a bull calf and a horse.[6]

In addition to her diaries Margaret's archive contains an uncatalogued miscellany of documents. She was a prolific letter writer and many of her first drafts and duplicates of letters have survived. She also kept itemised accounts of payments and receipts, records of rents collected and deferred, dairy production of salt butter, cream and cheese and day books listing hourly payments to her workers. Her early school copybook from 1848 provides examples of her precocious fluency, with descriptive exercises and drafts of her weekly letters home to "*My Dearest Mamma*", written in a tutored cursive style which was later abandoned in her diaries. She also retained much of her incoming correspondence and many of these letters, some still in their stamped envelopes, from friends and relatives complement her own writings and serve to illustrate the considerable interchange of correspondence which took place before the local introduction of the telephone. From these sources an impression of several key attributes of Margaret's character emerge: she was a forceful, independent, practical, active, sociable and influential person, respected by local society, admired by her circle of friends and regarded with considerable affection by her extended family of relatives.

Margaret's diaries, correspondence, notebooks, photographs and *cartes de visite* constitute a uniquely personal commentary on the activities, pleasures and tribulations of her daily life. She recorded the significant and mundane details of her interactions and relationships with the many individuals who inhabited different spheres of her life and she also revealed the difficulties of attempting to monitor the management of those who were responsible for her various sources of income. Both her social and financial environments provide the main underlying themes of her narrative.

Margaret's Social Environment

The census of April 1871 contains details of the people who lived in Garth House and its environs at the time when Margaret was writing the first of her surviving diaries. The census enumerator listed Margaret as unmarried, aged 37 and a landowner. Also in residence were her first cousin Elizabeth Jones (aged 18), her general servant Elizabeth Evans (45) and her maiden aunt Gwenllian Price (65) who was visiting for a few days from her home in Tretower near Milford in Pembrokeshire. Elizabeth Jones, invariably referred to as Lizzie, was Margaret's constant companion and, with an age difference of nearly 18 years, was regarded more as a surrogate daughter than a cousin. Her servant Elizabeth Evans, always called Betty, was another permanent if sometimes annoying presence and she gave Margaret forty-one years of devoted service.

At this time Garth House was an unpretentious stone-built structure in an imposing location. On the ground floor was a hallway, off which were a parlour and a drawing room, both overlooking a front lawn down to the main road from Pontardawe to Gwauncaegurwen and the Upper Clydach river below and up to the panoramic heights of Carn Llechart mountain. At the rear of the house was a small dining room which faced the steep slope of Garth mountain. On the first floor were four bedrooms, including Margaret's White Room, and over the stairs in the attic were two small bed spaces for the female domestic servants. An open courtyard led to the kitchen, dominated by an iron range with a coal fire, water boiler and bread oven, and to a dairy, larder and lamp room. Above the kitchen were sleeping quarters for the two male servants. Unlike the mansions of local industrialists and landowners of larger estates, the house contained few domestic comforts. There was no internal water tap, every room was heated by coal fires and lit by candles and oil lamps. Mountain water was collected in pitchers from a pipe (which Margaret referred to as the "*pistle*" for the Welsh *pistyll*) embedded in a retaining wall in the back lane. An outside closet with two wooden seats had been erected over a mountain stream among the trees below the same back lane. Apart from necessary maintenance and redecoration there was no upgrading of the structural amenities of the house during the remainder of the century. Between the house and the farm were stables, sheds and a small coach house, and beyond these were the farmyard and large stone barns for keeping hay, animals and machinery.

In the next door property, referred to variously as Garth Lodge or Garth Farm in the census returns from 1851 to 1891, lived John Day (50) who was the tenant farmer of Margaret's land, his wife Anne (31) and their two sons, Charles (12) and James (8), and six others. These included John's father James

Garth House
(Photo: D. M. Bateson)

Garth dairy and farm
(Photo: D. M. Bateson)

(78), a widower and 'annuitant' (i.e. funded by an annuity from a trust or investment), an unmarried niece Mary Arnold (25), who was a dressmaker by trade, an unmarried general servant Mary Ward (66), a young farm servant Thomas Willis (17), a visitor William Adams (45) who was a labourer in the tin works and his daughter Elizabeth Anne aged 4. With the exception of young Elizabeth Anne, all the occupants of John Day's home were English incomers, having been born in Devon.

The daily activities described in the early diaries mainly revolved around Margaret, Lizzie, Betty and John Day, with walk-on parts for a miscellany of others. These included workmen and servants, relatives and close friends, family members of local tenant farmers and landowners, industrialists, clergymen, solicitors and medical practitioners, together comprising a dynamic tapestry of social interaction. Despite Garth's relatively remote location there was a constant flow of callers with Margaret at the hub of this network of people who represented a cross-section of the middle and lower classes of society. She was conscious of her gentrified status in a predominantly working class and deferential society and expected as her customary right the observance of a code of behaviour which was rooted in tradition and respect for her position. In her first diary over eighty visitors were separately identified and whilst many provided some service to her and the estate, only a select few appear to have been regarded as equals and to provide her with interactive and affective pleasure. Prominent among these were the families of substantial landowner Herbert Lloyd of Plas Cilybebyll, of the industrialists William Gilbertson of Ynysderw and his son Arthur of Glanrhyd, and several others representing the professional and commercial strata of society. It was a cohesive and mutually supportive class-based structure and one within which Margaret moved with an easy acceptance.

Of especial importance to her were the Jenkins family who lived in Bryn Syfi House in Swansea and the Price family who lived in Glan Twrch House in Ystalyfera. Bryn Syfi was built around 1830 on the south facing slope of Kilvey Hill, overlooking the terraced streets of Swansea's St. Thomas area and the constantly busy railway sidings and docks. Beyond the clamour of activity was the panoramic sweep of Swansea Bay from Mumbles lighthouse in the west to the industrialising areas of Neath and Aberavon in the east and, on a clear day, the distant outline of the Devonshire coast. The head of that household in 1871 was John Borlase Jenkins, a bachelor aged 47 who was the owner of the Dinas Brick Company outside the neighbouring town of Neath. His refractory firebricks made of silica and lime were in constant demand for lining the many iron, copper and later steel furnaces throughout south Wales

Bryn Syfi House
(Photo: West Glamorgan Archive Service)

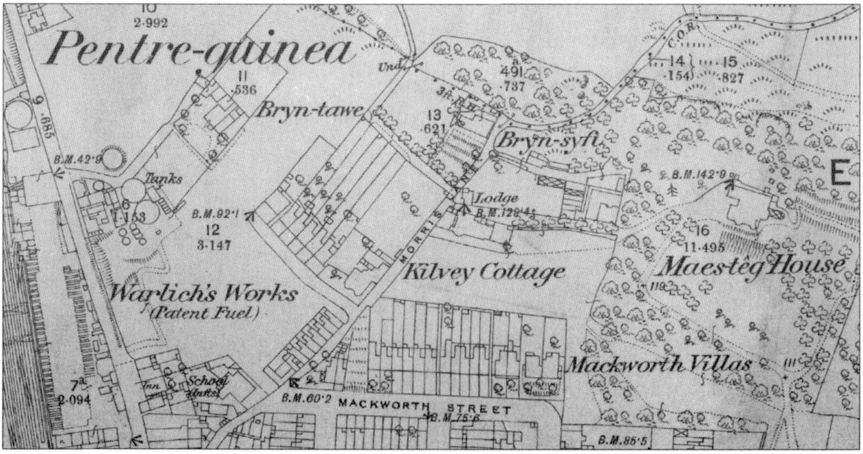

Location of Bryn Syfi House in St Thomas, Swansea, from the First Edition 25-inch Ordnance Survey map of 1879

and further afield. Living with him in Bryn Syfi were his two elder spinster sisters Mary, aged 60 and listed as housekeeper, and Rachel (56). There was one young female general servant. All had been born locally in Llansamlet or Swansea. Their nearest neighbours along the same contour of Kilvey Hill in Maesteg House was the family of the eminent Pascoe St. Leger Grenfell, the wealthy owner of the Middle and Upper Bank Copper Works in the Lower Swansea Valley.[7] Margaret's regular visits and frequent overnight stays at Bryn Syfi were welcome diversions from the daily routine at Garth and its bucolic serenity, and afforded her the opportunity to shop in Swansea's many stores for clothes and domestic supplies which were not available in such diversity or quality in Pontardawe. Her visits also allowed her to consult John's brother, solicitor Richard Jenkins in York Street, and to obtain medical and dental treatment for her persistent physical ailments.

Her other favourite venue was Glan Twrch House in Ystalyfera where Penderel descendant Dr. William Price, J.P., M.D. and his family lived (see Appendix 3). Unlike Bryn Syfi's vista over Swansea's commercial eastside, their home was set in a sylvan location in the upper reaches of the Swansea Valley and was described in 1871 as "*a very pretty residence, between the rivers Twrch and Tawe, with extensive grounds and romantic walks . . . beautiful views of the valley, the hills of Breconshire, with some magnificent woodland scenery*".[8] Dr. Price, aged 68 in 1871, had an established reputation as a medical practitioner and was the brother of the Gwenllian Price noted earlier. He and his wife Mary (59), a cousin of the Jenkins family of Bryn Syfi, had two unmarried daughters, Jane (24) and Dora (23). Visiting them on census day was Ellen Lloyd (20), the second daughter of wealthy landowner Francis Edwardes Lloyd of Plas Cilybebyll and who, in the following year, was to marry Arthur Gilbertson, heir to the growing Pontardawe iron, tinplate and galvanising works and a future major steel manufacturer. Margaret's frequent visits to Bryn Syfi and Glan Twrch provided her with many pleasurable interludes and served to reinforce the close kinship bonds which were important alternative substitutes for the intimacy and satisfactions of a family of her own. She shared their lives and their meetings were all recorded in the diaries and further supplemented by the many letters which passed between them.

By 1871 Margaret was an accepted member of the local rural gentry. She had been in sole charge of Garth for six years and was a prominent and commandingly conspicuous presence in the district, whether riding her pony or attracting attention in her monogrammed phaeton driven by her liveried coachman. Portrait albums provide additional information and show her to have been tall and slimly built, whilst her surviving tailored dresses have a 26" waist and a length of 5'8". Finely attired in the most fashionable styles of the time she presented the outward appearance of an elegant, if somewhat austere, lady. Beyond the sombre assurance conveyed by the camera's lens, however, was a physically vulnerable woman who was partially crippled. Whether her disability was congenital or acquired from an early accident is nowhere recorded nor is its severity, but the earlier diaries contain several references to her need to wear a built-up shoe and leather sheathed leg irons. She walked with a limp but her mobility does not appear to have been greatly affected, for there are numerous references to walks she undertook and she was capable of riding her pony to Llangiwg Church and to the neighbouring village of Rhyd-y-fro. There are, however, many diary references to her illnesses and painful episodes. Family hearsay suggests that Margaret may have suffered from epilepsy, but there is no written corroboration of such a condition. Occasionally an entry recording an illness is accompanied by a marginal code of several dots whose purpose may have been to note the recurrence of an irregular episode which was too private or personally sensitive to describe even in her confidential diary. Speculation as to their meaning is fruitless, but she recorded every bodily ailment including recurrent toothache which imposed further stress on what appears to have been a generally fragile constitution. Her frequent and early rejection of invitations to formal social gatherings, such as wedding receptions, on the grounds of her expectation of illness at the designated time, might suggest her foreboding of possible embarrassment, physical discomfort or a chronic lack of confidence stemming from her poor general health.

Margaret never married but there is evidence to suggest an early and close friendship with a naval surgeon named Daniel Saunders from Llandovery who was a trusted friend of Margaret's father. Two of his letters to Margaret in 1860 have survived, the first expressing such endearing sentiments as "*my dearest Margaret*", "*you little incorrigible tease*", "*my little charmer*" and a declaration which possibly implies a developing affection, despite what he perceived to be Margaret's "*cautious and reserved*" response: "*You naughty but dear little girl, in spite of all I have told you, still will obstinately persist in measuring my affection by your own – such must be the case – for you do really very far moderate mine – you cannot my dear short little thing in common reason compare the feeling of affection of a few days growth only – with that which has been the growth of years – deeply and maturely formed – daily gaining in strength until perfectly established, so much now as to form a part of my very existence . . .*". Margaret's reply appears to have encouraged him to hope and prompted him to respond in his second letter "*that monosyllable 'Hope'! cheers me wonderfully.*"[9] Unfortunately there is no further correspondence to clarify

Daniel Saunders, Surgeon RN
(Photo: courtesy of Mrs J. Morris)

the possible continuation of the relationship but in Margaret's archive were photographs of Daniel and copies of memorials of his death on active service in July 1865 which extol his "Heroism in rescuing a wounded Marine" and his "noble Self-devotion and Gallantry". Enclosed with his second letter was his photograph, separately wrapped in plain paper and bearing in his handwriting Elizabeth I's motto *Semper Eadem*, possibly a declaration of his promise to Margaret to be 'Always the Same'.[10]

Following Daniel's death there appear to have been no marriage suitors and Margaret remained a spinster throughout her life. While she may have been appreciative of the blessings which married life could bestow, she expressed no musing regrets of her spinster status in her writings. Unlike many middle-class Victorian ladies, Margaret was untrammelled by the need to subordinate herself to a husband and a family of children and had the freedom and financial security to live an independent life. She was the mistress of her home and a prominent landowner, and employed servants for all household chores and tenants to work her farms.

Margaret and her cousin Lizzie

Living with Margaret, possibly for companionship since Margaret's father's death, was her young cousin Lizzie. Almost eighteen years her junior, Lizzie was treated as a much-loved surrogate daughter, the lodestar of Margaret's life and her abiding concern. As the daughter of a landowner and farmer, Lizzie had no formal training for any occupation and is only occasionally recorded as physically working in the kitchen, dairy or garden. She appears to have lived a generally leisured and indulged life and filled her days in Margaret's company or in visiting her widowed father at Llwynyronnen Farm, Betws, or practising her needlework skills. Freed from the need to work for a living and unprepared by privilege, education or expectation for any utilitarian activity, Margaret and Lizzie might have succumbed to the boredom and frustration of weary days and empty evenings which are alleged to have been the lot of many middle-class ladies.[11] However, the diary entries suggest a lifestyle which was fulfilling and varied and there were few hints of any domestic tension which might have threatened their close relationship. Their bond of affection was that of a doting mother for her favourite daughter and was always caring, supportive and unconditional. In a letter to Lizzie on 4 November 1871 Margaret outlined her precepts for a virtuous life:

> *"I hope you are a good & steady girl & doing nothing that I would disapprove of now you are out of my sight. Remember that by the fruit*

Lizzie Jones
(Photo: courtesy of Mrs J. Morris)

the tree is known & you are now of an age for people to judge of your character by your manner, conversation & general conduct & perhaps thereby make a lasting impression of your future life. So be careful & bear in mind that one wrong action cracks the confidence as successfully as one hand knock cracks the China Vase – it will be a blemish to the end. Always carry in your every thought & action the tonic of a wholesome pride that will never stoop to any thing mean or degrading & shun as you would a poison the idea of any thing that is not strictly just & honourable. Be guided with whom you associate, never forget that 'a Man is known by the company he keeps' & that 'a good name is better than wealth'. Better alone than in bad company is an old & true saying.

You will think I am giving you a scolding – I am not, it is only that I greatly wish to impress upon you, that it is entirely in your own power whether now, when you are about stepping from the little girl into the young woman you wish to be considered & looked upon as a steady, well behaved, sensible girl who respects herself & by that means commands respect from others, or spoken of as silly, thoughtless, ill mannered girl who cares not what people say or think as long as she can gratify her own whims & fancies.

If you choose the good path you will always find in me a kind & sincere friend. Since you have lived with me I have at all times endeavoured to set you a good example & to give you good advice & to see you reward my efforts by shining forth a bright example of every thing that is good & noble, will be to crown my advancing years with the only happiness this world can now give.

If you take the road that leads to evil you will when too late repent the choice for your own sake, and in the mean while bitterly grieve the heart of your Cousin Margaret who has, as far as she was able, given you the care of a Mother."

Margaret's birthday gift to Lizzie on her twenty-fourth birthday in 1875 was a book entitled *Maternal Counsels to a Daughter.*[12] Her card on Lizzie's twenty-sixth birthday was inscribed: "*For dear little Liz with Mother's best love*" (7/7/1877). A measure of the depth of her feelings for her young cousin was occasionally more lovingly articulated. Saved among Margaret's possessions is an undated Valentine card with the dedication: "*For darling Lizzie with Margaret's affectionate love*" and its verse, entitled 'My Little Blossom', was unequivocally sentimental: "I honour manhood's glory,/I bow to woman's grace,/I love the tell-tale blushes/That flush sweet girlhood's face./But dearer far than these things/Oh! dearer far to me/Than all the things this side of heaven/The love I bear to thee!" A diary entry in 1880, during a painful illness when Margaret had been diagnosed with a life-threatening ovarian tumour, expressed a mother's anguish, heightened by an awareness of her mortality, for one who she perceived to be her dependent daughter: "*I believe my time on earth is very short. Poor dear little Liz. I wish to live for her sake for she will be a lonely little waif without her old Mam & this World is a cold one*" (4/1/1880). There is only one surviving letter in which Lizzie referred to Margaret as her *Mam* but on her birthday in July 1883, just six months before her marriage, Lizzie colluded in this innocent pretence by ending her letters to Margaret with the subscription "*I am my dear Margaret/ Your affectionate little girl*" (7/1/1883). The "*little girl*" was then 32 years of age.

Margaret and Lizzie were regarded by all as *de facto* mother and daughter and when one of Lizzie's male admirers, the Rev. Nathaniel Thomas, curate of Pontardawe and Llangiwg churches from 1874 to 1878, expressed an interest in establishing a closer relationship, Margaret proved to be a cautious guardian and forbade him to write to Lizzie after his transfer to another parish. Lizzie's most persistent suitor was Thomas Jones, the son of a Llandeilo brewer, and when he sought Margaret's permission to marry Lizzie, Margaret's letters to him in October 1878 were politely discouraging. She finally relented, however, and when Lizzie married Thomas Jones in Llangiwg Church on 10 January 1884, Margaret was one of the witnessing signatories. As with many a doting parent, she possibly signed the marriage certificate with an outward show of happiness diluted by the poignant realisation of her own impending solitude. She was now to lose her *affectionate little girl* when Lizzie left Garth to become mistress of her own home in Llandeilo. They would thereafter occupy separate spheres and no longer would she have Lizzie's constantly reassuring and dependable presence to support her nor to fill the long hours with intimate conversations and reminiscences of shared experiences. Although she was not socially isolated in Garth, Margaret was now required to endure the forlorn loneliness of separation from the one comforting love in her life.

Several weeks after Lizzie's marriage, Margaret wrote to Lizzie to confirm the transfer of domestic items from Garth to help the newly-weds in setting up their home.[13] The letter has a certain poignancy and reveals how deeply affected Margaret was by Lizzie's action in dissolving their close partnership:

> "*I have just looked over the lists of plate & linen written out last night. I think you will find them a correct inventory of the things sent, if not please let me know the surplus or deficiency.*

Thomas Jones
(Photo: courtesy of Mrs J. Morris)

There are yet a few things to be sent you such as a plate basket & brush & crumb brush, pair of carver rests, &c. & then you will have all you require & all that you have been used to in your old home & I hope you will take the same good care of them that you have always taken of ours (mine now since you dissolved the partnership).

Tomorrow will put you & I in possession of separate homes & the care of separate houses. You have health, youth and spirit for your household cares and duties. I have neither. Still I must do my best.

Wishing you both comfort & happiness in your new home & with kind love."

In a nostalgic mood she later wrote to Lizzie about her lone attendance at a church service when Lizzie's absence was commented upon by those who were accustomed to seeing them always together: "*The old Church looked very well. I thought of you during the Service continually – it made me very sad to see all as usual but no Miss Lizzie by my side. Jones Ystalyfera came & asked me 'How is she that was Miss Lizzie'? That was his only comment & I thought it contained Volumes . . . Mrs K. & two pews full of girls, she Polly & 3 others with me. The Font looked the prettiest I ever saw decorated. How I longed for you to see it. I feel sure they all missed Miss Lizzie's pretty, bright face & eyes.*"[14]

Lizzie's departure was a watershed in Margaret's life. Although there were frequent visits and a regular, sometimes daily, correspondence, Margaret was now alone in Garth, possibly for the first time in her life and with only her domestic staff as her daily companions. The diaries for 1883 to 1887 are unfortunately missing so that the preparations for Lizzie's wedding and the following four years are only partially illuminated by several of Margaret's letters during this period. They provide fragmentary glimpses into her life and her pragmatic adjustment to her new situation and, a little later, to her new role as surrogate grandmother to Lizzie's children. As they had no surviving grandparents, the children were brought up to refer to Margaret as their Nanna and Lizzie would reinforce the newly acquired status by ending her letters with an amended subscription: "*I am dear Nanna/Yours very affectionately*".

Margaret and the local community

Female employment and educational opportunities were severely restricted by law, convention and prejudice, and in 1871 the catalyst of women's suffrage was an aspiration which would not be attained for another four decades. From

1869 Margaret would have benefited from the Municipal Franchise Act which gave the vote to women rate payers in local elections and from the Education Act 1871 which allowed women to vote for and be elected to the new school boards. Also in 1871 the Married Women's Property Act recognised the principle that wives, in specific circumstances, could retain control over their own earnings, savings and legacies. Margaret's prominence in the community, her right to vote as a registered rate payer and her ability and willingness to express herself forcefully, led her to champion projects which she felt to be socially beneficial and where she could exert some personal influence. She focused her attention on Rhyd-y-fro whose inhabitants she knew personally and whose values and language she would have shared. Her expectations of those who held public office were exacting and her letter in April 1870 to William Griffiths, one of the Poor Law Guardians for Llangiwg, required his full commitment and accountability in the performance of his public duties:

> "*Sir, I have just voted for you as Guardian with the hope that if you are elected you will exert yourself & look into matters. The Poor & Highway rates of this Parish are very heavy, all are compelled to pay & why should not a return of the expenditure be sent to each ratepayer once a year. At present we are quite in the dark of how the money goes. A very large amount is collected of that there can be no mistake & I think it but fair that the contribution to that amount should have a clear & plain statement of how matters are carried on. There is ample room for improvement & trusting the coming year may bring satisfaction to every one.*"

Community improvements and self-interest were combined in her advocacy of a regular postal service in Rhyd-y-fro. In 1876 she was encouraged by Dr. Walters, the Vicar of Llansamlet, who offered to ask the head postmaster in Swansea to visit the village "*to see about it*", while a separate survey of potential usage was undertaken. At the same time Margaret succeeded in persuading Howel Gwyn of Dyffryn, a prominent local landowner, friend of her late father and a former High Sheriff, local politician and Conservative M.P., to advise and support her application to the Postmaster General. She asked her cousin, the Rev. Richard Pendrill Llewelyn to prepare a rough draft of the petition and produced a legible copy which she sent as a *'Memorial'* for "*having a Pillar Post letter box*" to Gwyn. His reply recommended that the petition should be as "*strongly worded as possible – stating the number of the population & the Works & Collieries & other matters of that kind – & also the distance from the Post Office in Pontardawe*". He anticipated that "*you know of some respectable Shopkeeper or other person who could keep the office*" and hoped that "*the Person recommended will be a Churchman*". Margaret amended her draft only slightly, ignored the recommendation to include the number of works and collieries, collected local signatures and posted the petition to Gwyn which he, in turn, forwarded to Lord John Manners, the Postmaster General, "*with a letter from myself & do what I can for you*". He asked for her assurance that the post office would not be "*at a Public House*". The petition was successful and on 5 August Margaret wrote to Howel Gwyn to thank him "*very much*" for his support: "*It is indeed a great boon to find that we are to have a Post Office in Rhyd-y-fro, and I am sure you will have much pleasure in thinking you have so greatly assisted in obtaining it.*" She recommended "*a young woman named Mary Lewis, a Church woman (grand daughter of the late Richard Lewis of Wern ddu formerly I believe a tenant of yours) would be suitable. Her Father David Lewis is Tenant & Land Agent to Mr. Gwyn Jeffreys & keeps the 'Travellers Well' at Rhyd-y-fro. If she gets the appointment her Father will immediately build a suitable house in the Village combining Shop & Post Office. Until this is ready a private room can be had close by for the purpose.*" A few days later she wrote again to Howel Gwyn to reassure him that she believed "*Mary Lewis to be a trustworthy & reliable person for Postmistress at Rhyd-y-fro*". She added that "*There are some things respecting this appointment which perhaps it would be well to talk over, & if you would wish to see me about it I will meet you at any time tomorrow either at the Castle Hotel Neath or if more convenient to you at Dyffryn.*"[15]

Also in August, and possibly elated by her earlier success, she lent her support to another petition and wrote directly to the Postmaster General recommending the establishment of a post office at nearby "*Cae Gurwen . . . which is getting a large Village*" and where the Cwmgors valley "*abounds in Coal, Stone Quarries &c. and likely to become a populous district as houses are rapidly springing up*".[16] Almost a decade later on 16 October 1886 she again asked Howel Gwyn for his help "*respecting the further development of postal improvement in this neighbourhood*". She enclosed a copy of a letter she had written to the Secretary of the General Post Office and asked Gwyn "*if you will kindly use your influence with the Post Master General to further this matter I should indeed feel greatly obliged*". She referred to their long and amicable association by adding "*Knowing the true friendship that always existed between you & my late Father & your very kind letter to me on hearing of his death induce me to come to you in time of need, and trusting you will pardon the liberty I take.*"[17] Gwyn replied on 16 November acknowledging her letter "*with the memorial about an additional Post Office for Cwmgorse which I was able to hand to Mr. Raikes myself as he came to us that day for a large meeting in Neath that evening. Of course I warmly support your application. No doubt you will hear from him shortly about it.*"[18] On 18 June 1887 she wrote to E. H. Oakden, head postmaster in Swansea, requesting "*a suit of livery*" for "*our Postman* [*who*] *is an obliging, steady young man and true to his time*". She justified her request by suggesting that as 1887 was the year of Queen Victoria's Golden Jubilee "*I feel that it cannot be celebrated in this Valley by a more loyal or lasting remembrance than by clearly seeing our Postman in Her Majesty's Uniform. I should indeed be truly glad if the Clothes could be ready by next week.*"[19] Mr. Oakden's reply was immediate, brief and courteous, stating that "*I am sorry to say the Department do not provide it* [clothing] *for Officers of this class. The allowance to provide for the Service is made to the sub-postmaster of Pontardawe, and he in fact employs the man to perform the duty.*"[20] There is no record of Margaret's further pursuit of the matter.

A permanent focus of Margaret's interest was Llangiwg Church, where her ancestors had worshipped for many years and where her grandfather and father had served as church wardens. Margaret was possibly a regular attender in her early years but her Sunday attendance from 1871 was irregular and was largely influenced by the state of her health and mobility or the weather which could make access difficult. Even when she was absent her diaries rarely missed noting the clergyman who officiated at the Sunday service and there were constant visits by the clergy to Garth House where they were always welcomed. She had a maternalistic regard for her church and contributed substantially to its general maintenance, repairs and improvements, could be critical of its lack of cleanliness and warmth, paid the choir leader, harmonium player and the cleaner, to whom she supplied cleaning brushes, funded the Vicar with loans and in 1882 organised a concert in Rhyd-y-fro School to aid the restoration fund. Her great affection for the church was expressed in a diary entry on Sunday 11 July 1880 when she wrote: "*I think I never was so glad to see the dear old place, I really cried with joy to be once again in the old Church, & the Communicants (18) seemed so glad to see me.*" On Christmas Day in the same year she recorded that "*the dear old Church looking so 'serchus'* [beloved] *with the sun shining in, a good congregation. It quite gladdened my heart to see all so cheerful & bright & so nice. May God bless every hand & heart that in any way helps to keep up dear old Llanguicke.*" Margaret also provided the land and helped to finance the establishment of St. Catherine's Church in neighbouring Brynaman, laying its foundation stone on 7 October

Llangiwg Church
(Photo: courtesy of D. Roderick)

1880, and subscribed generously to the building of St. Margaret's Church in Ystradowen, which was presumed to have been named after her.

In addition, Margaret played a prominent role in helping to establish an elementary school in Rhyd-y-fro. The Llangiwg School Board was formed on 23 February 1875 with Margaret holding the responsible office of Treasurer. Her diary entry for 12 February 1876 recorded her contribution of ten shillings, possibly to its building fund, and at the School's official opening on 10 September 1877 she provided tea and cakes for the children.[21] Thereafter she collected and banked the "School pence" until her resignation in June 1882.

Margaret's Working Environment

Margaret's employment relationships with her tenants and sundry workers were personal and formal. They lived and worked in an environment where the prevailing class structure was reinforced by traditionally accepted behavioural norms and conventions, and the disciplined formalities of daily life are implicit in Margaret's writing and may be inferred from her conduct and actions.

Farm Tenancies

Margaret's income was partly derived from her farm tenancies where written agreements stipulated the conditions which a tenant was required to fulfil in respect of the regular payment of rent and taxes and the upkeep of the buildings. There was also an expectation that the land would be farmed efficiently and that livestock would be adequately cared for to produce a profitable return. Throughout the tenant farming community concerns had long been expressed over the lack of compensation paid to tenants who had improved the productivity of their holdings. Parliament was drawn into the growing debate over 'tenant right', namely the amount payable to an outgoing tenant for improvements which he had funded and worked to achieve and the crops which remained in the ground when his contract was terminated. As a result an innovative, but permissive, measure of statutory control was introduced with the Agricultural Holdings Act in 1875 which provided tenants with a limited level of compensation for the value of their improvements and for crops in the ground, allowed tenants the right to remove fixtures they had introduced, doubled the period of the Notice to Quit to twelve months and established an agricultural disputes resolution procedure. In a display of reactionary assertiveness Margaret's response (13/04/1876) was to require each of her tenants to contract out by signing notices "*objecting to the new Act of 1875*".

While preserving her customary rights, Margaret's personal relationships with her tenants and their families appear to have been generally authoritative but approachable. Her tolerance of delays in rent payments and acceptance of valuations in lieu of cash suggest a different image from that of tenant exploitation by avaricious landlords which was portrayed by political radicals during the nineteenth century. Her local birth and upbringing, her ubiquitous presence, her fluency in the Welsh language and her long association with the farming community, complemented by her many contacts at all social levels, would have nullified the socio-cultural divisions which characterised many of the larger lowland estates where English or Anglicised landlords and a Welsh peasantry co-existed in an often alien relationship. She also shared with the local community a common history and an awareness of the events which had shaped the recent past. Her parents would have witnessed the effects of the post-Napoleonic depression on rural Wales and on the farming sector, with widespread poverty, food scarcity and starvation, a banking crisis, fluctuating stock prices and rents and a harshly enforced poor relief regime. Their experiences would have helped to define Margaret's early perceptions of her environment, and her understanding would later have been reinforced by tales she would have heard of violent expressions of agrarian discontent in neighbouring counties, starting with the burning of Narberth workhouse in 1839, followed by the sporadic destruction of toll gates through south west Wales and culminating with attacks on the toll gates of nearby Pontardulais and Hendy.[22] Such events at a formative time in her life would possibly have influenced the young Margaret's attitudes to the farming community and later to her own tenants. She was to remain rooted in this rural environment, understood its values and never expressed a desire to leave it.

The agreements between Margaret and her tenant-farmers would have been determined by the terms of their contract of tenancy which was normally based on prevailing local custom.[23] The Garth archive contains the original memorandum of agreement dated 10 June 1850 and signed by Margaret's father which let "*Part of Cwmllynfell Farm to William Griffiths the present Tenant, during my natural life.*" An accompanying map showed seven numbered areas enclosing Cwmllynfell colliery "*which I Keep in my own possession.*" The conditions of the memorandum required William Griffiths to "*Rent £36..0..0 per year, commencing on the 25th day of March last past, to be paid half yearly* [*and*] *To Keep the whole Building in good Tenantable repair & all the fences &c. together with all Taxes.*" When Margaret inherited Cwmllynfell Farm in 1864, William Griffiths was paying £20 each half year for part of the farm and blacksmith's shop with Margaret paying for all farm repairs, improvements

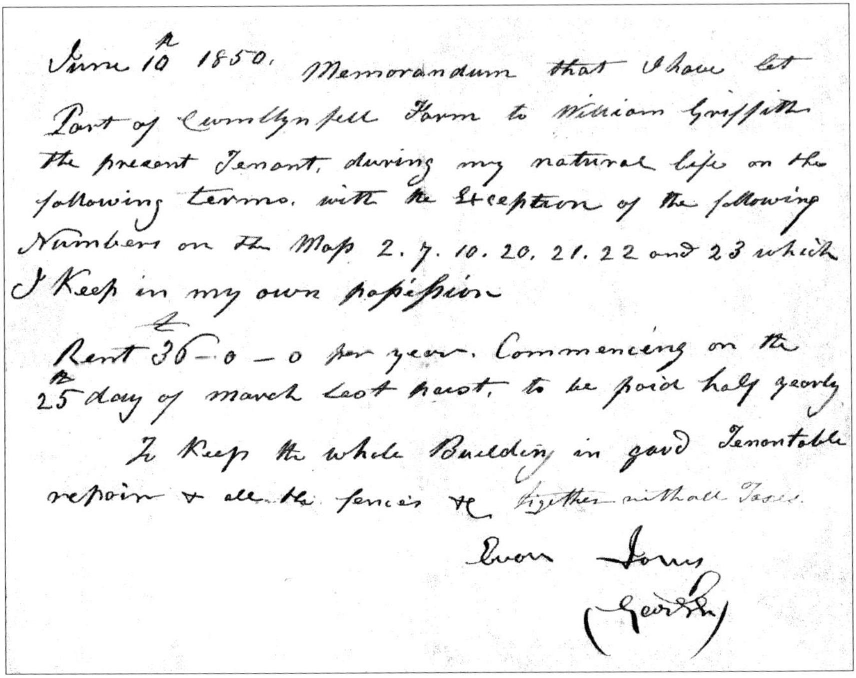
June 10th 1850. Memorandum that I have let
Part of Cwmllynfell Farm to William Griffith
the present Tenant, during my natural life on the
following terms. with the Exception of the following
Numbers on the Map 2. 7. 10. 20. 21. 22 and 23 which
I Keep in my own possession

Rent £36–0–0 per year. Commencing on the
25th day of March last past, to be paid half yearly

To Keep the whole Building in good Tenantable
repair & all the fences &c together with all Taxes.

Evan Jones
(Garth)

Tenancy letting of part of Cwmllynfell Farm, 10 June 1850
(Photo: courtesy of Mrs J. Morris)

and income tax on the farm and cottages. The rent remained constant until its increase to £22..10..0 from 25 March 1879. When William Price took over the tenancy in September 1889 he required various improvements and compensation for their cost totalling £10..9..9. Such compensation was, by that time, a statutory requirement following the passing of the Agricultural Holdings Act of 1883, and in this instance was offset against the full amount of rent due.

Margaret's largest holding was that of Garth Farm with 141 acres and where from September 1867 tenant John Day was required to pay £36 each half year. By 1872 he was finding it difficult to pay regularly and from October 1872 to September 1873 paid in four unequal instalments. From November 1873 to June 1875 he made ten separate payments to make up his deficit. In September 1874, Margaret reduced his half-yearly rent to £33..10..0 but Day was obviously struggling and, on the 16 September 1876, with two years' arrears of rent, Margaret gave him his second notice to quit. His stock was auctioned on 5 October and he paid off his arrears of £135..10..0 with promissory notes for

£128..19..6 payable on 5 February and a cheque for £6..10..6. Margaret gave Day a £5 note "*as a present for I found him honest in this business.*" Day and his family left Garth Farm in March 1877 for Tarenni Gleision and his final rent payment was calculated by valuation. This comprised clover bills valued at £3..8..8, sowing and harrowing 15/-, lime £5..17..10, haulage of lime £7..12..0, heap of manure in yard £10 and a cash payment of £5..16..6.

He was succeeded by John Jones who immediately encountered difficulty in making regular biannual rent payments and in 1878 contributed seven cash payments of varying amounts and one of butter whose estimated value was £1..9..7½. By 29 September 1880, he owed Margaret £93 and was given notice to quit. Her rent book shows that he was allowed to make contributions towards his rent arrears with two cash payments totalling £13, a cheque from Martin Scale, a Neath solicitor, of £1..10..5 and separate contributions of 42½ lbs. of beef at 8d. (£1..8..4), tongue to the value of 1/6d., butter and cream valued at £1..1..9 and grass for the calf for 9 weeks valued at 9/-. On 30 December 1880, Margaret told John and Esther Jones that if they "*could not give good security for the arrears of rent*" she would meet them in Scale's office to resolve the deficit. Her diary entry for that day described her tenant's desperation: "*John came after me & begged me to wait until this day week. Said I would.*" During early January 1881, John and Margaret disagreed over his valuation for improvements and over aspects of their Agreement of Tenancy and the issue was not resolved until March when the bailiff had been authorised to take possession of John's cattle until his rent arrears to the previous September had been paid. His last rental payment on 21 March 1881 was covered by a cheque from Martin Scale and was made up by agreed valuations for repairing the boundary hedge between Waun-hir and Nant-y-gwin (18/-), cutting small surface gutters (£1), making a bank fence on Waun Daniel (£1), hauling and spreading 113 loads of dung on Waunpedairerw (£19..15..6) and 2 heaps of earth and dung on Waun Fawr (6/-), a Note of Hand for £3..11..6 and "*Labour &c &c as per bill*" (£1..19..0). Her diary comment that day stated that John Jones spoke to her and "*cried & seemed very penitent*". He and his family left Garth on 14 April 1881 and Margaret's final assessment was that "*he proved himself at the last a very disagreeable man and a rogue. I hope I may never meet his like again.*" Margaret's poor opinion of John Jones resurfaced on 1 October 1881 when she consulted Martin Scale "*for the notes of hand John owes me*". He advised her to take the dispute to the County Court and the case was heard on 6 December in Margaret's favour.[24] John Jones was replaced as tenant by David Morgan of Cilpentwyn Farm from 21 April and Margaret hoped that he and his family "*will prove good tenants &*

that we shall get on well." Their subsequent relationship proved to be amicable and he regularly paid his half yearly rent of £28 by cash, free of all taxes, from 29 September 1881 to 1896.

Margaret's third inherited farm was Gelliluog Isaf with 74 acres of undulating land which had been occupied by John and Hannah Williams since 1861 on a half yearly rental of £15 which was increased to £17..10..0, including income tax, in September 1865. Margaret had planned to increase the annual rental to £40 from March 1879, but John Williams found it difficult to pay the rent due in September 1879 until 8 May 1880 when, in explanation of the delay, "*he complained of the times*", and Margaret set the rent at £18..15..0 a half-year. By March 1889 Margaret was actively seeking another tenant and a sale of stock was arranged for October, by which time her tenant owed her a year's rent. John Williams and Jordan the auctioneer together settled the outstanding amount before the tenancy was taken over by Lewis Walters from 29 September 1889 at a yearly rent of £40. Unfortunately Walters died in the following July but his wife retained the tenancy until September 1891 when Thomas Jones took the tenancy at a reduced half yearly rental of £17..10..0, remaining at that rate until Margaret's last entry on 25 March 1897.

The two neighbouring farms of Crachlwyn Ucha and Crachlwyn Fach, located high on Cefn Gwrhyd alongside the mountain track to Cwmllynfell, were late additions to Margaret's holdings. They had been farmed from around 1850 by John Jones who also held the post of Collector of Poor Rates for Llangiwg parish. On 1 September 1877 he deposited the deeds of both properties with Messrs. David Jones & Co., Llandeilo bankers, as collateral security for monies advanced to him and by 2 February 1885 his account was heavily overdrawn by £1,253..6..11d.[25] He agreed "*to execute a legal mortgage of Crachllwyn*" at his own expense "*whenever called upon to do so*" by the bank.[26] On 5 June 1886 the two farms, lands and hereditaments were mortgaged to the bank to secure £1,357 at an interest rate of 2%. By the Indenture John Jones covenanted to pay the principal and interest to the bank on 5 December 1886 and after that date to pay the same interest half yearly on the outstanding principal. He also agreed "*as beneficial owner*" to convey Crachlwyn Ucha (71 acres) and Crachlwyn Fach (28 acres) to the bank, provided that if the principal and interest were paid the properties would be reconveyed to him. He was also required to insure both properties and produce receipts for every premium paid and, as the bank's tenant, to pay a yearly rent of £67..17..0 half yearly on 5 December and 5 June. John Jones failed to meet these conditions and the bank exercised its right to enter the properties and "*determine the tenancy hereby created without giving the said John Jones (party hereto) any notice to quit*".[27] The bank initiated a judicial foreclosure of the mortgage, John Jones was declared a bankrupt and both farms passed into the hands of the Official Receiver for Glamorgan.

The Conveyance of the properties from the bank to Margaret was not signed until 25 June 1888.[28] However, her diary entries during the early months of that year record Esther Jones's distress at the loss of her home, her despairing attempts to sell her life interest in Crachlwyn Ucha to Margaret and John Jones's initial refusal to sign the conveyance. Margaret found "*the Crachllwyn business*" deeply upsetting and was anxious to sell the farms immediately for £1,675, the amount she had paid, and to be repaid £141 owed to her by John Jones. From 29 September 1888 a half yearly rent of £25 was paid by the putative "*Occupier*" Hopkin Jones, the eldest of John and Esther's nine children. The family's financial difficulties continued and in September 1893 they were forced to sell their crop and cattle, but remained Margaret's tenants.

Early in 1894 Margaret informed a potential purchaser that the rent was £50 a year and the "*price of surface & minerals £3,000*". This costing was based on an earlier report which she had commissioned from John Roberts, "*the well known Engineer*", on "*the minerals lying under the Farms*". He had stated that there were vast unworked seams of anthracite coal beneath Crachlwyn's acres and concluded that "*I estimate the property to contain workable coal 1,374,543 tons*".[29] This remarkably tempting inducement may have been the prime motive for Margaret's purchase of the two farms but, after her earlier problems with the lessees of Cwmllynfell Colliery, the enormity of embarking on another such venture in coal mining may have lost its initial appeal and retrenchment appeared a more comforting alternative. In May 1895 Hopkin Jones's erratic rent payments comprised two instalments totalling £19..5..0 and 40 yards of blankets valued at £5..15..0, and on 15 January 1896 a year's rent of £50, due on 29 September 1895, was paid in full. Subsequently the required payments appear to have been made regularly until May 1898, although Margaret's last rent book entry for £25 was dated 3 March 1897. Esther Jones remained in occupation of the property after Margaret's death and was recorded in the 1901 census as living there with one of her sons and his family.

These data provide a bare summary of Margaret's rental income from her farms. They also illustrate the financial difficulties faced by tenant farmers in the upland areas of south west Wales throughout this time. Pastoral farming provided a frugal living compared with the coal and metallurgical industries which were expanding and offering alternative work and more attractive life-style opportunities for workers from the rural areas. Tenant farming was not for the faint-hearted and the instances of bankruptcy were too evident.[30]

Margaret's diary entries over these years convey insights into the harsh practicalities and human costs of failure for her tenants and their families and into Margaret's responses to their problems. With no estate manager or agent to provide a measure of professional scrutiny and advice, such as she adopted to keep a critical watch over the management of Cwmllynfell Colliery, and no systematic control or regular personal monitoring of her farms, she had little alternative but to accept rent arrears, irregular payments and valuations in kind, or hope to attract enterprising tenants or buyers.

Cwmllynfell Colliery

Margaret's most contentious problem from 1864 to 1877 was also her main source of revenue. Cwmllynfell colliery had provided her family with an annual income since at least 1815 when her grandfather Richard had signed Articles of Agreement with George Walker of Swansea to extract coal from seams known as the Great Vein and the Brass Vein "*in or under the Tenement of land called Cwmllynfell*".[31] In 1824 her father Evan anticipated greater expansion and agreed the terms of a lease on Cwmllynfell colliery with Evan James of Hendreforgan and Jenkin Davies Berrington of Swansea, both neighbouring landowners, which permitted the lessees "*to take so much land as shall be required to for the erection of furnaces & for yards, cinder banks and building cottages and all other sorts of buildings connected with the Colliery or Furnaces for which a Rent of 20/- per acre per annum be paid*". The agreement was for a term of 60 years, sleeping rent of £100 for coals and iron, a royalty of 6d per ton, a royalty of 12/- per barge of coal sent down the Swansea Canal and, to ensure transparency in their dealings, "*a proper Book of Accounts was to be kept*". The lease also provided for "*the grant of all water flowing over or by the said estate with liberty to divert & use the same & to make any watercourse or weirs necessary*".[32] A few weeks later Evan instructed his solicitor Richard Jenkins to draw up a lease which permitted James Aubrey and his partner Christopher James to remove "*Stone coal and Culm and Iron Stone minerals under Cwmllynfell Tenement . . . for a term of 60 years commencing 1 January 1825.*" The sleeping rent on coal was kept at £100, the royalty on coal at 6d per ton and the royalty on iron at 7d per ton. A further lease in 1840, between Evan Jones and John Reynolds, formerly of Baglan, Christopher James and Richard Aubrey confirmed the previously agreed term, rent and royalties.[33]

Margaret shared her father's suspicions of the trustworthiness of those managing the colliery, distrusted the accuracy of monies paid to her on production tonnages and wayleave dues and was consistently worried by the damaging

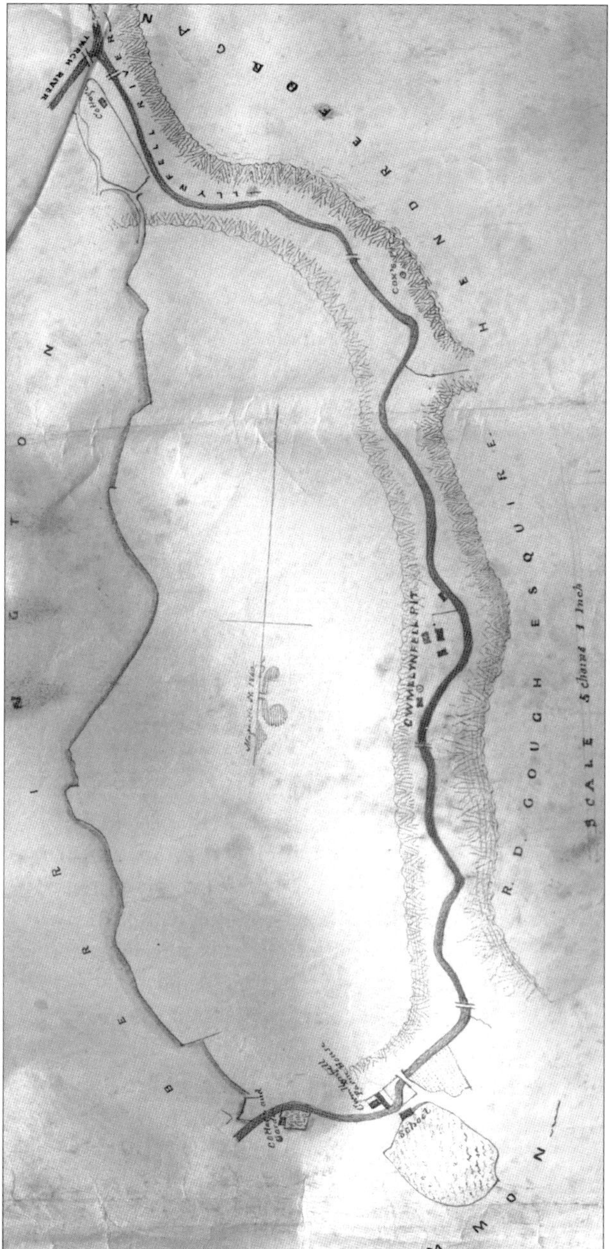

Map attached to a lease of coal, culm and ironstone minerals to Messrs James & Aubrey, 22 August 1840
(Photo: West Glamorgan Archive Service)

environmental effect of dumping colliery waste on her land. She therefore employed a mining surveyor Joseph Jones to provide her with a detailed annual report on the colliery's output and associated activities. On 8 June 1865 he reported on "*a most excellent quality as anthracite*" in the Big Vein and calculated that "*the quantity yet remaining unworked . . . to be about 40 acres which would produce something like 5,000 Tons per acre, making a total of 200,000.*" The "*most extensively*" worked seam was the Brass Vein where there were "*about 12 to 15 acres*" totalling about 65,000 tons which were unworked. He complimented the company secretary Mr. Rees for his "*method of accounts of coal worked*" and "*also his uniform kindness in showing me everything I needed*", but was critical of the colliery's management: "*I am sorry however to reverse the picture as regards the management generally underground. Some portions of the Colliery workings being at complete variance with the present system of mining.*" The report also drew attention to the lack of concern shown by Alexander Bain, the owner of the adjoining Hendreforgan farmland, stating "*Mr. Bain . . . appears not to pay much attention to agreements over Cwmllynfell Boundary &c. as he is still tipping mine rubbish to the River which will cause much confusion in the matter.*"[34] In the following year Joseph Jones returned to the worsening river pollution problem: "*I wish to say a word respecting Mr. Bain Hendreforgan – The River is still left running out of its proper Channel – no road for the Public use, and moreover he has commenced a very large tip to the River a little above his old Engine Houses, which threatens, if proceeded with, not only to wash away your Lands situate between River and railway but also the Railway itself. I have desired him to desist but to no purpose, therefore there is no other plan left now to remedy this matter but to place it in the hands of your Solicitor.*"[35]

The threat of flooding Cwmllynfell farm land remained a perpetual worry for Margaret and her diary entries show her recurrent frustrations. Despite her ownership of the colliery she had no operational control or effective influence on its management. She could monitor the colliery's activities from the reports of surveyors Joseph Jones and John Davies (from 1864 to 1877) but she was powerless to intercede unless she took legal action. In 1868 the colliery manager George Brock implied that a lady could not understand the world of business and also maligned the competency of John Davies, her land and mineral surveyor, who did "*not understand the nature of underground working*". Margaret had studied Davies's report and was not to be dismissed so lightly, disarmingly replying that as she was "*quite unaccustomed to business matters*" she had better consult her solicitor Richard Jenkins regarding Brock's suspect accounting in the "*deduction of Engine Coal when no Engine is used*".[36]

James & Aubrey in a/c with Margaret Jones

	£ .. s .. d		
1864	131 .. 4 .. 7	Coal, Ironstone & Wayleave	
1865	125 .. 4 .. 7	" " "	
1866	175 .. 2 .. 1	" " "	
1867	230 ..19 .. 4	" " "	
1868	370 ..17 .. 3	Coal 14214 tons @ 6d	335 .. 7 .. 0
		Ironstone 189 " " 7d	5 ..10 .. 3
		5 yrs. land under rubbish	10 .. 0 .. 0
1869	105 .. 3 .. 0	Coal, Ironstone	103 .. 3 .. 0
		Surface damage	2 .. 0 .. 0
1870	148 .. 7 .. 3		
1871	152 ..18 ..11	Coal 4112 tons @ 6d	102 ..16 .. 0
		Ironstone 130 " " 7d	3 ..15 ..10
		Wayleave 18410 " " ½d	38 .. 7 .. 1
		Surface damage	8 .. 0 .. 0
1872	184 ..16 .. 1	Coal 550 tons @ 6d	137 ..14 .. 0
		Ironstone 172 " " 7d	5 .. 0 .. 4
		Wayleave 16362 " " ½d	34 .. 1 .. 9
		Surface damage	8 .. 0 .. 0
1873	156 .. 2 .. 4½	Coal 4704 tons @ 6d	117 ..12 .. 0
		Ironstone 161 " " 7d	4 ..13 ..11
		Wayleave 12395 " " ½d	25 ..16 .. 5½
		Surface damage	8 .. 0 .. 0
1874	122 ..13 ..11	Coal Dead rent*	100 .. 0 .. 0
		Ironstone 45 tons @ 7d	1 .. 6 .. 3
		Wayleave 5944 " @ ½d	12 .. 7 .. 8
		Surface damage	9 .. 0 .. 0
1875	147 .. 3 .. 2	Coal 748 tons Dead rent	100 .. 0 .. 0
		Ironstone 181 " @ 7d	5 .. 5 .. 7
		Wayleave 20103 " @ ½d	41 ..17 .. 7
		Surface damage	-
1876	130 ..11 .. 6	Coal 48 tons Dead rent	100 .. 0 .. 0
		Ironstone 105 " @ 7d	3 .. 1 .. 3
		Wayleave 13206 " @ ½d	27 ..10 .. 3
		Surface damage	-
1877	117 ..13 .. 5	Coal 3644 tons Dead rent	100 .. 0 .. 0
		Ironstone 122 " @ 7d	3 ..11 .. 2
		Wayleave 6774 " @ ½d	14 .. 2 .. 3
		Surface damage	-

* Dead or certain rent guaranteed landowners a basic minimum rent regardless of how little coal was worked and was almost invariably calculated on the acreage of the mineral undertaking.

The early 1870s were boom years for the south Wales coal trade but the accompanying data, abstracted from her Rent Book, show that Margaret's entries of annual income from the colliery increased from £131..4..7 in 1864 to a peak of £370..17..3 in 1868 but thereafter never exceeded the sum of £184..16..1 in 1872. On visiting the site in October 1873 and having seen "*a high tip on the Cwmllynfell side and thereby obstructing the old road way*" she felt that "*closing up the only road way is a great injury.*"[37] This infringement, possibly aggravated by her declining income from the colliery, may have prompted her to consider selling her Cwmllynfell land and on 13 April 1874 she wrote to Brock stating that "*I will not fail in my promise of giving you the first offer of Cwmllynfell.*"[38] Other contributory factors may have been the coalfield's wage disputes and three major stoppages between 1871 and 1873.[39] Margaret's diary entry for 8 October 1874 refers to a stoppage at Cwmllynfell colliery which had lasted throughout the previous twenty-two weeks. Such stoppages would have affected production and reduced her royalties and wayleave entitlement. As trade declined, another wage dispute shut most of the south Wales coal industry for the first five months of 1875. Margaret's diary entry on 24 February 1875 stated that she told her solicitor Richard Jenkins that she "*wd. like to sell Cwmllynfell*". On 10 January 1876, her surveyor John Davies wrote to Richard Jenkins stating that he had "*carefully considered my Valuation on Cwmllynfell Surface & Minerals made a few years ago & amounted to £6,060.*" He added that "*The Value of Wayleave on the adjoining Minerals was then left out. I consider the present value of the same to be £50 per annum & say 20 years purchase would be £1,000 & added to the former Valuation would make a Total of £7,060 which amount I consider fair and reasonable.*"[40] A week later Davies wrote to Jenkins stating he was "*quite clear in my opinion that Messrs, James & Aubrey cannot work the Minerals under Coedfald & Barringtons except thro Cwmllynfell without going into a very large outlay by making new openings on both properties & also a Branch Railway from Barrington's Property. I think Miss Jones stands in a good position to obtain a good price.*"[41] On 10 February 1876 Margaret saw her solicitor "*about Cwmllynfell rubbish*" and additional rubbish from other properties which had been dumped "*on my land as it ruins it for ever*". She instructed him to offer her Cwmllynfell land for sale for £10,000. In July 1877 John Davies reported that the colliery had not worked in January and February "*and only worked a small quantity in March owing to a strike and the depressed state of trade*".[42]

Cwmllynfell Colliery was offered for sale by public auction at the Mackworth Arms Hotel, Swansea, on 10 December 1878. The leasehold portion included "*the Colliery, with the pits, shafts, levels, and engine houses, smiths' and carpenters' shops, sawing machine, offices, and cottages, and the coal, culm, iron-stone, and iron-ore under the farm called 'Cwmllynfell' containing 80 acres, or thereabouts, held for the term of 60 years, from the 1st day of January, 1825. Extensive railway sidings have been constructed by the lessees on this property to connect the Colliery with the Midland Railway . . . The Colliery is open for a considerable daily out-put, and is in constant work, the trade connection being extensive and much of it of long standing, so that the good will of the business is of considerable value.*" Full details of the various other properties, rents of lessees, royalties on coal and access to the ports of Swansea and Llanelli were also included.[43]

Attending the sale on Margaret's behalf was her cousin, Richard Pendrill Llewelyn, Vicar of Llangynwyd, whose report was a comprehensive indictment of the event: "*I attended the so-called sale when naught was sold, save the cottage called 'Gellie', & the attendants – about 35 in the room. There was not a bid for aught else.*" He expressed his suspicion of a man "*connected I believe with the Colliery*" who displayed plans "*of the same Kidney as the one I sent you – but with this most useful difference – that the Coal-Veins &c were, to a certain extent, delineated thereon – but Cwm had the merest minimum set down.*" He pointed out the discrepancy to John Davies who "*said it was not right.*" R.P.L. also suspected the impartiality of the auctioneer: "*Indeed I observed throughout a very strong inclination – as I thought – to depreciate your property. The Auctioneer said – that Miss Jones' property – the lease thereof had nearly expired – but he doubted not Miss Jones would renew – but if she did not see fit to do so – there were other most convenient outlets for the coal &c &c. He uttered almost the very words with which you have been pestered – & I have not a doubt but that he was taught his lesson, & ordered expressly to say what he did. But Margaret – be not bamboozled. I told Davies that I thought the Auctioneer maltreated your property & he Davies said so too.*" He assured Margaret that opening new outlets or pits to remove the coal "*will be a most expensive job, & any one will think twice – ere abandoning your pit to indulge in making a new.*" He referred to the Bank suspension which had "*caused quite a panic*" and that attempting to sell property "*in the murky gloom which overhangs all trade is the height of madness. Your property is valuable – say they what they will of it . You ought to have a man to look after it, one who knows mineral property & will act or do what is right.*"[44]

Margaret had no man to look after it and there is no evidence in her diaries or letters to show that Messrs. James & Aubrey wished to renew or extend the lease at its expiry on 31 December 1885, nor was the market sufficiently buoyant to attract the speculative interest of other investors. Replying to a letter from Swansea solicitor Edward Strick on 25 February 1879, Margaret acknowledged Messrs James and Aubrey's "*kind offer*" to relinquish possession at Midsummer 1879 "*but as I do not see that that will benefit either party. I think it is as well to wait until the given Notice terminates which will be 1st Jan. 1880.*"[45] She banked a cheque for £100 from the company on 23 January and wrote again to Strick on the 27 March 1880 complaining about the company's demolition of colliery walls and theft of the stones and in July expressed her concern over actual trespass on her property. When she and Lizzie visited the colliery site on 30 October 1880 she recorded that "*The place looks desolate, all the works being stopped & all the rails & every thing removed & houses empty . . . House formerly occupied by Mr. Brock, sadly pilfered & stripped of every thing.*" A year later, in response to an inquiry from a potential purchaser, she gave the Pontardawe bank manager "*particulars & the price of the farm & minerals £7,000.*"

Cottage Rents

Margaret received half yearly rents from the occupants of the six cottages (onc cottage near Garth House, two near the colliery and three in Cwmllynfell) on which she paid rates. Her diaries record the rent payments made by each tenant and her Rent Book records that between 1893 and 1897 William Morgan, William Williams, Hannah Williams and Mary Rees each paid rents of £1..10..0 per half year for Plas-y-bryn; David Williams and John Pugh paid £2 each for Llynfell Cottage; William Rowland paid £4 a year rent for Cwmllynfell Cottage until he bought it from Margaret for £130 on 23 April 1896; and for renting Colliery House Thomas Davies and Thomas Jones each paid an annual rent of £4..10..0 in 1893. From 1894 to 1896, Thomas Jones and Henry Stephens each paid between £5..10..0 and £4..10..0 and taxes of 15/- to 16/6d annually.

Personal Loans

Margaret charged interest on loans to a restricted number of individuals. The Rev. David Jones, Vicar of Llangiwg, was possibly her most prominent creditor and despite his position in society she was prepared to take legal action against him in November 1889 for non-payment of interest on a bond of £400, issued on 30 June 1871 at 5% p.a., and a separate loan. His death at the beginning of 1892, and the knowledge that he also owed £100 to another person, stimulated Margaret to contact her solicitor to ascertain her position regarding the outstanding interest and the bond signed by the vicar and his wife. Another pillar of the community who owed her money (£140) was the local postmaster and merchant Zephania Evans, who was threatened by Margaret with legal proceedings on 26 July 1889. Also recorded in the diaries (5 June 1875 and 11 February 1876) was a loan of £1,918 at 5% p.a., to a Miss Harris as part mortgage of a house in Neath. Margaret's notebook of 'Money Received' recorded that in 1893 Bridget Lewis paid £6 interest on a loan of £120; J. Jones paid £5 interest on £160; T. Jones paid £16 on two loans totalling £500; and in 1895 John Pugh paid 2½ years' interest of £39..8..4 on a loan of £525. In the five years from 1893, the interest paid on these loans totalled £194..7..8.[46]

Miscellaneous Sales

Throughout the text there are many references to Margaret's sales of her home-made dairy products, calves, bacon, timber, meadow hay, scrap iron and old newspapers. She was keenly aware not only of the price of every commodity but also of the value of waste items.

Margaret's Final Years

In the last years of Margaret's life when her physical strength was diminishing she devoted less time and energy to her diaries and the daily entries became fewer as the years passed. There were only seventy-four entries in the 1895 diary and during the early months of that year she rarely emerged from her home, recording that she "*felt very confused & stupid*" (3/3/95) and "*sleepy & stupid*" (15/3/95). On 2 May she visited her garden for the first time in three years and on 22 August she walked to the adjoining meadow with Lizzie, possibly for the first time in four years. Lizzie and Tom visited her frequently and the children were sent for days on end, accompanied by Lizzie's young maid Esther, to provide her with the stimulation of their company and the contact comfort she had always craved. On 18 June 1895 Lizzie wrote to Margaret to thank her for her "*newsy letter*" and commented encouragingly on Margaret's capacity "*to see to things bit by bit . . . and I trust you will be able to get the Coachhouse doors painted before rain.*" Lizzie's children were staying in Garth at the time and arrangements were to be made for Colin and Esther to return, but "*We all hope to be with you on the 7th and half of us on the*

5th. If they come please dress little Colin in Doddy's sailor suit, and only send what he requires for change for we can wash his things." Lizzie wrote again on the following day asking that Colin and Esther should catch "*the 2 train from Garnant*", adding Doddy's thanks for Margaret's letter to him and saying "*I told him the other day that you were ill and he said I hope she will live until next week for me to go to Garth.*" Another letter on 23 June thanked Margaret "*for the care you have taken of Colin, and Esther is quite pleased with her visit to Garth and will be quite ready to go back next week. I am so glad she was happy there.*" The fourth letter on 18 July referred to Margaret's illness and hoped that "*your head will soon be better.*" Her son Colin was staying with Margaret at that time and was soon to be joined by the other children. Margaret was advised to "*make the most of Esther now before the boys come, for afterwards I am afraid that much work will not be done. If you find the 3 too many for you I will have Colin here.*" On her sixty-second birthday on 2 September Margaret wrote in a foreboding and prophetic mood: "*T.J., Lizzie, Douglas, Doddy & Colin here. Perhaps we shall never all dine together again.*" There were only thirteen entries in her diary for 1896 and only twenty entries in that for 1897, the last being on 16 September. Her final letter was dated 30 November 1897, when she wrote to Lizzie in a style which was reminiscent of her precise and business-like manner of earlier years, describing the interview she had conducted with a possible tenant for Garth Farm. Margaret died on 16 June 1898 in Garth House.

NOTES

1. Gwynedd O. Pierce, *The Place-names of Dinas Powys Hundred*, University of Wales Press, Cardiff, 1968,(i)159.
2. Margaret Jones to Dr. Williams, her father's physician, 14 June 1864.
3. *Probate of the Will of Mr. Evan Jones Deceased, 21 July 1864.*
4. *Post Office Directory of Monmouthshire and South Wales 1871*, 374.
5. The Pontardawe Historians, *Around Pontardawe*, Chalford, 1996, 19.
6. Margaret Jones to the Pontardawe Magistrates, 20 April 1883.
7. "Delightfully situated under the brow of Kilvey Hill stands Maesteg House . . . which commands a splendid view of the town and bay. Contiguous to it there are several very genteel residences." John Lewis, *The Swansea Guide*, 1851, 67. The 1871 census records that the Grenfell family members in residence on Census day were the unmarried daughter Eleanor Catherine (aged 26), widowed daughter-in-law Georgina (42), and two grand-daughters Catherine (17) and Eleanor du Pre (16).
8. *Slater's Commercial Directory*, 1871.
9. The letters are dated 21 July and 22 September 1860. A window in the nave of Llanfair Church, Llandovery, was dedicated to Daniel Saunders by the Officers of HMS *Conqueror* and Royal Marine Battalion, Japan, 1865.
10. This motto is also inscribed at the head of the memorial to Richard Penderel (Trusty Dick) in the Parish Church of St. Giles-in-the-Fields, London, and commemorates his "Fidelity & Eminent Services" in helping to save the future Charles II from Oliver Cromwell's soldiers after the Battle of Worcester, 1651 (see Appendix 5).
11. Angela Holdsworth, *Out of the Doll's House*, BBC Books, 1988, 9-14.
12. Matilda Marion Pullan, *Maternal Counsels to a Daughter*, published in 1855 was "designed to aid her in the care of her health, the improvement of her mind and the cultivation of her heart".
13. Letter dated 23 March 1884. The list is reproduced in the 1884 section.
14. No date but the content suggests that the letter was written in late March or April 1884.
15. Letters from Margaret Jones to Howel Gwyn, 5 and 9 August 1876.
16. Margaret Jones to P.M.G.
17. Margaret Jones to Howel Gwyn, 16 October 1886.
18. Henry Cecil Raikes was Postmaster-General, 1886-91.
19. Margaret Jones to E. H. Oakden, 18 June 1887.
20. E. H. Oakden to Margaret Jones, 19 June 1887.
21. C. Lloyd, *Rhyd-y-Fro Primary School Centenary 1877-1977*, commemorative pamphlet, May 1977.
22. Keri Thomas, *The Rebecca Riots at Pontarddulais and Rhydypandy*, Clydach Historical Society, Newsletters 90 (2005), 91 and 92 (2006).
23. M. Alan Griffiths, 'Agricultural Development in South Wales 1830-1875: The case of some Glamorgan parishes', *Morgannwg*, Volume XVII, 1973, 42.
24. The 1891 census recorded John and Esther Jones farming Cilmaengwyn Isaf and living there with their adult children Eynon and Mary and 2 grandchildren.
25. *Schedule of Deeds* and *Memorandum 1 September 1877*, Carmarthen Record Office.
26. *Memorandum from John Jones to David Jones 2 February 1885*, Carmarthen Record Office.
27. *Mortgage John Jones to William Jones 5 June 1886*, West Glamorgan Archive Service [hereafter WGAS].
28. *Conveyance William Jones to Margaret Jones 25 June 1888* and *Esther Jones and John Jones to Margaret Jones 7 August 1888*, WGAS.
29. Copy in Margaret Jones's handwriting of a letter purported to be from John Roberts, n.d., Garth Archives.
30. Apart from the few large estates, almost 90% of Welsh land was worked at a near subsistence level by small-scale tenant farmers with fewer than 50 acres and where "there had been for

decades, a low margin of profitability for landowners; agricultural technique was relatively backward; capital input was at a consistently low ratio. Most landowners and their agents seemed more concerned to maintain amicable relations with their tenants, most of whom had been settled on their farmsteads for generations, rather than strike out boldly for agricultural improvement or innovation". Kenneth O. Morgan, *Rebirth of a Nation Wales 1880-1980*, OUP/UWP, 1982, 81.

31. *Articles of Agreement*, 16 February 1815, WGAS, Acc. 3474, 1/8.
32. *Lease on Cwmllynfell Colliery*, 24 November 1824, WGAS.
33. *Lease*, 22 August 1840, WGAS, Acc. 3474, 2/8.
34. Joseph Jones to Margaret Jones, 8 June 1865, WGAS, Acc. 3474, 2/8.
35. Joseph Jones to Margaret Jones, 24 May 1866, WGAS, Acc. 3474, 2/8.
36. Margaret Jones to G. R. Brock, 2 May 1868.
37. Margaret Jones to John Davies, 22 October 1873.
38. Margaret Jones to G. R. Brock, 13 April 1874.
39. J. H. Morris & L. J. Williams, *The South Wales Coal Industry 1841-75*, UWP Cardiff, 1958, 152, 272-83.
40. John Davies to Richard Jenkins, 10 January 1876, Garth Archive.
41. John Davies to Richard Jenkins, 17 January 1876, Garth Archive.
42. John Davies to Margaret Jones, 19 July 1877.
43. *The Cambrian*, 6 December 1878.
44. R. P. Llewelyn to Margaret Jones, 11 December 1878.
45. Margaret Jones to Edward Strick, 25 February 1879.
46. All rent data abstracted from Rent Book 1861-98.

THE DIARIES
1871–1897

Winter view of Garth house and dairy
(Photo: courtesy of Mrs J. Morris)

Snowscape from Mynydd y Garth over Garth and the Upper Clydach Valley
(Photo: courtesy of Mrs J. Morris)

1871

Sunday 1 January: Very cold. Lizzie, Betty & I in the house all day. T. E. John called in his way to Cwmgorse. Recd. a letter from Mrs. Morgan Ashford.

Monday 2 January: A heavy fall of snow last night several inches deep.

Tuesday 3 January: Made 4lbs of apples into jam. Paid John Davies Blacksmith as per book to 31st Decr. by cheque £2..3..6. Paid him also 4/- for Williams the Painter's lodgings last April when he was here papering and painting.

Wednesday 4 January: D. Morgan (Mason) came to see how we were, too much snow to work. Betty to Pontardawe on Fly, had 40 lbs. of flour. Paid Mr. Evans Post Office as per book for shop goods to Decr. 31st £11..4..6 cheque. Paid Davies the Ironmonger Pontardawe as per book to 31st Decr. £4..6..0 cheque. Wrote to Mrs. D. M. Morgan.

Thursday 5 January: ***** A rapid thaw after the severe frost. The front trough had become quite frozen & the water came pouring into the Drawing room & White room. Day went up to the top of the trough & broke the ice with a chisel so as to make a passage for the water to escape. I never saw it so before.

Friday 6 January: Died at Hereford Janry. 4th aged 67 years Revd. Charles Maybery of Brecon, 40 years Rector of Penderyn, a great friend of the Pendrills particularly Uncle Michael, I think he was the Clergyman that buried him at Ystradgynlais 1831.

Saturday 7 January: Lizzie went to see Old Pal and to fetch me some Penny Royal.[1]

---

1. Penny Royal was a popular medicine derived from a species of mint *(mentha pulegium)* and used as a remedy for various ailments including colds, stomach and menstrual problems and as an abortifacient.

Sunday 8 January: Lizzie to Church on Gronow. Betty to Church. I at home all day not well. Sacrament D. Jones.

Monday 9 January: Mended the sleeves of my stripe alpaca frock. Mr. John Cook Surgeon of Glais near Clydach died yesterday aged 58 years, he was a clever Doctor and the first to say my Poor Father's heart was affected. We all liked him.

Tuesday 10 January: Lizzie & I received a pretty little Valentine each from Jane her sister. Tomorrow the Annual Hospital Ball (the 3rd) at Swansea. The Cambrian[2] speaks of it in High terms as successful. The Gilbertson's there.

Wednesday 11 January: Miss Jenkins Birthday. Lizzie sent her an Antimacassar[3] by 1st train. Betty took it to the Station. Mr. Jones Llanguicke [Church] called at 5.30 p.m., stayed to tea & left at 10 o'clk., he was very pleasant & friendly. Spoke to him about building a stable at Llanguicke. Heard of Kate G's engagement. 1870 seems to have been a lucky year for the young ladies of the Swansea Valley to find Husbands! Dotty Williams, Dora Price, Netta Lewis, Kate Gilbertson. All 4 have my best wishes to be happy.

Thursday 12 January: Paid Garth Tithe by Cheque £2..12..0. William Thomas of Garn Wen's (Gwinfe) daughter to see Gronow, bought her for £11. She is an excellent & faultless pony but is getting old. Betty went to see her Father who is very poorly.

Friday 13 January: Margaret Howard came here for Pontardawe Pew Rent, she collects the money now instead of Mr. Woodman.

Sunday 15 January: Very wet no one to Church. Betty to see her Father.

Monday 16 January: Betty Williams here paying £1..10..0, ½ a year's rent for Plas-y-bryn due last September. I gave her the ½ yrs Income tax (9d.) which I forgot to allow in 1869.

Wednesday 18 January: Mrs. Day to Neath had by her 7 pints lamp oil, 2 lbs. candles, 6 lbs. sugar, 2 quarts peas. Had a load of soft coal 16 cwt. 7/- paid &

2. *The Cambrian* was the first English language newspaper published in Wales and from February 1804 its weekly issue carried news and comment on local and national events until 1930.
3. A cloth covering placed over the backs of chairs as a decoration and as a protection from Macassar oiled hair.

a load tomorrow 16 cwt. 7/- paid. As I have sold Gronow there is about ½ a wheelbarrow full not used of the coal had Nov. 5th.

Thursday 19 January: Margaret Thomas of Garn Wen near Llangadock came for Gronow which she bought of me this day week. She is an exceedingly pretty pony & as good as she is handsome without a blemish & without a fault. I never expect to meet her like again £11..0..0 paid. Rose the bacon up to dry, did not wash the flitches.[4] A load of soft coal, the cart axle broke in Heol y Cefn. D. Morgan hurt his hand badly.

Friday 20 January: Revd. D. Jones, Mr. John Davies & Charlie up this way shooting snipes. They called at 5.30 p.m. & took some beer & wine. The servant brought up the Phaeton[5] to meet them at 5 o'clk. Recd. a letter from Mrs. Bowman & Lizzie a little card, they were at the Paddington Hotel just arrived in London from spending 8 weeks in Clifton. Margaret Gellyluog here with £15..0..0 on a/c of Rent.

Saturday 21 January: Begun the little black Pot of butter last night for tea. Put clean cap in my bonnet.

Sunday 22 January: Lizzie to Church on Fly. Betty to Church. Wm. Lewis came here.

Tuesday 24 January: Paid Evan Jones Butcher as per bill in full up to Decr. 31st 1870 £4..0..0 Cheque. Wrote to Mrs. D. M. Morgan to ask how Mrs. Dixon's boil was. Betty to Pontardawe for flour, told her to take my boot strap to be mended, replied "No indeed I will not"! Asked her how she could think of giving me or even any one such an answer. I almost think her mind is wandering at times or she would never be so odd. She believes herself to be perfection & that no one else knows anything.

Wednesday 25 January: Betty washed a piece of Calico 18 yds to be made into Chemises, also the short muslin blinds of bedrooms. Jane & Dora Price returned from a visit to the St. Johns at Tenby, they had been to the Hunt & Fancy balls. Jane dressed as a Welsh Girl, Dora in a Swiss Watteau Costume. Mr. Vaughan was at the ball.

---

4. A side of salted and cured pork.
5. A light open 4-wheeled carriage drawn by one horse or a pair of horses.

Thursday 26 January: Paid John James Gotregarth the Income tax (by Gwen his daughter).

1 year ending 5th April 1871 for Garth Schedule A @ 4d, Schedule B @ 2d on £50	£1..5..0	
Garth Cottage Income tax 1 year ending 5th April 1871 @ 4d.	1..0	
Garth Land tax 1 year 14/7d.	14..7	It used to be only 12/6, this is the first time I have paid so much & why it is increased I do not know.
	£2..0s..7d Paid	

Friday 27 January: Day drove me as far as the Mountain, walked from there to the Vicarage, stayed to tea. Mary Watkins & Miss Richards there. Day met me at the Schoolroom at 6.30 brought back Lizzie who had been staying with Mrs. Thomas since Monday. She has a dreadful earache & sore throat. Called at Mrs. Jones Hendreforgan, she had a bad cold & Mrs. Evan Jones Aberdare there very ill since Monday.

Saturday 28 January: 1 load of Llwynrhidie coal,[6] 17 cwt. 2/10d., brought by Fly alone having sold poor little Gronow. D. Morgan & John cutting hangers at Gellyluog for fencing at Garth. ***** Lizzie very poorly with earache, sore throat and cold.

Sunday 29 January: Betty to Church. Lizzie in bed all day with earache &c. I at home.

Monday 30 January: Mary Watkins dined here. John Derrybach took her home in the Phaeton at 8.30 p.m. Expected Miss Thomas & her brother but they did not come owing I think to a little snow in the morning. Heard of J.M. & T.J. fighting at the station! 21st inst. Sam Morris married at Ystrad Meurig to Miss Evans Henblas. A grand wedding. Paid Mrs. Williams Nant-y-gasseg for 1 stack of wheat had Decr. 30th £1..0..0 Paid.

---

6. Opened as a drift mine by Garnant shopkeeper Joseph Thomas in 1850 into an outcrop of the Red Vein on the land of Llwynrhydie Farm and produced about 50 tons of coal per week. Abraham Evans, 'Cwmgors Colliery', *Ein Cyngor*, Spring 1964, 40.

Tuesday 31 January: Recd. a letter from Miss Jenkins saying Miss Rachel was very poorly & had had Mr. Hall & that they had all had colds &c. Wrote to Laura Jones. Wrote to Mrs. Bowman 1st time since her marriage to 13 Sheffield Gardens Kensington.

Wednesday 1 February: Lizzie recd. a letter from Mary Watkins with pattern of antimacassar. Poor old Mrs. Roderick of Llanwrtyd Wells died today aged 80 years. I had known her since I was a child & always found her very kind.

Thursday 2 February: Went to see the hedge D.M. & John were steeping between Iron Gate & the Cottage, <u>not at all pleased</u> that they had cut the trees <u>close</u> to the Cottage. They looked so pretty overhanging the water, all looks now so bare & naked. Lizzie wrote to Miss Thomas & Mary Watkins. Mrs. Day put manure over my rhubarb.

Saturday 4 February: Cleaned the carpets of my room, shook & folded them up.

Sunday 5 February: L[izzie] *****. Betty to Church. Lizzie & I at home all day.

Wednesday 8 February: John & D. Morgan finished cutting down all the Larch trees in the strip between Front field & Cae Barriwns, after getting 20 feet high they seemed to wither & die as if the roots were decaying. John took Hampers to Station, called at Post Office & had 5 Currant casks to put over rhubarb roots.

Thursday 9 February: John took 2 loads 24 cwt. 3 qtrs. of wood to Pontardawe Chemical Works, the white thorn from the hedge in Cae front. Tomorrow John takes down 3 loads of wood 36 cwt.1qtr. making in all 3 tons 1 cwt @ 15/- per ton. This wood includes <u>white thorn</u>, stumps & branches of <u>alder</u> from the hedge steeped between Iron gate and Cottage also branches of Oak from Big field. Paid for April 1st. £2..5..9 Paid.

Friday 10 February: Recd. letter from Mrs. Bowman from 7 Pembridge Crescent Bayswater London, she speaks of these lodgings as very clean & comfortable & wishes me to come up to London very soon. Wrote to her today. Mr. Popkin, Solicitor of Llandilo died today aged 72 years.

Saturday 11 February: Alltwen Fair. John & D.M. put up oak stumps by the Closet to prevent its being seen from the road now the trees are cut. Mrs. Ford, Miss Ford & Kate Gilbertson called. They all walked up & I walked back with them to the Saron Milestone, the first time I had been so far since I sprained my foot. They spoke of Kate's engagement to Mr. Richardson of Liverpool.

Sunday 12 February: Very wet. Lizzie & I at home all day. Betty to see her Father.

Monday 13 February: John raking up the stones tidy on Heol-y-ty & carrying stuff from Quarry to throw into the stones to harden them.

Tuesday 14 February: Paid Garth Poor Rate to J. Jones Crachllwyn as follows:

Garth farm	£47.. 0..0	@ 10d	)	* Less
Garth Cottage	2..0..0	" "	)	Commission
3 Cots Cwmllynfell	7..10..0		)	2..10..2½
Smith shop	1..15..0		)	* 2..4½
1 Cot Craig Llanguicke	2..0..0		)	£2..7..10
	£60..5..0			By cheque Paid

Wednesday 15 February: Miss Kate Grenfell married to Mr. Edw. Henry Thornton at Kilvey Church. 70 persons to the breakfast. Wrote to Mr. R. Jenkins asking if he had recd. Mr. Davis' account of the coal & saying I wanted Messrs. James & Aubrey to settle for 1870 & that I had had no money.

Thursday 16 February: Betty to the Mill grinding the stack of wheat had from Nant-y-gasseg.

Flour	142 lbs.	
Coarse Flour	10 lbs.	
Bran	48 lbs.	all bags deducted
	200 lbs.	

Put a poultice of Briony roots to my foot which is very painful since Tuesday. Recd. a letter from Mrs. Bowman.

Friday 17 February: Recd. a letter from Mr. R. Jenkins saying Mr. Davies had been very ill, but that another Surveyor had been to Cwmllynfell [Colliery] & that he would write for the account. D. Morgan & John finished carrying off the fir poles &c from the strip by Cae front & finished the ditch.

Saturday 18 February: Had 2 loads of Llwynrhidie coal 16 cwt each @ 2d., 5/4. D. Morgan commenced trashing Wain Pedr Erw hedge.

Sunday 19 February: My foot very painful. No one from here in Church. Very wet. Lizzie & I in the house. Betty to see her Father. Wm. Lewis came from Church with letters.

Tuesday 21 February: Young John Morgan & others hunting here, caught 3 or 4 hares. Recd. a letter from Miss Jenkins & a list of the people at Miss K.G.'s wedding breakfast. Recd. a letter from Mrs. Morgan. Wrote & asked her to send me a paper with an account of the battle, also said I did not at present require their Carriage as I was undecided about horses.

Wednesday 22 February: Betty ill in bed nearly all day. Recd. a news paper from Cape Argus, left there 14 Janry. D.M. trimming fruit trees in both Gardens. John putting manure with the roots of the Currant trees in New Garden.

Thursday 2 March: Lizzie & I went to Swansea 1st train. Lizzie returned midday & I stayed the night at Bryn Syfi. Paid the following bills up to 31st Decr. Richmond, Arkell [*Shoemaker*], Butt [*Shoemaker*], D. & J. Williams, Herbert Jones [*Bookseller*], Davie [*Chemist*]. Had lamp shades & chimnies from Scantlebury [*Thomas Scantlebury, Retail Ironmonger, 4 Castle Square, Swansea*]. 2 Dozn. Beer, ½ Gallon Gin, ½ Gal. Brandy, ½ Gal. Whisky, 1 bottle of Rum, the 1st this year. <u>All Empties returned to 31st Decr</u>. Spoke to Day in going to the Station about the Hedges, that he must cut the briars & not stuff in dead branches to fill gaps.

Friday 3 March: Kate G. called on horseback. I had not returned from Swansea. Mr. Scott [*Frederick C. Scott, Dentist, 9 Fisher Street, Swansea*] stopped 2 teeth for me & altered the lower false tooth. Saw Mrs. Scott. Came up last train. called to see T. E. John who is getting better. Lizzie was waiting with the Phaeton at Maes Iago. Poor Mr. Gough in the train, he is <u>very aged</u> & <u>altered</u>.[7] Heard T.J. had to pay a fine of £25. Mrs. Rawson died age 80, Mrs. Budd's Mother.

---

7. Richard Douglas Gough (1800-86) of Ynyscedwyn House, Ystradgynlais, J.P. for Breconshire and Glamorgan.

Saturday 4 March: John took salt butter to Post Office (Black Pot & small cask) 95½ lbs. @ 1/3d, £6..0..4 paid, brought Hampers &c from Station, also beef from Evan Jones' Ynysmeudw. D.M. digging between fruit trees in old garden. John planted 3 little Scotch fir in old garden grown from seed by sawpit. Finished putting wardrobe in White Room tidy after shaking & airing the things.

Sunday 5 March: Betty to Church. Lizzie & I at home. Recd. Mr. Davies Colliery report for 1870.[8]

Tuesday 7 March: Llangavelach fair. D.M. & John trimming Wain Pedr Erw hedge. Mrs. Day put cucumber seed in flower pots to transplant to Garden when fine. Wrote to Mrs. Bowman 7 Pembridge Crescent Bayswater London.

Wednesday 8 March: Betty to Llangavelach fair for flannel. Recd. a letter from Mrs. D. Morgan.

Sunday 12 March: Lizzie to Church on Fly. Betty & I at home. Daniel, T. E. John's son here to borrow a £10 [note] of Betty for her Father to go to Taff's Well.

Monday 13 March: Yesterday at Royston House Llandovery, Mrs. H. Thos. Gwynne Vaughan of Erwood Hall Breconshire of a son (formerly Miss David Thomas, Royston House). I think this is the 1st child.

Wednesday 15 March: Lizzie waisted Grey alpaca Petticoat that I made for myself.

Thursday 16 March: Snow & very high wind all night, blew 2 branches off Scotch Fir by the Kitchen window. Mr. George Mowat (late Surgeon of the Swansea Infirmary) married to Patty Martin only child of the late Joseph Martin. Wrote to Kate G. saying I was sorry I had not been able to call & that I was in Swansea when she called 3rd inst.

Friday 17 March: The woman of Tymawr brought me a stack of oats, 18/- Paid.

---

8. Margaret had commissioned John Davies, Land & Mineral Surveyor, Llwydcoed Llannon, near Llanelli, to provide her with an annual report on the management and tonnages of Cwmllynfell Colliery.

Saturday 18 March: John the Blacksmith put lock on Betty's Bedroom door after he repaired it. John also made 2 little pieces of iron to fit the sheath in my Boot for the shoemaker to have the size as I cannot let them have the iron I wear. I think it was a good idea to have it made. I hope it will answer. I finished putting drawers in my room tidy.

Sunday 19 March: Revd. Walter Jones, Cil-y-bebyll preached at Llanguicke 1st time. I rode Fly, left her at M. Jones' & walked to Church. Lizzie & Betty in Church, 1st time for me since Xmas.

Monday 20 March: Lizzie drove me to Maes Iago, called at the Gilbertsons, & from there walked to call at the Parsonage the 1st time, they made me stay to tea & their man drove me home. I intended going to stay a few days at Bryn Syfi but had a letter by train to say the Prices (Jane & Dora) were coming there to stay tomorrow so I preferred not going. Kate gone to Neath to meet Miss Drake. Fanny told me they had dined at the Prices this day week to meet Tom Vaughan.

Tuesday 21 March: D. Morgan cutting ivy on kitchen stable &c. John brush harrowing Cae Cwtta & meadow, had the loan of Gellyluog mare to put with Fly. Old Pal spreading mole earth. Wrote to Miss Jenkins & also to Miss Price saying I hoped she wd. come here on Saturday next to stay. Paid Garth Highway rate to Thos. y Gove £1..3..6 (£47 @ 6d.).

Wednesday 22 March: Catherine Rowland here paying one year's rent £3..0..0 due next Saturday the 25th inst. Recd. a letter from Mrs. D. Jones asking me to Dotty's wedding & to the Breakfast on the 13th April. Tomorrow write to Mrs. D. Jones begging them to excuse my coming on the 13th as it is uncertain whether I should be well enough. Biddy here, her hand very sore. Sent silk skirt to Sally to take the lace out of the breadth. John finished harrowing all my fields at 4.30 p.m. Took Gellyluog mare back.

Thursday 23 March: D. Morgan finished digging up the flower beds & filling them with leaf mould, cutting around the edges, removing fuchsias &c & I making the place tidy. John rolled the Green & Betty swept it, the front is now quite tidy. D.M. & John took stones off front field & then off the Croften & commenced carrying the heap of lime & earth over the Croften. Lizzie to Swansea on midday train for crochet cotton.

Friday 24 March: Old Pal & Hannah gathering stones off Cae Cwtta. I walked up to see the Croften & the fields, in returning met a woman by the Iron gate who spoke to me & seemed quite pleased to see me, she was Mrs. Roberts the Smith's wife & sister to Old Betty who lived here a Servant in Mama's time. I did not remember her until she told me.

Saturday 25 March: Put Betty's room ready for Miss Price. Cleared out the Hall.

Sunday 26 March: Rode Fly to Church. Left her at Cefn llan (Griffiths). Met Olwen Llwynmeudw who asked why I did not bring the horse there, that I was quite welcome to do so. Mrs. Lewis here. Lizzie & Betty in Church. Shonny, Betty's brother & his little girl came here from Church.

Monday 27 March: D.M. & John finished at 4 p.m. carrying lime & earth & the manure & earth over the Croften, it has had a <u>thick</u> & good dressing & ought to give a good crop. They have been <u>very busy</u> for the heaps were <u>very large</u>.

Tuesday 28 March: I went to Swansea 1st train, called at Mr. Scott's, he was from home. Called at Bryn Syfi, gave [Cwmllynfell Colliery] coal a/c to Mr. Jenkins & borrowed £9..0..0 of him. Rachel Jenkins going to Glan Twrch midday train. Miss Price came here to stay from Tretower. Met her at 3 p.m. at the V.N.R. [*Vale of Neath Railway*]. Had load of Llwynrhidie coal, 14 cwt 2/4d. Day sowed ½ bus[hel] of vetches[9] & bus. of oats in the Croften for me.

Wednesday 29 March: Had yesterday from Messrs. Williams 1 dozn. Porter, ½ dozn. Sherry, ½ dozn.Tarragona, ½ dozn. Marsala, 1 dozn. Champagne, 1 Hamper.

Saturday 1 April: D.M. & John finished setting potato seeds &c in New Garden, all but cabbage plants wh. Mrs. Day will bring from Swansea this evening. Wm. Lewis came here to say he had just been all through Gellyluog wood. There are some 3 or 4 trees cut, but nothing of any consequence. Recd. money from wood to Chemical Works by John Derrybach, 3 tons 1 cwt. @ 9d. per cwt £2..5..9 paid.

Sunday 2 April: Lizzie to Church. Miss Price, I & Betty at home all day. Rain tonight, the ground very dry.

---

9. Vetch is a plant of the pea family largely used for forage.

Wednesday 5 April: Miss Price called at the Griffiths' Bryncelyn & from there by midday train to Glan Twrch. Lizzie & I drove her as far as Maes Iago & Day fetched her last train. Mr. & Mrs. Lloyd & Russell lunched at Glan Twrch, Nellie staying there. Evans paid for salt butter had March 4th (Pot 45 lbs. Cask 50½) 95½ lbs. @ 1/3 (1/- over) £6..0..4 paid.

Thursday 6 April: John brought ½ a ton of soft coal from Pontardawe with Fly, 4/- pd. Begin it next Monday. Paid Neath Insurance by postage stamps, 7/6 paid.

Good Friday 7 April: Only Lizzie to Church. John digging up large stones by front gate on the road & on the walk. D. Morgan trimming hedges.

Saturday 8 April: John carrying sand & gravel &c the refuse after screening for mortar to walk by front Gate. The hedge between Wain Pedr Erw & before the house took fire from burning brush too near the hedge. Went down & told Day I was very angry. Had 2 dozn. Beer by Mrs. Day. Sold little pot of butter to Mrs. Nott Swansea, 5½ lbs. @ 1/6d., 8/3 paid.

Easter Sunday 9 April: Lizzie to Church. Miss Price, I & Betty in the house. Betty to see her Father after tea.

Monday 10 April: Recd. letter from Mr. J. B. Jenkins yesterday saying he had seen his Cousin & that I was entitled to the Colliery keeping rent as the coal was not worked up to the amount. Lizzie finished the antimacasser for Dotty Williams. She commenced it last Friday fortnight, 24th March. Gave her 10/- for doing it.

Tuesday 11 April: Miss Price left here midday train for Milford, Alice joining her at Landore. Miss Louise M. M. Jones of Pantglas married to Revd. Henry Donald Maurice Spence, M.A., Professor of Modern Languages at Lampeter, at Llanwenny Church Cardiganshire. Very wet.

Wednesday 12 April: Recd. a letter yesterday from Mr. Ed. Price saying Sir J. Bailey's man (the one he thought wd. suit me) saw my wages low, 14/- in all & not worth changing as he has now 13/- at Glan Usk (Williams by name). Sent Charlie with antimacassar to the Parsonage, a wedding present to Dotty & a letter with good wishes. Old Captn. Evans Vale of Neath Brewery died today aged 77 years.

Thursday 13 April: Dotty Williams married today at Pontardawe Church to Mr. S. G. James (Bristol).[10] A very grand affair. I was asked to the Breakfast but declined going. There was a Party in the Evening. A damp misty morning but cleared up in the afternoon.

Saturday 15 April: John cleared gutter in Heol y Ty. Recd. a letter from Miss Price saying Alice & herself arrived safely at Milford on Tuesday. Oysters there 5/- a hundred!! Mrs. Day brought me a new pair of Boots from Mr. Butt, they fit nicely & the iron fits in the sheath comfortably.

Sunday 16 April: Lizzie rode Fly to Church. Betty to Church. No Clergyman came. I at home.

Monday 17 April: John Derrybach cutting dead branches from trees both sides of Heol y Ty & carrying away the mud &c raised from Gutter on Saturday. Day carried the branches off for firewood. John planted 3 little sycamore trees in Cottage garden hedge. Wore new Boots had last Saturday, the 1st with John's pattern iron for sheath. I think it answers well. John & Lizzie washed Nero 1st time, he enjoyed it.

Tuesday 18 April: Jane & Dora Price & Miss R. Jenkins to the Mumbles for a week.

Thursday 20 April: Peggy Daniel came for 2 cwt. of short hay @ 2/9d, 5/6d paid. Lizzie scolded John Derrybach for speaking rudely before her, Lizzie seeing the hay weighed as I was in bed not well.

Friday 21 April: Lizzie to Bryn Syfi 1st train. Sent Mr. Jenkins the £9..0..0 I borrowed of him March 28th. He wrote a receipt for me to give James & Aubrey. Lizzie paid Miss Symonds for making my light jacket, 8/6d. Sent a receipt to Mr. Brock for cheque recd. yesterday.

Sunday 23 April: Lizzie to Church. Betty to see her Father. Wm. Lewis had Fly to go to Carmarthenshire, he slept here last night.

Tuesday 25 April: Lizzie went home on Fly & returned this evening, Nero the dog went too. Fly was restless in opening a gate, tore skirt & stirrup & a most

10. Sarah Fox Williams (20) married Stephen George James (27), a brewer of Bedminster.

fortunate thing Lizzie did not hurt herself. William Evans Llwynrhydie buried today at Carmel aged 72. Mary Arnold went home. Away 5 months 1 week.

Thursday 27 April: Mr. Lewis Bishop (Dolygarreg) Solicitor Llandilo married to Miss Neville from Devonshire.

Friday 28 April: Betty took letter to Mr. Kirkhouse with Epsom paper & £3..0..0 for 2 Sofa rugs. Sent cheque to Mr. John Davies of Llwydcoed Llanelly for £37..16..0, the amount of his bill up to 1st Jany. last for surveying Colliery at Cwmllynfell.

Saturday 29 April: John Thomas Gwernllwyn here buying all the long hay I have to sell, 14 cwt at 4/6 (Paid for June 15th) £3..0..0 paid. His nephew John carried it off today.

Sunday 30 April: L*****. No one to Church. Betty to see her Father, sent him a bottle of Porter.

Monday 1 May: D. Griffiths Cwmllynfell sent down his boy with £1..0..0 which with the £2..0..0 recd. in Nov. makes 1 year's rent for Smith shop due 1st June '70, £3..0..0. Lizzie went for a ride on Fly round the Garth & then to Morgan Jones' with a £1..0..0, my subscription to Joseph the Clerk for '70. Paid Cwmllynfell & Gellyluog [Farm] Insurance to E. Phillips Pontardawe Agent, 9/- paid. D.M. & John finished ditching road side of Coed cae y Gwraetheg hedge to saw pit from the Gate. It is now very tidy, begun last Tuesday.

Tuesday 2 May: Had 2 loads of Llwynrhidie coal, quite out of this coal, 30 cwt. 5/-. Went to Swansea midday train, came up last. F[anny] & Kate G[ilbertson] to Swansea too, also Netta Lewis & Mr. Thornley. Mr. Scott stopped a tooth for me. Paid his bill £22..10..0. Spoke to him about Lodgings in Bath.

Wednesday 3 May: Betty fetched Sally from Llwynypreved to cut out my black dress, Victoria cloth 3/- a yard 33 inches wide. Recd. receipt from Mr. Davies of Llwydcoed Llanelly for cheque £37..16 sent him last Friday for surveying & mapping Cwmllynfell Colliery up to 1st Janry. last.

Friday 5 May: I lunched at the Gilbertsons, they were very friendly. Mrs. G, Fanny & Kate walked back with me as far as D. Lewis' Rhydyfro. Day met me there with the Phaeton. Lizzie finished making my old Cheltenham silk cape into a Tunic which I wore today. Sally here making sash for Lizzie's grey Carmelite dress & putting velvet on the jacket. The little white cow brought He calf.

Saturday 6 May: Recd. a letter from Miss Charlotte Scott from Bath saying she had seen lodgings she thought would suit & when I wd. require them. Wrote to thank her & to say I shd. be up on Saturday if possible. Felt very poorly all day liver sadly out of order making me feel wretched.

Sunday 7 May: Lizzie, I & Betty to Church. I left Fly at M. Jones' & Lizzie & I drank tea there. I went for ride by Coed cae Mawr, Lizzie came on foot to meet me above Nant-y-Gwin. Francis here.

Monday 8 May: John took 4 cwt short hay to Joseph Rees Abernant Brewery @ 2/6, 10/- paid. Had 2 loads Llwynrhydie coal 30 cwt, 5/-. Dl. Jenkins & D.M. sawing poles for railing. Betty washed my flannel shawl & Lizzie's.

Tuesday 9 May: Paid John Jones Crachllwyn Garth Poor Rate by cheque £60..5..0 @ 1/-, £2..17..4 paid. Day thought he had lost the Ram but it was found at Nant-y-Gasseg. Betty wonderfully annoyed! by their wanting to know Shonny Peggy's Surname in case they suspected him. I never saw a girl behave so silly & wrong. D.M. mowed Green 1st time this year. John carried all the long hay to store room & cleaned out Hay House, the boards are quite rotten from hay sweat.

Wednesday 10 May: E. Jones Butcher bill paid by cheque yesterday to this date, £2.. 15..0 paid. Mr. & Mrs. Jones Llanguicke called, stayed to tea & supper left at 11 o'clk. They were very friendly & brought me a large piece of Wedding Cake, Dotty's. Mrs. Jones had not been here a very long time. Gave Revd. D. Jones cheque for £100..0..0. Paid Pastoral Aid money. Sent bottle Cod Liver Oil to Margaret Joseph by Revd. D. Jones. Recd. letter from A. Gilbertson about the fishing in the River "Egel".

Thursday 11 May: John & D.M. railing between saw pit & Wain Daniel. All the road fence on both sides is in thorough repair, safe & looking tidy.

Friday 12 May: D. Davies Forchegel came here. I had sent for him to know about the River "Egel". He is very glad Mr. Lloyd & Mr. Gilbertson are going to preserve the fish, he will do all he can to help them & to prevent poachers.

Saturday 13 May: Lizzie & I left Garth 1st train for Swansea thence by Express to Newport where we had to wait ½ hour for train to Portishead & Bristol, thence without any delay to Bath which place we arrived at 4.30 p.m. Miss Scott met us at the Station & brought us to our lodgings, 9 Pierrepont Street North Parade. Very nice rooms & pleasant situation. Roberto Lena Apartments, 2 Bedrooms & Parlour £1..10..0, Kitchen fire 2/6d, Parlour fire 3/6d Gas. Looking very nice & clean.

Sunday 14 May: In the house all day.

Monday 15 May: Lizzie & I went for a walk up Pulteney Street, Laura Place, &c. The chestnut trees are in beautiful blossom. There is a cold wind & we are glad of a fire. Mrs. & Miss Scott called & were very pleasant & kind. Bought 2 combs at Hatt's Milsom Street [*T. J. Hatt, Hairsetting & Shampooing*]. Lizzie had her hair cut. Took G.C.R.'s prescription to Mr. Clarke Smith, Chemist, such a nice kind man. He said I was quite out of health, liver the great enemy. John Jones Bryn Amman died aged 76 yrs., he had broken his leg some weeks ago.

Tuesday 16 May: Mrs. Scott came at 10 a.m. Walked with us round the streets to see the shops. Went with Mrs. S. to see the Pump Room, a fine handsome room & the hot water comes through a pretty fountain, the cups &c nicely arranged for use. Bath Races: Lizzie & I went past the York Hotel & saw lots of Carriages & all sorts of traps going to the Race Course. Went to Camden Terrace & back thro' Walcot. Mr. [William Abraham] Cox the Surgeon called, said I was very much out of health.

Wednesday 17 May: Recd. letter from Revd. D. Jones saying they wd. like to have £300 in addition to the £100 given this day week. Recd. card from Laura Jones saying she knew of one & only one man in the Parish likely to suit me, wants to know the wages I give &c. Write to say it is 12/- in money, house, coal, &c equal to 2/- per week making in all 14/- per week.

Thursday 18 May: ***** Mr. Cox the Surgeon called, said my Kidneys & Liver were greatly deranged owing he thought to too much anxiety & perhaps a long standing cold. Said I was very weak, exceedingly so & that I must keep quiet taking only very moderate exercise. He is a very nice old Gentleman & takes much pains to find the seat of disorder. Lizzie & I went to order Banner Screen, also to see Vezey's Carriages [*E&H Vezey, Coach Builders & Harness*

Makers, 19 Milsom Street], then to the Crescent & Park, the Circus, &c all very beautiful.

Friday 19 May: Went for a drive through the Park and Weston Road.

Saturday 20 May: Went to see the Market a.m., fish, flesh, fowl, fruit, flowers, vegetables, &c beautifully arranged, looking so tempting & every thing so nice, the building is of peculiar form & the prettiest market I have ever seen. Had little Scarbro' brooch & locket mended. The 2 Miss Scotts called asked us to tea (yesterday).

Sunday 21 May: Neither of us to Church. Lizzie went a walk p.m., I in the house all day.

Monday 22 May: Went to "Hamper" Draper [*Hamper & Son, Mercers & Drapers, Northgate Street*] to see for stays & cloth jacket for me, none suitable. Had my Hair cut at "Finagans", 30 Milsom Street [*L&S Finigan, Coiffeur, Perfumier & Ornamental Hair Manufacturer*], not well done, the boy thought more of himself than of his business.

Tuesday 23 May: Lizzie & I went in a Pony Carriage up to Combe Down, thro Claverton & back along the Warminster road, such a lovely drive & such pretty views of Midford, & Farley Castles, Bathampton, Larkhall & the whole of the City & surrounding Country. It took us 2¼ hours. It was very dusty which is rather unpleasant. Felt very poorly in the afternoon. Went to bed 4.30.

Wednesday 24 May: Lizzie went to Wool Shop to be shown how to make Crochet pattern bought there last week for antimacasser. Mr. Cox called, gave me a bread seal made by him 45 years ago (The Oak). Lizzie & I called on Mrs. Scott, 13 St. Mark's Place & from there went for a walk up the hill & down to Lyncombe Vale, such a lovely quiet place & home a pretty way by the toll bridge.

Thursday 25 May: Recd. letter from Evans saying "Fly" had been kicked & was quite lame, the cow too was not well. Recd. letter from Laura Jones about Man Servant (John Jones), says he is honest, sober & industrious & knows him well. Recd. letter from Gwen Price (Tretower) Jane & Dora in London, also Dora Starbuck. London very full. Gwen had seen Morgan Bolgoed & T. Vaughan in passing thro' Brecon, the latter on duty with the Militia.

Friday 26 May: Mr. Cox called, told me to take a bath. Went in a "Fly" for a drive through the Park & Weston Road, Mrs. Scott, Lizzie & I at 3 p.m., the country looking lovely & the air very pleasant after the rain of yesterday. Took a Bath 100° at the New Royal Baths joining the Grand Hotel. Enjoyed it very much, the arrangements & accommodation perfection.

Saturday 27 May: Lizzie wrote to her Father & Miss R. Jenkins. Mr. Cox called. Went to look at bonnets & hats at Miss Weller's Bond Street, none to suit me. All too old & too young.

Whit Sunday 28 May: Lizzie & I to the Cathedral 11 a.m. Not out afterwards. Had the Baby to nurse p.m.

Whit Monday 29 May: A bright warm day. Lizzie & I went over the Abbey Church. They are making great improvements, restoring the Nave & throwing it into the Church. It is a beautiful place, the painted Windows are magnificent. Went p.m. to see Mrs. [Samuel] Richardson's (Down House, Upper Bristol Road). Musical boxes, very pleased.

Thursday 1 June: D. Morgan took White Cow's Calf to E. Jones Butcher, 96 lbs. @ 7d. £2..16.

Friday 2 June: I called at 4 p.m. at 13 Bennett Street (near the Circus) upon Miss Pendrill (my dear Mother's 1st Cousin). She was out so I left my card & afterwards wrote to say I had called & who I was. Mrs. Cox 54 New King Street called. Lizzie & I went to Misses Evans & Owen, Bartlett Street [*Silk Mercers & Linen Drapers*]. To see Willie Paddison, I hardly knew him, he knew my voice.

Saturday 3 June: Miss [Mary] Pendrill & her niece Miss M. Mackenzie came to call upon me, the former is an old lady with very white hair, beautifully & suitably dressed, very stout, handsome, rather short but very stately & dignified in manner, quite a lady & one who undoubtedly has moved in the best society. The niece is a very nice, pretty, unaffected lady-like person. They seemed pleased I had called & asked me there on Monday evening.

Sunday 4 June: Went to the Roman Catholic Chapel a.m. Willie came at 4 p.m. & stayed till 10.15, he is a nice boy & I think very good.

Thursday 8 June: Miss Pendrill & Mrs. Mackenzie called in a Carriage & Pair 11.30 to take me for a drive. Went up the Wells road to Combe Down, came home by the North road, Sydney Gardens & Pulteney Street, it was a lovely morning, the views extensive & pretty, the air bracing & clear – a lovely drive – & one I enjoyed very much. Miss Mackenzie's arm was too painful to bear the motion of the Carriage. I never met with more kindness & politeness, they are real Ladies & Mrs. Mackenzie so handsome & a fine woman also.

Friday 9 June: Stayed in Bed until 12 o'clk. as Mr. Cox wished to examine my back & spine, he said I was wonderfully thin & weak & required great care & nourishment & on no account to fatigue myself. He thinks there is no organic disease but that my whole system is delicate & the circulation very weak & languid. Mrs. Scott dined with us, took her home in a Fly & after tea went to buy a black trunk, gave 14/- for it.

Saturday 10 June: I called at 13 Bennett Street at 12 o'clk. to wish Miss Pendrill Good bye. She was very kind & begged me to come & see her if I came again to Bath, gave me a little Book written by her Niece. Mrs. & Miss Mackenzie out which she regretted so much. They are very nice kind people & seemed so glad to have seen me & so glad I called. If I had been the Queen they could not have shown me more respect. Lizzie & I left 9 Pierrepont Street at 2 p.m. for Swansea, thence to Garth by Fly, here at 10 p.m.

Monday 12 June: Some man from Cwmllynfell came here with letter from Levi Rees[11] saying he had seen Mr. R. Jenkins & that the School Room lease was ready to be signed & asked if I could attend at the Court Leet on Thursday to have my name placed on the Rolls.[12] Lizzie to Bryn Syfi with a letter from me to Mr. Jenkins asking what I had better do about the above letter (midday

---

11. Levi Rees was employed by the Cwmllynfell Colliery Company and lived in Cwmllynfell Cottage. Visiting him on census day was George B. Brock J.P., who was listed as a merchant.
12. Court Leet: originated in the Court Baron, a feudal court in which the lord of the manor exercised jurisdictional rights over his tenants and bondsmen in respect of his manor's administration. It was a court of record, would hear presentments on matters of local concern and could form a jury of freeholders to hear and punish offenders within its jurisdiction. It exercised a controlling surveyance over the condition of watercourses, ditches, roads and paths and any encroachment on public rights, e.g. in respect of enclosure, common lands, abuse of pasturage, the inspection of food, weights and measures. Gradually superseded by county J.P.'s and later magistrates' courts, but remained in many areas as a form of civil administration well into the 19th C. Its legal jurisdiction was abolished in 1977 but a few exemptions have survived to re-enact traditional ceremonies.

train came back the last). Mr. Jenkins gone to Merthyr so she did not see him. Thos. Jenkins here seeing Fly's foot. Paid him 15/- for 3 journeys also 6/4d. the amount of Hibbert's bill for medicine to this date.

Wednesday 14 June: Recd. a letter from Mr. J. B. Jenkins saying he has seen his Cousin & that it was not necessary that I must attend at the Court Leet tomorrow, as the matter of placing my name on the Court Rolls could be done at Mr. Kempthorne's office at Neath. D. Morgan to Cwmllynfell with a letter to Levi Rees saying that if I was not well enough to go to the Court Leet tomorrow I wd. attend to the matter at Neath as soon as I was able.

Thursday 15 June: John Thomas Gwernllyn here paying for long hay had 29th April, 14 cwt @ 4/6 £3..3..0. Leet Court at Gwain Caegurwen Leigh Arms.

Friday 16 June: Lizzie walked home this evening left here at 6 o'clk., took her photograph & the spectacles case bought at Bath for her Father.

Sunday 18 June: I & Betty at home all day. Expected Evans the Post Office, did not come.

Monday 19 June: Lizzie returned at 11 a.m. says her Father's ankle is very painful.

Wednesday 21 June: Miss Thomas Cwmamman & Miss Anne Morgan Llansamlet walked here stayed to tea, Lizzie & I walked home with them as far as Cwmgorse farm. Met lots of people coming from Llandilo fair. Fly's leg was bad or we wd. have driven them home.

Thursday 22 June: Wm. Rees Gellylucka brought the pig here that Wm. Lewis bought of him for me last Monday, £2..9..0 paid.

Friday 23 June: Henry Jones carpenter Craig Llanguicke whose shop & a large quantity of timber was burned down a few weeks ago came here with an appeal. Gave him a Sovereign £1..0..0. Betty very disagreeable, saying she was not well & could not do her work if she had to go messages such as for ham, flour, &c. She is <u>the most</u> detestable or at least <u>one</u> of the most detestable beings in Creation, of that I am certain. Mary Williams here with a duck 2/6d. She had the little boy (Evan) a very nice baby 7 months old gave him 2/6d.

Saturday 24 June: I went to Bryn Syfi midday train to stay a week or so with Miss Jenkins, Miss Rachel at Bridgend. Lizzie drove me as far as Gellygron.

Wednesday 28 June: Went to Mr. R. Jenkins to tell him to draw a Bond out for securing £400 which I am going to lend Revd. David Jones, Llanguicke.

Saturday 1 July: Mr. J. Morgan of Bolgoed dined at Bryn Syfi & left at 8 p.m. for Growen where they are all staying. He & his family intend leaving in a few weeks for Germany (Bonn I think). 2 Dozn. Beer, 1 Dozn. Porter by Mrs. Day.

Monday 3 July: Paid Mr. Shepherd's bill for last year by Mr. Jenkins, £1..14 paid. Swansea Wool fair. Miss Jenkins & I called at Mrs. Matthews, after tea Richard walked back with us as far as toll bridge.

Tuesday 4 July: Miss Rachel returned from Bridgend looking better.

Wednesday 5 July: Recd. a letter from Revd. Dd. Jones saying Mrs. Jones & himself had been at Mr. Jenkins on Friday, that they had had the money (£400) & signed the bond for it. Came home from Bryn Syfi midday train, Miss Jenkins came with me as far as Pontardawe in her way to Glantwrch to see how Mr. Price was, he has been very ill. Mrs. Walters of Ystrad in the train. Lizzie at the Station to meet me.

Thursday 6 July: Peggy Rees 18 lbs bacon @ 10½d., 15/9d. paid.

Sunday 9 July: Lizzie & Betty to Church. I at home all day. Mrs. Herbert Lloyd a daughter.

Monday 10 July: John Derrybach came over this evening to mow the hay, the weather is so wet & unsettled that I am afraid for him to begin for a few days. Mary Dai Shone Williams here paying 6 months rent for Graig Llanguicke cottage occupied by her daughter, £1..10..0 due 1st last June. Recd. an invitation note from Mr. Gilbertson to Kate's Wedding Breakfast August 2nd.

Tuesday 11 July: John mowing thistles &c on front field until dinner time. John took the Hereford Cow (Minny) calf to Ynysmeudw. In his way back brought 5 cwt of soft coal, 2/6 paid. Betty took Banner Screen & holder to Mr. Gilbertson's (my wedding present to Kate), also a letter to her with kind wishes & a letter to Mr. G. declining his kind invitation to the Breakfast as I am not well enough.

Wednesday 12 July: John to E. Jones to weigh the calf, 109 lbs @ 7d (£3..3..7), it was 5 weeks yesterday & turned out well which I am glad of as the Collins all dine at Pontardawe tomorrow had calf's feet with hair on. Recd. 9 Gallon Cask of Beer from Brewery, 9/- paid.

Thursday 13 July: Netta Lewis Alltycham married today at Pontardawe Church to Mr. Robert Thornley.[13]

Friday 14 July: Recd. a kind note from Kate Gilbertson thanking me very much for the Screen & very sorry I was not coming to the Breakfast, she says "If on the 2nd August you feel strong enough to come down, pray do so, we should be so pleased to see you".

Sunday 16 July: I rode "Fly" to Church, left her at Mr. Jones'. Last time I was in Llanguicke was May 7th. Lizzie in the house, Betty to Church. Church very dirty. Spoke to D. Davies about it & told him to see to it.

Monday 17 July: John Williams Gellyluog brought me £15 on a/c of rent. Recd. a letter from Gwen Price saying her brother had been to Taff's Well & was better. She thought North Wales wd. be a good change for me & recommended "Penmaenmawr" in Carnarvonshire where Mrs. D. Morgan of Milford & her daughter who is delicate are going to. Miss Price says "O! how I should like to be taken with you. I wd. Iron [for] you, or do any other kind act". Jane Herbert, Alice W. & Mrs. E. Morris at Llandrindod Wells, they have been as many as 60 persons at table.

Tuesday 18 July: John Derrybach began mowing Cae Barriwns hay. D.M. mowing the Green. D. Morgan clearing Hay House and carrying in the remainder of the fern rick to put under the hay. Recd. letter from Levi Rees saying the Rubbish Tip going towards the Wood has been stopped & that he recommends not cutting the wood until the Spring being out of season when in leaf. He says "I do not think you ask much more than their value". The money I ask is £12 – price named by Surveyor.

---

13. Anna Jennet Lewis (23) married Robert Thornley (27) of Bickenhill.

Wednesday 19 July: Went on "Fly" to Gellyluog & D. Morgan to see about steps or ladder to go to Chaff room over stable, & also about a roof over the oven.

Thursday 20 July: John finished mowing Cae Barriwns midday & then commenced "Wainhir". Such a good & heavy crop of short hay & of such improved quality after all the lime & earth carried over it. It plainly shows how top dressing improves land, & how it pays.

Saturday 22 July: Mrs. Day brought me 1 Dozn. Jam pots from Swansea, 2/6d. paid.

Sunday 23 July: No one in Church, heavy showers.

Monday 24 July: Lizzie recd. a letter from her Sister saying her Father wanted to see her. She went home at 4 p.m., very wet & raining when she left but she wd. go, altho' I wanted her to wait till tomorrow owing to the rain.

Tuesday 25 July: Sold Rachel Thomas	4 lbs Bacon @	10½d	3s..6d
	28 lbs Cheese @	2½d	5s..10d
		Paid	9s..4d

Willie Paddison rode over from Gelly to see me. Stayed to tea & went up to the meadow with me & all about to see what I had done. D. Morgan putting pebbles to keep up the earth from Gate to Pistle.[14]

Wednesday 26 July: Daniel Jenkins nailing & closing boards of Chaff room above Gellyluog stable. I rode over after tea.

Thursday 27 July: Lizzie returned 6 p.m. Carried Cae Barriwns hay in good condition altho it had had a great deal of rain since it was mown, begun carrying 1.30 finished 7 p.m., all the Days, their Horse & Gambo helping.

Friday 28 July: John Derrybach for a load of hard coal. Cart broke on the road, 16 cwt 2/8d.

Sunday 30 July: No one to Church, very wet.

---

14. Pistle is a corruption of the Welsh *pistyll* meaning waterfall or water spout.

Y Pistyll
(Photo: courtesy of Mrs J. Morris)

Monday 31 July: Recd. a letter from Mrs. D. Morgan from Barmouth, she went there on Thursday & likes the place.

Wednesday 2 August: Kate Gilbertson married today at Pontardawe Church to Wm. Fisk Richardson of Liverpool.[15] A very gay wedding. A lovely day, so bright & warm.

Thursday 3 August: I feel very poorly & often in much pain, particularly in my head & eyes. I feel very different to usual & have no heart for anything.

Saturday 5 August: John Derrybach and John the Blacksmith finished mowing Ty Cwtta field at 12 o'clk., the hay is now all cut.

Sunday 6 August: Betty to Church.

15. Catherine Anne Gilbertson (25) married William Fisk Richardson (25), a Cotton Broker of Tranmere, Cheshire.

Monday 7 August: Morgan Jones called, sorry to see me so poorly. Wrote for him to J. W. Vaughan about Penbrindod buildings. Had Meadow hay, a wonderful crop after the lime & earth. ***** p.m. My head & eyes are exceedingly painful. I am much vexed about them.

Tuesday 8 August: Very poorly all day, eyes & headache. I feel exceedingly weak, it is quite an exertion for me to move or think.

Wednesday 9 August: Finished having all my hay in in good condition. John Derrybach went home at 3.30 p.m. to cut his own hay. Very hot. I am not at all well. Nero howls dreadfully at night. My Chest burns very much. I have not suffered from my chest for more than 15 years. Wrote to Mrs. D. Morgan at 2 Ael y don Barmouth.

Thursday 10 August: Dl. Jenkins & D.M. sawing rails & posts to make a gate way to the hill opposite the Hay House. Recd. letter & plan of Bridge on Tonmaen Owen (Cwmllynfell) from Kempthorne. Mr. Campion called here about the plan & said he thought I ought to be paid for the land. Recd. letter from Mrs. Lena Bath saying her 2nd Baby a boy was a month old.

Friday 11 August: Daniel & D.M. putting down post in 4 stones in Hill gate way by Hay house. Lizzie to Pontardawe with letters to Post & to fetch 100 nails @ a 1/- for railing. She walked in 1¾ hours leaving here at 9.50 returning at 11.35, it was very warm but she said she did not feel very tired. She often has been 2½ hours in cold weather.

Saturday 12 August: D.M. left here at 10 a.m. to go to his sister-in-law's funeral (Herbert's widow). Daniel finished putting up Hill gate way opposite Hay house, the railing looks very tidy & the little gate & spring so useful about the house is now very nicely & prettily enclosed & safe from the hill & all trespass. How my dearest Mama wd. have enjoyed seeing it. She was so pleased with tidiness & neatness & such a good clever woman in every thing & the best Mother & Wife in the World.

Sunday 13 August: Thunder. Lizzie to Church.

Tuesday 15 August: Recd. letter from Mrs. Morgan saying they left Barmouth last Thursday & were now at Ashford. John mowing rushes on the Hill for thatching Rick on Meadow.

Wednesday 16 August: Rode Fly to Cwmllynfell & John Griffiths walked with me, went to see about the bridge & new road over Tonmaen Owen. Rees said they were tipping Rubbish to the Meadow & wanted me to come down & see it but I could not. It was the first time I had been to Cwmllynfell since I sprained my foot. Very warm & distant thunder.

Thursday 17 August: Recd. letter from Miss Price saying Alice was coming to Tretower on Saturday.

Paid J. Jones	Poor Rate £60..5..0 @10d	£2.. 7..10
	Highway Rate on Cottages	6..10
		£2..14..8 Paid

D.M. & D. Jenkins at Gellyluog putting up roof over the Oven & putting wooden steps up to Chaff room.

Friday 18 August: Went down to Bryn Syfi midday train to stay a few days. The 2 Miss E. Stricks went in the same carriage, they had been calling at the Gilbertsons.

Saturday 19 August: Mrs. Price called at Bryn Syfi. Miss Jenkins & I went with her to Swansea in the Fly. Mrs Bankent & her 2 children staying at the Mumbles, they were in Swansea but I did not see them. Tom Price also in the Mumbles. Called at Mr. R. Jenkins, he was in the country. Bought in the Market teapot & dishes &c., 2 loads Coal 31 cwt @ 2d by J. Griffiths 5/2d, 2 Dozn. Beer, 2 Dozn. Porter, ½ Dozn. Sherry.

Sunday 20 August: Betty to Church. Lizzie in the house. I at Bryn Syfi.

Tuesday 22 August: Miss M. A. Williams & her little niece Katie Gunter dined at Bryn Syfi.

Wednesday 23 August: Went to Swansea with Miss Rachel. Called at Mr. R. Jenkins Office, told him about the Cwmllynfell New Bridge. He has not yet got my papers for the Court Rolls ready for the sale of the house at Neath, he is the most dilatory man I ever met with & annoys me very much. Saw Mr. Shepherd about the pain in my side & chest, he thinks there is nothing serious, but the result of Pleurisy in '65 at Cheltenham.

Thursday 24 August: Came home from Bryn Syfi midday train. Very stormy & damp. Miss Jenkins gave me a fowl. The man recommended by David Ystradamman came here this morning. I had not come home, he comes again.

Friday 25 August: Sally here putting fringe on the black silk cloak she had turned for me a little time ago (new in '57), it looks nice. She also cut out white muslin Garibaldi[16] for me & takes it home to make.

Saturday 26 August: Lizzie finished making white petticoat for herself to wear with her new grey & brown Barège[17] with tucks. Henry (the lame man) finished thatching the short hay rick on the meadow, he was 2 days & John attending him, 7/- paid. D. Morgan trimming road side hedges.

Monday 28 August: D. Morgan (Mason) told me a neighbour of his who works in Cwmllynfell Colliery told him yesterday that about 150 tons of Coedfalda coal comes up daily thro' Cwmllynfell pit. I am supposed to be paid a ½d a ton wayleave for every ton coming thro' my pit, but I greatly doubt the correctness of the account.

Tuesday 29 August: David Davies the man recommended by David Ystradamman came here yesterday afternoon to see me, & to know if I wd. engage him, told him the wages I gave were 12/- a week in money, house coal, garden & manure besides, which I consider equal to 2/- a week making in all 14/- a week. After my return home he comes on a month's trial at 15/- a week. Met the Budds under Cae Barriwns on my way from Meadow yesterday.

Thursday 31 August: Lizzie & I left Garth 8.30 a.m. for Garnant, tickets 2nd Class to Shrewsbury £1..10. Arrived there 2.30 p.m. Stayed the night at the Raven Hotel (Ladies Coffee Room) all very nice & comfortable. Our train company consisted of 2 young Ladies going to Edinburgh where they lived, they had been visiting friends in Wales. Went to Redmays in the Square where I bought Lizzie black cloth jacket open front & myself a kind of black cashmere cloak with bow behind. Jane came with us to Cross Inn. Rather a damp morning but cleared very fine.

Friday 1 September: Went for a walk to the Quarry, the trees a lovely Avenue along the banks of the Severn. Saw St. Chad's Church, it is Circular in shape

16. A loose blouse originally made of bright red material.
17. Silky gauze made from wool.

and has a magnificent Chancel Window & 4 other handsome stained windows & several good tablets & a beautiful font cushioned all round. It is a very nice Church & well kept. Lodgings (Shrewsbury) recommended Mrs. Wilson, Music Shop, The Square. Left Shrewsbury 11.33 a.m. for York, getting there 5.40. Stayed the night at N.E.R. [*North Eastern Railway*] Hotel (tickets 2nd Class £1..12..6). A young lady very nice from Newport travelled with us to Scarboro'. Met Miss Symonds at Leeds going to Ilkely. She knew me first.

Saturday 2 September: A damp morning squall rain. Left N.E. Hotel York 9.45 a.m., arrived in Whitby about 1 o'clk. Met & travelled with a very kind Gentleman from Leeds. We had lunch at the "Crown Hotel" & he came out with us after lunch to look for lodgings & to show us the town. Took rooms (sitting room & bedroom) at 4 Wellington Terrace, £2..0..0 per week. They are not what I like, being small & draughty but I cannot get others the place is so full.

Sunday 3 September: ***** Lizzie & I went to the Iron Church (St. Hilda) 10.30 a.m. The Rector Mr. Keane did the duty in a Chair being paralysed.

Tuesday 5 September: In the house altering cloak a.m. Went for a walk p.m. along the Cliff to the Brickworks & home by the road & St. Hilda's Terrace, went into the Nursery Gardens, the ferns looking very nice & altogether a very nice walk & very pretty sea & land views. I never saw any thing look so pretty as the boats do with their dark & white sails. Recd. a letter from Miss Jenkins, Miss Rachel went yesterday to Glan Twrch to stay with Jane. Mrs. Price & Dora going to Buxton.

Wednesday 6 September: Whitby Races on the sands. Lizzie & I sat on the Cliff to see them. Not well a bad face ache. Recd. letter from Mrs. Scott (Bath) in answer to my letter of the 27th on the death of her Daughter-in-law, Mrs. F. Scott. She died rather suddenly on the 24th.

Friday 8 September: Lizzie & I went over the bridge into old Whitby, went to see where the Herrings were pickled, smoked & packed for the London & other markets. Went to see the Parish Church (St. Mary's), it is a peculiar building 197 steps I think to get to it, the Church overlooks the sea on one side. We went from there to St. Hilda's Abbey, a fine old Ruin close by the Church & well worth inspection, the view from it magnificent of land & sea & gives one a good & correct idea of the situation of the town of Whitby & its neighbourhood.

Saturday 9 September: In the house all day, raining all the morning & until 3 p.m. Face ache very bad. Wrote to Mrs. Tuttle, Miss Price & Miss Jenkins. Recd. a letter from Miss Jenkins 9 a.m. & from Miss Price 7.30 p.m. Miss King is now staying at Tretower.

Sunday 10 September: Lizzie & I went to the Congregational Chapel close by here a.m. & p.m. Very much pleased with Mr. Jackson & his sermons, his voice is so clear & pleasant. Texts: a.m. Peter Ch. 3 Verse 18, p.m. St. John Ch.1 verse 48.

Monday 11 September: Very fine morning. Lizzie & I walked to the Cemetery, ground very neatly kept & nicely laid out with shrubs & greenhouse plants. The earth like a garden & without a stone & the view very pretty, such a nice & peaceful resting place for the remains of those who are gone. I like to see a grave yard well kept & tastefully laid out, it lessens the sadness of death & makes us think of the beauties of Heaven. Walk from there to Ruswarp & back by the train, the country round very pretty. The best view I have seen of Abbey is from the Cemetery, it is lovely. 4.30 p.m. took a walk on the Cliff & went to inside of the Congress Hall. Went at 7 p.m. to a Prayer Meeting in Silver Street.

Tuesday 12 September: Whitby Flower Show in the Congress Hall, did not go. Lizzie finished the body of her Barège frock. I went in the afternoon for a walk by myself along the Cliff towards sands end till I came to a wayside Inn & then returned.

Wednesday 13 September: A cold morning. Recd. a letter a.m. from Mrs. Tuttle naming the lodgings at Scarbro'. After breakfast walked on the sands to a little wayside Inn towards sands end & returned by the Cliff, a nice healthy & pretty walk. At 4.20 posted letters, took a turn in the town, then past St. Hilda's Terrace to the field across the Esplanade & down the Pier to see the fishing boats going out, some taken by the Tugs (6 & 7 fastened by ropes to one Tug). The sea rough & the boats much tossed. The Pier is most substantial & the best I have ever seen, a credit to the town. Bought book of views &c.

Friday 15 September: Went to the Pier a.m. to see the boats come in & landing fish on the sands (low water), saw 2 casks packed for Swansea, a pretty sight. Met Miss Symonds in Cliff Street, she had been to the Post Office to see for letters. Her friend & herself had come to "The Royal Hotel" last night, they leave for Scarbro' tomorrow at 1 o'clk. She came to our lodgings & I gave her the address of lodgings recommended by Mrs. Tuttle & the Scarbro'

Gazette with which she seemed much pleased. Miss Barricks took us to see the Jet Workers. It is a dirty & unhealthy business & requires taste & skill. Took warm bath at 6 o'clk (1st). Walked on the Cliff p.m.

Sunday 17 September: Went to Chapel a.m. & p.m. Mr. Jackson gave a very good sermon on Singing a.m., Psalm 33 V. 2 & 3; p.m. Forgiveness of Sins, Acts 13 V. 38-39. Very good & plain. I wish we had such a Minister at home.

Monday 18 September: A cold morning. A.M. in the house writing letters. Recd. letter from Miss Jenkins, she said Dora's engagement with T. Vaughan was broken off, wh. I had heard of before. Lizzie began making twilled Night Gown for me. P.M. went for a walk down the Cliff path to the sands up to the Battery Upgang & back along the sands as far as the Pier & up road by the donkeys' home. No one hardly walking on the Cliff, it looked so desolate & so different to when we came when the place was so full. People are now going away rapidly. The waves were rolling in, rather roughly & no boats out, only 2 or 3 in the distance.

Thursday 21 September: Recd. letter from Miss Price saying why T.V. & D.P. broke off. Recd. letter from Miss Jenkins, Mrs. Price & Dora expected home on Saturday from Buxton. A.M. walked on the Pier to see the Packet "Confidence" to Saltburn, had a talk with the Coast Guard about Naval Matters &c. Such a nice pleasing & intelligent man & such a good open cheerful face, a nice figure & altogether so gentlemanly. Went to the Museum, lots of fossils, ores &c., but nothing else particular. Took a bath, rained in coming home so it did me no good. Miss Barricks very kind, warm shawls &c.

Friday 22 September: A.M. Lizzie took umbrella back that was lent us by the Bath woman last night, came back for me & we went to the Cliff. It was so cold we went for a walk to the Station to look for time table (none to be had), walked on to Esk Terrace, called at No. 12 to enquire the price of lodgings. Drawing room & two Bedrooms all included £2..2..0 now, in the Season £3..3..0. Looked very clean & comfortable & well furnished & Mrs. Wear a very nice pleasant woman. (Very cold wind).

Saturday 23 September: Lizzie & I to a Bible Meeting last night at the Iron Church 7 p.m. & were much pleased. Mr. Edwards (the B.S. Deputation) spoke and made a most interesting & instructive address, his voice & manner clear & pleasing. He travelled a good deal abroad in Spain, France & Italy & said the whole of the Continent of Europe was now open for the free circulation of the Bible wh. he had never been able to say until this year.

Sunday 24 September: I went to Chapel a.m. Mr. Jackson gave a good Sermon Zach. 2 verse 5 (wall of fire). Lizzie to Parish Church (St. Mary's), Mr. Kane preached. Both to Chapel p.m. Mr. Jackson preached on Temperance, Eph. 5, V. 17, 18, 19. Very good.

Friday 6 October: Watkin Davies called, stayed to tea, said Mr. Thomas our Curate was appointed Inspector of Schools.

Saturday 7 October: David Davies Forchegel here. Gave him £1..0..0 towards the repairs of the roof of Llanguicke Church, he being the Churchwarden.

Sunday 8 October: Lizzie & I at home. Betty to Church.

Tuesday 10 October: A load of Llwynrhydie coal 15 cwt 2/6d. by D. Morgan (Mason).

Friday 13 October: Wrote to 16 Railway stations &c to say my 2 missing boxes were found at Bristol & came here safely last night. Mary Watkins here to tea, she rode Mr. Richard's pony. Teddy Thomas called here in his way from School thinking his Mamma was here, she was not, he stayed to tea & left with Mary Watkins at 9 p.m.

Saturday 14 October: Wm. Lewis came here, he had been through Gellyluog Wood said it was very free from damage.

Sunday 15 October: Lizzie & I at home all day (wet). Betty to Ystalyfera to see Mary's son who had met with an accident. W. Lewis here from Church with letters.

Wednesday 18 October: Lewis the Tiler at Gellyluog, put roof over the Oven & in his way home came here to mend the Closet roof with mortar. Paid him for slating the back roof of Plas-y-bryn & taking off Welsh tiles with which the back was covered before in August last as per bill .... £1..7..8

1 day (today) 3/8 all paid to this date 3..8

£1..11..4

Friday 20 October: Recd. a letter from Mrs. R. P. Llewelyn asking for my Photograph.

Saturday 21 October: Put braid round bottom of black Moreen[18] Petticoat.

Sunday 22 October: Lizzie & Betty to Church. Biddy came up to tea & Wm. came for her.

Monday 23 October: Betty to the Mill for a stack of barley meal for the pig (1st) 4d. pd.

Tuesday 24 October: Had 2 loads of Llwynrhidie coal by D.M. (Mason) 16 cwt each 5/4. Sent D. Morgan for Bevans Gartheithen, he came when he came from his work, told him that his cows had damaged the fence between the road & Wain Pedr Erw & that if he did not keep his cows off the road I would pound them or fine him.

Wednesday 25 October: ***** Finished drawing the Potatoes in Cottage garden, a very poor crop, & very few fit for eating. Recd. a letter from Miss Price from Itton Court,[19] said Alice was going to spend the Winter with her Brother at Llandovery.

Friday 27 October: Lizzie went home for a few days, took Grey dress &c in my bonnet basket. I sent a pair of jet studs to each of her sisters. Morgan Jones called here in his way from Cwm Nanthopkin, said Mr. Kempthorne was full of having a railway up this Valley.

Saturday 28 October: Margaret Gellyluog brought me a Tongue & Heart, they had killed a Cow.

Sunday 29 October: Betty to Church. Very wet. Pastoral Aid collection. Revd. D. Jones preached.

Monday 30 October: The woman who lives near Llwynhir by Jenny came here to offer her husband John Jones as workman, he had been with Sir John Mansel & she had lived as Dairy maid with Mrs. Harris, Aberglasney. Morgan & Ellen came here, said they knew of a man likely to suit me now at Golden Grove, told them I would like to take him on a month's trial.

---

18. Ribbed woollen and/or cotton material.
19. Itton Court near Chepstow was the home of William Edward Carne and Annie, second daughter of Thomas King of Chepstow and a grand-daughter of Elizabeth Pendrill, a lineal descendant of John Pendrill, *Arch. Camb 1859, 114,229.* In his youth Dr. William Price of Glan Twrch had been indentured to Thomas King.

Tuesday 31 October: Wrote to Mrs. Kirkhouse asking her to make me a sofa rug to be ready by 13th Decr.

Wednesday 1 November: Recd. a letter from Mrs. D. Morgan.

Thursday 2 November: Thomas y Gove's sale. Had ½ ton of soft coal by David Gellyluog 4/-, David, horse & cart 3/-, 7/- paid.

Friday 3 November: Thos. Evans, Llandilo, the man recommended by Morgan & Ellen came here to see me & to know if I wd. engage him. I told him the kind of man I required & that the wages gave were 12/- per week in Money, house, coal, garden & manure besides, which I consider equal to 2/- a week making in all 14/- a week. He comes on a month's trial at 15/- a week. He is <u>very tall</u> which I <u>dislike very much</u> & I cannot say I am in <u>any</u> way prepossessed in his favour. D.M. cleaned the Pigsty & all about the Pistle & all the dead leaves from Stable, new garden &c. The back of the House is now <u>very tidy</u>.

Sunday 5 November: No one to Church. Betty to see her Father. I at home all day. Wm. Lewis here.

Tuesday 7 November: Mary, Betty's Sister-in-law here. Lizzie came back after been at home nearly a fortnight.

Wednesday 8 November: Jenny & Jacky came here tonight, bought the hind carriage wheels & axle. D. Morgan & I cleaned out the Coach House & took lining & stuffing out of old carriage.

Friday 10 November: Betty putting flower beds & green a <u>little tidy</u> & D.M. cleaning old garden. Paid Dd. Thomas the Star [Inn] for 18 yards of flags[tones] for Cottage which he brought today @ 2/- £1..16..0 Paid. Tied the 2 Cows tonight.

Saturday 11 November: D. Morgan finished putting the old garden tidy, the front is now tolerably clean. Mrs. Kirkhouse walked up to dinner. She very kindly brought me some herrings knowing I liked them. Said her sister Mrs. Hale had a baby (1st Child) 4 months old, Thos. Ferdinand. She walked home, gave her a pot of cream.

Sunday 12 November: Very fine day. Betty to Ystalyfera. Lizzie & I intended going to Church, but Daniel came & hindered us. He is going a Servant to Gellygron.

Monday 13 November: Daniel Harris' wife broke her leg in coming from Llandilo fair. The cart upset near Llwynhen Brewery.

Wednesday 15 November: Jacky came for the Wheels she bought this day week. Lizzie with letters to Post. Wrote to Thos. Evans Towy Terrace asking why he did not send me Mr. Brockie's address that I may write for his Character.

Thursday 16 November: Miss Watkins' servant came for antimacassar that she had lent Lizzie to copy & brought me the address of "Stephenson's Tooth-ache Pills." Had dreadful pain in my face all the afternoon.

Friday 17 November: Cleaned out my room.

Saturday 18 November: Slept in White room last night as my room was not quite dry. In dreadful pain with my face all night. As I am in so much pain with my face & have such bad nights Lizzie is to sleep with Betty in the White room.

Sunday 19 November: Lizzie & Betty to Church. I at home. Face very painful.

Monday 20 November: Betty Plas y bryn here paying ½ year's rent due last March £1..10 Paid. In bed all day with most dreadful face ache.

Tuesday 21 November: ***** In bed all day in dreadful pain with one side of my head & face, did not sleep a wink last night. I never suffered such excruciating pain before. Had fire in my Bedroom.

Wednesday 22 November: A load of hard coal 18 cwt fetched by D.M., 3/-.

Thursday 23 November: Jacky y Nailer's son here cleaning the Clock, it had been standing nearly 2 years & is very dirty & getting rusty. He seemed to take great pains to clean it & I hope it will now go right.

Friday 24 November: Dd. Jones Cwmcoy here offering a man, he was a servant of his lately married & he thought he wd. exactly suit me. Told him I had partly engaged a man from Golden Grove, if he wd. not suit I wd. be glad of the one he spoke of.

Saturday 25 November: Gwen Price came to Glan Twrch from Itton Court where she had been staying 5 weeks.

Sunday 26 November: Lizzie to Church. Betty at 6 p.m. went to see her Father. My face painful.

Monday 27 November: Wrote to Mr. Brockie Golden Grove asking the Character of Thos. Evans, one of his Workmen who offers himself to me as manservant. Mrs. Thomas Cwmamman & her nephew Willie Hyde called here, stayed to tea. Lizzie & Day took them home in the Phaeton as far as the "Mountain [Inn]". Daniel Thomas Gellyluog Ucha killing the Pig, 1½ hour exactly doing all. Rachel John here helping & cleaning.

Tuesday 28 November: Mr. Price came down to see old Mary Ward, he drove Aunt Gwen to see me & they both lunched here. Miss Jenkins walked up from Pontardawe midday train to see me, knowing I was very ill with dreadful face ache, brought me a fowl.

Wednesday 29 November: Jane Jones Hendreforgan walked down to see me having heard I was very poorly, & a message from Mrs. Jones Tirbach saying she was sorry she could not come as her Father was ill. Jane stayed the night. Miss Jenkins left last train. Lizzie & Day took her to the Station. Recd. a letter from Mr. Brockie saying Thos. Evans was honest, sober, truthful, steady, good workman & had been on the Estate 8 years.

Thursday 30 November: Jane Jones left at 6 o'clk. Lizzie walked part of the way with her.

Friday 1 December: Biddy came up to see me, hearing I was so ill. David Gellyluog brought ½ ton of soft coal 4/-, David, horse & cart 3/-, 7/- Paid. D. Jones Cwm Coy here asking if the Golden Grove man was coming, told him I had recd. a good Character of him from Mr. Brockie & that I intended having him on a fortnight's trial.

Sunday 3 December: Betty to Church, Lizzie in the house with me. Sally came up to see me.

Monday 4 December: John Evans (Jacky y Nailer's son) came here to see if the Clock he cleaned Nov. 30th was going all right. I am glad to say it does & so far keeps time very well. I think he took great pains to clean & repair it & that his work is a success.

Tuesday 5 December: Paid John Jones Crachllwyn Garth Poor Rate @ 10d in the £, £2..7..10. D. Morgan manure to mix with earth in Cae Cwtta, 14 loads. Lizzie with letters to Post. Gave her tonight a new Sovereign of 1871 to keep for my sake. Says she will & seemed pleased to have it. Wrote to Mr. J. B. Jenkins asking him to buy the set of Harness of Mr. Davis, if he thought it would suit me.

Wednesday 6 December: In dreadful pain with my face, in & on the bed nearly all day. D.M. mixing manure & earth heap in Cae Cwtta. Recd. a letter from W.H.L. Cape of Good Hope dated Oct.19th.

Thursday 7 December: D.M. finished mixing manure & earth heap in Cae Cwtta at 12 o'clk.

Friday 8 December: 2 loads of Llwynrhidie coal by D.M., 14 cwt. each @ 2d., 4/8d. Nero howled very much at 1 o'clk this morning. Betty carried Galvanised Iron from Chaff room to Kitchen loft. She also cleaned Chaff room & put it tidy.

Saturday 9 December: Lizzie very sick & ill this morning. D.M. & Lizzie cleaned the Stable &c. I mended Fly Cart Collar with Flannel. My face a little easier today. I hope I am now going to get better for I have suffered great pain since Nov. 15th with the right side of my head & face.

Sunday 10 December: Lizzie to Church. Betty at home with me.

Monday 11 December: Thos. Evans (Golden Grove) came here this day 12 o'clk. on a fortnight's trial. He begun digging & spading up the stumps in Plantation between Cae Barriwns & Front field.

Tuesday 12 December: Rev. Jones Llanguicke & Mr. Davies called asking permission to shoot snipes. I said I refused their request with reluctance for that I allowed no one to shoot on this land as Poachers had done so much damage to my fences & Day's crops. I dare say they were offended by my refusal, which I am sorry for, but I have made up my mind that for this year no shooting shall be.

Wednesday 13 December: Thos. Evans put new washers to Phaeton wheels & oiled them. Mr. Price came to see old Mary Ward. Gwen Price came with him to see me, they both lunched here. Mrs. Price in Clifton, both girls at home. Paid Dl. Jenkins for all work done to this date (this year) 9 days £1..16..0 Paid.

Thursday 14 December: ***** Mr. Jenkins came up midday train, he walked up from the Station. Thos. Evans spading up Flower beds. Bought 5 bushels of Oats of Samuel Williams Bagelegel 15/-. Mr. Essery Snr. died at Tirbach. His body was taken by here in a Hearse & 4 horses today 10 a.m., 1 Mourning coach.[20]

Friday 15 December: Mr. Jenkins left midday train today. Thos. Evans drove him to the Station.

Saturday 16 December: Thos. Evans went to meet his wife & child to Garnant Station. She comes over to see if she likes the place. Arthur Gilbertson & his sister Madalena called here on horseback, they had heard from the Price's I had been ill. They did not come in, Lizzie saw them.

Wednesday 20 December: A great storm of wind & rain. Thos. Evans cleaning gutter in Heol y Ty. Mr. Elias Beor married today at St. James' Church Swansea to Miss Elizabeth Harvey Bell, only daughter of Lieut. Col. Bell, late 12th Reg. now living in Swansea. Lizzie finished making the Antimacassar she is going to give me Xmas day.

Thursday 21 December: Thos. Evans brought 10 cwt of coal from Pontardawe, 4/-. He left here at 9 a.m., came back & had finished putting the coal tidy in its place by 2.30 p.m., the quickest time I have ever seen it done.

Friday 22 December: Lizzie went to Swansea midday train to see for Game to send to London tomorrow, but cd. get none, & no promise of some tomorrow so I am obliged to send the Poultry without Game, only ½ hun[dred] Oysters to the Marryats. Paid Mrs. Day for Poultry as follows:

Mrs. Rees	1 Turkey	8½ lbs.	1 Goose	5¼ lbs.
Mrs. Marryat	2 Turkies	13 lbs.	Mrs. Matthews	5 lbs.
Mifs Jenkins	1 Turkey	4¾ lbs.	Mifs Jenkins	5¼ lbs.
Mrs. J.	2 Turkies		Mrs. Evans	4¾ lbs.
Mrs. Kirkhouse	1 Goose	5 lbs.	Mrs. Jones (Station)	3¾ lbs.
				24 lbs. all @ 11d. per lb.

20. T. B. Essery, 78-year-old father-in-law of John Jones, medical practitioner.

Did not like to trouble Miss Jenkins as Miss Rachel is not well & her servants are rather high about carrying things, she used to send the Hampers off.

Saturday 23 December: Sent Basket to Mrs. Rees, Goose & Turkey, to Mrs. Marryat 2 Turkies, ½ hun. Oysters. So very sorry I could not get Game. Mrs. Day took them to Swansea & sent them off by train. Thos. Evans took 6 Mahogany Chairs to Dl. Jenkins Carpenter wh. he bought of me last night @ 7/6d. each, hair bottom & very good they were in White room, £2..5..0 Paid. Had load of hard coal 13 cwt.

Sunday 24 December: Betty to see her Father. Lizzie & I at home.

Monday 25 December: Very wet a.m. Cleaned a little p.m. Llanguicke at 11 o'clk. a.m. No one to Church. Lizzie & I at home all day. Betty too in the house all day. Lizzie gave me the Rose Antimacassar, it is nicely made & looks handsome. She also gave me a pretty little card. I gave Lizzie a little Book. Sent Jane a card, also Mrs. Bowman & Laura a letter, all posted yesterday. Recd. a kind letter from Miss Jenkins also a Xmas card from Mrs. Tuttle. Kind letters from Mrs. Morgan & Mrs. Kirkhouse yesterday.

Tuesday 26 December: Recd. a kind letter from Miss Rees today acknowledging the Goose & Turkey & wishing me to come & stay with them & to see a first rate Dentist. They are very kind to me at all times.

Wednesday 27 December: Recd. a kind letter from Mrs. Marryat, they have removed to 61 Warwick Street, Belgrave Road. Thos. Evans went to Neath for the New Plated Carriage Harness bought of Davies the Saddler, he says they are home made & of the best quality. Had the Carriage Lamp from Mr. Samuel wh. I lent him a long while ago.

Thursday 28 December: Very wet. D.M. dressing flags for Cottage & Thos. picking up the floor ready for laying them down.

Sunday 31 December: Betty to Church. Lizzie at home with me. My face very much swollen, right side from toothache.

1872

Margaret Jones's diary for 1872 is unfortunately missing but copies of some of her letters and of letters which she received during the year have survived. They help to provide a measure of continuity in several key features of her life.

Margaret Jones to Alexander Bain, Colliery Owner, Hendreforgan Farm

Garth Febry. 6th 1872

Mr. Bain, Sir

I am sorry I am not well enough to come to Cwmllynfell as intended. In reply to your letter of the 29th ult. I beg to say I have no one to send up with whom you can consult as to what you should do to prevent damage to my property. I have no doubt that it would have been easier for you to keep the River in its proper channel than to put it so now. Whatever may have been the first cause of making it deviate a little out of its course you must have been fully aware that your tipping rubbish into it would be the certain means of throwing it out of its bed thereby some day causing serious mischief. Considerable damage has been done to my land by your tipping into the River & I am sure you will see it just & right to make good the past damage caused by your acts & prevent future injury from the same cause.

Hoping to find you using every endeavour to meet my request,

I remain Sir, Yours obediently

Margaret Jones

Delivered by D. Morgan (Mason)

Margaret Jones to William Griffiths

Garth Febry. 6th 1872

Mr. Wm. Griffiths, Sir

I have seen Mr. Kempthorn's letter to Mr. Jenkins. I have no wish to incur any expense either to myself or the Highway Board respecting the Road. I know the part through which the road passes & all I require is a written promise from the Board that they will be at the expense of putting up a good fence of White Thorns on each side of the road to prevent trespass to my land. When I receive that promise they shall have my sanction to take the land shown on the plan.

Yours truly

Margaret Jones

James Kempthorne was Superintendent Registrar, Perpetual Commissioner & Commissioner in all courts including the Highway Board for the district of Neath.

John Davies to Margaret Jones

Llwyndcoed Llanelly
Feby. 17th 1872

Miss M. Jones Garth Pontardawe

Miss,

According to your request I have examined my papers respecting Cwmllynfell Colliery and am sorry to say that I found a little mistake in adding up the last half year's account. It was done by my assistant in a hurry. I will take great care in future & I beg most respectfully to apologize for my neglect this time.

The Colliery was visited last year in January, July & January this year. I am sorry I could not attend quarterly last year, it was owing to a most severe attack of Typhoid fever which kept me in Doors for 13 weeks. I am glad to say I am now able to follow my usual work. I will visit the Colliery in future the 1st week in April, 1st week in July, Octr. & January.

The Company are tipping Rubbish from all parts of the Colliery upon Cwmllynfell farm, they are tipping now since June last upon the meadow above the works which I have included in the last measurements.

Cwmllynfell Coal & Culm	*Tons*	
½ year ended June 30th 1871	*1671½*	
½ year ended Decr. 31st "	*2440½*	
	4112 @ 6d	*£102..16..0*

Mine		
½ year ended June 30th	*58*	
½ year ended Decr. 31st	*71½*	
	129½ @ 7d	*3..15..6½*
Wayleave		
½ year ended June 30th	*8762½*	
½ year ended Decr. 31st	*8975½*	
	17738 @ ½d	*36..19..0*
Surface damage		*8.. 0..0*
		£151..10..6½

I am Miss

Your most obed Sert,

John Davies

Mrs Frances Lloyd to Margaret Jones

Plas Cilybebyll
Swansea
S. Wales

April 21st

My dear Miss Jones

My daughter is to be married on 31st and as the wedding is to be comparatively quiet (only relations coming to it) we wish our friends if they wd. care to do so, to come here on Monday next the 27th to any afternoon from 4 to 6.30 & see my daughter, her wedding dress & presents. If you have nothing better to do we hope you will come?

Believe me yours sincerely,

Frances H. Lloyd.

Arthur Gilbertson married Ellen Lloyd on 25th July 1872 at Cilybebyll Church.

Margaret Jones to George R. Brock, Merchant

May 9th 1872

Dear Sir,

I send you a statement of what is due to me from Messrs. James & Aubrey for Royalty, Wayleave &c. to the 31st Decr. last according to the account given me by Jno. Davies the Surveyor & I shall feel obliged by you sending me a cheque for the amount.

Yours sincerely
Margaret Jones

Cwmllynfell Coal & Culm	*Tons*	
Year ending 31st Decr. 1871	*4112 @ 6d*	*102..16..0*
Mine	*130 @ 7d*	*3..15..10*
Wayleave a/c year		
Ending Decr. 31st 1871	*18410 @ ½d*	*38..7..1*
Surface damage		*8..0..0*
		£152..18..11

Swansea May 18th 1872

Recd of James & Aubrey by cheque the sum of One hundred, forty nine pounds eight shillings & ten pence for a/c rendered for Royalties, Wayleaves, Surface damage at Cwmllynfell for year 1871.

£149. .8..10
3..10.. 1 less tax
152..18..11

J. H. Rowland, Glamorganshire Banking Company, Neath to Margaret Jones, 9 October 1872

Dear Madam,

I believe that by the death of Mrs. Jane Llewellyn you are entitled to the £1,501..19. Now 3% standing in the name of H. S. Coke Executors, W. Coke having been the surviving Trustee of Mrs. Pendrill's Will. I saw Mr. W. H. Francis one of the Executors yesterday and he told me that if you could satisfy Messrs. Dod & Longstaffe Ltd 16 Hanover Street London, that you were entitled to the money, the transfer would be made to you.

If you will inform me how you are entitled I shall have pleasure in communicating with those gentlemen.

If you have the Probate of Mrs. Pendrill's Will that would probably be all that would be required.

I am

Dear Madam

Yours truly

J. H. Rowland

Ellen Lloyd to Margaret Jones

Cilybebyll
July 20th

My dear Miss Jones

I hardly know how to thank you enough for the beautiful present you have so kindly sent me and which will find a place on my drawing room chimney piece.

The enclosed note from my sister in law was written when your messenger arrived. I therefore send it with mine.
Hoping to see you on the 25th

Believe me

Most sincerely yours

Ellen Lloyd

Margaret Jones to John Davies, Land & Mineral Surveyor

Garth Novr. 30th 1872

Mr. John Davies, Sir

The recent floods have so surrounded & endangered the Cottage at Cwmllynfell near the River that the tenant has been obliged to leave. I expected that you would long ago have decided & concluded the boundary question & I cannot refrain from expressing my great surprise & dissatisfaction at your continued delay, knowing as you did how matters stood, and the urgency of the case. You will I presume write at once to Mr. Bain & also see that my property is safely & properly secured by him from at least further damage. Waiting your reply.

Yours &c.

Margaret Jones.

From John Davies, Land & Mineral Surveyor, to Margaret Jones, 3 December 1872

Madam,

I am in receipt of yours of the 30th ult. The weather has been so very bad all this time is the only reason that the matter has not been settled. If this fine weather continues for a few days we will be able to complete early next week. I will ride up tomorrow to see Mr. Bain & the place & let you hear from me as soon as possible.

Your most obed. Sert

John Davies

Margaret Jones to J. H. Rowland, 5 December 1872

Mrs. Eliza Tuttle & William Harries Francis Esq. (Executors of the Will of the late Henry Simmons Coke Esq.)

I hereby acknowledge that the transfer by you of £1501..19 New 3 per cent Annuities through your Attornies, Isaac Braithwaite, Henry Waite, Alfred Braithwaite, Albert Leland Noel & Charles Branch all of the Stock Exchange Gentlemen appointed at my request by a Power executed by you dated the 29th day of Novr. 1872 is in full satisfaction and discharge of all claims that I have upon you as Executors, of the late Mr. H. S. Coke as surviving Trustee of the Will of the late Mrs. Catherine Pendrill formerly of Pontardawe Cottage in the parish of Llanguicke in the County of Glamorgan Widow, and I undertake whenever called upon by you or either of you at my expense in all things to execute to you or either of you a proper release in respect of the said Stock and all other claims & demands arising under the Will of the said Mrs. Catherine Pendrill against the said Mr. Coke or his Estate in respect of the trusts thereof.

Dated the 5th day of December 1872

Margaret Jones

This is the copy of a Document sent me by Mr. Rowland from Messrs. Dod & Longstaffe Solicitors London, which I signed & returned to Mr. Rowland.

Margaret Jones to Lizzie Jones

Garth
Decr. 31st 1872

My dear Lizzie

I enclose a little card. May the New Year which is just opening bring you much happiness.

With my kind love & many thanks for the many little kindnesses you do me.

Believe me

Dear Lizzie

Yours affectionately

Margaret

1873

Margaret's diary for 1873 recorded another full and active year. She continued to exercise a close control over her domestic and financial affairs, detailing every transaction from the payment of rates and rents to the sale of hay and pots of salt butter and the replenishment of her stocks of coal and alcohol. Betty's illness and prolonged absence forced Margaret to search for a suitable replacement servant, whilst Walter's departure in late March left an outdoor vacancy to be filled. Margaret spent the greater part of June in Bath, although only 3 days were recorded, and in September enjoyed a fortnight in Rhayader with Lizzie and the two Misses Jenkins. The deaths of Mrs. Day's two month old daughter in January and of a favourite aunt Gwenllian Price in November were particularly distressing events. She maintained a critical watch over developments affecting her land around Cwmllynfell colliery and her concern over boundaries, noted in the 1872 letters, resurfaced.

Thursday 2 January: John Thomas Gwern-llwyn here paid me for the trees he bought Octr. 4th 1872, £2..6..0 paid. Betty ill in bed all day.

Friday 3 January: Betty in bed all day.

Saturday 4 January: Betty in bed all day. Sent D. Morgan for Mary her Sister at 10 a.m. She & Shonny came down about 7.30 p.m. Shonny went back & Mary stayed here.

Sunday 5 January: Mrs. Day's little girl christened at Llanguicke. Lizzie to Church.

Monday 6 January: Mary came down this evening with medicine for Betty.

Tuesday 7 January: I went to Bryn Syfi midday train to see about a girl, Betto's daughter, did not think she wd. suit so did not see her. Returned last train. Mary, Betty's sister, met me at the Station going to Ystalyfera. Said Betty was still poorly & that she wd. be down tomorrow to take her home to see the Doctor. Called at Mrs. A. Gilbertson's saying I wd. spare her some salt butter. Pd. Davies Ironmonger's bill [£2..10..9]. Met Mrs. Clarke at Pontardawe Station.

Thursday 9 January: Walters took Mary and Betty to Ystalyfera in Day's Car. Gave Betty a bottle of the best Sherry, a pot of jam, some biscuits &

arrowroot, & said if she liked to come back here when she was better, one of two servants, she was quite welcome to do so.

Friday 10 January: Hannah Gellyluog & I cleaned down kitchen loft. Paid Llwynrhidie Coal bill up to 31st Dec. 1872 [£6..2..4]. Paid John James the Income tax (by his son William):

1 yr. ending 5th April 1873 for Garth	£..s..d
Schedule A @ 4d. Schedule B @ 2d. on £50	1..5..0
Garth Cottage 1 yr ending 5th April 73 @ 4d.	1..0
Garth Land tax 1 year	14..7
By chcque	2.. 0..7

Recd. cheque for £49 from J. B. Jenkins being the Interest on rent paid by Samuel when buying the House at Neath.

Saturday 11 January: Walters took 27 lbs of salt butter to Mrs. Arthur Gilbertson at 4½, £1..12..7. paid. Mrs. Day to Swansea by train, 1st time since her confinement (Decr. 7th). Walters fetched the New Cart from John Davies, Dynevor Arms. Had ½ sack flour from P.O. & 1 cwt bran. Miss Jenkins birthday, 62 today. May she live many years.

Wednesday 15 January: Mr. Clarke here. Sent Walters to Neath with a letter to Mrs. Clarke asking her to send Margaret Owen here tomorrow, the girl she spoke of, to talk to me.

Thursday 16 January: Margaret Owen came here to see me. Engaged her for a month on trial at the rate of £12 a year. She comes on Tuesday.

Friday 17 January: Walters took 26lbs salt butter to Post Office @ 1/1½d, paid for this day. £1..9..3. paid.

Saturday 18 January: Mrs. Day took down 30 lbs salt butter to Miss Jenkins @ 14½d. £1..16..3.

Wednesday 22 January: ***** a.m. very little. Recd a letter from Mrs. Arthur Gilbertson inviting me to a dance on the 31st. Paid John Davies (Dynevor Arms) £11..0..0 by cheque for a new Cart had from him the 11th inst. He said he had made it of the best materials & that with my light work it ought to last 20 years. He said he would give £6 for the phaeton.

Thursday 23 January: Margaret Owen (whom we call Mary) from near Narberth came here on a month's trial, she had been a few months with Mrs. Clarke at Western Moor [Neath]. I give her at the rate of £12 a year.

Friday 24 January: David Gape paid Walters the 6/- he owed me for 2 cwt of meadow hay had May 4th 1872. I had often sent to ask him for it & said if he did not pay I would put him in the County Court & so I would even if it cost me £6. Sent Walters with a letter to Mrs. Gilbertson saying I was afraid of Neuralgia to venture to their dance on the 31st. Walters planted Billy Woodford's roses in the Green.

Saturday 25 January: Sold Griffith (Biddy's cousin) last year's rick of meadow hay in the presence of Wm. Lewis for £9. It is considered to be 3 tons 15cwt to 4 tons.

Sunday 26 January: No one to Church. Very wet.

Monday 27 January: Settled this day with John Williams Gellyluog all accounts to this date.

John Williams		Margaret Jones	
To Margaret Jones		To John Williams	
24 lbs Bacon @ 10½		1 load of lime	
had Sept.1872	£1..1..0 Paid	4½ tramloads @ 1/3 a trl.	5..7½
		ditto	5..7½
		Haulage of lime	10
		Gates	8
		1 Tram soft coal	12
		Haulage	4
			£1..17..11 Paid

Tuesday 28 January: Went to Bryn Syfi midday train to stay till Thursday

Wednesday 29 January: Jane (Lizzie's sister) came here and stayed a week. She brought Lizzie 2 pairs of brown woollen stockings.

Thursday 30 January: Returned from Bryn Syfi midday train. The two Miss Jenkins came with me as far as Pontardawe. They were going on to stay at Glan Twrch till Saturday.

Friday 31 January: A dance at Mrs. Arthur Gilbertson's. William Cwmllynfell here paying ½ a year's rent due last Sept. Levi Rees here with him.

Saturday 2 February: Snow. Several lives lost in some places. Lizzie, Jane & Mary walked to Church. Lizzie got tired & waited at Davies Forchegel until Mary took "Fly" for her. I at home all day.

Monday 3 February: Mrs. Day's little girl (Mary Elizabeth) died this afternoon at 3.25 in convulsion fits. She was 2 months old last Saturday & the prettiest Baby I ever saw.

Wednesday 5 February: Jane (Lizzie's sister) went home today. We walked with her to near the Star [Inn, Cwmgors] & then turned in to see Thomas the Blacksmith who is ill, & then down to Pal's who is also not well.

Thursday 6 February: Mrs. Day's little baby buried today at Llanguicke.

Monday 10 February: Mr. Jones, Llanguicke called. Stayed to tea.

Wednesday 12 February: Mary (Betty's sister) & Mary Shonny came here for Betty's every day boots. Said she was still not well & that the Dr. said her nerves were weak, & that she wd. not get better until the warm weather came. I told them I was quite willing for her to come back here when she was well enough as one of <u>two</u> servants but not as one.

Thursday 13 February: Sarah Joseph came up with a letter to me from <u>Mrs.</u> Price Glantwrch saying Revd. D. Jones had called to say that Day had a Cow & Calf to sell. She wished to know the breed, age & price, & that Mr. Price wd. see about it. She sent up the letter from Pontardawe on her way to Neath & I wrote for her to have the answer on her return.

Friday 14 February: Paid J. Jones, Garth Poor Rate 1 quarter as follows:

Garth Farm	47.. 0..0)	
" Cottage	2.. 0..0)	
3 Cots Cwmllynfell	7..10..0) @ 8d.	2.. 0.. 2
Smith Shop	1..15..0)	1..11*
1 Cot Craig Llanguicke	2.. 0..0)	£1..18.. 3
	£60..5..0)	* less commission

Sent Messrs. James & Aubrey the Coal a/c of '72.

Saturday 15 February: Thos. Davies (Blacksmith) buried today at Baran [Chapel]. Walters & Day to the funeral. Little Walter Jeffreys brought up the little shawl I lent his Mother some time ago, he is at Mr. Samuel's school.

Sunday 16 February: I rode Fly as far as where we turn to the fields & Lizzie rode up & I walked. Mary, Annie & Jenny also in Church.

Monday 17 February: John Morgan "Salutation" son came with a letter from his Father asking if I could meet him at Ystradgynlais tomorrow, that the Tomb was ready.[1]

Tuesday 18 February: Telegraphed to Swansea for a Fly to go up to Ystrad.

Wednesday 19 February: Took Lizzie to Mr. Shepherd. He examined her chest & gave her medicine. Wished to see her again in a fortnight.

Friday 21 February: Went on Fly to Cwmllynfell to meet Mr. Campion about the new fences by the new road, he was prevented coming & sent his servant up with a letter desiring me to express my wishes to Wm. Griffiths & Levi Rees & that he would carry them out.[2] They told me Wm. Evans had kept £20 towards the fences. I said I would be willing to take that sum to make the hedges & exonerate the Highway board from further trouble if they were willing. Mr. Jones Llanguicke called, he had been shooting with Mr. Davies.

Sunday 23 February: No one to Church (snow).

Tuesday 25 February: Walters cleaned the Dish Covers.

Wednesday 26 February: I cleaned out all the Cupboards & Mary gave the little Kitchen a thorough scrubbing.

Thursday 27 February: Lizzie went home on Fly to stay until tomorrow. Mary cleaned the Dairy & Cheese loft & gave the benches a good washing.

Friday 28 February: Mary finished cleaning the kitchen & tins, it all looks very clean.

---

1. The Pendrill tomb in the graveyard of St. Cynog's Parish Church, Ystradgynlais.
2. Alfred Bryant Campion held the offices of Neath Borough Surveyor, District Surveyor of Highways and Surveyor to the Rural Sanitary Authority.

Saturday 2 March: Mary to Church, also Mrs. Day, Annie & Jenny. Lizzie & I at home.

Monday 3 March: Morgan Jones Llwynhên brought his Mare for me to see as he heard I wanted a horse. She was tried with Cart & Saddle & I thought the Mare would do, but as I had spoken to John Gellyluog about getting me a horse I said he should come up & decide whether she would suit me. John went up & he said he did not like her at all for me but that she may be very good for a farmer, price £35..0..0.

Tuesday 4 March: Walters cut the yew trees by the front door, it looks very bare & naked now but I hope they will grow again.

Wednesday 5 March: Mr. Clarke here. Walters removing the stumps further & putting ivy cuttings to the wall by the coal after cleaning away the coal & removing the old iron.

Thursday 6 March: Walters told me he intended leaving here in about 3 weeks as he was far from his Mother.

Friday 7 March: Walters picked over the potatoes in the Cowhouse & took them all up to the Storeroom. Walters made all by the coal tidy. I feel sure some of the coal is stolen, we weighed some in the coal box & as far as I can judge it is about 80 lbs of coal (lumps & balls) we use a day with 3 fires, Parlour & two kitchens, for I have had no fire in my bedroom all the Winter. Told the Days of it & asked them if they missed coal, they said NO.

Saturday 8 March: Walters to Swansea 1st train to see Mrs. Melville's rhododendrons &c. Had 2 cwt of potatoes (Scotch Macks) for setting of Somerville 8/- per cwt. 2 Dozen Beer. D.M. cleaned manger in Cowhouse, very dirty kept by Walters. Sally taking crepe off my black silk & repairing the sleeves, put lace back on trims.

Sunday 9 March: I rode Fly to Church. Mary to Church, Lizzie in the house. Sacrament Mr. Jones.

Monday 10 March: Had 2 cwts of Llwynrhidie coal, 30 cwt which we began this afternoon, there being only about 3 buckets full of balls. Sally here doing up my bonnet, putting the lace & taking off the crepe.

Tuesday 11 March: Walters had garden hoe made by John the Blacksmith. Sent Walters to see D.M. who we hear is very ill. He is better this evening.

Wednesday 12 March: Lizzie went to Swansea 1st train to spend the day with Mrs. Matthews & returned the last. She called at Bryn Syfi and brought up the Pomatum 6 pots.[3] Mrs. Price with her to & fro in the train, said Miss Price was at Glan Twrch & Dora at Liverpool with Mrs. Richardson. Walters to Swansea for shrubs & rhododendrons. Had cart collar from Morgan Jones Llangatock after being repaired & stuffed, 4/-.

Thursday 13 March: Cleaned out spare bedroom. Recd. letter from Mrs. James (Dotty Williams) asking for Epsom votes. They are promised to Ernest Lewis through Mrs. Peak. Walters planted ½ hun[dred] cabbage plants.

Friday 14 March: Snow this morning 3 inches deep by front door.

Monday 17 March: Mr. Clarke here, he had been to Glynmeirch, gave me some white broom seed & Cape gooseberry seed.

Tuesday 18 March: Asked Mary if she would stay another month to see if she would improve, said she would. She is not at all a girl to suit me but I do not know of any girl.

Wednesday 19 March: Lizzie went on Fly to see D. Morgan, he is still very poorly. Walters put kidney potatoes in the garden, our own seed. He also made a little parsley bed among the currant trees.

Thursday 20 March: Mary went home at 6 o'clk for some stockings & is to return tomorrow 12 o'clk. White cow brought a she calf.

Friday 21 March: Walters put in carrots, parsnips &c. in Garden. The red cow Minnie brought calf on the hill, the calf was dead when Walters found it, whether it died from cold or how we know not. A He calf. Sent Walters up to the "Salutation" with cheque £49..0..0 to John Morgan, his charge for repairing Ystrad Tomb. A very high charge I think.

3. Pomatum, a perfumed oil or ointment commonly used for dressing the hair and occasionally for treating the skin.

Saturday 22 March: Mary did not return yesterday but came today 3 o'clk, said her Sister was confined yesterday. Walters to Swansea today midday train. He has now quite settled to go to Mrs. Melville next Monday week 31st. I am sorry in some things he is leaving, he is such a steady, respectable man & in some things he is very inefficient. Mr. A. B. Campion's breach of promise in the "Cambrian", he has to pay Miss Fanny Bishop £450.[4]

Tuesday 25 March: I went to Swansea 1st train, returned last. Walters met me with the mare by Gellygron. Had a long talk with Mrs. Morgan who was on the road by front gate. Called on Mrs. E. Strick about a Servant (Mary Lewis). She had arranged to stay until Mrs. Strick went to London in May. Called on Mrs. John Jones. Paid Miles for 8 pieces of paper @ 1/6, used for my bedroom last August. Saw Lewis the Cabinet maker about stuffing sofa & dining room chairs. Bought 10 yds unbleached calico @ 9d for sheets for Servants bed. Bought large earthen pan 2/6, also large water pitcher, 10d.

Wednesday 26 March: Walters to the Station this evening for things bought in Swansea yesterday. Betty came here this evening. She is very thin & still feels very weak. She has not been near here since she went away ill Janry 9th. Walters took 58 lbs salt butter to Post Office @ 1/1d. £3..2..10 paid.

Thursday 27 March: Lizzie went home on Fly, left here 11 a.m. returned at 5 p.m. A lovely day. She called to see D. Morgan, took a letter from me to D. Morgan Llwynrhidie Colliery asking him if John Jones the Brothin would like to apply for this situation as Walters was going away & he had offered himself twice before. D.M. said it was not convenient for him to leave.

Friday 28 March: Walters putting leaf mould between the rhododendrons he had planted opposite the front door & sowed lawn seed in it. He finished digging between fruit trees in old garden. Mr. Wm. Jeffreys (late of Nantdu) & his eldest son called in their way from Brynamman to Swansea, they took lunch. I had not seen him for many many years (15 or 20), he looks very well.

Saturday 29 March: Walters finished putting leaf mould & seed about the yew tree &c & down to the Nook. Finished cutting off branches of laurel, arbutus, laurestina &c on the Green, the shrubs are now very tidy. Walter Jeffreys came up from School & stayed to tea.

---

4. Miss Fanny Eliza Bishop of Neath sought damages of £3,000, *The Cambrian*, 21 March 1873.

Sunday 30 March: Came on to rain at midday. No one to Church.

Monday 31 March: Walters left here by midday train to go to Mrs. Melville about Gardens in Swansea. He had been here 24 weeks this day at 18/- per week.

Tuesday 1 April: Mr. Clarke here.

Wednesday 2 April: Griffiths who bought the rick of short hay here saying he could not get anyone to carry it away & that cattle would not eat it. He wanted for it to remain on the field during the Summer but I told him I insisted upon its being carried away by the 12th inst. & that I wd. wait for the money £9 until the middle of May. He has I think behaved badly about it & I never will have any more dealings with him. Mr. Evans P.O. & the two boys here in Mr. Thomas' phaeton, brought it up for me to see, I don't much like it & he asks high for it £28.

Friday 4 April: D. Morgan & I sorted out old Iron that had been carried from the green by the coal, & put what I thought of use with old carriage springs in Cart Shed & the rest ready to be weighed as old iron to John Gellyluog on top of chaff stairs.

Sunday 6 April: Lizzie to Church on Fly, Mary also and 4 from Days. I at home all day.

Monday 7 April: Mary Watkins came down in Bryn Amman Carriage which was passing to meet midday up train at Pontardawe, stayed to dinner & tea & we walked a little way back with her.

Tuesday 8 April: Mary made 6 lbs butter & took it to Post Office this evening, the 1st Butter made this year. Wrote to Morgan Jones, Sadler, Llangadock who had written to say he thought he knew of a man to suit me, who had been a servant at Glan Twrch, he does not come.

Wednesday 9 April: Lizzie to Swansea 1st train to send off basket to Mrs. Marryat. Quarter of lamb, 8 eggs, 1 bottle Cream. She called at Bryn Syfi & returned midday.

Thursday 10 April: John Gellyluog here with cart & horse helping D.M. to carry out lime & earth to the Strip to put in vetches. He also carried manure to Cottage Garden.

Good Friday 11 April: Lizzie & Mary to Church, Llanguicke at 11 a.m. William Lewis came here at 6 p.m. after being through Gellyluog wood. He said there was not much damage. Recd. a very kind letter from dear Mrs. Marryat, the bottle of cream & 4 eggs broke in going.

Easter Sunday 13 April: Lizzie, Mary & I in Church. Also Mrs. Day, Annie, Jenny & Charlie. Sacrament.

Tuesday 15 April: Mrs. Maber & her brother Tom came down to call & stayed to tea, the 1st time we had seen her since her marriage. We walked back with them as far as Cwmgorse, the wheel of the phaeton broken so we could not drive them home. Mrs. Maber gave Lizzie the Watch stand. Paid Gellyluog & Cwmllynfell Insurance to E. Phillips, 9/-.

Wednesday 16 April: John Gellyluog here sowing & harrowing in the vetches.

Thursday 17 April: Evan Jones, Butcher came here to see the calf. Sold it him for £3..0..0 or 9d a lb., the former was the least trouble so I sold it off hand 4 weeks today.

Friday 18 April: D. Morgan put up Stumpery by Closet after the Winter's wind had blown it down & took away all the old branches & rubbish from between the trees. All the front now looks very tidy.

Saturday 19 April: Recd. letter from Tatchell from Worcester saying he thought he knew of a man to suit me. Also a letter from Mrs. Maber saying the girl she spoke could not leave her brother. Sent letter to Mary Watkins by D.M. saying I was in correspondence with a man but that I wd. let her know the decision on Saturday so as to tell the man she spoke of. Lizzie went home on Fly with patterns of dresses for her Sisters to see.

Sunday 20 April: I rode Fly to Church. Mary to Church. Lizzie in the house. Betty's nephew (David) here saying she had been worse since she was here.

Monday 21 April: Wm. Lewis came up tonight to say Sally could not come up to make my dress until after some meeting as she is so busy. I am very much annoyed for I want a black dress. Put oil on Pantry window to make it open easily & also on the Kitchen window.

Wednesday 23 April: Mary with 8 lbs butter to Post Office.

Thursday 24 April: John Gellyluog here with a horse harrowing front fields & a little in Cae Barriwns, Cae Cwtta & Meadow too dry to brush harrow.

Sold John 3 cwt of old iron		7..6
Old cart		2..6
	Paid	10..0

Lizzie not well, put her in a warm bath.

Friday 25 April: Lizzie in bed after dinner with a severe pain in her back & sides. Agreed with Mary (Margaret Owen) for 6 months until November in the third room, in Lizzie's presence gave her 1/- loan. Wages £6. Betty came here, she looks very ill.

Saturday 26 April: Recd. Mr. Davies' account of coal from Cwmllynfell, also his bill & other charges which I think high.

Sunday 27 April: No one in Church very cold.

Monday 28 April: Lizzie spent the day at the vicarage with Mrs. Maber. She rode Fly, back at 9 p.m. Mr. Clarke came here at 3.30 p.m, he had been to Killay.

Tuesday 29 April: Recd. a letter from Tatchell saying the man would come on a month's trial on the 7th May.

Tuesday 6 May: Lizzie & I went to Swansea 1st train, returned last train. Fanny and Ellen G. in the train. We called at Gellygron on our way up, I wanted to see Mrs. Morgan about the cleaning of Llanguicke Church. 2 Dozen Beer, ½ Dozen Marsala, ½ Dozen Tarragona, ½ Gall Gin.

Wednesday 7 May: Betty & Mrs. Day to Neath to see Hibbert. Had 1½ bus. Aberthaw lime, ½ cwt soap, 17/6. Sweeping brush 2/-. New buckles put to cart reins & my bridle mended.

Thursday 8 May: Had a letter from Tatchell saying the man would be at Neath this evening 4.45 train & if I would meet him, his wife & some luggage. Charlie with horse and Car[riage] to meet them & took them direct to Rachel Thos. y Gove's

Friday 9 May: At 10 o'clk a.m. Charles Thomas & his wife came here from Worcester. They were so grand in dress & with such high notions I knew in a moment they wd. not suit, & they decidedly were dissatisfied or disappointed with the place from having no shooting that I advised them at once to return. Gave them a Sovereign towards their expenses.

Sunday 11 May: Mary broke "The Turk" on Dining room chimney piece. Lizzie to Church on Fly, Mary to Church. Betty & I at home. Sacrament.

Monday 12 May: Hannah Gellyluog here cleaning the fields with D. Morgan. Wrote to Mrs. Peak, Oak Grove Chepstow with the Epsom Balloting Paper giving all my votes to Ernest Lewis.

Tuesday 13 May: Mrs. Kirkhouse & her little girl came up to tea. Gave her the Epsom subscription £1..1..0. I gave here a cheque for £3..3..0. as she wanted to send that sum to Dr. Johnson & she gave me £2..0..0.

Wednesday 14 May: Paid Mary Owen balance of wages up to tomorrow 16 weeks @ 4/7½ per week being at the rate of £12 a year. She went to the fair with the Day's as far as Pontardawe, left them there to change her dress at Sally's.

16 weeks @ 4/7½		£..s..d
Going home	10/-	3..14..0
Mending Boots	3..2	1..13..8
Dress lining &c.	11..9	£2.. 0..4
New boots	5..9	Paid her this day
Pan & Jug	3..0	The balance £2..0..4
	£1..13..8	

Thursday 15 May: Very poorly all day. Mary came back at 5 o'clk p.m. saying she might have got £18 or £20 a year in the fair & that she had agreed to go to Aberdare.

Friday 16 May: Spoke to Mary this morning about staying away Wednesday night without leave, & that as she could get £18 or £20 a year I would free her in a month & for her to give me back the 1/- loan, which she did in the Kitchen in Lizzie's presence. Mr. Clarke called, did not come in. D.M. cleaning the Walk.

Sunday 18 May: Walters came up 1st train saying he thought he had seen a phaeton to suit me. No one to Church.

Monday 19 May: Went to Swansea 1st train to see the phaeton Walters spoke of yesterday at the Gore House. It is not what I like & therefore I do not buy it. Called at Bryn Syfi & stayed the night.

Tuesday 20 May: The 2 Miss Jenkins went to Maesgogllwyn to stay because Mrs. Jenkins was ill. I came home midday train. I came home in a Fly from Rosser [*James Rosser, Coach Builder & Livery Stables, 35-36 Wind Street, Swansea*], 1 horse 11/-, man 3/-.

Thursday 29 May: Left Garth by 1st train for Swansea, thence by express to Bath, got to 9 Pierrepont Street at 5 o'clock.

Whit Sunday 1 June: A.M. Went to the Abbey, the service is now held in the Nave which is finished & looks so nice. P.M. Went in a chair to the Park, it looked lovely.

Thursday 19 June: Intended going home today but I was very ill & obliged to send for Mr. Davies, who said I must keep very quiet, & that I was not equal to the journey. He was so kind & came in twice to see me, he telegraphed himself to Williams the Livery Stables, to stop the Fly ordered to Landore & to tell Lizzie that I could not come today.

Saturday 21 June: Left Bath for Garth, Lizzie met me at Landore with a Fly from Williams.

Thursday 26 June: Betty went up to Cwmtwrch to see Eliza Griffiths, who had been a Servant at Gellygron & at Cwm y Scwd to know if she would like coming here as Servant, said she would & that her Mother & herself would come to see me on Monday.

Monday 30 June: Eliza Griffiths & her Mother came here. I have engaged her until Nov. at the rate of £12..0..0 a year. She comes July 10th when Mary Owen leaves.

Thursday 3 July: John Gellyluog here with a mare he had bought for me yesterday in Swansea fair to see if I liked her. She is not sufficiently broken in for a carriage. I told him he must keep her & try her to see if she was likely to suit me, if not he must sell her. I gave him a cheque for £40..0..0, the amount he paid for her. Martha our old Servant & her little stepson came to see me, she is staying a day or two with her sister Mary Williams.

Monday 7 July: Lizzie's Birthday, gave her a pair of Studs & a book "Dora Hamilton".[5]

Saturday 19 July: Had in part of Cae Barriwns hay.

Sunday 20 July: I rode Fly to Church. Lizzie in the house not very well & the two girls, Mrs. Day, Charlie & Jenny in Church.

Monday 21 July: Finished turning in Cae Barriwns hay.

Saturday 26 July: Poor Jane Herbert died.

Tuesday 29 July: Lizzie & I went to Swansea 1st train. Called at Mrs. Matthews. The Carriage I bought of Vezey came in by Packet at 7 o'clk. We took tea at the Cameron Arms & came up in it with a man & horse from Bullin's Stables [*Ll. & T. Bullin, Livery Stables and Fly Proprietors, Belle Vue Street, Swansea*]. Ordered bonnet for me & hat for Lizzie at Evans, Temple Street. [*B. Evans & Co., General Drapers & Haberdashers, Swansea*].

Friday 1 August: Lizzie's Cousin (Anne) Mr. Joseph Jones second daughter died today, buried at Pontardawe Church the 4th inst.

Tuesday 12 August: I went down to Bryn Syfi midday train, stayed there till evening train of Thursday.

Wednesday 13 August: Went into Swansea to have the flower in my new bonnet changed & black feather put instead of coloured flower in Lizzie's hat, which is also new as we both have to go into slight mourning.

Saturday 16 August: Walter Jeffreys and little Glover came up & stayed to tea. D.M. (Mason) up to this day, he is going to Llanwrtyd Wells on Monday, he is not at all well.

5. Mrs. W. H. Coates, *Dora Hamilton or Sunshine and Shadow*, Religious Tract Society, London, *c.*1870.

Sunday 17 August: Eliza went home, I gave her leave to stay the night. Lizzie to Church, Betty & I in the house.

Monday 18 August: Paid J. Jones Crachllwyn rates as follows by cheque:

Garth Poor Rate 2 qrs.	)	£.. s.. d
on £60..5..0 @ 1/-	)	5..14..9
Caergurwen Highway Rate	)	7..8½
£9..5..0 @ 10d	)	
Mawr H.way rate on £2 @ 6d		1
		£6..3..5½ Paid

Tuesday 19 August: D. Lewis Rhyd-y-fro & Isaac Gellfowy bought as much hay as I would not require on Wain hir Ucha at £2..2..6 per chain acre (standing or unmown). There is a very heavy crop of hay on the Meadow.

Friday 22 August: The 2 Mary's from Ystalyfera came to see Betty. Lizzie rode up to Garnant & sent off by train the antimacassar (she had done for me which I returned as she had no time to make another). She gave it Mrs. Hughes for the Bettws Bazaar which is to be on Wednesday next, also £2..12..6 subscription towards Bettws Church.

Thursday 28 August: *****

Wednesday 3 September: Lizzie & I went to Bryn Syfi by the last train. Charlie took down the Phaeton to Burchell to be repaired.

Thursday 4 September: The 2 Miss Jenkins, Lizzie & I left Bryn Syfi for Rhayader by 12 o'clk. train from Victoria Station, had to wait some hours at Builth Road for the train to Rhayader, arrived at the Red Lion Hotel about 7 o'clk. They sent a wagonette to meet us at the Station.

Friday 5 September: Went for a walk on the Builth Road, Lizzie & I turned into a tan yard to see the skins taken out of the water, the 1st time I had seen a tan yard.

Saturday 6 September: In walking past turned in to see the Rhayader Church.

Sunday 7 September: Lizzie & I to Rhayader Church in the morning. Communion. No sermon.

Monday 8 September: We all went for a walk to the Station to ask about the train to Llanidloes & from there to see Cwmdeuddwr Church.

Tuesday 9 September: I asked Mrs. Jones if she knew of a man servant likely to suit me, she said Mr. Lloyd of Nantgwillt Coachman was going to leave & that he might do, he happened to be in the house & came up to speak [to] me. I explained the kind of place & wages & told him to consult with his wife & let me know on Thursday.

Wednesday 10 September: Sent down Mrs. Marryat by 3 o'clk. train to London a quarter of mutton 10½ lbs & a couple of chickens.

Thursday 11 September: Thomas Price (Nantgwillt) came in at 3 o'clk & said he would like to come on a month's trial & that he was quite willing to take general work & referred me to Mr. Lloyd for his Character.

Friday 12 September: Received a letter from Mr. B. Lewis Lloyd, Nantgwillt saying he had found Thomas Price honest, sober, truthful & industrious, temper fairly good & obliging, had occasionally waited at table but not during the past year. Agreed with Thos. Price for 18/- a week, or 14/- a week with house, coal, &c. to come Oct 6th on a month's trial. Went for a walk a.m. on the Builth Road, p.m. on the Aberystwith Road, a very pretty walk.

Saturday 13 September: Received a very kind letter from dear Mrs. Marryat acknowledging the parcel in excellent condition.

Thursday 18 September: Left Rhayader by the 12 o'clk train & travelled together as far as Llandilo where Lizzie & I waited until 6 o'clk for the Garnant train. The 2 Miss Jenkins going on direct to Swansea. Lizzie & I had tea at the Cawdor Arms, liked the butter very much & ordered a pot of 20 lbs for winter use, saw the Church, ordered boots for Lizzie of Thomas the Shoemaker, I bought 2 little jugs & gave Lizzie a mug. It was a lovely afternoon & the view from the Station very beautiful. We enjoyed it much. Charlie met us with the P.O. Dog Cart at Garnant.

Friday 19 September: *****

Tuesday 23 September: Betty went to Pontardawe for maize for fowls, heard there that Mary Shonny was very ill, her throat having broke in several places, Betty went up to see her, I sent a bottle of wine & 2/6.

Sunday 28 September: Lizzie, Eliza & I in Church. Mr. Jones begged us to come to the Choral Service on the 1st, offered to send his phaeton for us, but I declined. Mrs. Jones in Clifton.

Monday 29 September: Eliza limed the Court & took off the old irons that held the Kitchen trough & limed where they had been. D.M. swept Kitchen roof & cropped ivy shoots on wall.

Tuesday 30 September: D. Jenkins here making box in the coach house window for brushes, &c. & cutting cross door lower, so as to be able to step over it without removing it. Mary John Thos y Gove carried fern from the hill over my fence by the Cottage without asking leave. D. Jenkins painted inside of front trough white & stopped cracks with putty. Lizzie painted Kitchen window.

Wednesday 1 October: Wm. Evans the Tailor here putting down new floor cloth & recovering green baize door, the others had last 22 years, they were put new in 1851. D. Jenkins mended floor by Parlour door in the passage. Harvest Thanksgiving at Pontardawe.

Friday 3 October: Took sofa out of little Kitchen, it wants to be re-stuffed. I repaired the paper about & above the window & other bad places. It now looks very tidy & will last the Winter. Put new muslin blinds.

Saturday 4 October: Sent a letter this evening by D.M. to John the Blacksmith telling him to come & see [me] respecting trespassing over my fence on the 30th ult.

Sunday 5 October: All of us in Church. Had a long chat with Mr. Jones in the Porch. Mrs. Jones still in Clifton.

Monday 6 October: Lizzie went home on Fly & returned this evening, brought the little pincushions Jane gave us from the Bazaar. John Harries & his family came to Gartheithen to live.

Tuesday 7 October: Lizzie & I went this evening to see them at Gartheithen.

Wednesday 8 October: Thomas Lloyd from Rhayader came here as Servant on a month's trial at 18/- per week. Dl. Jenkins finished making Hen-house above the pigsty. Samuel Jenkins (who has just returned from America) here sawing poles for rails with D.M.

Thursday 9 October: Gave Lloyd 2 brushes for harness leather, 2 new towels, sponge, paste & polish & told him that the better he kept things the better I should be pleased. Took Fly into the stable.

Sunday 12 October: Lizzie, Eliza & I in Church & Mrs. Day. Mr. Jones Llanguicke & Mr. Davies Clydach both did duty. Sacrament. D. Lewis, Rhyd-y-fro a Girl born.

Monday 13 October: Lloyd removed chaffcutter from the storeroom to the Hay house, as I wish the chaff to be cut in the Hay house. It will be the means of keeping the Coach house tidier. Lloyd to Pontardawe for 3 bus. oats for the mare, also ½ bus. linseed which he says is better than bran or any thing else for her breath & cough. Had 1 cwt of barley meal for pig. Recd. a letter yesterday from Dora Price from Tretower saying her Aunt Gwen was ill & in a very helpless state. She has been there a week.

Tuesday 14 October: Jane Isaac paid ½ a year's rent, also John Jones wife (late a maid at Mr. Bain's) they took the house when Wm. Williams left. Gave them geraniums. Mrs. Harries, Gartheithen came here to borrow the Cart, the first time she was here. Sold the old side saddle to her for 10/- paid. D.M. clearing old Polka from Cae shed hedge. Lizzie went to see Wm. Lewis who is ill, took him 6 eggs. Lloyd raking leaves off Green & Walk.

Wednesday 15 October: ***** D.M. & Lloyd putting rails instead of old Polka by Cae Shed hedge. Finished mending black dress (Henrietta cloth) after Eliza washed it, it looks very tidy & will last a good bit for every day. Rhydderch took Lizzie's boots to Llandilo.

Thursday 16 October: Lloyd in the Garden taking up potatoes. D.M. beating Wain pedr Erw ditch with wooden sledge & mending the gaps. Lizzie took the best surplice to Llanguicke after it had been washed, also book markers. Tied the 2 Cows.

Sunday 19 October: Eliza went home, returned 8 p.m. Lizzie & I to Church, Betty in the house. Little bird tapping Kitchen loft window. Mr. Jones the Curate.

Monday 20 October: Put carriage harness in Kitchen loft, the sulphur in Coach house spoils the plate. Spoke to Eliza about keeping Kitchen loft tidy & clean. Lloyd over to Gellyluog to see New Mare, he does not like at all for a Carriage, "She is too heavy & has no life in her".

Tuesday 21 October: Lloyd carried the last of the hay off Wainhir Ucha to the manure heap in Cae Cwtta. Asked Lloyd how he liked his lodgings at John the Blacksmith's & what he paid per week, he [said] 2/9d it is a great imposition to charge so much & I have arranged for him to come to Mrs. Day's at 2/- & for her to wash his shirts, stockings & handkerchiefs & keep them mended at that price. Walters only paid 1/8 a week, but everything is rising.

Wednesday 22 October: Wrote to Mr. Davies Llwydcoed about Mr. Bain's making a great tip on the Cwmllynfell side & thereby obstructing the old road way to the Colliery.

Thursday 23 October: Nant-y-Gasseg sale. Paid Daniel Jenkins Carpenter for all work done to this date, £1..18..6. D.M. finished beating the Ditch from Gwyndwn Hir to Cottage garden, it looks very tidy & is well done.

Monday 27 October: Lloyd drove me in the new Carriage (1st time) to Garnant to meet the 11 o'clk. train to Llandilo.

Saturday 1 November: Poor Gwen Price died at Tretower aged 68. She had been ailing some time. She is to be buried at Cwmdu Church.

Monday 3 November: Received a letter from Dora Price saying her Aunt Gwen died on Saturday last. Lloyd to Swansea to fetch the phaeton from Burchell after it had been painted & had new wheels & axles &c. &c.

Tuesday 4 November: The re-opening of Bettws Church. Lloyd drove Lizzie in the phaeton to Cross Inn to go there at 11 a.m. He was back here at 1 o'clk, & the worse for beer, but I said nothing to see if it would occur again.

Wednesday 5 November: Fanny Gilbertson called yesterday on horseback, asked Lizzie & I to come there to lunch tomorrow. Lloyd fetched Lizzie from the Garnant Station at 12 o'clk.

Thursday 6 November: ***** Lloyd drove me in the phaeton to lunch at the Gilbertsons & came for me at 4.30. They were very kind & seemed glad to see me. Mr. & Mrs. G. Llewellyn, Baglan, called there & stayed to lunch & the G's drove them to Llansamlet to meet the train for Swansea. Mr. Gilbertson had a bad cold. Mr. & Mrs. A.G. in London coming home tomorrow. Saw the baby (Francis William) for the 1st time, he is a fine boy. Called at Wm. Lewis, he has been very poorly. Walter Jeffreys came up & stayed to tea. Gave Lloyd a Water Brush for the mare's feet, 2/6.

Friday 7 November: Walter Jeffreys came up & stayed to tea.

Saturday 8 November: I went to Swansea midday train, came up the last. Called at 9 Dynevor Place to ask Mrs. Jeffreys if she knew of a maid to suit me. She did not.

Sunday 9 November: Lizzie to Church & Betty. Very windy, the Chancel window broken. Eliza went home this afternoon, returned tonight (no, it was to Pontardawe).

Tuesday 11 November: Lizzie went to the Ddufadfa to see if they knew of a maid. She stays the night there & meets me at Llandilo tomorrow. I went to Swansea midday train, called on Mrs. Jeffreys & drank tea there. Her mother came there to see me. I slept at the Mackworth Arms.

Wednesday 12 November: Left Swansea by the 8.15 a.m. train to Llandilo fair to see if I could meet with a maid, Lizzie came to the Station to meet me. Engaged a girl that was at the Post Office recommended by R. Evans the Saddler's wife. She is a native of Pumpsaint near Froodvale, name Mary Lewis. Wages at the rate of £12 a year. She knows nothing of Dairy work. Came up from Swansea in a Fly being too late for the Swansea Vale train through losing the train at Llandilo.

Friday 14 November: D.M. & Lloyd swept Kitchen chimney & tomorrow the little Kitchen chimney.

Saturday 15 November: I went to Swansea morning train and came up midday. Mrs. Price & Dora in the Carriage going down, Dora & Jane coming up. They were all very friendly.

Paid Burchell by cheque for repairing the Phaeton & painting it.	28.. 0..0
Whip 17/- Mat 10/6 Chamois 3/- Candles 1/6	1..12..0
	29..12..0
By Cheque	£29..10..0

Lizzie & Lloyd met me at the Station. Saw Mr. R. Jenkins about his Dairy maid.

Sunday 16 November: Lizzie & I to Church. Called at Cefn llan to see the twins, gave them 3/-, drank tea there. Evans the P.O. and his son there too. Mary (Betty's niece) and Maryanne here when we were in Church.

Monday 17 November: Margaret Howard here for Pontardawe Pew rent £1..1..0 Paid. Wm. Lewis came up for a turn, he has been very poorly & is now far from well.

Tuesday 18 November: John Harries's (Gartheithen) wife & her sister-in-law Jane Tynewydd took tea here. Lizzie went down to Sally's to have her Linsey body fitted.[6] It was not ready & she had to wait a long time which made it late when she came home. I am not at all pleased about it. Lizzie left here 2.50 p.m. & returned 6.45. Lloyd in Pontardawe with the cart for oats & to the mill for barley meal for pig.

Wednesday 19 November: Eliza Griffiths from near Cwmllynfell left this morning for Neath fair.

Thursday 20 November: Eliza came for her clothes. She had been here 19 weeks today at the rate of £12 a year, paid her £4..7..6. Wrote to Mrs. Jenkins to say I would take her Dairy maid, Margaret Jones on a month's trial at the rate of £12 a year & pay her expenses up. Wrote to Mary Lewis, Bryneinon Pumpsaint to say I had the offer of a girl that cd. take Dairy & housework & that I was going to engage her for a month. If she did not suit I wd. take her at the end of that time, but that any how I wd. pay her a month's wages.

Friday 21 November: Paid J. Jones Crachllwyn, Garth Poor Rate 1 quarter as follows:

---

6. Possibly linsey-woolsey which is a coarse twill or fabric combination of linen and wool.

Garth Farm	47.. 0..0)			
" Cottage	2.. 0..0)			
3 Cots Cwmllynfell	7..10..0)	@ 10d.	2..10.. 2½	
Smith Shop	1..15..0)		2.. 4½	less
1 Cot Graig Llanguicke	2.. 0..0)		£2.. 7..10	commission
	£60.. 5..0)		By Cheque	

Saturday 22 November: Margaret Gellyluog brought a tongue, 1s.6d paid. Received a letter from Mrs. Jenkins, Marchagllwyn saying her servant M. Jones had been offered £14 a year & that she had changed her mind & would not come here. This puts me to great inconvenience for I wrote on Thursday to decline Mary Lewis the one I engaged at Llandilo fair & now I have no prospect of a girl.

Sunday 23 November: Lizzie to Church on Fly, Betty & I in the house.

Tuesday 25 November: Hannah Gellyluog here making balls & washing out the White room.

Thursday 27 November: Lloyd drove me to call on Mrs. Arthur Gilbertson. She was out, met Mr. & Mrs. A.G., Mrs. & Miss Ford on my return by Davies the Ironmonger. Received a letter from Mary Lewis saying she wd. be here tomorrow by last train at Garnant, telegraphed to tell her to come by midday the last is so late. I am glad she comes as the Marchagllwyn girl disappointed me. Evans the P.O. here paying 1 yrs. interest on £50 due last August. He is very anxious to lease Garth Coal as the railway is likely to come this way shortly. Promised him 1st offer of it.

Friday 28 November: Lloyd took Car to meet Mary Lewis at Garnant station 12.30 train. She is the girl I engaged at Llandilo fair. She is engaged at the rate of £12 a year for 6 months that either Mistress or Maid can give a month's notice, this is clearly understood by her Mother who brought her here & who seems a hard working woman. She had posted the letter saying she was coming before she recd. mine of the 20th telling her not to come & wd. not have known what to do if she had not had the telegram yesterday. So far it all turns out well for me.

Saturday 29 November: The morning was so wet that I sent Lloyd with a Car to take Mary's Mother to Garnant Station for which she seemed much obliged.

Sunday 30 November: Lizzie & Betty to Church. Mary to Saron a.m. I at home all day. Lizzie wrote to Margaret & I to my uncle.

Monday 1 December: Richard Jones Craig Trebanos (the clockmaker recommended by Evans the Post Office) came up to clean the clock. Paid him 3/6. He is to keep it going 12 months.

Tuesday 2 December: Margaret Jones Llwyn-yr-Onen [Lizzie's eldest sister] married today at Bettws Church.

Thursday 4 December: Morgan Jones Cefnllan called here on his way from Cwmgorse.

Friday 5 December: Lizzie called at Gellygron to ask how Mrs. Morgan was. She is better & able to come down stairs. She had had a mild Paraletic Seizure in one side some days ago.

Saturday 6 December: Lizzie called at Cwm y scwd to ask how little David Forchegel was. He is better but had been very ill with quinsy. Spoke to Lloyd of the untidy way he kept the dunghill, & that he must take the old manure to Cae Barriwns.

Sunday 7 December: Lizzie walked to Church.

Monday 8 December: D. Morgan commenced trashing hedge by Heol Hugh from the road to the Pill, he is to steep the hedge and ditch it well up, it now looks so untidy. I am ashamed to see it & Day has <u>no</u> idea of how to make a hedge tidy. Lloyd commenced carrying manure to Cae Barriwns.

Tuesday 9 December: Lloyd fetched a load of coal, Fly would not bring it up Heol-y-Cefn, obliged to borrow Day's mare. Lloyd said he would leave this day month, said he would never wish a better Mistress than I was but that he could not make himself comfortable as <u>outdoor</u> Servant. The truth is I think he is vexed at having clipped the mare & made such a figure of her. Lloyd drove Lizzie & I to the Vicarage. We stayed to tea & supper & left there 9.40. Mr. & Mrs. Jones were very friendly.

Wednesday 10 December: Lloyd carrying manure to Cae Barriwns.

Saturday 13 December: Lizzie went to Swansea 1st train. She called at Bryn Syfi, Mrs. Matthews & Mrs. Jeffreys & Mr. Jenkins came up with her last train. Lloyd met them at the Station.

Sunday 14 December: Only Lizzie in Church. Sacrament.

Monday 15 December: Lloyd rode to Neath with Basket for Mrs. Rees to be sent off by train. 1 Turkey, 1 Goose, 2 Woodcocks (tomorrow). Mr. Jenkins left midday train. Lloyd drove him to the Station.

Friday 19 December: Went to Bryn Syfi 1st train. Thought to go into Swansea but it came on to pour the rain.

Sunday 21 December: Lizzie, I, Betty, Mrs. Day & Jenny to Church. Wet coming home. Mary to Saron School.

Monday 22 December: Lloyd took the Carriage to Swansea to have the Crest erased & my monogram put instead. Sent off basket to Mrs. Marryat with 2 Pheasants, 1 lb. cream, 1 hun. oysters & a tin with 9 eggs. Sent my desk to be repaired to Lewis the Cabinet Maker Swansea.

Tuesday 23 December: Paid Richard Jones Graig Trebanos 12/- for cleaning & repairing the Clock that was in the Attic, it is now put in the Kitchen. He is to keep it going 12 months. Wm. Evans Gellygron Mill brought up meal for pig, barley for fowls & oatmeal. Paid him in full for all I have had up to this day.

Wednesday 24 December: Betty to Pontardawe for suet. Heard there that Ianto her brother was missing since Monday night. Sent Lloyd for Rachel's Car, he took her up to Ystalyfera immediately & left her there. She is in sad trouble poor girl.

Thursday 25 December: A damp misty day & very mild. Not at all like Christmas. Lizzie to Llanguicke 11 a.m. on Fly. Lloyd to Pontardawe. The Church Choir (10 little boys & their 2 leaders) came at 3.30 p.m. & sang most beautifully several pieces by the front door. It really was a pleasure to hear them. Gave them beer, apples & oranges and 10/- with which they seemed very pleased. Lloyd, Mary, Annie & Webber to Pontardawe Church at 6 p.m. Came back at 10. I was at home all day.

Friday 26 December: Anne wife of David Thomas Mason who lives in the Cottage on Graig Llanguicke here saying they were going to leave & had taken a house near Llwynhen Brewery. She brought another woman with her who is willing to take the house on the day she leaves it. David Tirlan came to say that Ianto had slept Monday night in Swansea & gone to Brecon on Tuesday.

Saturday 27 December: Lloyd took the phaeton to Swansea for Burchell to make the wheels &c. steady & brought up the Carriage after the Crest had been erased & monogram put on. David Phillips came to say that they had heard Ianto was in Merthyr.

Sunday 28 December: Lizzie to Church. Mary to Chapel. I at home all day. Mrs. Day to Cwmtwrch.

Monday 29 December: Lloyd to Swansea for the phaeton. Had a letter from Dr. Rees acknowledging the game & poultry. Dl. Jenkins here sawing rails for fencing, paid him 4/6 for today, as I have settled all with him before & now <u>everything</u> is paid him to <u>end of this year</u>. Gave him 5/- towards collection for Wain Gurwen Schoolroom.

Tuesday 30 December: John Peggy killed the pig. Rachel John here helping. It bled very little, weighed 309 lbs. Pigs are now about 11/6 a score.

Wednesday 31 December: Paid Richard James, Blaenegel, Garth Highway rate £47. @ 8d, £1.11s.4d. Lloyd drove Lizzie & I to call at the Gilbertsons on (Kate) Mrs. Richardson, they were <u>all out</u>. Lizzie fell out of the phaeton when we got home in alighting & fainted. She was not hurt but frightened.

1874

Despite the recurrence of several painful and debilitating ailments, one of which drove her to apply a leech to her aching gum, Margaret continued to record the significant happenings of most days with an assured precision. She supervised improvements to her Garth property and, while contemplating its expansion, maintained a watchful scrutiny over her tenants and Cwmllynfell colliery. There were frequent visits to her relatives and she enjoyed several weeks in Bath during March and September and a fortnight's sightseeing holiday in London with Lizzie and the Jenkins sisters. The hiring and retention of competent indoor servants and outdoor workers caused some concern. Lloyd's decision to remain in her employment and his upgrading to indoor servant and coachman, dressed in distinctive livery and driving her new phaeton, enhanced her visible presence in the community. Following a fall in July, her health declined to a point of despair when, on her 41st birthday on 2 September, she felt the imminence of death and that it might be her "last birthday on Earth". A brief entry in late October regarding the condition of Dora Price's lungs was to have a tragic outcome in the following year.

Thursday 1 January: Mary Dai Shone Williams here saying she would keep on the Cottage on Graig Llanguicke even if her daughter Anne Thomas would leave. Mrs. & Miss Ford & Ellen G. walked up to see me. They admired Lizzie's Bookmarkers, promised to send Miss Ford fir cones for picture frames tomorrow. Paid Llwynrhidie coal bill £6..18..0 up to 31st Decr. 1873 by cheque.

Friday 2 January: I went to Swansea 1st train. Saw Mr. R. Jenkins, told him to prepare an agreement to allow Mr. Bain to tip into the river to protect Mrs. Rowland's house. Called at Mr. F. Price's office, paid the Duke's [Duke of Beaufort] rent, 4 years last Sept, 8/-. Spoke to Mr. Price about taking a lease of 60 years upon the two pieces of waste land & that I shd. like to rent more of the hill so as to prevent any nuisance or disturbance by searching for stones or coal. Said he wd. come up & that I shd. have what I wished at a reasonable price. Called at Bryn Syfi to say Lizzie wd. come & stay there after Jane Price had left. She went home this morning for some school treat & returns tomorrow.

Saturday 3 January: Margaret Cwmllynfell came here with a little pot of butter 16 lbs. pot included. She paid ½ a year's rent due last September £20. It was a very wet morning. Lloyd fetched & took her to Pontardawe Station in the Blacksmith's Car. ½ Gal Gin, ½ Gal Brandy, ½ Gal Whisky, 1 doz. Sherry.

Sunday 4 January: I rode Fly to Church, came to snow. Betty to Church. Lizzie in the house all day.

Monday 5 January: Lloyd spoke to me Friday night in coming from the Station saying that he had not heard from Mr. Jenner of Newport about his situation, & that he had partly agreed to go to the Ystalyfera Hotel but that on further consideration he wd. not do so, & that he now had no place in view. I told him I was not suited with a man so that if he wd. like staying here & be sober, I wd. engage him for a few months. He said he would like staying & I promised to take him as indoor servant for 3 months from next Saturday at 8/- a week.

Friday 9 January: Dl. Jenkins down to Pontardawe to see for boards for partition &c in Kitchen loft.

Saturday 10 January: Lloyd came as indoor servant this evening, but is to sleep at Day's until I have altered Kitchen Loft. I have agreed with him for 3 months at 8/- a week if he suits & continues here he is to have a suit of clothes for driving. He promises to be sober. Mary, Betty's niece from Ystalyfera came here. No news of Ianto.

Sunday 11 January: No one to Llanguicke. Lizzie all day in bed with ear & face ache. Walters came to see us & had tea (he is now at the Vicarage).

Monday 12 January: Dl. Jenkins putting a wide board on Kitchen loft instead of wall fitting. Samuel putting screws in bedstead & mending it.

Tuesday 13 January: Lloyd to Pontardawe for grains, board & flour. Fly wd. not come up Heol-y-Ty but kept backing cart & standing on her hind legs, obliged to bring her up Heol-y-Cefn. D.M. levelling jamb on Kitchen loft & Dl. put a wide board on it.

Wednesday 14 January: Margaret Gellyluog here paying ½ a year's rent due last Sept. Lloyd to Ynismeudw to see if a mare Mr. Rees had for sale would suit me, he says she is too heavy & has puffed legs.

Thursday 15 January: Mended sleeves of my grey linsey.

Friday 16 January: Mary not well in bed all day. Walter Jeffreys called, he could not stay to tea.

Saturday 17 January: Lizzie broke a pane of glass in dining room by trying to shut the window with her knee. I had told her some time ago not to open the window as it was so difficult to shut in wet weather, but she was disobedient as the result shows.

Sunday 18 January: Very wet. No one to Church. John Gellyluog here.

Wednesday 21 January: ***** Lizzie went down by the Brecon train 1.7 p.m. to stay at Bryn Syfi. I went in the Phaeton as far as the Post Office. Went to the Pontardawe Bank for the 1st time. Poor old Day very poorly.

Thursday 22 January: Betty to Ystalyfera to see if there was any news of her brother Evan, they had heard nothing. D. Morgan (Mason) cutting down the thorn hedge between Cae shed & Gwndwn Hir. Jane wrote to Lizzie saying her Father had had two teeth taken out & that he was much better.

Friday 23 January: Lloyd to Pontardawe for 1 cwt Bran, 5 bus. Oats & 40 lbs of Flour. D.M. finished cutting hedge at 12 o'clk & went to steep Wain Fawr hedge. The Duke of Edinburgh married today at St. Petersburgh to the Grand Duchess Marie of Russia!![1]

Sunday 25 January: Betty to Church, Mary to Chapel. I at home all day.

Tuesday 27 January: Paid John James Garth Income Tax (by his son Daniel) 1 year ending 5th April 1874.

	£ .. s .. d
Schedule A @ 3d. Schedule B @ 1½d on £50	18..9
Garth Cottage 1 yr. ending 5 April 1874 on £3 @ 3d.	9
Garth Land tax 1 yr.	14..7
By Cheque	£1..14..1

Friday 30 January: Miss Jenkins & I went to see Miss Price of Bridgend, found her very weak & ill in bed, but very glad to see us. I had never seen her before, she was quite pleased with me & said she was so sorry not to have known me before & then I could have come to stay with her. She always liked Kate Pendrill & was so glad to see her daughter.

1. Prince Alfred Ernest Albert married Grand Duchess Marie Alexandrovna.

Saturday 31 January: Went to Swansea. Met Mrs. Ed. Strick in Martin the Jeweller's, Mr. Jones Llanguicke in Goat Street, Dr. Walters in Castle Street & Mrs. Walters in the Bank, & Mrs. Kirkhouse in Wind Street.

Sunday 1 February: At home all day. Betty to Church & Mary to Chapel.

Tuesday 3 February: Sent bottle of Orange Brandy & a few eggs to Miss Price of Bridgend by train.

Thursday 5 February: D.M. & Lloyd cut down 8 large trees between little walk & Hay house. They [are] decaying fast & now there will be room for a young plantation of firs. The place is getting very bare & exposed. Dl. Jenkins putting partition up on Kitchen loft. Recd. a very kind letter from Miss Price Bridgend acknowledging the Brandy &c. & saying she was very weak yesterday.

Friday 6 February: D.M. & Lloyd carrying thorns from Cae shed hedge to shut hill fence.

Saturday 7 February: Mr. Jenkins brought Lizzie back by the 5.30 train. She had been staying at Bryn Syfi a fortnight last Wednesday. Dl. Jenkins finished putting sacking to Kitchen bedstead & altering the loft, it will be a tidy bedroom after it has been ceiled.

Sunday 8 February: No one to Church. Mary to Chapel at 6 p.m, the first time at that hour & she came back in good time.

Monday 9 February: Mr. Price & Jane (the latter has not been here since '66) called when we were at dinner to ask Miss Pendrill's address in Bath that Dora who was now in Clifton might call there. They took lunch & took Mr. Jenkins down to Pontardawe with them to meet the 4.13 train to Swansea. I was much annoyed they met here as I know it was unpleasant to Mr. Jenkins in as much as he always refuses to go to Glantwrch.

Monday 16 February: *****

Saturday 21 February: Lizzie took tea at Gartheithen. Betty came back, she & Mary had been yesterday & today to Penclawdd, Lougher & Spitty Works to look for Ianto. No one had seen him there.

Sunday 22 February: No one to Church (very wet) except Lloyd a.m. Mary to Chapel at 6 p.m.

Wednesday 25 February: D.M. putting pebbles each side of Walk in New Garden by fruit trees towards Hill gate, Lloyd clearing up & assisting him.

Thursday 26 February: Wrote to Misses Davies Lower Market Street Carmarthen declining the mare Lloyd had been to see, he was afraid she was too light for the Cart, although suiting the Carriage nicely, price £44.

Friday 27 February: D.M. nailing currant trees to garden wall & trimming them.

Saturday 28 February: D.M. & Lloyd cleaning between here & Day's.

Sunday 1 March: Lizzie, Betty & I in house all day. Mary to Chapel, Lloyd to Church a.m.

Saturday 7 March: Recd. a letter from Lizzie. Wrote to Lizzie. Dr. Davies called to see me, said he saw me looking better than when I left Bath last June, but that I must be very careful about myself. Miss Longlands called, said her sister was not at all well. I called to see Mrs. Lena, she has a little girl born this day fortnight. Mr. Lena in Rome.

Sunday 8 March: Went to St. James Church 11 a.m. A very good sermon on the Communion. To the Abbey 6.30 p.m. It now seems all finished & looks a magnificent Church.

Monday 9 March: Miss Drewe who is now in lodgings with a Miss Pinch, 34 Henrietta Street called to see me.

Tuesday 10 March: I dined at Miss Pendrill's this evening to meet Mrs. Morgan (formerly Louisa King). She lives near Taunton but is now on a visit here to her stepson. She looked very well & is a cheerful pleasant woman, a widow's dress suits her. It is very cold, quite as cold as at home. Snow falling all day off & on.

Wednesday 10 March: Called at Phipps in Gay Street to ask if he would make me a pair of boots, said he would. He made a pair for me last year with a stiffening in the ankle, I wish him now to make them for the Iron. Had my watch cleaned by Clarks in Bartlett Street, paid 2/6. Miss Drewe took tea with me, said Ellen Longlands had had 2 teeth out yesterday. Wrote to Miss Jenkins.

Thursday 12 March: Mrs. Morgan & her sister Mary King called, they were very pleasant. I called at Mrs. Mackenzie's. She made me promise to dine with her on Saturday at 5 o'clk. Called at Miss Pendrill's, she was very kind & asked me to come to tea on Saturday at 7.30 to meet the Kings, which I promised to as Mrs. M. retires early. M.M. [Mary Mackenzie] called here when I was out, I was sorry to have missed her.

Friday 13 March: Miss Longlands called & asked me to lunch with them tomorrow at 1 o'clk. which I promised to do. Went in a chair to call on Mr. Cox & took him the sofa rug. Mrs. Cox was out & he was engaged so I did not see either, went from there to the Park & then to the Dentist, he was from home. He will be back Monday & I have made an appointment to see him at 1 o'clk.

Saturday 14 March: ***** Very poorly all day, very sick & giddy. Mr. Davis told me to be very quiet. Wrote to Miss Longlands, Mrs. Mackenzie & Miss Pendrill, saying I was very poorly & obliged to decline their kind invitations for today in consequence. Mr. Cox Junr. called said his Father was not well & that his Mother wd. call on me on Monday. Very ill & faint at 7 p.m. Obliged to send for Brandy & go to bed. Miss Aston & maid very kind & attentive.

Sunday 15 March: Not at all well in the house all day. M.M. came to see me. Miss Longlands sent her card & to know how I was at 3 p.m.

Monday 16 March: Lloyd to Carmarthen to see a mare of Davies the Flour Merchant.

Tuesday 17 March: I called on Mrs. Morgan & Mary King at 14 Charlotte Street, they leave tomorrow. Recd. a kind letter from M.M. saying her Aunt wished me to come & stay a week at least with them before I left, called at 13 & decided to go there on Thursday. Miss E. Longlands there. She looked very flushed & poorly. Called at Mrs. Mackenzie's, she was very kind & glad I was coming next door.

Saturday 21 March: Had two teeth (lower jaw right side) taken out by Mr. Parkinson under the influence of gas.

Sunday 22 March: In house all day.

Monday 23 March: Poor Mrs. Rees of London died this morning between 9 & 10 o'clk. a.m. She was always a kind friend to me & I am very sorry after her. She was so true and sincere. I shall greatly miss her kind welcome when I go to London.

Friday 27 March: Called to wish Mrs. Lena good bye & also to see her after her Husband's death. Called to wish Miss Drewe good bye at 34 Henrietta Street. Called also at 7 The Vineyards to wish the two Miss Longlands good bye.

Saturday 28 March: ½ Gal. Pale Brandy, ½ doz. Marsalla, ½ doz. Tarragona, 2 doz. Pale Ale.

Tuesday 31 March: Ellen Gilbertson & Miss Edwards walked up to see me.

Wednesday 1 April: Lizzie to Llanguicke with old surplice after being washed & brought the rest to be washed. Lloyd to Llanguicke to clean my dear Mother's grave. Mr. Clarke here. Revd. Nathl. Thomas the new Curate at Pontardawe called, stayed to tea, the 1st time he was here. He said he came to say that Service wd. be on Good Friday at 3 o'clk.

Good Friday 3 April: Lloyd to Pontardawe Church at 11 a.m. Recd. a very nice letter from Mary Mackenzie.

Easter Sunday 5 April: Lloyd to Pontardawe a.m. Lizzie, Betty & Mary to Llanguicke. Biddy came back with them & Wm. came afterwards. I had gone to bed with a bad headache & very bad toothache.

Monday 6 April: Mary asked to leave to go to Llandilo to meet her sisters. Said she should & that she may stay until tomorrow.

Tuesday 7 April: Mary returned at 7 p.m.

Thursday 9 April: Lizzie walked home over the hill, took bag for potatoes. John Harris Gartheithen came here for the churn. I think they will find it too large so I said they could return it if it did not suit them.

Friday 10 April: Lizzie returned by 12 o'clk. train to Garnant, she walked from there. Lloyd to Garnant to fetch bag of potatoes sent from Llwyn-yr-onen. John Gellyluog here asking if I would lend him Fly a few days next week to plough.

Saturday 11 April: Lloyd to Neath for trees sent by Wheeler & Son Glos'ter.

Sunday 12 April: ***** Lizzie, Betty, Day & his wife to Llanguicke. The Pontardawe Welsh School there repeating verses & answering questions.

Monday 13 April: Lloyd's 3 months up last Saturday. Agreed with him at the same rate (8/- per week) for 6 months with the understanding that he keeps <u>all tidy</u> & does his best in everything.

Garth

April 13, 1874

Dear Sir,

On the receipt of your letter on Saturday I looked over Mr. Davies's Report and found the error was <u>mine</u> by entering Surface Damage £10 instead of £8. I am sorry this mistake should have occurred, it was quite unintentional. I enclose a cheque for £2 and send a receipt for £103..19..7 which I think makes all right. You can easily see Mr. Davies when he is at the Colliery or if you wish to write his address is

Llwyd Coed
Llanelly

I will not fail in my promise of giving you the first offer of Cwmllynfell.

Yours sincerely,

Margaret Jones

G.B. Brock, Esq.

Wednesday 15 April: Lloyd forking & raking up the ground for planting the trees tomorrow. Eliza Goetregarth came to see how I was, showed her anti-macassars, &c. Mrs. Williams came to see how I was as she had heard I had been so ill with toothache. Day sowed oats & vetches in the strip. Charley harrowing with new mare & Fly.

Thursday 16 April: Lloyd planted Austrian pine & Scotch firs &c. had from Wheeler & Son Gloucester in plantation between here & the Closet. Mr. Clarke here, brought me some trout. D. Lewis Rhyd-y-fro paid for the Meadow hay bought by him & Isaac Gellyfowy last August, 3 acres @ £2..2..6 per acre, £6..7..6. Allowed the 7/6 as the harvest was bad, he gave me a cheque for £6..0..0.

Friday 17 April: Lloyd commenced digging in Kitchen garden.

Sunday 19 April: I am very poorly & <u>sick</u>.

Tuesday 21 April: Mrs. Thomas Cwmamman, Mrs. & Miss Day came here to tea & supper. Mr. Day drove them down & Lloyd took them home in my new Carriage. The harness broke on the road & they had to wait a long time to have it mended with cords. I was <u>so vexed</u>.

Wednesday 22 April: I went to Swansea midday train & stayed the night at Bryn Syfi. Settled to go to London with the Jenkins the week after next.

Thursday 23 April: Had straps of harness broken last Tuesday mended by Burchell. Came home through Garnant thinking to call at the Vicarage but I had a letter from Mrs. Day saying they were all right so I called on Jane Jones & asked her to call there for me & to say I was glad they were all safe. Lloyd met me with new mare in the new Carriage the 1st time I was after Polly.

Friday 24 April: D.M. & Lloyd finished setting Kitchen garden.

Saturday 25 April: D.M. & Lloyd carrying away the thorns from Cae hedge. Lloyd broke the stone post of Gate between here & Day's by letting the Gambo knock against it, it was thorough carelessness & I am very angry. I called at Gotregarth hearing Betty was so ill. She is much better.

Monday 27 April: Lloyd took new mare to be shod before breakfast, did not come back until 11.15. Lloyd cutting <u>Ivy</u> by front door. Mr. Clarke here, left for Garnant before tea. Intends going to London tomorrow. Sally came up to make Lizzie's dresses.

Tuesday 28 April: Lloyd cutting the <u>Ivy</u> on the kitchen & Day's house, finished tonight <u>except</u> carrying it away. I went up to see Cottage garden, hill fence, meadow & the road fence after D.M. had done it. The road fence has been steeped by D.M. from Wain Daniel to Wain Hir & looks exceedingly neat & tidy all the way, & seems growing nicely.

Wednesday 29 April: D.M. & Lloyd cleaning stones &c. off Cae Cwtta & also clearing rubbish after old rick on the meadow. Set 2 hens, 1 on 9 duck eggs & 1 on 9 hen eggs. Lloyd to Pontardawe at 6 p.m. for 1½ hun. potatoes for setting, also bran & flour.

Thursday 30 April: D.M. & Lloyd setting potatoes in Cottage Garden.

Friday 1 May: Lloyd drove me in the Phaeton with new mare to Swansea, left here at 2 p.m. Went down in an hour & a half exactly, returned home at 9.15. Went to Bryn Syfi to see if they had arranged about lodgings in London, they had not decided. Called at Andrews in Wind Street to return patterns of livery. Bought Lloyd a new hat 12/-.

Saturday 2 May: Went to the Stable before breakfast, found poor old Fly not cleaned. All mud up to her knees. Spoke to Lloyd about it & told him I was very displeased at his neglect of her, particularly as I had said when he first came here that I valued her past services & that I wished her well cared for.

Sunday 3 May: Lizzie to Church, also Mrs. Day, Jenny & Annie & Charlie. Betty, Mary & I in the house all day.

Monday 4 May: D.M. & Lloyd carrying clay.

Tuesday 5 May: D.M. cutting Polka lower end road side of Wain Pedr Erw. Lloyd cutting suckers off currant & gooseberry trees in old garden & raking the Walk.

Wednesday 6 May: Paid Mary Lewis her 6 months wages from Nov 28th to May 29th as agreed at Llandilo £6..0..0 for the coming six months. I have agreed with her for £4..10..0. She is not a competent servant, therefore I reduce her wages, & wages too are lowering owing to The Works stopping & all the tinworks girls are idle. She goes home tomorrow for a fortnight's holiday while Lizzie & I are in London and Betty takes charge of the house.

Saturday 9 May: The 2 Miss Jenkins went in a cab to Rotten Row & Lizzie & I walked there. We all sat there an hour to see the Ladies ride & to see the Carriages. We also saw the Horse Guards ride through to Knightsbridge. Such a lovely sight.

Sunday 10 May: L. ***** & I went a.m. to All Souls Church opposite the Langham Hotel. The others remained at home all day. Mr. Rees called.

Saturday 16 May: Mr. & Mrs. Bowman called to see Miss Rachel, brought some strawberries & roses.

Sunday 17 May: No one to Church. Miss Rachel feeling poorly last night. Lizzie sat up until 6 a.m. At 4 p.m. Lizzie & I walked in Regents Park.

Monday 18 May: Lizzie & I went by the 9.35 train from Charing Cross to Reigate where Mr. Bowman met us with the Carriage & drove us to his house at Brockham Green. Mrs. Bowman received us very warmly & we spent a very pleasant day, returning to London in the evening.

Tuesday 19 May: Lizzie & I walked down Wigmore Street looking at shop windows & to Madame Tussaud in Baker Street to see the Wax Works, returning to dinner at 3 o'clk. At 4.30 I went in a cab to 61 Warwick Street, Belgrave Road to see the Marryats. They were both so glad to see me. Mrs. Marryat looked very aged & broken but Mr. Marryat looked very well considering his serious illness some time ago. They seemed very comfortable & many of their own nice old things about them. Mr. Jenkins had come by Express when I arrived. I saw the Royal procession from Aldershot with the Emperor in Belgrave Road.

Wednesday 20 May: In the morning Lizzie & I went in a cab to Ken. Palace Gardens & walked past Ken. Palace to the Albert Memorial which is a lovely piece of architecture & well worth seeing. We walked past Rotten Row & home in a Cab from Hyde Park Gates Piccadilly. We walked again in the afternoon with Mr. Jenkins to Hyde Park where we saw the Four in hand Club (34 drays 4 horses in each) drive out through Hyde Park Gates in Piccadilly. The park was thronged with Carriages.

Thursday 21 May: Mr. Jenkins, the 2 Miss Jenkins, Lizzie & I left 33 Harley Street, Cav. Square for Paddington thence by Express to Swansea. Poor Miss

Rachel bore the journey much better than we expected. Mr. Richard Jenkins, Jane Matthews & their old Servant Susan met us at the Swansea Station. We had some difficulty in getting Miss Rachel into a Cab, she was carried in a chair up the steps to Bryn Syfi. We stayed there the night.

Friday 22 May: Lizzie & I left Bryn Syfi for Garth by the 3.20 train, Lloyd meeting us at Pontardawe with Fly in the Phaeton. Mary Lewis returned at 9 p.m. from Garnant. She had been home to Pumpsaint during the time we were away. Day bled the white cow's calf to death. There was something the matter with its legs from birth, it could not stand.

Saturday 23 May: Took Lizzie in the new Carriage as far as Cross Inn Station (she was going home until Wednesday). Lloyd halted the mare at the Cross Inn & we then drove home. Met Mrs. Perkins going to Mr. Hughes. She said 3 of Mr. Morris Pontamman's grandchildren died lately from scarlet fever.

Whitsun Monday 25 May: D.M. finished paving the Hay house. He now goes to prepare pebbles for building his nephew's house in Cwmamman. Some gathering on Gellyonen Mountain. Lloyd went there after dinner. Rose drawing room carpet.

Wednesday 27 May: Put down Drawing room carpet & put the Grate & Curtains for the Summer. It all looks clean & tidy. Told Morgan & Ellen I wanted a man that Lloyd was likely to leave. Lizzie returned at 12 o'clk. Her father is much better & able to go out a little.

Thursday 28 May: John Gellyluog here for Gate Post which I promised him long ago, had 4 poles enough to hang 4 gates. He said he had borrowed Fly when I was away in London & hoped he had not done wrong. I said he had made more free than welcome & that I was not at all pleased he had come to borrow things from my Servants when I was away & that he must never do so again.

Friday 29 May: Lloyd drove Lizzie & I in the New Carriage to call on Mrs. Day Cwmamman. We intended calling at the Vicarage but she said Mrs. Thomas had gone to Kidsgrove, Mrs. Maber having a little girl. Went to see Morgan Tyllwyd & took him a bottle of wine. He is very weak, but very glad to see us. Returned to the Day's & took tea. They were very kind & gave us a Pot of Seedlings for planting. Lloyd put the Carriage at Raven Inn. Met & spoke to Mr. Charles Morgan. Also met Mrs. Morgan & her niece but she did not speak.

Saturday 30 May: Planted seedlings in Stumpery & some geraniums in one bed. Asked Lloyd for garden fork, it was long in coming & he was obliged to acknowledge he had lent it to Day. I found fault with him for doing so & I also told Day he or his wife should always come & ask me for anything they want to borrow & not allow the children to ask Lloyd. I think both parties are much to blame & I told them so. Mrs. Kirkhouse walked up to tea. Lloyd took her home in the Phaeton. Paid her £1..10 for Rug.

Sunday 31 May: ***** Lizzie to Llanguicke on the new mare 1st time. Lloyd walked with her. Mary to Chapel at 6 p.m.

Monday 1 June: Went to Swansea 1st train. Went to Bryn Syfi. Miss Rachel not quite so well today as she has been. Bought new matting for little kitchen at Goodalls. Paid for polishing desk at Lewis' 18/6. Paid for Lloyd's hat at Jenkins, 12/-. Had Gin, Brandy, Whisky, 1 Gal. each from D & J Williams. Settled in full with Fulton. Returned 3.20 train. Called at the Gilbertsons. They had gone to lunch at Glantwrch. Lloyd said his month wd. be up next Friday. Said he had not had a place to suit him. I said I had not had a man & that if he liked he could stay another month. He said he liked this place & was quite satisfied.

Tuesday 2 June: Lloyd to the Station for things bought yesterday. Had carrots, parsnips & onions from Mrs. Kirkhouse to transplant as our seeds had failed. Had a letter from Miss Price Bridgend saying she was very weak, & that she wd. be very glad to see if I would come & see her, & if I could stay the night.

Wednesday 3 June: Sowed parsnips & turnips this evening, the seed first sown having failed by so much dry weather.

Thursday 4 June: Lizzie not well, did not get up until 1 o'clk. Put leech to my gum as my tooth ached so much.[2] Paid Dl. Jenkins Carpenter for all work done by himself & Son up to this day. By cash £1..17..0 paid. When he heard I was in London last month he said he was in trouble, fearing I should meet with some accident or be killed & that no one wd. believe I owed him money & that he shd. not be paid! I shall never think so well of him again, he did not care for my life, only his money. Lloyd earthing the potatoes in the garden.

2. "Until the middle of the nineteenth century, the leech was used enthusiastically to treat almost any illness . . . [and] . . . in cases of inflammation and localised swelling, it would have been an effective treatment." J. Eastoe, *Victorian Pharmacy*, 101.

Sunday 14 June: ***** Lizzie in the house. I rode Fly to Church. Sacrament. The Cloths were very dirty & also the Plate. Told Sarah Joseph so & brought them home with me.

Monday 15 June: Sarah Jones Llwyn-yr-Onen [Lizzie's sister] 25 years old today.

Tuesday 16 June: Williams late of Nant-y-Gasseg came here to mow my hay. He begins the Meadow this day. Lizzie went home for the day, took Jane the black & white muslin skirt she had made for her. She also called on Mrs. Hughes & took Mr. Jones Llanguicke's subscription £2..2 towards Bettws Church. Lloyd drove her to meet 1st train at Garnant & fetched her by the last. A Choral Meeting at Llandovery. Mr. Jones & 2 Curates there with their Choir. Lizzie came with them from Cross Inn. Mr. Nathaniel Thomas came, had a lift to the bottom of this road.

Wednesday 17 June: Gave Lizzie a scolding this morning for not mending her old stay. She had worn her best some time, & then got Betty to buy one in Neath without telling me. Lizzie very naughty this afternoon in going to a nest in the Kitchen wall by Cowhouse & bringing a young bird without feathers & putting it quietly on my lap. It <u>frightened</u> me <u>very much</u> & I was very poorly all the evening.

Thursday 18 June: Lizzie went to stay at Bryn Syfi. I went with her to the Station last train S.V.R. Called at Gartheithen in coming back from Pontardawe & paid for the cheese Mrs. Harris bought me 28 lbs @ 4½d, 10/6 paid.

Friday 19 June: Went to the meadow a.m. to see the hay. In coming back in Heol y Cefn saw a Snake by the wall. Called to Jacky Ty Twt who was digging for coal on the hill to come & kill it, he came directly but the Snake had run away. He came to the house with me & had a glass of beer.

Sunday 21 June: I rode Fly to Church. Mary to Chapel in the morning. Betty in the house all day, not feeling well. She fainted after dinner.

Monday 22 June: William commenced mowing Cae Barriwns hay. Finished carrying the meadow hay, also the little Garden Croft. The hay has not had one drop of rain. I hope it is well harvested, it was very bad last year it had so much rain.

Thursday 25 June: Went to Bryn Syfi last train S.V.R. to see Lizzie who was not well. She had taken a Tablespoonful of her medicine instead of a teaspoonful. I wonder it did not half kill her for it was powerful Iron. I hope she will be more careful in future.

Saturday 27 June: Carried Cae Barriwns hay today. John Harris & his wife came to help, Day & Charlie, their horse & cart. Day said he thought the hay was not fit. Williams said it was. Griffith Thomas paid £3 on account of hay had in 1873.

Sunday 28 June: Lizzie at Bryn Syfi. I at home all day, had a very bad head all the afternoon.

Monday 29 June: Williams commenced cutting fern for me.

Tuesday 30 June: Lizzie returned last train from Bryn Syfi. She gave me a steel brooch & little blue scarf. Mr. Jenkins gave Lizzie an Album for Photographs. Mary complained of feeling ill yesterday after dinner. Mr. Saunders of Llansamlet brought a horse for me to see, price too high £65.

Friday 3 July: Mary feeling ill since Monday & not able to do anything. Sent Lloyd for Mr. Rees Tirbach. He said it was weakness & indigestion & that she must keep up her spirits, she wd. soon be well.

Monday 6 July: Let out the calf for the first time, tied him to a stake in Cae Barriwns. I went out to see the calf & she ran round & got the rope round my ankles so that I fell instantly on my back.

Tuesday 7 July: Lizzie's birthday (23 years). Gave her a book "The Two Cities" by Charles Dickens. Fanny G. & Miss Ford called in the little Pony Carriage, said Kate had a son since Friday, her 2nd child. Mr. Jones called, stayed to supper.

Thursday 9 July: Betty very ill all last night with the toothache. She went this morning to Griffiths the Doctor & had her front tooth out. Mr. Rees the Doctor came down to see Mary, he said the same as before that there was not much the matter & that she must rouse herself.

Friday 10 July: Lloyd drove me in the Phaeton to call on Mrs. Charles Morgan. She said it was years since she had seen me. She seemed very glad I returned her call & hoped I would not be ceremonious but come to see her as often as I could.

Saturday 11 July: Wm. Griffiths Cwmllynfell here. I was very poorly, fainted several times.

Sunday 12 July: I rode Fly to Church & Lloyd walked with me. Took Communion Cloths, Chalice & Paten back after being washed & cleaned. Sacrament.

Monday 13 July: Mary's Mother came here at 1 o'clk. Lloyd took them both in the Cart to the Garnant Station to meet last train. Rachel Tom here washing.

Tuesday 14 July Mrs. Day returned from spending a week in Devonshire. Miss Elizabeth Lloyd of Glanhonddu late of Nantgwyllt married to Revd. W. Williams of Llandefaelog Fach, Brecon.

Saturday 18 July: Finished carrying Ty Cwtta hay, all the hay is now carried & in very good condition but a very thin crop partly owing to the dry Summer. Rachel cleaned Kitchen Tins.

Sunday 19 July: Lizzie to Church on Fly. I at home all day, my back very painful.

Monday 20 July: Williams, Lloyd & Rachel Tom finished making Fern rick and putting hay tidy in hay house. Mrs. Williams (Rhoda Attwood) died at Lota, Chile, aged 42 years. Her eldest daughter was married some months ago in Chile.

Tuesday 21 July: Lloyd at last finished earthing Cottage Garden potatoes.

Wednesday 22 July: D. Morgan came to see me having heard from Jane Isaac that I was very poorly after the calf threw me down.

Thursday 23 July: Lloyd to Swansea to change scythe & do other errands for me. He missed the 10 o'clk train & had to wait until the 1 o'clk. It was 7.30 when he came back here, he was not drunk but he had I think been drinking.

Sunday 26 July: No one to Church. Lizzie not well with toothache.

Tuesday 28 July: Lizzie & I went to Bryn Syfi by midday train. Went to Mr. Scott's to have Lizzie's tooth taken out (the 1st). He gave her Mitheline to make her insensible. She felt rather poorly & we returned to Bryn Syfi in a Cab. She got hysterical after tea & Mr. Shepherd came up at 10.30, he said there was no danger.

Wednesday 29 July: Mr. Shepherd came to Bryn Syfi at 12 o'clk. this morning to examine my back which is very painful since the calf threw me down 3 weeks ago. He thought there was no injury to the spine but that I had received a great shock to my whole system & that I must lie down a good deal & keep quiet & not ride.

Thursday 30 July: Lizzie & I went into Swansea. Called on Mrs. Matthews, she was very glad to see us. She is feeling very poorly & looks a good deal swollen. I returned home this evening last train & Lizzie stays a few days with Miss Jenkins. 1 Gal. Gin, 1 doz. each beer & porter.

Friday 31 July: William Cwmllynfell here in his way from Neath fair. Pd. half a year's rent due last March. Said James & Aubrey were likely to work Ystradowen coal thro' Cwmllynfell pit. His cousin Billy brought a horse for me to see, it was not at all a nice one & I declined it. Sent Frock, Jacket &c. to Bryn Syfi for Lizzie by last train.

Saturday 1 August: John Gellyluog paid half a year's rent due last March. Settled as follows all accounts to this date.

£ .. s .. d	John Williams	Margaret Jones	
	to	To	
	Margaret Jones	John Williams	£ .. s .. d
	(Rick of Meadow	2½ days Man & horse	
	(hay had Janry. 1873	in April 1873	12.. 6
		Leg of Veal 11 lbs @ 9½d	8 8½
		4 Calfs feet	8
		Paid	£1..1..10½

Sunday 2 August: Had sea weed for my back. No one in Church very wet a.m.

Monday 3 August: Feeling very poorly all day. Flower show at Mr. Grenfell's.

Tuesday 4 August: Lizzie came back last train from Bryn Syfi. Lloyd met her with the Phaeton at Pontardawe Station. Recd. cheque for £8..6..7 from Mr. Jenkins, half year's interest due last month on £520 (Neath House). Mary Anne Gotregarth married to John Cwmbryn her 2nd husband.

Wednesday 5 August: Betty fell down on the Store room stairs & hurt her arm very much. Recd. a letter from Levi Rees saying the Gwain cae Gurwen Coal Company were digging the foundation for a house on the Common without asking the permission of either the Court Leet or the Homagers & as they intended holding another meeting about it he wished to know if I was for or against it.[3] I wrote saying I was against it without permission from the proper Authorities.

Monday 10 August: Very poorly all day. Great shooting pain in my right bosom, the first time I felt it. I do not remember having had any blow on it. I think my whole system is very much shaken since my fall July 6th for I have been very poorly & in much pain ever since.

Tuesday 11 August: Feeling very poorly. Lloyd drove me after dinner as far as D. Morgan's to get his Hatchet & Billhook for cropping hedges. I think the air did me good. Recd. a letter from Jane Matthews saying Richard & herself wd. come and stay over Sunday if convenient.

Wednesday 12 August: ***** Lizzie to Swansea midday train. Took French beans to Bryn Syfi. Lloyd fetched her by the last S.V. train. It was pouring with rain. Mary Shonny & Maryanne here, stayed the night it was so wet. Mr. J. W. James' eldest daughter (Esther) married today at St. James Church Swansea to Edward Henry eldest son of Mr. Edward Bath.[4] A very gay wedding & a ball in the evening at the James', 70 or more at the Breakfast. A fine morning but very wet afternoon.

Thursday 13 August: Margaret Gellyluog had 10½ lbs bacon @ 1/- per lb. 10/6 paid. D.M. & Lloyd cleaning the Walk.

---

3. Court Leet: see footnote for 12 June 1871. Homager: originally a vassal but later attributed to anyone who owed or paid homage to a superior in return for the use of land, e.g. a tenant.
4. Esther, daughter of John William James, Harbour Superintendent, married Edward Henry Bath, merchant of Brynymor, Swansea. Henry Bath was one of the Trustees and Executors of the will of Elias Jenkins of Kilvey House.

Friday 14 August: Put down carpet in my room. Willie Paddison rode down to see me, he has a fortnight's holiday. He is so changed, getting quite a man with whiskers &c. & he is grown. He is in Westbourne Grove London with Wm. Owen & getting on very well. He is a steady good boy & I hope success will attend him. Lizzie went with Lloyd in the Phaeton to meet Jane Matthews who comes here to stay until Monday.

Saturday 15 August: Lizzie & Jane Matthews went up to Garnant in the Carriage to meet Richard who was at the Colliery. They returned in time for tea 5.30 p.m.

Sunday 16 August: Very wet, could not go to Church. It cleared about 4 p.m. & after tea Lizzie, Jane & Richard went for a walk up the hill & back through Rhydyfro.

Monday 17 August: Jane & Richard Matthews left by 1st train. Lizzie went with them to the Station. Heard Mrs. Morgan Gellygron had had another fit on Friday. Lloyd drove me down to see how she was this afternoon. She has not spoken nor eaten any thing since Friday evening when she was taken ill.

Tuesday 18 August: Poor Mrs. Morgan Gellygron died this morning at 6 a.m. aged 65. Feeling very poorly & my back very painful, it seems as if the pain went up my spine into my head & made my head heavy & giddy. I have not felt this until today. Lewis the Tiler here preparing lime for plastering kitchen loft. Louisa Price!! married today at Sherborne to Capt. Gilbert.

Wednesday 19 August: Very poorly all day & often in great pain in my back & all through my sides & chest & bosoms.

Thursday 20 August: Lloyd all day at Gartheithen helping to carry the wheat, a very hot & sultry day.

Friday 21 August: Poor Mrs. Morgan Gellygron buried today at Llanguicke, a public funeral leaving the house at 3 p.m. Betty, Lloyd, Day & his wife there. Very fine day & a large funeral.

Saturday 22 August: Lloyd with Gambo & mare helping Day to carry hay from 10.30 to 3 o'clk. Walter Jeffreys here to tea, Lloyd took him down in going to meet Mr. Jenkins who came up by last train. Mrs. Kirkhouse &

Georgy came here at 5.30, had tea & left again at 7 o'clk. Paid her for the Rug. Edward Clarke M.D. died at Wood Green London, he was youngest son of Revd. Thos Clarke, Vicar of Pontardulais.

Sunday 23 August: Lizzie to Church. Mr. Jenkins walked as far as Gotregarth to meet her. Very hot. Mr. Jenkins very poorly after tea. G. Lewis Hussey, M. Smith, G. Rees, the two sons in Church after Mrs. Morgan.

Monday 24 August: Mr. Jenkins left by the Brecon train going from here 3.45. I met Lloyd returning at the bottom of the road & he drove me as far as Daniel the Carpenter's. I think a little going out does me good & I can't walk much. Biddy came up to see me & brought me a few plums & pears.

Tuesday 25 August: Lizzie went home on Fly. Took a bottle of jam, a few apples & a cucumber to her Father. Mr. Jones Llanguicke & Mr. Thomas the Curate came here about 5 o'clk, had tea & left at 7 o'clk, having a prayer meeting at the Schoolroom. They came in the Dog cart. Lloyd carrying road scrapings to Cae Cwtta.

Wednesday 26 August: D.M. & Daniel the Carpenter sawing poles for rails. They also cut down 3 large trees lower side of Walk going to front gate, the trees were quite dead, not a leaf on them. J. W. Vaughan of Velin Newydd Breconshire, cousin to T.G.J., 21 years this day. Grand doings there.[5] Lizzie returned 12.15. The Policemen went up the hill after Poachers, they caught the dog. Called to ask me who the Lord of the Manor was & who his Agent. I gave Mr. Price's address to Brynamman Policeman. Mary, Betty's sister here. Gave her 2 hens for her 2 sons.

Thursday 27 August: After dinner Lloyd & D.M. taking trees cut yesterday to the saw pit ready for Daniel when he comes.

Friday 28 August: Lloyd & D.M. carrying some of the heap of earth by the hedge over Cae Cwtta field.

Saturday 29 August: Felt very poorly before dinner. Lloyd drove me in the Carriage to within a mile of Cross Inn. Lizzie got out at Garnant to go & call at the Vicarage. When I returned Richard Matthews & herself were waiting for me on the road, Richard going by train to Swansea from the Colliery.

5. Son of John William Vaughan JP, landowner and former Lieutenant of Breconshire.

Sunday 30 August: Lizzie walked to Church. Wm. Lewis here. I can hardly move with a severe & acute pain in my back & thighs.

Monday 31 August: Betty very grumpy & speechless because I told her yesterday to change her old ragged & patched bedgown that I was ashamed to see it. She is certainly one of the most disagreeable persons I ever met with. No wonder other Servants don't like her, it is quite her own fault to be so ill tempered & insinuating in her remarks to & of people. Lizzie & I called at Gellygron in the Carriage after Mrs. Morgan's death. Saw only Mary Smith, Mrs. Rees gone to Alltycham.

Wednesday 2 September: My birthday! 41 years old. A sad & miserable one to me for I am feeling very ill, great pain in my chest, pit of stomach, left side & back, indeed all through my body & head. I have very little hope myself of ever getting better. My own belief is that this pain in my chest is the beginning of something serious & that my time in this world will not be long. Perhaps this will be my last birthday on Earth. God only knows. I wish oh! how I wish I felt prepared to die. Lizzie gave me bookmarker "Think of me".

Thursday 3 September: Recd. a letter from Mrs. R. P. Llewelyn with Olwen & Llewelyn's Photographs. She said Tom's daughter had left for Boulogne to live with her Uncle, her Mother's brother as their place was too quiet. She had been with [her] 4 years. Feeling very poorly & on the bed nearly all day. Great pain in my chest & pit of stomach. I have often great pain in breathing. Lizzie & I were to have gone to Bath today, lodgings taken. I was too ill to travel, also the day wet. Lizzie wrote to 9 Pierrepont Street to say we wd. come Saturday.

Friday 4 September: Sold the new mare (Polly) back to John Gellyluog for £40 to be paid the 2nd of March next, that is the money I paid him for her & altho' horses are lower in price now than then I think she is well worth the money. She is an excellent mare for farm work, so quiet & free from vice, but is too heavy, & her fore legs not good for Carriage. Gave John £1..0..0 for trouble of buying her last year. The usual sum given a jockey for buying a horse.

Saturday 5 September: ***** Lizzie & I left Garth at 8.50 in time for 1st train to Swansea, thence by Express to Bath, arrived at 9 Pierrepont Street 5.45 p.m. Called at Bryn Syfi to see Miss Rachel who seemed more cheerful than when last I saw her. Mrs. Kirkhouse & her School children going to spend the day at Langland.

Sunday 6 September: Lizzie & I in the house all day.

Monday 7 September: Recd. a telegram from Mr. Jenkins saying he would come & see us tomorrow if convenient. Telegraphed back to say it would. Mr. Davies the Doctor came. He said I was in a very weak & delicate state of health & that I must be very careful of myself in every way. He said "Your pulse is weaker than an infant's 2 months old. You must be careful indeed."

Tuesday 8 September: Bought Lizzie a pair of buttoned boots at Phipps Gay Street. Paid 14/6. Mr. Jenkins came here at 4.40 p.m. Lizzie intended meeting him at the Station but the train arrived sooner than we expected.

Wednesday 9 September: Took Mr. Jenkins to see the Royal Baths, Pump Room, &c. I came back to wait for the Dr. & Lizzie & he went on to the Park. Very wet & thunder in the afternoon, after tea I went with him for a walk across North Parade bridge, along Pulteney Road & home through Pulteney Street.

Thursday 10 September: Mr. Jenkins, Lizzie & I went to Fluke's the Photographer in Milsom Street. The two former had their photos taken. We afterwards had a walk all around the Park & back to dinner. At 3 p.m. had a Landau & pair from Strange's & went for a drive up the Wells Road & back the North Road. It was a nice afternoon & we enjoyed the drive & the different views we saw.

Friday 11 September: Mr. Jenkins left for Bryn Syfi by the 11.40 train. We took him to the Station, it turned out a miserable wet day.

Saturday 12 September: Went for an hour p.m. in a Chair & Lizzie walking to Henrietta Park, Cleveland Bridge, Pulteney Road & back thro' Pulteney Street.

Sunday 13 September: Lizzie & I to the Abbey a.m. Lizzie to the Roman Catholic Church at 6.30. I lying on the sofa not very well.

Monday 14 September: Recd. Mary's letter saying her Mother had been over the day we left home for this place & that she was still not very strong. She had been to Aberaeron. Lizzie wrote to Mrs. Grenfell to thank her for her photograph. I wrote to Mrs. Jones Lion Hotel Rhayader to ask if she knew of a maid. Lizzie & I went up to the [Kennet & Avon] Canal & down Bathwick Hill. A lovely morning.

Saturday 19 September: Lizzie & I called on Mrs. Scott at 15 Bathwick Street, she seemed glad to see us. The Yeomanry left Bath. Saw a detachment of them assemble at the Royal Hotel & then leave the City. Miss Drewe took tea with us.

Sunday 20 September: Lizzie & I to St. James' a.m. Miss Pendrill called at 3 p.m. to see how I was as I was not well yesterday. She was so cheerful & kind. Lizzie & I to the Abbey at 6.30.

Monday 21 September: Mr. Davies called, he examined my back & chest. Said my spine was a little curved & that I must be very careful not to strain myself in any way. Lizzie & I called at 13 & 14 Bennett St. to wish them good bye at 6.30. Mary Mackenzie had gone out to some musical friends. Miss Charlotte Scott called, she looked very well & was so kind & friendly.

Tuesday 22 September: Bristol Races. Lizzie & I left Bath for Bryn Syfi where we remain until Saturday.

Saturday 26 September: Mr. Jenkins birthday, 51 years today. Lizzie & I left Bryn Syfi for home by the S.V. train 5 p.m. We had been away 3 weeks today. I feel rather better than when I left. Lloyd met us at the Station, he had a very bad arm. Dora Price & Tom Whittington called on horseback about 3 p.m. Jane Price returned from Buxton where she had been 2 months with Mrs. Hart.

Sunday 27 September: No one to Church.

Tuesday 29 September: Lizzie took Day a Notice paper to leave on the 25th March next as he had been so disagreeable about my mare Polly jumping into his fields & saying my hedges were not good fences & that the hedges were his as long as he paid for the land &c. In an hour or so he came in to ask if he was really to leave. I told him I gave him a fortnight to consider what was best.

Friday 2 October: Paid John Griffiths Timber Merchant Pontardawe £8..0..0 by cheque being all the money I owe him up to this day.

Saturday 3 October: ***** Wm. Lewis here saying he had lately been all through Gellyluog wood. Some ash had been cut but no damage of any value done. He advises me to sell the wood. Paid Garth Insurance due 29th September 18s 9d.

Sunday 4 October: No one to Church, a heavy shower came on to prevent Lizzie. Annie had a tooth taken out by Griffiths, face much swollen.

Monday 5 October: A fine day. Hannah Gellyluog here washing servants' bedclothes, 3 blankets & sheets. D. Morgan went back to sleep with Lloyd, his arm is now getting better.

Tuesday 6 October: Revd. D. M. Herbert, Vicar of Tremaine married today at Penally to a Mrs. Evans of Cilgerran a clergyman's widow. His 1st wife (Jane Whittington) only died 12 months last July (26th). He soon forgot her poor thing.

Wednesday 7 October: D.M. cutting privet hedge & cleaning in the front. Mary, Betty's niece, came here & stayed the night. She had been home from her service ill some weeks & intended returning on Friday until Novr.

Thursday 8 October: Jane Isaac here paying half year's rent due 25th last March, £1..10..0. Mary (J. Jones wife) here paying 1 year's rent for Plas-y-bryn due 29th last Septr, £3..5..0. They said Cwmllynfell Colliery had ceased working owing to the strike 22 weeks next Saturday. D.M. cleaning Green & between trees. Paid Tom Daniel £1 for painting gates & 18/7 for paint.

Friday 9 October: D.M. finished cleaning the front, he has done it thoroughly, raking the grass well & getting out all the dead grass & leaves. I wish Lloyd would take pains & try to do it the same, but he has no idea of garden work. Had a tram of Ynisderw coal 10/6. Morgan Gartheithen here for hauling it 5/- paid.

Saturday 10 October: Mr. Jenkins came up last train. It was so wet I did not expect him altho. I sent Lloyd with the Phaeton to the Station in case he may come. David Gellyluog married!! at Neath to Rachel Gellyllucka. Daniel broke his leg in coming from the wedding.

Sunday 11 October: No one to Church.

Monday 12 October: Mr. Jenkins left in time for the 4.13 train. Lloyd drove him with Fly. Lizzie went as far as the Mill to see for oats & to know how much I owed. The man had gone to Swansea.

Tuesday 13 October: Paid J. Jones Crachllwyn two quarters Poor Rate as follows:

		£ .. s .. d
Garth farm	£47.. 0..0 @ 10d	1.. 19..2
" Cottage	2.. 0..0	1..8
3 Cots Cwmllynfell	7..10..0	6..3
Smith shop	1..15..0	1..5½
Cot Craig Llanguicke	2.. 0..0	1..8
	£60.. 5..0	£2..10..2½
	Less Commission	2..4
	3rd quarter	2.. 7..10½
	4th quarter	2.. 7..10½
	By Cheque	£4..15.. 9

Lizzie walked to the Crachllwyn to see if they had butter for Miss Jenkins. Esther has a young baby christened yesterday Benjamin her 14th child.

Wednesday 14 October: Lloyd & D.M. drawing in the garden potatoes. Recd. a letter from Tom Whittington thanking me for leave to come shooting here. John Harris Gartheithen paid me for the Barrel Churn £1..15..0 made by Jack yr Hooper. Cost my Father £3..10..0.

Thursday 15 October: Mary Soar called to say she knew of a girl as a Servant, but that she did not know whether she would suit, her Mother & herself would come over next week to see me if I liked. Told her to tell them to come.

Friday 16 October: Went to Bryn Syfi by the 4 o'clk. train, found poor Miss Rachel in bed & not so well.

Saturday 17 October: A very wet morning. Could not go into Swansea to meet Mrs. Day so wrote a few lines to say about meat required.

Sunday 18 October: Miss Rachel very poorly. Wm. Lewis dined here. The daughter of Nant-y-Gasseg married to the son of Havod.

Monday 19 October: Lizzie came to Bryn Syfi midday train. She remained there & I returned last train. Mr. Josiah Rees called at Bryn Syfi, he had just come from Narbeth. Mr. Rees & Mr. Jenkins took me to the Station in their way to Swansea. Mr. Jones Llanguicke came up with me.

Tuesday 20 October: Mrs. Rees & Mary Smith called in the Phaeton, said they were going to have a housekeeper at Gellygron. They begged I would come there to tea some evening. D.M. & Lloyd drawing Cottage Garden potatoes. Dl. Jenkins here putting Kitchen loft ready for Lewis the Tiler, boarded by pigsty & put post to tie the calf. Recd. letter and powders from Dr. Davies, Bath.

Wednesday 21 October: Recd. a letter from Lizzie saying poor Miss Rachel was a little better. Put new fringe round the tunic of striped alpaca.

Thursday 22 October: Margaret Cwmllynfell sent me a present of a goose by the servant girl. Returned the jar the butter came in last Winter. Went to Bryn Syfi this afternoon to stay till Saturday.

Saturday 24 October: I returned last train. Lizzie stays until Monday. Mrs. Price called at Bryn Syfi but did not see Miss Rachel. She said they feared Dora's lungs were affected.

Sunday 25 October: Very wet, no one to Church. Lizzie at Bryn Syfi. She went to hear Mr. Trotter at the School room (Mission Week at Killay).

Monday 26 October: Samuel Williams Bogelegel & his brother-in-law John Thomas 3 Counties Foundry Cwmtwrch here, the latter wanting to leave Wm. Rowland's house & the land adjoining to build a house. Told him I had promised the first offer of a lease to Wm. Rowland. John Thomas had agreed to rent the Smith shop & garden now in the occupation of Dr. Griffiths from 1st Janry. next at £3 per year. Lizzie returned last train from Bryn Syfi. Mrs. Williams Maesquarra buried today.

Tuesday 27 October: Recd. 18 yds of Barathea from Shoolbred [*Tottenham Court Road*]. Sally brought it up & took it down with her to make a dress for me. Wrote to Mrs. Matt, 26 Thackerey Street, Toxteth Park, Liverpool giving Mary Lewis Pumpsaint's character which she wrote for. Sale at Pontardulais Vicarage (the late Revd. Thos. Clarke). Day killed the Bull.

Wednesday 28 October: Finished cleaning out the Pantry. Betty has limed it with Aberthaw lime. Walter Jeffreys called for a few minutes. Day took 4 steers to Neath but could not sell, cattle are come down very much in price, owing to a scarcity of food.

Thursday 29 October: Lloyd sweeping up leaves & cutting dead branches off larch tree by front gate & trimming the ivy on it. D. Morgan ditching thorn hedge between Gwyndwr Hir & Cae Shed. The Day's had it in very nice order but they have left it go into a shameful condition.

Friday 30 October: I went down to Gartheithen. John Harris & his wife had taken one pig & a half to Pontardawe to sell. They had 11/- a score. Morgan had gone to Llanybydder fair to buy sheep.

Saturday 31 October: D. Morgan spreading earth over Cae Cwtta. Lloyd fetched two loads of coal.

Sunday 1 November: Lizzie & Betty to Church. Miss Rachel Jenkins birthday, 60 years old today.

Monday 2 November: Lewis the Tiler & his workman here putting ceiling to Kitchen loft. I am feeling very poorly & have been so for some time with a pain in my chest & side, very severe at times. Altogether I am very far from well & am quite half my time either in or on the bed & when up I feel too poorly to do hardly anything. It makes me quite sad to feel so different to usual. I have never been well since the calf threw me down July 6th.

Tuesday 3 November: Lizzie went home walked over the hill. Took them 2 of her photos.

Wednesday 4 November: Recd. letter from Miss Jenkins saying she was sorry to hear I was not well & that her Sister was worse, getting so very excited at times. Cleaned out Dining Room & put down carpet. Lizzie returned at 6 p.m. & brought little white dog.

Thursday 5 November: Went down to Bryn Syfi by 1st Brecon train, found poor Miss Rachel much worse being every now & then in such an excited state, & afterwards weak & not inclined to move out of bed even to the chair. I am so sorry for them all. I was not at all well on leaving home & felt very poorly in the train & became very sick when I got to Bryn Syfi. After vomiting I was a little better but still uncomfortable. Took Miss Walford a little jar of butter about 6 lbs. She seemed very pleased.

Friday 6 November: Called at Mrs. Matthews, she is very poorly & very much swollen in her bowels. Paid Richard for having old sideboard lock repaired & new key to fit, 1/6. Paid him for key for kitchen cupboard had some weeks ago 9d. Returned home last train leaving poor Miss Rachel in a very excited state.

Saturday 7 November: Mr. Jenkins came up by last train. Wrote to Evans, Close Glas, Llandilo saying the price he wants for a mare (50 guineas) is higher than I intend giving.

Sunday 8 November: Lizzie to Church. Mr. Jenkins to meet her where we turn to the fields. Sacrament.

Monday 9 November: Went to the Pound to see John Thomas the Carrier's horse, a good mare seemingly but not a pretty one having 3 white legs & heavy, 14½ hands £35. D. Griffiths wife brought £2..0..0 on account of rent. Told her they must abide by the Notice I gave 30th Octr. & give up possession of the Smith's shop on the 1st Decr. next & pay all rent due to that day. She begged to continue as a tenant but I refused. Mr. Jenkins left.

Tuesday 10 November: Recd. a note from Miss Jenkins saying poor Mr. Edward Price died suddenly last Friday evening. The sad news was telegraphed to Glantwrch on Saturday morning. Lizzie went home on Fly to see about Thos. Rees' mare.

Wednesday 11 November: Lizzie came back & Thomas Rees with her, on his mare. Lloyd tried her in the Phaeton. She is not a carriage horse but he warrants her quiet, free from vice & a good useful mare, able to bring up a ton weight. She is rising 6 years & one he reared himself. Being greatly in want of a horse & afraid of risking a fair I bought her and gave him a cheque for £45..0..0. I think the price very high as she is very low in condition but he wd. not sell her under. He gave me 2/6 back and 2/- to Lizzie.

Friday 13 November: D.M. & Lloyd finished Heol y Cefn. It is now a very good road with a good thickness of broken stones laid on & then some earth from the quarry grown over them so as to make it a nice hard road for the carriage. How my dear Mama would have liked to have had it down so in her time. She was so tidy & neat in every thing & such a judge & admirer of what was tidy & properly done.

Tuesday 17 November: Lloyd fetched 3 cwt ¾ of straw for chaffing with hay from Isaac Jones, Glynmeirch @ 3/9 per cwt, 17/9 paid.

Thursday 19 November: Hannah Gellyluog here cleaning & liming Lloyd's room after Lewis had put ceiling to kitchen loft.

Friday 20 November: I went to Bryn Syfi 1st S.V. train & returned by the last. Miss Rachel very excited & had taken a great dislike to animal food. Heard Mr. Clarke had left Miss Powell £250 for her life & the house in Picton Place.

Saturday 21 November: Saron Eisteddfod. Lloyd went at 11 a.m. & came back at 5.10 p.m. He did not go to the Concert at 7 p.m. Recd. a letter from Ithel Llewellyn saying his Mother died last Thursday, 19th inst. about 1 o'clk. The daughter of Nant-y-Gasseg died. She had only been married a month this day. Diphtheria or throat disease, only ill a few days.

Sunday 22 November: Wm. Lewis here stayed to dinner & then went to Nant-y-Gasseg. Lizzie to Church.

Monday 23 November: ***** Hannah Gellyluog here washing. Catherine Rowland here paying half a year's rent due last September & asking if I would grant them a lease that they may repair & improve their house, told her I wd. grant them a lease to expire with the Colliery lease which is 10 years next Janry. They see that time very short. I have promised to think the matter over & let them know before Christmas. Lloyd carrying manure to Cae Cwtta heap to mix with it.

Tuesday 24 November: The Daughter of Nant-y-Gasseg buried at Carmel. Lloyd to the funeral & Mrs. Day. D.M. mixing heap in Ty Cwtta field. Old Mr. Evans of Eaglesbush near Neath died yesterday aged 78 years. He was Barrister at Law of the Inner Temple London & J.P. for Glamorganshire.

Thursday 26 November: Tom Bevan (late of Gartheithen) little boy William buried today at Pontardawe Church. Scarlet fever. Mrs. Day & Charlie to the funeral. John Thomas Cwmtwrch here asking if he could commence repairing about the Smith shop. Told him No until I had finally settled with Wm. Rowland, said I wd. let him know in a fortnight. Lloyd carrying manure to mix with earth heap in Ty Cwtta field.

Friday 27 November: William Evans, Tailor & his man here doing up sofa. D.M. finished mixing heap in Ty Cwtta field.

Monday 30 November: D. Griffiths wife brought me £2..10..0. The rent is now all paid up to tomorrow Decr. 1st. She said they wd. not give up possession of the Smithshop tomorrow, that they were not obliged to leave without 6 months notice.

Tuesday 1 December: Sent D. Morgan Mason to Cwmllynfell to ask for possession of the Smithshop of David Griffiths, the month's notice expiring today. He refused possession in the presence of Wm. Rowland, said I might [have] the garden or gardens whenever I liked, & that he would give up the Smithshop as soon as he could get a place to suit him.

Wednesday 2 December: Yesterday Lewis the Tiler here finishing the ceiling of kitchen loft. It is now looking very tidy & will be very warm & comfortable.

Lewis 5 days @ 5/6	£1..7..6)	£ .. s .. d	
Man 4 days @ 3/6	14..0)	2 .. 1 .. 6	
Paid Lewis for going to Llanguicke	)		
and Cwmllynfell some time ago	)	8 .. 6	
Paid him all I owe him up to this date for work done.		2 ..10 .. 0	Paid

Thursday 3 December: Betty to Neath yesterday with Fly & Day's car, had

½ soap	16 .. 6	
½ cwt of Salt 1/9d. 1 large bag 2/3d	4 .. 0	
1 sack of flour (Leather tie)	1 ..19 .. 6	
Mrs. Day went with Betty to Neath	£3 .. 0 .. 0	Paid

Dl. Jenkins here sawing rails. I went to Swansea. The new mare took to backing the Phaeton by D. Lewis, Rhyd-y-fro & again by the Dynevor Arms & Canal Bridge.

Saturday 5 December: Mrs. Jones Ffynnon Eiddon near Kidwelly died this day (her birthday). Poor Laura will miss her greatly. Old Captain Wm. Jones (Glanbrane near Neath) died aged 87 years. He was Miss Place's uncle & she had lived with him some years of late.

Monday 7 December: Lloyd to Swansea with Mrs. Day & Charlie for barley from Michael's Stores. I had 15 bushels @ 3/-, £2..5..0. The sea water had gone over it in the vessel, it does as well as the best for pigs, fowls, &c. as the grain is quite good. The Days had the same quantity for their pigs &c.

Tuesday 8 December: Hannah Gellyluog here cleaning down kitchen loft after the Tilers & putting all the things in their places. It looks now very nice, clean & tidy with no old lumber of any kind.

Wednesday 9 December: Lloyd & D. Morgan went back to sleep in kitchen loft. They like their room very much & say it is very warm & comfortable. I am glad they are pleased, it is some recompense for the expense & trouble of doing it.

Thursday 10 December: Lloyd & Betty finished picking the potatoes on the Storeroom and brought them to kitchen loft.

Friday 11 December: Betty to the mill with 3 bushels of the barley had Monday to grind for the pig. She took it on Fly.

Saturday 12 December: Put the sofa in the Dining room after covering it with chintz & making a Horse hair cushion for seat. It looks pretty tidy & is comfortable. I have had a great deal of trouble with it as I was obliged to undo Wm. the Tailor's work. He had no idea of making a proper seat. Cleaned out cupboards & gave the little Kitchen a thorough cleaning, also the Dining room before putting sofa in. Biddy came up to know if we wanted Sally, that she had returned from Swansea. Said I did to make Lizzie's black frock at home.

Sunday 13 December: No one in Church.

Monday 14 December: Sally came up to cut out Lizzie's black frock. Took it home to make. The clockmaker Richard Jones here to Kitchen Clock. He repaired the screw of my looking glass & put glass of barometer safe. Gave him 1/-. Hannah Gellyluog here washing. Cleaned the Drawing room.

Tuesday 15 December: Lloyd to Swansea with Mrs. Day for barley from Michael's Stores.

Thursday 17 December: Paid Wm. Griffiths Lime burner 6/- for one load of lime had this last Summer for ceiling Kitchen for mortar. This is all I owed him up to this date.

Friday 18 December: Sent Basket to dear Mrs. Marryat, 61 Warwick Street, Belgrave Road, with couple of fowls, 1 Pheasant, 1 Partridge and 2 tins of Cream. Sent a Goose of 7 lbs to Miss Jenkins. Lloyd took the things to Swansea, he brought up 4 dozn. Beer from Fulton with him by train & had to pay 1/- for its carriage. The Station Master wrote to tell me it was merchandise & the charge a legal one. I never was charged for any luggage before coming with a passenger.

Saturday 19 December: The band of Good Templars from Alltwen came up to play tonight, gave them 10/-.

Sunday 20 December: No one to Church.

Tuesday 22 December: The Pontardawe Glee Party came up to sing at 8 o'clk. We expected them. They sang in the Kitchen, 8 men and 3 women, conductor Daniel Howells. The women had tea & cake, the men bread & cheese & beer. I gave them 10/-. They sang very well. It was a very cold evening & a bright clear moonlight, a good deal of snow on the ground & a hard frost. Recd. cheque from Revd. D. Jones for £20 being 1 year's interest on £400 due last June.

Wednesday 23 December: Lizzie to Swansea. She walked down to the train & Lloyd fetched her back in the Phaeton. A very disagreeable evening, snowing & the roads very slippery. She called at Bryn Syfi & at Mrs. Matthews, the latter very poorly & very swollen. Recd. Xtmas cards from my old Servant Mary Lewis now in service in Liverpool & a letter thanking me for giving her character to Mrs. Matt, 26 Thackeray Street, Princes Road. Lizzie wore her new black Barathea dress 1st time.

Saturday 26 December: Lloyd went home by the 11.30 a.m. Brecon train to stay until Monday. Richard Matthews came to see us by the 11.30 train, as there was nothing doing in the Office. Was here to dinner & tea & left to meet the 7.30 Brecon train. The roads were slippery with the frost & snow, & he must have found it disagreeable walking down.

Sunday 27 December: Lizzie walked to Church. Very few in Church & no Clerk.

Tuesday 29 December: Lloyd to Cwmllynfell for cheese, he brought 2 in a bag on the mare's back. He had a nasty day there being a good deal of snow on the hill in some places & it was coming on to snow when he came here at 5.10 p.m.

Wednesday 30 December: The wife of Nant-y-Gasseg buried today at Carmel. A heavy fall of snow last night. It measured 8½ inches deep on the Court this morning & no doubt is much deeper in exposed places. It seems by the Papers to have been general every where & greatly impedes travelling being several feet deep in many places. We have not had such a severe winter of frost & snow for many years.

1875

The early months were overshadowed by the deaths of four of Margaret's close relatives. On 27 January Dr. Price's daughter Dora died in Bath, aged 27 years, on 23 March Miss Rachel Jenkins died at Bryn Syfi "after a lingering illness", on 1 April Lizzie's father David died at the age of 71 at Llwynyronnen, Betws, Carmarthenshire, and on 8 April Miss Sarah Jenkins, after "many years an invalid", died aged 55 at her home in Clifton, Bristol. The emotional effect of these deaths on Margaret is not recorded. Domestic and external work at Garth continued normally with all tasks chronicled and every cost itemised. Lloyd and D.M. laboured in the fields and outbuildings, calves were born, pigs were killed and trees were blown down. Indoors Margaret continued to improve her home, complained about the high sulphur content of the coal and its effect on her silvered tableware, scolded Lizzie for clumsiness and suffered intermittent pains in her head and back. The culpability of Cwmllynfell colliery's lease-holders in the flooding of Cwmllynfell farm rekindled her animosity. Possibly in deference to her bereaved relatives she took no holiday trips with Lizzie, unless they occurred during the 36 unrecorded days in May and June. Overall there were 125 blank days in the 1875 diary.

Friday 1 January: A thaw commences this day. We had a heavy fall of snow last Tuesday night, it measured 8½ inches deep on the Court and was many feet deep in exposed places. It was very deep on the leaden gutter on the top of the house. Lloyd went up to clean it away. Lizzie, Lloyd, Betty & I are the only people here. Samuel the Carpenter married at Neath to John Cwmgorse's daughter (Sally).

Saturday 2 January: Paid David the Blacksmith's bill yesterday up to 31st, £1..10..0 paid. Pd. Sally yesterday for all work done in 1874, done by her at home & here for Lizzie & I, by cash £1..15..1 paid. Pd. Mr. Z. Evans, P.O. yesterday by cheque as per book to Decr. 31st, £25..0..0.

Sunday 3 January: Lizzie to Church on Fly. I at home all day. Betty to Ystalyfera to see Ianto. He came last night from Aberdare. He is a little ashamed at having run away a year ago.

Monday 4 January: Lloyd went up to Gwaun Cae Gurwen for coal, but [could] <u>not</u> get under a truck of <u>5 or 6 tons</u> so he returned empty to Llwynrhidie & brought a load from there. I wrote by him to D. Morgan saying their coal was <u>so bad</u> & contained so much <u>sulphur</u> that I was determined to try another pit. D.M. said he warranted the coal had today [was] free from sulphur. Hannah cleaned Lloyd's bedroom & turned the Barley.

Tuesday 5 January: Lloyd to Pontardawe for a load of soft coal, 15 cwt 10/6 paid. The Bettws mare brought it up herself, but it was too heavy a load for one horse by right & the roads were so heavy and muddy after the rain & snow. She is an <u>excellent</u> cart mare & will I believe <u>pull</u> to the <u>last breath</u>. I wish she would take the phaeton nicely, she <u>backs</u> in that. Lloyd had sack of oats (Swansea) for horses, 4½ bus[hels]. D. Morgan came to see how we were, he has had a long holiday owing to the snow <u>& looks the better</u> for it. Tom Witt here gave him 6d & told him <u>not</u> to come again as he never came to Church.

Wednesday 6 January: Sent 5/- to Z. Evans for him to divide between the clerk & letter carrier, they sent a letter asking for a Xmas box. Sent Lloyd with a note to Mr. Howell Rees Surgeon Cwmamman with 18/- enclosed, the amount of his bill for attending (Servant) Mary Lewis last July. Pd. Dl. Jenkins, Carpenter, for work <u>done up to 31st Decr. last</u> by cash £1..7..6. paid, <u>entered in payments of 1874</u>.

Thursday 7 January: Went out this morning at 10 o'clock, found Hill Gate, Cae Barriwns Gate and Road Gate all three wide open, found fault with Lloyd for not keeping them shut & said I was much displeased with such carelessness

& neglect. Lloyd carrying manure to the Garden, 2 loads to the hill side and loads to the yard side. John Morgan this way hunting.

Saturday 9 January: Paid Llwynrhidie coal bill by cheque £6..14..0. Told D. Morgan that the coal was so bad & contained so much sulphur that it ruined every thing, turning the plate quite black & that unless I had better in future that I must try for coal elsewhere. He said he wd. see that better was sent.

Sunday 10 January: Lizzie to Church on Fly. Cefn Llan children ill either in measles or scarlet fever. Sacrament.

Monday 11 January: Lloyd took salt butter to the Post Office. Mr. Thomas, Cwmamman called & took tea. Some of the cattle ate Lizzie's Cuffs & Collars on the hill. Our little calf we think. Lewis Brynheulog sent his man up with a note asking if Mr. Sutton & himself should shoot here on Wednesday next. Wrote back & said he should.

Tuesday 12 January: Paid John James Garth Income Tax (by his son Daniel) 1 yr ending 5th April 1875.

		£ .. s .. d
Schedule A @ 2d. Schedule B @ 1d. on £50		12 .. 6
Garth Cottage 1 yr ending 5 Apl/75 on £3 @ 2d		6
Garth Land Tax £3		14 .. 7
	By cheque	£1.. 7 .. 7
Paid Wm. Evans Gellygron Mill up to this day by Lloyd.		£1.. 7 .. 9

Wednesday 13 January: D.M. at Gellyluog cutting *Polion a Bangors* [stakes and wattle fence rods] for steeping the hill fence by Heol-y-Cefn road gate. Lizzie went midday train to Mrs. Matthews. Stayed the night there & then to stay at Bryn Syfi. Lloyd took her in the phaeton to Pontardawe.

Thursday 14 January: Lloyd with Gambo fetching a load of *Polion a Bangors* from Gellyluog. Lloyd cleaned Dish Covers, they are nearly ruined by the sulphur in coal. I cleaned all little Kitchen cupboards & dusted the walls.

Friday 15 January: ***** Lloyd cleaned Parlour candlesticks as they were quite black from smoke. I never saw the coal & chimneys so bad as this winter spoiling everything. Mrs. Day's cousin John West killed on the S.V. [Swansea Vale] railway this morning. His work was to clean the Engines.

Saturday 16 January: Lloyd cleaning about the house a little, front & back. Washed Parlour antimacassars. John Gellyluog paid £14 on a/c of rent. Gave him 10/- towards Saron Schoolmaster.

Sunday 17 January: No one to Llanguicke. Lizzie at Bryn Syfi. Lloyd to Pontardawe. Charlie had loan of saddle to go to Neath.

Monday 18 January: Mrs. West's son buried. Mrs. Day went to Swansea by 1st Brecon train, sent by her Lizzie's linsey frock to Bryn Syfi. Annie went by midday train to Llansamlet to meet the funeral. When they came back Jenny & Charlie quarrelled in playing & Day interfered which ended in a great row. Charlie came to sleep with Lloyd & said he would leave. Lloyd to the Mill with stack of Barley for pig.

Tuesday 19 January: Hannah Gellyluog here washing. Lloyd & I cleaned out the two upper shelves of kitchen cupboard, wiped & washed the dinner & tea things (yesterday).

Wednesday 20 January: Lloyd took the mare in the phaeton as far as the Station just to practise her as she has a trick of backing.

Thursday 21 January: Lloyd & D.M. at Gellyluog for fencing wood. Snow-storm at 3 p.m. which soon passed off.

Saturday 23 January: Lloyd finished putting the front tidy. Lizzie & Mr. Jenkins came up last train. Lloyd met them with new mare. The train was very late, it was 10 minutes to 8 o'clk. when they came here just an hour after the usual time.

Sunday 24 January: Mr. Jenkins here. No one to Church. Very heavy showers & windy. Large tree blown down by the Nook across the stumpery, it was quite dead.

Monday 25 January: A very stormy night last night & a good deal of thunder. Mr. Jenkins left 3.20. Betty ill nearly all the morning on the bed, went to bed directly Mr. Jenkins left.

Tuesday 26 January: Began 3 lbs of London tea today.

Wednesday 27 January: Lloyd & D.M. cutting down Portugal Laurel by the Nook, that it may sprout out again, & removing the tree behind it that was blown down by the wind last Sunday. It looks very bare without the laurel branches. I hope they will grow again. Rachel the Blacksmith here, paid her all I owed her up to this day. Poor Dora Price died at 5.30 p.m. at 5 South Parade, Bath aged 27 last Novr.

Thursday 28 January: Lloyd to Pentwyn to see for straw, none to be had. Gave Mrs. Day a drake. I intend killing the duck as they constantly run into their yard. D.M. planting young thorns had last Tuesday in the gaps in the hedges. Gave Lloyd new carriage sponge.

Friday 29 January: Poor Dora Price's body brought to Glan Twrch tonight by train to Neath then in a hearse.

Saturday 30 January: Recd. a letter from Miss Jenkins saying Miss Rachel had had another fit last Sunday. Also that poor Dora Price died last Wednesday 5.30 p.m. in Bath. Wrote to Mrs. Price saying how sorry I was to hear the sad news, sent Lloyd up on horseback with the letter. Wm. Cwmllynfell here paying ½ year's rent. Paid him for 2 cheese 93 lbs @ 4½d £1..14..11. Owen Pen-y-Garn here buying front wheels, axle & springs of old carriage, 15/- paid.

Sunday 31 January: A fine Sunday. No one to Church.

Monday 1 February: Went down to Bryn Syfi thinking Miss Jenkins wd. like going to Glan Twrch. Lost the Brecon train, went to P.O. to telegraph for Fly to meet me as the old mare could not go all the way. Mrs. Evans & John going to Swansea so I had their horse put in our phaeton & Lloyd drove us all down. He drove through the Strand to the Halfpenny Bridge & I walked to Bryn Syfi. Miss Jenkins had been to Glan Twrch yesterday.

Tuesday 2 February: Daniel Thomas did not come to kill the pig as he promised. Poor Dora Price buried at Ystrad Church today. Age 27 years last Novr. Returned last train from Bryn Syfi. Lizzie & Lloyd met me. Miss Powell & Mrs. Ed. Careless & little boy called at Bryn Syfi.

Wednesday 3 February: Sent Lloyd to ask Evan Pen-y-Garn to come & kill the pig. He came at 11 o'clk. I think he is a very clean good Butcher & very particular about bleeding & the proper heat of the water. Shonny Peggy killed our pig last year & he used the water much too hot which made the rind & meat very hard & it wd. not take salt properly & was not so nice tasted. I think this pig is very well bled & killed.

Thursday 4 February: Little calf not well after her fall on Monday. Sent Lloyd for Thos. the Farrier. He brought medicine from Hibbert & Thos. comes tomorrow. Evan Pen-y-Garn came to cut up the pig. He charged 1/9d for killing and 1/9d for cutting, 3/6. The pig weighed 15 score 18 lbs.

Friday 5 February: Recd. a letter from Mrs. Price saying she wd. take it very kindly if I came up to see them, that Jane was unable to realize Dora's death & Mr. Price quite broken down. They intended going to Clifton today & hoped I wd. come up on their return. Lloyd took 3 loads of manure to cottage garden. Thos. the Farrier here to the calf. He bled her a good deal & thought she wd. come all right.

Saturday 6 February: Betty salted the pig, the rind is very soft & nice & I hope it will prove good bacon. It was not rubbed at all, merely laid on salt & covered with salt. D.M. and Lloyd fetched fencing wood from Gellyluog.

Sunday 7 February: Lizzie to Church on Fly. Young David Forchegel read the lessons.

Monday 8 February: ***** P.M. D.M. & Lloyd cutting down trees by the Closet & a large tree that injured lower yew tree. Lloyd cut down holly & planted berberry tree by the Closet also the Scotch fir had from Llandilo. D.M. cutting ivy all round Kitchen &c. Sent cheque for £31..10..0 to Mr. Davies Surveyor & said I would settle in full after I had seen Mr. R. Jenkins. He is paid for surveying up to 1st Janry. 1874.

Tuesday 9 February: D.M. trimming currant trees in old garden. Lloyd taking up root of tree cut yesterday.

Wednesday 10 February: Lloyd to Gurnos or Cwm Twrch with Gambo for 10 cwt of hay that David Forchegel said we could have of Wm. Davies Pwlldu of Yniscedwin field. The man not at home so Lloyd was obliged to come back without it as there was no one to weigh it. The Government Surveyors here surveying about the house for making new maps 25 inches to the mile. D.M. planting young thorns in gaps of hedge between Cae Shed & Gwndwn Hir.

Recd. letter from Mrs. Bowman saying her brother William was engaged to Mary Bowman.

Thursday 11 February: D.M. taking up stumps lower side of walk. Lloyd planting small laurel & another tree behind the yew tree by Closet walk. Alltwen fair.

Friday 12 February: D.M. & Lloyd cutting down the large dead fir tree lower side of Walk that had the ivy creeping through its branches, also cutting down branches of laurel hoping they may all grow into a thick hedge to form some shade & shelter. Lizzie & I cleaned lower shelf of kitchen cupboard. It is now all cleaned out & tidy.

Saturday 13 February: Lloyd cutting down all the branches of the Portugal laurel. All the laurels are now cut low to the front gate. D.M. taking up the stumps of trees cut last year lower side of Walk, to plant young trees. Lloyd took wheels, axles & springs to Owen Pen-y-Garn living now near the Cross Hands.

Sunday 14 February: Very wet. No one to Church.

Monday 15 February: Lloyd & D.M. quarrelled this morning about the pickaxe & shovel. D.M. said Lloyd had removed it from where he put it Saturday night. Lloyd said he had not. D.M. said he was a liar. I do not at all know where the blame lies, so that I have nothing to say between them. Lloyd gave me notice to leave as he cd. not put up with D.M. Lloyd to Swansea for 4 sacks of damaged oats. Charlie & Mrs. Day for 50 bushels of the same. John Thomas Garnant Colliery came to see the mare if she wd. suit them. She was in Swansea.

Tuesday 16 February: Lloyd & I measured the oats this morning. They are 19 bushels strike measure. They ought to have been 20 bus. according to what I paid for them, 1/6d per bus, £1..10..0. Gave Mr. Jones £1. The Pew rents are this year given up at Pontardawe Church & the voluntary Sunday collections made instead. This plan is only a trial & for this year. Each Pew owner retains his Pew. As I never go to that Church, I gave my usual £1 & said that if I went I shd. not give at the collections. Mr. Jones Llanguicke, Minnie & Miss Curtis came up in the Dog cart at 4 p.m. They stayed to tea & left at 7 o'clk. Mrs. Jones in Clifton. Dotty has lately been confined of her 3rd child.

Wednesday 17 February: Lizzie spent the day at Revd. D. Jones. She walked down & was there by 12 o'clk. Lloyd fetched her in the phaeton, he left here 6.20 & they were back 7.40. The mare behaved very well both ways. Lloyd took mare at 1.15 to Garnant to see if she wd. suit John Thomas. She was too high to go into the Level. D.M. cutting turf for top of wall until midday, then forking up earth between currant trees in old Garden.

Thursday 18 February: D.M. finished forking between currant trees in old Garden. Lloyd carried down 2 loads of turf from the hill. Also 3 loads of earth from Wain Fawr heap, for the front it is very good stuff being so sandy. It is old road scrapings.

Friday 19 February: D.M. & Daniel Jenkins sawing rails. Lloyd carried 6 loads of earth from Wain Fawr heap to the Front, lower side of Walk. Lloyd went to Cwrt-y-Barriwns to see for oats & hay. The son going to Llandilo fair tomorrow. He will let us know if his Uncle has hay to sell. Measured barley that was left from feeding pig & fowls, 13 bus. which is put in two bags, 5 bus. each & 3 bus. in Gwrn fach. It is to be kept for feeding the pigs in Summer & the damaged oats to be given the fowls.

Saturday 20 February: A slight fall of snow last night. Lloyd planted 7 young laurels near front gate lower side of Walk. D.M. taking stones out of earth carried yesterday & digging between trees. Lloyd to Post Office p.m. for a sack of oats.

Sunday 21 February: No one to Church. Lloyd to Chapel at 6 p.m. Betty had cramp in the evening. The ground covered with snow this morning.

Monday 22 February: Lloyd drove me to Pontardawe, called at the Bank & put £30.

Tuesday 23 February: Ballot voting at Pontardawe School room about School Board Committee. Each voter had 7 votes. I went down & gave my votes at 1 o'clk. John James & Ben Evans elected & five others. Paid Davies the Ironmonger up to the 31st December 1874 in full by cheque, £5..17..0. Went to Swansea midday train to Bryn Syfi where I stayed until Thursday. Met R.P.L. [Richard Pendrill Llewelyn] at Shaws. He looked better than when I saw him before.

Wednesday 24 February: Went to Gower Road Station to see Shaw's nurseries. Selected what trees I wanted & when the frost is over they will be sent by rail to Pontardawe. Called at the Inland Revenue Office, saw Mr. Rice Davies [*Surveyor of Taxes, Russell Place*], said I thought he had rated the House too high, £25. He thought not & said it looked a nice residence & was surprised at my thinking it high. He promised to lower it to £20 & when passing would call up & see it then if he considered it worth more he would rise it & if worth less he would lower it. Called on Mr. R. Jenkins said I considered Mr. Davies charges very high. He said he thought so too & would write to him. Told him I wd. like to sell Cwmllynfell.

Thursday 25 February: Had 4 dozen beer of Fulton & Co. to come on Saturday. This is the first beer had this year from them. Paid for beer 10/-, bottles & case 10/-, £1 paid. Fulton's bottle a/c all correct to 31st Decr. last. They say I owe £1 in last year. I don't think it is so much. Returned home last train from Bryn Syfi. Paid D. & J. Williams bill yesterday, £10..13..6 to the 31st Decr. last. Had 2 doz. Beer, 1 Gal Gin, the first things had this year.

Friday 26 February: Lizzie broke off one foot of looking glass in spare bedroom by cleaning it roughly & loosened the other, which afterwards came off in my hand. Scolded her & said it was through her clumsy handling & carelessness that she had done it & so I believe it was. She was much better & more careful when a child than she is now & much nicer in every way. It is a sad pity to see people get worse as they get older. She cried a great deal & said she wd. go home tomorrow. I said she cd. not as Mr. Jenkins was coming unless she wrote in the morning to prevent him wh. she could by train.

Saturday 27 February: Lloyd took Mrs. Day to the Station and brought up parcel left there by me 25th. Mr. Jenkins came up last train. Recd. a letter from Mrs. Bowman saying they were going to have their house painted &c. & if I would have her here either for the 5th, 8th or 9th March (next week). F.G. & Miss Ford called. The Walk in a horrid mess. They asked Lizzie & I there to lunch next week. 4 dozen of Fulton's beer begun this night.

Sunday 28 February: Mr. Jenkins here. No one to Church. A damp day.

Monday 1 March: Lizzie had a letter from Mr. Josiah Rees thanking her for the socks she had knitted him. I wrote to Mrs. Bowman saying I should be glad to see her on either the 8th or 9th inst. & that she must excuse our untidiness.

Mr. Jenkins left at 3.30 p.m. The mare backed at the large doors & was very provoking. Ianto came to see Betty, I had not seen him for 6 or 7 years. He looks stouter but much altered having lost all his teeth.

Wednesday 3 March: Lloyd to Maes Llan to ask if they had any hay to sell. They had none. Mrs. Day & Thos. Coitcae Mawr to Swansea for damaged oats 50 bus. each. Wm. Lewis here, he had been through Gellyluog wood. He said there was very little damage done. Four oak trees are giving way at the roots owing to the water working under & one small ash tree blown down & dead.

Friday 5 March: ***** P.M. Lloyd before dinner carrying off the laurel branches from Front field that were cut from the Walk. After dinner went for a load of coal. Recd. a letter from Mrs. Bowman saying she intended coming here the 11th. Recd. a letter from Laura Jones saying she would come & stay here 10 days if I would have her. She was uncertain as to when she wd. be leaving Ffynnon Eiddon.

Saturday 6 March: Lloyd to Swansea with Gambo for hay, brought 15½ cwt @ 7/6, £5..16..0. 2 cwt had of Day last Tuesday (2nd) 15/-. Our own hay quite finished on that day. It is dreadful to be short of food for animals. I hope it may never occur again. Lloyd took back hamper with Jar and 3 dozen bottles to Williams, all right to 31st Decr. 1874.

Sunday 7 March: No one to Church. Very wet. I am not at all well, back very painful. I feel sure <u>my spine</u> is injured from the fall.

Monday 8 March: Hannah Gellyluog here cleaning out <u>Dairy</u>, <u>Pantry</u> & <u>Kitchen loft</u>. Rose the pig out of the salt.

Paid J. Jones Crachllwyn Poor rate as follows 1 quarter

			£ .. s .. d
Garth Farm	£47 .. 0 .. 0	@ 1/-	2 .. 7 .. 0
" Cottage	2 .. 0 .. 0	"	2
3 Cots Cwmllynfell	7 .. 10 .. 0	"	7 .. 6
Smith shop	1 .. 15 .. 0	"	1 .. 9
Cot Graig Llanguicke	2 .. 0 .. 0	"	2
	£60 .. 5 .. 0	"	£3 .. 0 .. 3
	Less commission		2 .. 9
	By cheque		£2 ..17 .. 6

Tuesday 9 March: Daniel here mending the feet of Looking Glass broken 26th ult. Also putting shelves in sideboard. Recd. cheque of James & Aubrey £71..10..11. Had trees from Shaw. They came by train from Swansea to Pontardawe & the Railway Carrier brought them up here, for wh. he charged 4/-. A great imposition.

Wednesday 10 March: Sold the Bettws mare to a man from Neath sent up by Mr. J. B. Jenkins received for her £48 paid.

Thursday 11 March: Went to Swansea midday train to meet Mrs. Bowman who was coming by Express & fearing we should be too late to catch the last Brecon train 5.30 p.m. I ordered a Fly & we drove all the way, were here by 7 p.m. The last time she was here was in 1866. She seemed very glad to see me & the old place again.

Friday 12 March: Fanny G. rode up to call on Mrs. Bowman.

Sunday 14 March: Lloyd drove Mrs. Bowman & I to Pontardawe Church.

Monday 15 March: Recd. a letter yesterday from Mr. Jenkins saying Miss Jenkins was very poorly & in bed. Lizzie went down by morning train today to see how they were. I could not go as Mrs. Bowman was here. She came back by 4 o'clk. train. Poor Mrs. Matthews buried today at Llansamlet.

Tuesday 16 March: Mrs. Kirkhouse came up to tea & to see Mrs. Bowman. Dr. Humphreys of Clydach & J. Morgan Gellygron drove her up, & Lloyd took her part of the way home.

Wednesday 17 March: Lloyd drove Mrs. Bowman & myself to the Gilbertsons to lunch. Mrs. Bowman had been asked there to dine & stay the night. I was not & returned home about 5 o'clk.

Saturday 20 March: Mrs. Bowman left. I went with her to Swansea by 1st train & saw her off by the Express for Gloucester where she was to meet her Husband & stay until Monday. We saw Mr. Jenkins at Swansea, he was very cold & stiff in his manner. Paid Shaw for the trees £2..11..6. I called at Bryn Syfi. The last time I saw poor Miss Rachel.

Palm Sunday 21 March: William Griffiths Maes Quarra came for Lizzie, her Father being very poorly. She went with him on Fly, leaving here 12.15. A fine day.

Monday 22 March: Lizzie returned this evening. Her Father is very weak & poorly & she sees a great change in him. She does not think he will get over it.

Tuesday 23 March: Lizzie went home this morning by 11 o'clk. train to stay a little with her Father. Lloyd drove us to the Mountain & I walked with her to the Station & saw her off, Lloyd waiting until I returned. A very nice day. Margaret Gellyluog here when I came back bringing balance of rent.

Saturday 27 March: Poor dear Miss Rachel Jenkins buried today at Llantwit near Neath. She had always been a kind friend to me.[1]

Tuesday 30 March: Returned home from Bryn Syfi through Garnant by evening train. Lizzie met me at Pant-y-ffynnon & came with me to Cross Inn, said her Father was very weak & could not last many days. I brought up a mattress for him from Swansea.

Monday 5 April: My Uncle buried today at Bettws Church. A very wet day.[2]

Thursday 8 April: Miss Sarah Jenkins (Mrs. Price's Sister) of 6 Berkeley Square Clifton died this morning aged 55 years. She had been many years an invalid.[3]

Sunday 11 April: I rode Fly to Church. Lizzie in the house.

Monday 12 April: Daniel Gellyluog here ploughing for vetches in the Strip by Cae Barriwns. Day sowed them this afternoon. Lizzie & I went down to Bryn Syfi by 4.13 train to stay with Miss Jenkins during the time her Brother would be in Bristol. She seemed very glad to see us.

---

1. Miss Rachel Jenkins died at Bryn Syfi on 23rd March "after a lingering illness" (*The Cambrian*, 2 April 1875).
2. David Jones died, aged 71, on 1 April at Llwynyronnen, his home in Betws parish, Carmarthenshire. His will was proved by his son John who farmed Llwynyronnen and was the sole executor. Effects under £200.
3. Miss Sarah Jenkins's will was proved in Bristol by John Borlase Jenkins of Bryn Syfi and her brother in law Dr. William Price of Glantwrch. Effects under £8,000.

Tuesday 13 April: Mr. Jenkins left Bryn Syfi for Clifton this afternoon to be in readiness for Miss Sarah Jenkins funeral tomorrow. Mr. Richard Jenkins went too, & from there he goes to London on business.

Wednesday 14 April: Miss Sarah Jenkins buried today in Clifton. Lloyd came down to Swansea midday train to be measured by Andrews for a suit of clothes [*C. J. Andrews, Tailor & Woollen Drapers, 18 Wind Street*].

Thursday 15 April: Mr. Jenkins returned from Clifton by the Express at 5 p.m.

Friday 16 April: Lizzie & I returned from Bryn Syfi.

Sunday 18 April: I rode Fly to Church. Lloyd came with me. Mr. Jones said he wd. speak to Mr. Gilbertson tomorrow about my Pew.

Monday 19 April: Sally came up midday to cut out Lizzie's parramatta skirt.

Tuesday 20 April: D.M. shutting hill fence in Cae Cwtta. Lloyd gathering stones there. Lloyd set fire at 2 p.m. to heap of rubbish by saw pit, a spark fell among the briars & in spreading on to the hedge by Wain Daniel the Hay house caught fire. Fortunately it was soon put out, a good bit of damage was done to the roof but it was a mercy it was not more as it might have been <u>most serious</u> for everything was <u>so dry</u>. Began 4 dozn. Beer had last Saturday.

Wednesday 21 April: Sally came up this morning about Lizzie's parramatta jacket & tunic. R.P. Llewelyn came here 12.40 from Swansea to see how we were. He had seen my uncle's death in the "Cambrian". He saw <u>me</u> looking <u>very ill</u>.

Thursday 22 April: Lloyd to Swansea for his clothes, they were not ready. Andrews said he could not get the cloth, hoped they would be next week. Lloyd took note to Mrs. Jones, 11 Page Street asking if her rooms were vacant as I wd. like going down for a week or two. They were not, a Lady coming in today. 1 dozn. Sherry (Williams).

Saturday 24 April: Lizzie went home on Fly at 3.15 p.m. Lloyd & D.M. in Cottage garden. Lloyd took Mrs. Day to the Station a.m. & brought back hamper of wine had 22nd. Cleaned out Drawing room & removed piano to the Hall.

Revd Richard Pendrill Llewelyn (1813-1891), Vicar of Llangynwyd
(Photo: courtesy of Mrs J. Morris)

Sunday 25 April: Minnie a she calf 1.30 a.m., Lloyd up all last night watching her. No one to Church.

Monday 26 April: Lloyd & D.M. setting potatoes in Cottage garden. Lizzie returned at 7 p.m.

Tuesday 27 April: ***** Lloyd fetched a load of coal this morning. In the afternoon had Gartheithen mare with Fly brush harrowing Cae Cwtta, Cae Barriwns & Cae front. D.M. spreading mole heaps before him.

Thursday 29 April: Miss Jenkins Bryn Syfi went up to Clifton with Mrs. Price.

Monday 10 May: Lizzie returned at 6 p.m. exactly. Lloyd & I ready to go & meet her to the Garnant. She had walked over the Hill with her cousin John. I went in the phaeton to Pontardawe, bought a corkscrew & small hammer at Davies & some stamps at Post Office. Paid Anne Lewis 5/- for receiving letters. Asked Williams Nant-y-Gasseg if he wd. mow & gather my hay this year. Said he wd. let me know again. Lloyd wore his new clothes 1st time.

Tuesday 11 May: R.P. Llewelyn came up to see how I was as I was so poorly when he was here last. He was very glad to see me better, he left for Swansea last train.

Monday 17 May: Lloyd, Day & D.M. cut down large fir tree, it was over hanging Hay House & in the way of making the little pond in Plantation. Lloyd to Gellygron Eisteddfod midday. Mr. Jenkins came up midday, left last train. We did not expect him.

Saturday 22 May: Mr. Jenkins walked up from last train. I did not send to meet him as I hardly expected him as it came on a heavy shower at 5 o'clk.

Tuesday 25 May: *****

Wednesday 26 May: Paid Hopkin Jones Crachllwyn Garth Poor Rate 1 quarter, £60..5..0 @ 10d, £2..7..10 by cheque. Mrs. Evans the Post Office came up to say they had 10 Bank shares to sell if I would like to buy. I do not at present.

Friday 28 May: Lloyd mowed the Green.

Saturday 29 May: D.M. laying down curb stones for gutter from house to the cow house. Lloyd took the yearling calf to Forchegel to graze for a month at 2/6 week.

Sunday 30 May: Lizzie walked to Church the 1st time since her Father's death. White cow brought a He white calf like herself.

Monday 31 May: R. P. Llewelyn & Olwen came up by last train. Lloyd met them at the Station. It was the 1st time I had seen Olwen.

Tuesday 1 June: R.P.L. drove Olwen & I as far as Cwmamman & back. Richard enjoyed the drive, it was a lovely afternoon. Mrs. Charles Morgan, Miss Chester Thomas & Miss Prothero called here at 5.30 in their way from seeing Pontardawe Church.

Wednesday 2 June: R.P.L. & Olwen left by 1st train for Swansea thence home. Lizzie went with them to the Station.

Thursday 3 June: Miss Jenkins returned from Clifton after being away 5 weeks to this day.

Friday 4 June: Samuel Jenkins & Morgan Thomas (Carpenters) came here to put up iron trough at the back of the house &c. Samuel & D.M. sawing rails. Morgan repairing hinges &c. of cow house door & making large doors easy to shut.

Saturday 5 June: Went to Swansea 1st train. Met Mr. J. B. Jenkins at the bottom of the steps, walked with him to Mr. Richard Jenkins Office where we met Mr. Fred Williams waiting at the Door with a large bundle of Deeds under his arm. They were the Mortgage Deeds of Miss Harris' farms &c. in the Vale of Neath kept by the late Mr. John Clark as security for the money lent Miss Harris' Father, the late Mr. Charles Harris of Neath £2000..0..0. That money is now paid Mr. F. Williams & he gives up the papers. I take up part of the Mortgage & gave Mr. Williams a cheque for £1393..8..3. The money paid for the House at Neath sold to Mr. Samuel for wh. Mr. J. B. Jenkins & Mr. Josiah Rees are Trustees is also placed as part of the Mortgage.

My own money	£1393.. 8..3
Money for the house	525..11..0
at Neath, J.B.J. and	£1918..19..3 @ 5 per cent
J.R. Trustees	
I had no papers given me.	

Tuesday 8 June: Lloyd drove me in the phaeton to call at Glantwrch. We left here at 3 p.m. & came back by 7 o'clk. Mr. & Mrs. Price were at home & received me very kindly. I have not been there since June 1868 when I met Mrs. Price in the train & she asked me to come up & see Jessie Lloyd who was staying there. Old Fly went very well, 1½ hours each way & she looked quite nice. I shall never have a mare as good as her.

Sunday 13 June: No one in Church. Very wet.

Tuesday 15 June: ***** A wet & very stormy day. Sarah Jones, Llwyn-yr-Onen 26 years today. Lizzie intended going home but it was too cold & wet. I am very poorly all day with a dreadful rheumatic headache and in bed until 4 p.m. when I came down for a few hours. Maryanne Gotregarth had 4½ lbs bacon @ 1/- a lb.

Thursday 17 June: Lizzie & I called on Mrs. Charles Morgan. She was not at home. We called on Mrs. Thomas, stayed to tea & promised to go & see Mrs. Maber & the baby after their return from Swansea. Heard for the 1st time poor Mrs. Hildebrand was dead. She died last Febry. 14th aged 80 years. Miss Shenton is staying at the Vicarage, she has been there 9 months. Mr. & Mrs. Jones Llan-guicke called just after we had gone. Lloyd put the mare at the Raven. In starting to come home she reared in the phaeton! I never saw poor old Fly do so before in a Carriage.

Saturday 19 June: Washed the paint of my bedroom door. In rising off the floor knocked my back against the edge of the bedstead. It was a severe blow & I felt it very much & was in much pain.

Sunday 20 June: Lizzie to Church. Wm. Lewis came from Church to see me.

Tuesday 22 June: David Jones Cwmcoy here with a mare for me to see, tried her in the phaeton as far as Cwmgorse. She seemed a good strong creature, very like Dallus I think, 15.1¾, price £50. I gave him no answer today as John

Gellyluog bought a mare for me yesterday at Llandilo & I must first see if she suits.

Wednesday 23 June: Mary Smith Gellygron & Mary Gwen came here to tea for the 1st time.

Saturday 26 June: D.M. limed the Court with Aberthaw lime. I never had seen it so dirty. Mr. & Miss Jenkins came up last train. Lloyd met them at the Station.

Sunday 27 June: Poor Miss Jenkins very sick in bed all day. Lizzie to Church, she had it wet coming home.

Friday 2 July: Mr. Price came in just as we had done dinner. He stayed to tea & seemed to enjoy the dry toast.

Sunday 4 July: Lizzie to Church. Mr. Jenkins walked up this morning, here at 10 a.m. He walked to meet Lizzie coming from Church.

Monday 5 July: John Harris (Gartheithen) begun mowing Cae Barriwns hay. Lloyd helping as much as he could. Mr. & Miss Jenkins left by Brecon train 4.13 p.m.

Tuesday 6 July: Finished cutting Cae Barriwns at 3 p.m.

Wednesday 7 July: Lizzie's birthday 24 years today. Gave her a book "Maternal Counsels to a Daughter".[4]

Saturday 10 July: ***** Morgan Gartheithen & Lloyd commenced cutting meadow hay.

Sunday 11 July: Lizzie to Church on Fly.

Friday 16 July: Lizzie, Jane & Richard Matthews went to Langland Bay.

Saturday 17 July: David Phillip & his son John came here midday to help us with the meadow hay. John Daniel & two other men came to help about 4 o'clk.

4. Written by Mrs. Matilda Marian Pullan and "designed to aid her in the care of her health, the improvement of her mind, and the cultivation of her heart". Published by Darton & Co., London, 1855.

Lizzie returned last train from the Matthew's. She called this afternoon at Bryn Syfi with Jane. Lizzie walked up. Brought me the egg beater.

Sunday 18 July: Lizzie & Betty walked to Church. Wm. Lewis came up to see me instead of going to Church.

Monday 19 July: Jane Matthews came up by 4 o'clk train. Lizzie & Lloyd to meet her at the Station.

Tuesday 20 July: John Witt's wife here asking if they should rent the Cottage.

Wednesday 21 July: Jane Matthews left last train. Lizzie & Lloyd took her to the Station.

Thursday 22 July: Betty went to Aberdare to see Ianto after his accident, he is still unable to walk.

Friday 23 July: Betty returned from Aberdare tonight. She was very poorly when she was away.

Saturday 24 July: Very poorly all day & most of it in bed. Mary Smith & Mary Gwen called. Lizzie saw them, I was in bed.

Sunday 25 July: Lizzie to Church on Fly.

Monday 26 July: Tom (alias Witt) came to live in the Cottage. Samuel Jenkins came down to measure Cottage windows which he makes at home. Lizzie to Gellygron to tea, walked both ways. I was not well enough to go.

Tuesday 27 July: Samuel putting new windows & one frame in Cottage, also new window seat, & in the slope a new mantelpiece.

Friday 30 July: Richard Matthews sent a note from Garnant to ask if he could sleep here tonight as he was afraid he could not finish paying the men in time for the Swansea train. He came here about 7 p.m., he walked down.

Saturday 31 July: Richard left this morning 1st train. Mrs. Maber brought the baby (Ethel Mary 14 months old) to see me, as I was not well enough to go to the Vicarage. Miss Shenton & Miss Day came too. Mr. Day drove them in the

Dog cart. Finished mowing the hay. The hay house is now quite full. No room even for the chaff cutter.

Sunday 1 August: No one to Church. Betty in bed all day. I not at all well. Lizzie went after tea to see Mary Gartheithen.

Tuesday 3 August: Lloyd & D.M. nailed a piece of zinc on top of Hay shed in Wain Daniel which was damaged by fire 20th April. Mary Phillips (Betty's niece) came here with Lloyd's stockings. She can stay some days as the Tin-works are not in full work.

Thursday 5 August: Rose dining room carpet. R.P.L. came here, left last train. He is 62 years old this day, a wonderfully active man for his age. Miss Wm. Cwmllynfell here paying half a year's rent due last March, £20..0..0.

Saturday 7 August: Very heavy & continuous thunder here all last night & some rain. A dreadful flood this morning in the Llynfell river doing great damage to my property there. The water about a foot deep in Cwmllynfell Farmhouse (a thing I never heard of before). Part of the Chapel yard wall carried away & the bridge much damaged. Wm. Rowland's family obliged to leave the house, the garden & the little crofts quite destroyed by all the water & slag. Wm. Griffiths came down to say.

Monday 9 August: Wm. Rowland's son came down to say that they had been obliged to leave the house Saturday morning & go to the "George" club room. The river was never known to have been so high. Samuel Jenkins here mending little Parlour floor. He tried to tighten the screws of White room bedstead & broke one side of bedstead thereby. Took it all down, the dry rot is in the wood but it can I think be repaired.

Tuesday 10 August: Put down little Parlour carpet. Mary Phillips cleaned the furniture well & the room is thoroughly clean. Willy Paddison came to see me. He took tea here. He is still with Wm. Owen, 12 Westbourne Grove, London.

Wednesday 11 August: Gave the Drawing room a thorough cleaning but did not raise the carpet.

Saturday 14 August: Mary Phillips left this evening after giving Parlour, Hall & little Kitchen a thorough cleaning. Paid her 6/-.

Sunday 15 August: Mr. Jenkins walked up from 1st train, it was rather a wet morning & we hardly thought he wd. come. It turned out a fine day. Miss Jenkins at Aberystwyth.

Monday 16 August: Mr. Jenkins left by Brecon train 4.13 p.m. Lloyd took him to the Station. Mr. & Mrs. Arthur Gilbertson & Madelena G. who seems a nice ladylike girl called at 5 p.m. D.M. commenced trimming roadside hedges.

Tuesday 17 August: R.P.L. came up 1st train. Lloyd took the phaeton to meet him.

Wednesday 18 August: R.P.L. looked over Cwmllynfell lease & made a rough calculation as to the value of the place.

Friday 20 August: R.P.L. left by 2 o'clk train. Said he would come here for my birthday. Wrote to Mr. Bain asking what he intended doing with regard to the damage done by the late flood. Betty limed the Dairy yesterday.

Saturday 21 August: Lizzie recd. "Ingoldby Legends" by first post from R.P.L.

Sunday 22 August: Lizzie & Betty to Church. I at home by myself.

Monday 23 August: Llandilo fair. Biddy brought up my parramatta dress which Sally had made, 10¼ yards.

Thursday 26 August: Lloyd returned after being home a week.

Friday 27 August: Went down to Gartheithen, paid John Harris for mowing my hay in July, 8¼ days @ 6/- per day, £2..9..6. (on his own food). Lloyd helped to mow the hay with John Harris.

Saturday 28 August: Lizzie went to lunch at Mrs. Arthur Gilbertson's (the 1st time). She walked down leaving here 11.45. Lloyd fetched her in the phaeton at 3.30. Mrs. G. sent books for me to read.

Sunday 29 August: No one to Llanguicke. It looked like rain. I am very poorly today.

Monday 30 August: John Morgan Gellygron sent his little nephew Arthur Rees on horseback to ask how I was. Fanny Gilbertson called. She was sorry to see me so poorly. I was on the sofa. Lloyd all day at Gartheithen helping to carry the wheat. Day had Fly to carry some corn. His horses in the lime.

Tuesday 31 August: Lloyd to Swansea 1st train. Took all empties back to F. E. Williams up to June 30th. Had 1 doz. Beer, Gin, Brandy, Whisky each ½ gallon, ½ dozen Port, ½ dozen Sherry (1st had since June 30th). I have paid the bill up to that day. Lloyd paid Williams Livery Stables 15/- for Fly had March 11th for Mrs. Bowman, which was all I owed him up to this day. He has given up the Stables to a man named Eslick. Lloyd to Bryn Syfi for little butter pot & glass mug. Lloyd drew all apples except little Winter ones. A very small crop.

Thursday 9 September: David Davies the Kilybebyll Schoolmaster (now living in Mr. Lloyd's Lodge) came here.

Friday 10 September: Mr. James Shepherd came up to Bryn Syfi & examined my back in bed.

Saturday 11 September: D.M. finished trimming hedges & putting them all tidy. He leaves today to build some Cowhouse in Cwmamman, probably I shall not want him again until the Spring.

Sunday 12 September: Lizzie went with Miss Jenkins to the Unitarian Chapel in Swansea.

Monday 13 September: Lizzie & I returned last S.V. train from Bryn Syfi. We drove as far as the Vicarage Gate & Lloyd went up for the Parish Map which Mr. Jones lends me for a few days to see the Cwmllynfell boundary.

Tuesday 14 September: R.P.L. came up by 4.50 train & walked up from Pontardawe. Lloyd fetched Post Office Dog cart in the evening that we may drive up to Cwmllynfell tomorrow to meet Mr. J. O. Jones & Mr. Davies. Morgan Harris Gartheithen brought a load of lime to the Garden, 1st load.

Wednesday 15 September: Lloyd drove R.P.L. & myself in P.O. Dog cart up to Cwmllynfell. We left here 7.40 a.m., at Cwmllynfell 9.10. Walked down to the "George Inn" to meet Mr. Davies and J. O. Jones. The former came at 10.45. R.P.L. walked up riverside & Railway with Mr. Davies & showed Levi Rees' enclosure of my land at Pwll Rhyd-y-Pynau. J.O.J. came to Cwmllynfell at 2.50 p.m. He promised to meet Mr. Davies this day week at Cwmllynfell to decide the boundary between Cwm & Hendreforgan. The 2 Surveyors, W. Griffiths & R.P.L. all say decidedly Levi Rees ought to give me a yearly payment for the land.

Friday 17 September: R.P.L. left by 2 o'clk. train. Lloyd drove him to the Station.

Saturday 18 September: Morgan Gartheithen brought a load of lime to the Garden (the 2nd).

Sunday 19 September: Lizzie to Church on Fly.

Monday 20 September; Tom Witt here thatching Fern Rick.

Tuesday 21 September: The son of Cwrt-y-Barriwns buried today at Gwynfe age 37, he died suddenly last Saturday.

Wednesday 22 September: Lloyd took white cow to Nant-y-Gasseg bull.

Thursday 23 September: Began 4 dozn. Beer tonight.

Friday 24 September: John Harris here a couple of hours helping Lloyd to cut down 2 trees in Cae front by Front Gate. Lloyd cut down a dead tree opposite Front Gate in Cae Shed.

Saturday 25 September: ***** Lizzie went home on Fly over the hill.

Sunday 26 September: No one to Church. Wm. Lewis came to see me from Llanguicke. Lizzie & her sister Jane to Mrs. Hughes to tea. Met there Mrs. Lewis Pontamman.

Wednesday 29 September: Mr. Jones Llanguicke & Mr. N. Thomas the Curate came to see me, they stayed to tea. Mr. Jones told me that John Morgan was going to the Vicarage tonight & that Minnie would be engaged with her Mamma's consent. Her late illness was doubtless a good deal put on, so that she may get them willing for her to have him.

Thursday 30 September: Blaenegel sale. Richard James is leaving & going to farm in Gower near Swansea.

Saturday 2 October: John Gellyluog paid ½ a year's rent due last March. He also paid £20 on a/c of the Mare he bought at Barnaby fair, the remaining £20 he is to pay next March. I paid him as follows (being all I owe him):

Daniel & 2 horses 2 days & a half @ 7/6	18 .. 9
The loan of a horse 1 day	2 .. 6
	£1 .. 1 .. 3

Sunday 3 October: No one to Church.

Monday 4 October: Jane Matthews came here, came up by 11 o'clk. train. Lloyd met her with the phaeton. Mr. Jones Llanguicke's servant man came for the Parish Map which I had the loan of this day 3 weeks, and which I ought to have returned before. Mary Anne the shop paid me for the bacon she had of me some time ago.

Wednesday 6 October: Jane Matthews & I called on Mrs. C. Morgan. She was very pleasant & glad to see me. Mrs. Hughes of Bettws was spending the day there & her little girl (Edith). Called at the Day's, Mrs. & Miss Day in Somersetshire. Met Miss Shenton. She asked us to the Vicarage to tea, but we declined. I said we wd. call again. Called at D. Morgan the Mason's gave his wife £2..16..0.

Saturday 9 October: Richard Matthews came here from Garnant. Jane & he left by the last train. Lloyd took them to the Station.

Sunday 10 October: No one to Church.

Wednesday 13 October: Lizzie walked to meet 1st Brecon train to go to the Matthews, & to go with them tonight to a lecture at Mount Pleasant Chapel by Mr. Murcell on David Livingstone, the late African explorer. I wanted Lizzie to go by the midday train, but she was ill tempered & disobedient & went by 1st train (Brecon) leaving me very poorly in bed.

Thursday 14 October: Lizzie returned last train from the Matthews. Lloyd met her with the phaeton.

Friday 15 October: Fanny & Madelena Gilbertson & Miss Ford called to see me, they walked up. Lizzie walked back with them as far as Gartheithen.

Saturday 16 October: Mrs. Kirkhouse & Jonah Jones' eldest little girl (Nelly) came up, they stayed to tea. Lloyd took them back as far as Gellygron. Wm. Lewis came here yesterday evening after being through Gellyluog Wood. He said it was very free from damage & trespass.

Sunday 17 October: Lizzie to Church on Fly. The little heifer brought a she calf. She is only 1 year & 7 months. I had cramp in my stomach after going to bed & was obliged to get up for an hour. Heard Lizzie singing "Gwenith Gwyn" in the kitchen!! p.m.

Monday 18 October: *****

Tuesday 19 October: Daniel the Carpenter here making a place for the calves in the Cow house & also a place to tie the heifer. It is very tidy & convenient. Lloyd to Pontardawe for sack of bran, 5 bus. oats & 14 flooring boards. Very wet evening. Lizzie when going for letters met Minnie Williams & her brother on horseback under Gotregarth. J. Morgan rode back with her.

Wednesday 20 October: Lloyd carried the rails from saw pit & put them up over the Cart house.

Thursday 21 October: Lloyd cleaning gutter from here to Day's. The place is full of water, we are having such continued rain.

Friday 22 October: Rachel John here asking me if I had Troed-y-Rhiw lease. Lloyd grinding hay & chaff knives at Gartheithen.

Saturday 23 October: Lloyd put little walk by the front gate into old garden tidy with fresh ashes. D.M. came here to say he had finished Cowhouse in Cwmamman & to know if I wanted him before he took another job. I said I did not but that I shd. be glad of him in Janry. or Febry. Richard Matthews ran up for a minute in his way from Garnant. Mr. David waiting in the Carriage on the road.

Sunday 24 October: Lizzie & Betty to Llanguicke. Lloyd thought he had lost a letter in coming from Church a.m. & went all the way back to Pontardawe. It had got inside the "Graphic" & was all right. Charlie came to see the Day's & me.

Monday 25 October: Lloyd putting manure round the rhubarb. Lloyd cutting & carrying fern for present use before beginning the rick.

Wednesday 27 October: R.P.L. came here 3.47 train. Walked up from Pontardawe Station in 50 minutes. It was a disagreeable damp afternoon, the roads very dirty & he had a heavy great coat on. Good walking for a man over 62 years. He said he had not walked fast & was <u>not</u> much tired.

Thursday 28 October: R.P.L. left 2 o'clk train. Day killed my little pig in his yard. Lloyd helped but <u>Betty</u> had <u>nothing</u> to do with it. Paid John Harris for 4 loads of lime that Morgan brought from Black Mountain £2..16..0.

Friday 29 October: Pig weighed 120 lbs by Day's steel yards. I bought this pig of the Day's 29th May last.

Saturday 30 October: John Harris (Gartheithen) here helping Lloyd to cut down the large trees between here & the Closet.

Sunday 31 October: No one to Church. Betty not well.

Monday 1 November: See entry of this day week 8th inst.

Wednesday 3 November: John Thomas Gwernllwyn here buying fir trees cut by Lloyd & J. Harris. Paid John Harris for 3 days cutting the trees 9/-.

Saturday 6 November: Lizzie went home 1st train. Lloyd drove her to Garnant leaving here 7.30 a.m. She took the money to her Brother.

Sunday 7 November: Lloyd to Pontardawe 11 a.m. Recd. a letter from Lizzie saying she got home safely. Betty & I at home all day. Very wet afternoon.

Monday 8 November: John Harris here cutting the trees. Lloyd drove me to Pontardawe. Took all the money I had at Interest out of the Bank.
Gave a cheque for the money £201..19..11

Principal	£200 .. 0 .. 0)	£201..19s..11d.
3 months Interest	1..19..11)	

There is a mistake in this entry – it ought to have been entered <u>1st Novr</u>.

Tuesday 9 November: Mrs. Day had the little heifer's calf. She is a pretty little thing 3 weeks old last Sunday. The mother had <u>very nearly</u> 2 quarts of milk each milking, <u>more</u> than I expected in one so young & this time of the year too. Price of calf £1..0..0.

Thursday 11 November: Mr. Jones & Mr. Davies here shooting, they did not call but sent in by Day 3 snipes. Lloyd commenced digging up the stumps between here & the Closet, ready to plant young trees in the Spring.

Friday 12 November: Betty limed the bottom of the Court this evening. Had the loan of Mrs. Day's liming brush.

Saturday 13 November: Cleaned out the 3rd room ready for Lizzie & Sarah. Rose stair carpet. Lloyd cleaned dish covers.

Sunday 14 November: ***** Very wet & stormy. No one to Church.

Monday 15 November: Wm. Rowland's son here saying they had returned to live in the Cottage but were afraid of the floods in the Winter until the place had been made safe. Told him to rent another house in case they shd. have to leave and that they shd. pay no rent for time until all was put safe. Tom Whittington called on horseback, the 1st time I had seen him since he was quite a little boy. He is now staying with Mr. Griffiths Surgeon Pontardawe. He goes to Neath in Janry. to set up for himself. Asked my permission to shoot here, said he should & that I shd. be glad to see him at any time.

Tuesday 16 November: Lizzie returned yesterday 2.30 p.m. Sarah came with her, they both walked over the hill. I had not seen Sarah since 18 [blank]. John sent me a bag of potatoes, a present. Lloyd for them to Garnant Station. John Thomas Gwernllwyn here carrying away Fir Poles bought 3rd inst. 110 solid feet & 11½d per foot, £5..5..5 paid.

Wednesday 17 November: In getting up this morning felt a pain & stiff peculiar feeling in my left arm. I feel convinced there is some mischief under my arm, the little lump has increased in size & it is painful to the touch & towards my bosom & chest. Day took 2 steers to Neath fair, failed to sell. Sarah & Lizzie went to see them at Gartheithen, took tea there.

Thursday 18 November: Sarah left at 1.45. Lizzie went with her as far as Nant-y-Gwin. Gave her my jet brooch the one I had from Whitby last May.

Tuesday 23 November: Lloyd digging up the stumps in Plantation. Recd. 3 photographs of R.P.L. They are very like him especially the one in standing position.

Wednesday 24 November: Recd. letter from Mary Mackenzie. Lizzie paid Peggy Daniel for the waistcoat Magdalene had repaired for Lloyd.

Thursday 25 November: My back very painful all last night. There is a kind of heavy, tight benumbed feeling quite across my back, and often great pain in my chest from my left arm to the little enlarged bone in my chest. My left arm too has a peculiar feeling of numbness & pain. I am now quite in despair of ever getting as well as I [blank]. Wm. Cwmllynfell here paying the rent up to Sept. last.

Friday 26 November: Lloyd carrying earth from Ty Cwtta field to the front to mix in the plantation where he has taken up the stumps.

Saturday 27 November: Williams (formerly Schoolmaster in Mr. Marryat's Schoolroom) here asking the valuation & acreage of Garth for the Pontardawe Union board. Lloyd & Morgan Gartheithen taking lime & earth from by Cottage to Cae Cwtta.

Sunday 28 November: Lizzie to Church. A new Clergyman there. John Harris's daughter Anne very ill. Had bottle of Port Wine & ½ pint of Brandy.

Monday 29 November: Lloyd took a notice to David Griffiths Blacksmith. Wm. Cwmllynfell went with him. He is to give up the Smithshop &c. on the 1st June next. Lloyd returned by train from Gwys.

Wednesday 1 December: Paid J. Jones Crachllwyn Poor Rate & Highway Rate as follows by cheque:

		£ .. s .. d
Garth Farm	£47.. 0..0 @ 8d	1 .. 11 .. 4
" Cottage	2.. 0..0 "	1 .. 4
3 Cots Cwmllynfell	7..10..0	5 .. 0
Smithshop	1..15..0	1 .. 2
Cot Craig Llanguicke	2.. 0..0	1 .. 4
	£60.. 5..0	2 .. 0 .. 2
	Less Commission	1..10½
		£1..18.. 3½

Caegurwen Highway rate
Mawr " "

R.P.L. came here at 5 o'clk. He walked up from Station.

Friday 3 December: R.P.L. left by 2 o'clk. train. Lloyd drove him to the Station & took Lizzie & I as far as Rhyd-y-Fro, we walked up to see Morgan Jones who has been poorly a long time. He was very pleased to see us & so was Mrs. Jones. Lloyd waited for us at Rhyd-y-Fro & we came home in the phaeton.

Saturday 4 December: Anne Blaennant (John Harris Gartheithen's daughter) buried today at Cwmllynfell aged 25 years. She has left one little baby a fortnight old (a little girl Christened today Margaret Anne). Lloyd & John Day to the funeral. A nice frost but very cold.

Sunday 5 December: Lizzie to Church. A nice bright frost. Biddy & William camc here at 3.40 p.m. to see me.

Tuesday 14 December: Confirmation at Swansea. Lizzie to the Confirmation with Miss Powel. Returned with her to dinner at 12 Picton Place. Miss Powel saw her safe in the train at 3.15. Revd. Nathl. Thomas walked up with her from Station. I returned from Bryn Syfi by 12.25 train, Miss Jenkins coming with me as far as Pontardawe in her way to Glantwrch where she stays the night.

Wednesday 15 December: John Harris here cutting down two trees, one by front Gate lower side the other a very large tree in the front by Hay house close to the little pond.

Sunday 19 December: I rode Fly to Church.

Monday 20 December: The Days killed a young steer.

Tuesday 21 December: Lloyd spreading manure on Front field. Recd. Mrs. Kirkhouse's photograph & those of her children. Revd. Nathl. Thomas called & stayed to tea.

Wednesday 22 December: John Morgan Gellygron married this day to Minnie Williams at Pontardawe Church, a very quiet wedding.[5] Three young men here playing the flute, gave 2/-. Lloyd to Cwmllynfell for cheese, had 2 weighing [blank] @ 5d. Also a small hearth brush price 9d. He also brought a Goose, a present from Margaret.

5. John Morgan (26) Colliery Proprietor of Gellygron House married Emily Jane Williams (20) of Llangiwg Vicarage at St. Peter's Church, Pontardawe.

Thursday 23 December: Wm. Cwmllynfell here, gave him £1 towards repairing Cwmllynfell bridge injured by the flood last Summer. Recd. by post Wedding Cake with Mr. & Mrs. John Morgan's compliments. Dl. Jenkins Carpenter here putting new lock on Front door & putting boards on Cart House wall. Lloyd finished spreading manure in Cae front. Lizzie recd. Mr. & Mrs. Bowman's photographs. Lloyd p.m. putting stumps round Closet wall.

Friday 24 December: Part of Pontardawe Church Choir (7 little boys) here last night. They sang very nicely. Gave them 3/6, 2 apples & a cup of tea each. Lizzie also gave them 1/-.

Saturday 25 December: Llanguicke Service at 1 a.m. Lizzie walked to Church. Revd. Nl. Thomas walked back with her as far as Saron. 4 little boys of the Church Choir came here at 4 p.m. to sing, they had tea & cake in the Hall, 2 apples each & 1/6d.

Sunday 26 December: I rode on Fly to Church, Lloyd walked with me. The last time I was at Llanguicke was after my Uncle in April last. I am unable to ride owing to my back. Lizzie & Betty at home. J.B.J. [John Borlase Jenkins] intended coming up but the a.m. was wet.

1876

Two events during the year have been noted in the Introduction, namely (i) the establishment of a postal system in Rhyd-y-fro, which owed much to Margaret's initiative and persistence, and (ii) the implementation of the Agricultural Holdings Act 1875 whose provisions stimulated her to ensure that her tenants' existing agreements were not changed. The issue of waste tipping continued to sour her relationship with the lessees of Cwmllynfell Colliery and she instructed her solicitor to sell the land for £10,000. At Garth Farm the hapless John Day, who had not paid his rent for 2 years, was given notice to quit and forced to sell his stock. Whilst Margaret's dedication to improving her home and its environment continued, her attention was drawn to the physical inadequacies of Llangiwg Church whose chilled interior was blamed for Lizzie's month-long illness. Financing the repairs required Margaret to confer with the curate Nathaniel Thomas whose earlier attraction to Lizzie now became apparent. Margaret's health appeared to have improved considerably, with few ailments noted, allowing her to walk the many miles to and from Llangiwg Church and to enjoy a week's "very pleasant jaunt" with Lizzie in Chester.

Saturday 1 January: The Gwaun Cae Gurwen Good Templars Band came here about 8.30 p.m. They played very well, gave them 10/-.

Sunday 3 January: Settled in full with Evan Jones the Butcher up to Dec. 31st, £5..0..0. He paid me for calf had last year £1..12..0.

Friday 7 January: Recd. letter from Mrs. Price saying that if convenient they wd. come here on Monday about 1 o'clk. Wrote back by return of post to say I should be glad to see them to lunch & if wet Monday the 1st fine day afterwards.

Saturday 8 January: Covered easy chair with chintz & put it in the Drawing room.

Sunday 9 January: Lizzie to Church.

Monday 10 January: Expected the Prices today to lunch, waited for them until 3 o'clk. but they did not come. Mrs. Kirkhouse & her 4 children came up at 4.20, stayed to tea & walked home, a nice dry moonlight night. Lloyd to Pontardawe & on to Biddy's. Had from her some shop goods & a few lumps of free coal to see how I liked it.

Tuesday 11 January: The Prices came today. They had my letter hurriedly & thought I had said Tuesday instead of Monday. They were very sorry for the mistake. Mr. & Mrs. Price, Jane & Jane Matthews. Mrs. Price has not been here since 186[ ]. She was very pleasant, they left here 4.15 to call at Gellygron, the wedding call on Mr. & Mrs. Morgan.

Friday 14 January: Lizzie walked home through Cwmamman. When at her sister Margaret's she found her Brother, Jane &c going to a concert at Llwyn-yr-Onen Chapel & she walked with them there & back. I suppose she walked in all about from 18 to 20 miles, enough to kill her. She was very wrong to go & they were very wrong to take her to the concert.

Saturday 15 January: Salted the pig. Lizzie came back this afternoon. She walked & felt quite done up after yesterday. No wonder.

Sunday 16 January: Mr. Jenkins walked up from 1st train. The last time he was here was July 5th 1875. No one to Church.

Monday 17 January: Mr. Jenkins left. Lloyd took him to the Station.

Bought 1 stack of Oats @ 3/6	£1.. 1..0
" 1 " " Barley " 4/4	13..0
of the man of the Trescrych	£1..14..0 Paid

Thursday 20 January: R.P.L. came here, Lloyd went to meet him by 11 o'clk. train, he wanted to see Mr. Rowland at Neath & had walked from there to Pontardawe in time to meet Lloyd on the Canal bridge going to the Station. Lloyd after dinner to fetch our oats from the Station 10 bus. damaged oats @ 1/-, 10/-.

Friday 21 January: R.P.L. left here at 8.30 a.m. in time to meet 1st train. Lloyd drove him to the Station, a most disagreeable morning snowing heavily which towards midday turned to rain. Day finished carrying the oats from the Station.

Thursday 27 January: Samuel Bogelegel brought 10 bushels of white oats @ 3/6, paid him £1..15..0 paid.

Wednesday 2 February: Lloyd drove Lizzie & I to the Vicarage. We stayed to tea, Mr. Jones was from home. Mrs. Jones seemed now very pleased that Minnie had married John Morgan Gellygron.

Saturday 5 February: Lloyd finished cutting down Portugal laurel by Front gate. Mrs. Morgan & her brother Charlie called here, she was very friendly & hoped we wd. soon come & take tea with them at Gellygron. John Morgan had gone to Swansea. They have a very smart Coachman in Livery (Claret Coat & Dark breeches & gaiters). Who wd. have thought 20 years ago Old John Morgan's son wd. have turned out in such style!!

Sunday 6 February: Lizzie & I walked to Church. Lloyd met us coming back by Saron, the 1st time I walked since 1868.

Monday 7 February: Lloyd cut down the large rhododendron on the Green opposite middle window, also some branches of Portugal laurel by the Nook. Dr. & Mrs. Walters Llansamlet Vicarage called, they stayed to tea & left at 8.15. They had a nice carriage and pair of clipped cobs, all very nice. They had called on the Goughs, Hibarts, on the Bride at Gellygron, who was out. They were very friendly & Dr. W. said he wd. speak to the Swansea Postmaster about having a Pillar Post at Rhyd-y-fro.

Tuesday 8 February: Samuel Jenkins came here yesterday to put Iron trough under Hay house side next to Green. Old Betty cleaning & sweeping the Green. Lloyd cutting away some of the Ivy on Day's house to enable Samuel to put up the trough.

Wednesday 9 February: Samuel putting up Iron troughs under Day's house, side next to the Green also under Stable & Cowhouse. Recd. letter from Dr. Walters saying he had seen the Swansea Postmaster (Mr. Oakden) about the Pillar Post & that he had promised to come to Rhyd-y-fro to see about it. Wrote to Dr. W. by return of post saying I wd. accept his offer of drawing out a Petition for the Pillar box & return it to him after having it signed by those to whom the Post wd. be a convenience.

Thursday 10 February: Went to Swansea 1st train. Saw Mr. R. Jenkins about Cwmllynfell rubbish. I object to the tipping of other rubbish from <u>other</u> Properties on my land as it ruins it <u>for ever</u>. I told Mr. R. Jenkins to offer Cwmllynfell for £10,000. 1 Gal. Gin. Lizzie received Church Service.

Friday 11 February: A thick fall of snow during the night & this morning. Mr. J. B. Jenkins gave me a cheque yesterday for £47..11..2. being a ½ year's interest due Decr. 5th 1875 from Miss Harris on £1,918..8..8. @ 5%. I asked J.B.J. to give me the papers as an acknowledgement that I had lent the money to Miss Harris. Said he had them but I have <u>never</u> had anything to show for the money.

Saturday 12 February: Walter Jeffreys called. He said he was going to London in October to the Hospital. John Thomas the Rhyd-y-fro Factory man called to ask if I wd. give something towards the Rhyd-y-fro British School. Gave him 10/- with which he was <u>much pleased</u>. Told him I was anxious to have a Pillar Post at Rhyd-y-fro. He said it was very much wanted & that he wd. gladly do all he could to assist in getting it. He promised to get an a/c of the letters brought up for the next fortnight.

Sunday 13 February: No one to Church there being a good deal of snow on the ground.

Monday 14 February: Rose the pig from the salt. It had been in salt one month.

Wednesday 16 February: Lloyd filling the ruts in Heol-y-Cefn road & putting it tidy. Recd. a letter from Miss Jenkins saying there was no Bank interest due from Janry. to June 1875 when the money was taken out. Why I don't know.

Thursday 15 February: My teeth were very painful all day. I have not suffered from toothache for a long time until yesterday when they commenced aching a little. A very wet day, it never ceased raining one minute all day. Lloyd cleaned Dish covers.

Saturday 19 February: Wrote to Laura Jones & Mrs. Bowman. Wrote to Mr. Lloyd Cilybebyll & sent him a cheque for £3 being subscriptions to Pontardawe Cottage Garden fund for three years 1874-5-6. Lloyd taking away trees from Cae front that had been cut some time ago, he knocked down a few of the pebbles off the top of the wall.

Sunday 20 February: No one to Church being very wet.

Tuesday 22 February: Lloyd commenced Bogelegel oats, the 10 bus. put in the Coffer. Lloyd to Swansea midday train thinking to bring up potatoes from Mrs. Olson but the charge 9s/4d was too great by passenger train. He took Shawl & Prayer book back to Bryn Syfi. 1 Hamper, 4 dozn. Bottles, 2 Jars returned to Messrs. D. & J. Williams today, being all due to them up to 31st Decr. 1874. Recd. a letter from Mr. Lloyd acknowledging cheque £3.

Wednesday 23 February: Lloyd to the Station for 4 cwt potatoes, came by luggage train charge 1s/4d. paid. D.M. came here to see what I wanted done. He is now working with his nephew John Morgan, Amman Inn, but will come here for a week or two, or longer whenever I like. Told him to come March 13th for a week unless he heard to the contrary from me. A very windy day, but I walked with him from Wain Pedr Erw to end of Wain Hir.

Thursday 24 February: Wrote to Garraway for trees & shrubs for planting in the Green. Fanny & Madalena G. called. They walked & were very friendly. Recd. letter from Dr. Walters asking how many Shops, Public Houses there were about Rhyd-y-fro to whom the Pillar Post wd. be a convenience.

Saturday 26 February: Poor old Mrs. Jones Cefnllan died this morning about 10 a.m. She had a fit yesterday afternoon. She was 84 years & exceedingly active & well up to the very last.

Sunday 27 February: Lizzie to Church, called to see Mr. Jones on her way. He seemed rather low.

Shrove Tuesday 29 February: Paid John Jones of Crachllwyn, Poor rate as follows 1 quarter:

		£ .. s .. d
Garth farm	£47 .. 0 .. 0 @ 8d	1 .. 11 .. 4
" Cottage	2 .. 0 .. 0 "	1 .. 4
3 Cots. Cwmllynfell	7 ..10 .. 0 "	5 .. 0
Smith Shop	1 ..15 .. 0 "	1 .. 2
Cot. Graig Llanguicke	2 .. 0 .. 0	1 .. 4
	£60 .. 5 .. 0	2 .. 0 .. 2
	Less commission	1 .. 11
	By Cheque	1 .. 18 .. 3

Ash Wednesday 1 March: Poor Mrs. Jones Cefnllan buried today at Llanguicke. Betty to the funeral. The Pulpit in bad repair & the door of it which was loose tumbled down during the Service. I had sent old Betty & Mary Witt up to clean the Church & light a fire. They took coal from here as there was none by the Church. It was a large funeral, a very cold day but dry.

Thursday 2 March: Lizzie went home this afternoon on Fly. Sent John a small round of beef wh. she took in a basket on her lap, it was cold but dry. Sent money to pay Sarah for the oatmeal, 1½ bus. of pilcorn [hulled oats] about 65 lbs. 10/- pd. Betty Gotregarth here for High Way Rate, Garth £47, Cottage £2, £49 @ 8d. £1..12..8 paid.

Friday 3 March: A very wet morning. It cleared a little between 2 and 3 o'clk, the wind was very high & very cold. Lizzie came back about 5 o'clk. Poor child she had an awful ride over the hill. She had warm clothes & I made her go to bed directly, & fortunately she was none the worse. She thought she had lost my whip but John found it in going home after coming to send her part of the way.

Saturday 4 March: Ground a bus. of barley for pig. Lloyd to Swansea midday to see if the shrubs had come by steamer from Bristol. They had & Lloyd saw them safely in a truck to come up by luggage train on Monday. He called at Bryn Syfi & brought up 6 lbs Tea & 3 lbs Coffee from London. Sent a pair of socks to Mr. Josiah Rees to Mackworth Arms that I had knitted.

Sunday 5 March: No one to Church.

Monday 6 March: D. Morgan (Mason) came here about 12 o'clk. to see how we were. He had heard this morning that I was dead & came over directly to see if it was true. We think it must have been a mistake in persons having taken me instead of Mrs. Jones Cefnllan.

Tuesday 7 March: Samuel finished putting pipes up by Day's house & our stable. After dinner Lloyd & Samuel cutting down two Oak trees in Cae Mawr hedge & trimming other branches. I was down on the road with them, it was very windy & cold but dry. Saw Madalena G. riding up this way. She looked very nice & was very pleasant. The man of Nant-y-Gasseg called with a mare for me to see. I rather liked her but she was too young, only rising 3 yrs. The price £37..0..0.

Wednesday 8 March: Lloyd to Pontardawe for flooring boards to board up Cart house the Green side, made the little door so as to push out for Gambo to go in. Lloyd took down a Gambo load of oak branches to the Chemical Works. They refused to take them as they were not properly cut, instead of bringing them back he tipped them by Wm. Griffiths the Tailor. Samuel went up to the Attic & opened the boards so as to get to the roof above 3rd room & my room to see the state of the Timber, rather damp.

Thursday 9 March: Margaret Gellyluog here paying rent. Paid her for the little pig had this day week then 3 months old, £1..5..6. paid.

Friday 10 March: David Jenkins & Samuel here sawing wood for Brush Harrow and Small Ladder.

Paid Samuel to this date

6 days @ 5/6	1 .. 13 .. 0
6 lbs Lead @ 4d.	2 .. 0
Cottage Window 7 ft @ 2/-	14 .. 0
	£2 .. 9 .. 0

Saturday 11 March: Lloyd & I planting some of the Laurels &c. sent by Garraway. A nice afternoon. We have had very boisterous weather all the week. Also formed out the Walk by Hay house to the little Pond &c. Shonny Tom Shone came here in his uniform as "Town Crier". Gave him 3/- to help in buying Donkey.

Sunday 12 March: Lizzie to Church on Fly. Very cold & no fire in Church. (Sacrament Revd. D.J.) A fall of snow last night wh. soon melted.

Monday 13 March: D. Morgan came back to cut & mend the hedges &c. after being away since 11th Septr. Last.

Tuesday 14 March: Lloyd got up root of tree in Cae Shed opposite front Gate. D.M. mending Hill fence.

Thursday 16 March: Lloyd digging & putting more good earth to roots of Ivy under Day's house. It will now be a nice border for something pretty to grow in & the new trough will keep it all dry. Lloyd to Garnant Station for sack of potatoes from Llwyn-yr-Onen. Brought 9 cwt of coal also from Llwynrhidie.

Friday 17 March: D.M. & Lloyd cutting down 2 old oak trees in road corner of Wain Pedr Erw to make a tidy wall instead of polka.

Saturday 18 March: Daniel Jenkins went to Swansea to select wood for front trough. D.M. about Wain Pedr Erw wall & gutter. A thick fall of snow about 8 a.m. soon melted. Lloyd raising turf a little higher between old Nook & little Walk & making the drive about a foot narrower. Expected Rhyd-y-fro School here to sing, but it came to snow about 7 p.m.

Sunday 19 March: No one to Church. Very cold & dry. Lizzie in bed until 5 p.m. Very poorly with pain in her chest & altogether not well.

Monday 20 March: William Cwmllynfell here in his way to Dynevor Arms sale. Said he was afraid the outhouses wd. not last another year. Lizzie very poorly & in bed till dinner time. Lloyd & I planting some of the Bristol trees. Shonny Betty's brother here.

Tuesday 21 March: Lizzie went home last train with the Ddyfadfa Notice to John. I took her to the Station (she is not at all well). I had it very cold coming back & it was snowing a little.

Wednesday 22 March: Daniel & D.M. sawing rails. The woman of Llwyn-celyn brought her little girl for me to see, poor child her face looks very bad, gave her some cream, 4 eggs and 2/-. She was very pleased.

Thursday 23 March: R.P.L. came here by 12.30, he walked up from Pontar-dawe. Evans the Post Office & Mr. Oakden the Swansea Postmaster called.

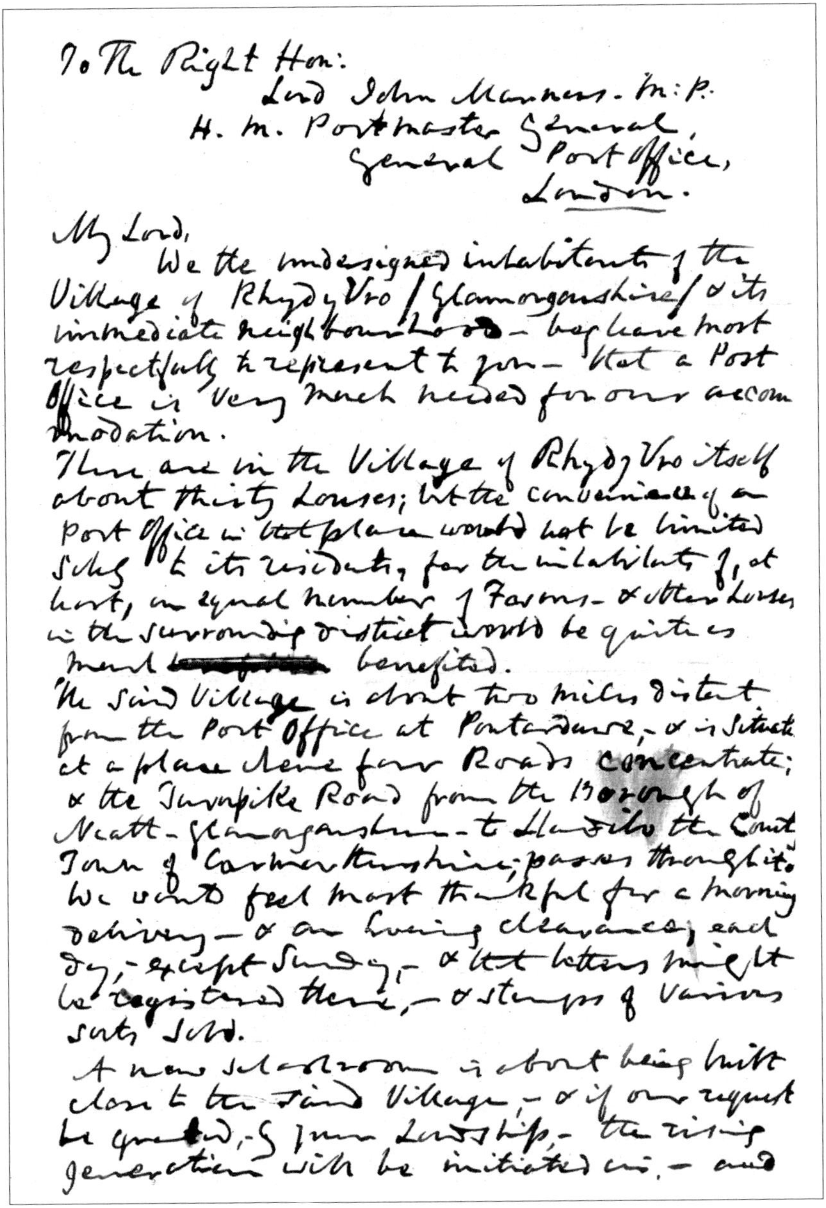

To The Right Hon:
Lord John Manners. M:P:
H. M. Postmaster General,
General Post Office,
London.

My Lord,

We the undersigned inhabitants of the Village of RhydyVro /Glamorganshire/ & its immediate neighbourhood — beg leave most respectfully to represent to you — that a Post Office is very much needed for our accommodation.

There are in the Village of RhydyVro itself about thirty houses; but the convenience of a Post Office in that place would not be limited solely to its residents, for the inhabitants of, at least, an equal number of Farms — & other houses in the surrounding district would be quite as much benefited.

The said Village is about two miles distant from the Post Office at Pontardawe, — & is situate at a place where four Roads concentrate; & the Turnpike Road from the Borough of Neath — Glamorganshire — to Llandilo the County Town of Carmarthenshire, passes through it.

We would feel most thankful for a morning delivery — & an Evening clearance, each day, — except Sunday, — & that letters might be registered there, — & stamps of various sorts sold.

A new schoolroom is about being built close to the said Village, — & if our request be granted, — by your Lordship, — the rising generation will be initiated in, — and

Richard Pendrill Llewelyn's draft appeal for a Post Office in Rhyd-y-fro, 1 April 1876
(Courtesy of Mrs J. Morris)

Wm. Morgan Ty Llwyd brought me 26 cwt of lime from the Kincoed Lime Works near Llandebie (Lime 7/6) paid.

Friday 24 March: Lizzie complained of feeling very ill at 7 a.m. directly she got out of bed. R.P.L. left 1st train. Lloyd took him to Station & telegraphed to Cwmamman for Mr. Rees the Surgeon who came here about 12.30. She had come down to the sofa. He ordered her to be taken to bed & the bedroom kept warm. Said she had "Congestion of the Lungs" & must be very careful.

Saturday 25 March: Mr. Rees here in the afternoon. Thought Lizzie better, said he wd. come on Monday.

Sunday 26 March: Sent for Mr. Rees at 11 a.m. He said Lizzie was worse.

Monday 27 March: Mr. Rees here. Jane left thinking to be in time for 11 train at Garnant but was too late. Lloyd went to Ystalyfera to ask Mary Phillip to come down for a fortnight or three weeks as Lizzie was ill.

Wednesday 29 March: Mr. Rees here. Teddy Thomas came with him. He is gone to look so manly with spectacles & whiskers &c. that I hardly knew him.

Friday 31 March: Mr. Rees here, thought Lizzie better but said she was very weak.

Saturday 1 April: Sarah, Lizzie's sister, came here to see her about 7 p.m. & to stay until Monday.

Sunday 2 April: Wm. Lewis & Biddy came to see Lizzie who was in bed.

Monday 3 April: Poor Miss Jenkins came up to see Lizzie as she heard she was so ill. She walked up from 1st train, we knew nothing of her coming until I saw her on the Green. Lloyd took her to meet last train. She thought I looked very ill, indeed I felt very poorly for I am so anxious about Lizzie & sleep & eat very little. Sarah left about 1 o'clk.

Tuesday 4 April: John Lizzie's brother came to see her.

2 Gal.	British Brandy
1 "	Gin
½ doz	Port
½ "	Sherry
2 "	Beer

Lloyd to Swansea for Garden seeds, Seville oranges, Brandy &c.

Wednesday 5 April: Mr. Rees here. Revd. D. Jones called this afternoon, went upstairs to see Lizzie. Told him she had taken cold in Church March 12th that there was no fire there, that John Morgan had neglected sending coal, & that old Betty Matthews had told him about it two or three times.

Saturday 8 April: Mrs. Morgan Gellygron called this morning at 10 o'clk. to ask how Lizzie was. She did not come in. I went out to speak to her & said Lizzie had taken cold in Church 12th March owing to there being no fire there & no coal. Katie Grenfell sent Lizzie a box of flowers, beautiful camellias &c. & a letter to me. Richard Matthews came from Garnant to enquire after Lizzie. Stayed to tea & left last train.

Tuesday 11 April: Mr. Rees here this afternoon. Lizzie came down to see him, he said he thought her improving & wd. not give her more medicine, that he wd. not come again professionally unless sent for. He said she was weak & delicate & must be very careful.

Wednesday 12 April: Revd. N. Thomas called, stayed to tea. He seemed rather anxious about repairing Llanguicke. I suggested having an Iron Pulpit & Reading desk as there was so much dry rot in the Church, & also removing them by the Chancel, also putting a Partition or Screen at the bottom of the Church to form a kind of Vestry. He liked the idea very much provided money could be had for it.

Thursday 13 April: Lloyd drove me to Pontardawe thinking to go 1st train to Swansea, but Z. Evans said Revd. D. Jones could give me copy of Notice to be given Tenants objecting to new Act of 1875. Mr. Jones came to Post Office & wrote them out for me. Z. Evans served the Notice to Wm. Griffiths Cwmllynfell who came to the Post Office. John Williams Gellyluog here putting vetches & Lizzie served him. She also served Mrs. Day who would give it her Husband.

Good Friday 14 April: Mr. Jones Llanguicke came here at 6.30 p.m., took tea & left at 11.20. Settled Church a/c.

Saturday 15 April: Eliza Gotregarth came to see Lizzie, said her mother was very poorly. Mary Phillip left gave her 6/-. Lizzie gave her new chemise & old brown frock. Mary finished cleaning out spare bedroom & putting carpet down.

Easter Day 16 April: Lizzie went out to the front for 10 minutes the 1st time since she has been ill. Betty to Llanguicke. The Pontardawe School there. Mr. Jones & Mr. Thomas there.

Easter Monday 17 April: Llandilo races. John Morgan Gellygron & his Coachman in livery went there. Opening of Cwmamman New Chapel. Bazaar at Neath.

Wednesday 19 April: Sally called here at 8 a.m. in her way home from Dl. Jenkins & the Cwmamman Chapel meetings. Wm. Rowland here asking if they shd. put potatoes in the Garden. They think the river will be safe for a while, but they are afraid to return to the Cottage to live until a weir has been put up. Told him to put what he liked in the garden & to take care of the Cottage that it was not damaged. Mr. Rees called stayed an hour, thought Lizzie better. His brother with [him] but did not come in. Lloyd carrying turf off the hill with Fly.

Thursday 20 April: Revd. Mr. Thomas Cwmamman Vicarage died suddenly age 71 years.

Friday 21 April: Jane Matthews walked up from Station was here by 12.35 to see Lizzie. She cd. not stay the night as Miss Davies was at the Mumbles. She left by last train. She walked down to the Station as poor old Fly's breath was too short to take the phaeton. I walked with her as far as Saron, a lovely afternoon. We thought it very kind to come up. She brought 2 soles.

Saturday 22 April: Morgan Jones, Saddler, Llangadock & a farmer near him named Davies came here with a Mare for me to see.

Sunday 23 April: No one to Church. Recd. letter from Mr. Gwyn enclosing one from P.M. General saying he wd. give the Rhyd-y-fro Petition his attentive consideration.

Monday 24 April: Heard that poor Mr. Thomas Cwmamman was dead. Sent Lloyd up with a note to Mrs. Thomas. He rode the New Chestnut Mare, left her at the Raven while he went to the Vicarage. Lloyd to the Bank this morning to cash me a cheque for £50 – had a new cheque book 5/-. Lloyd & I brought young fir trees from Cae Barriwns wood, planted them in old garden. Old Betty finished cleaning Front field. She has done it very clean all over with a rake.

Monday 8 May: ½ Gal. Brandy.

Sunday 14 May: I rode Fly to Church, Lloyd with me. Poor old Fly's breath very bad. Sacrament.

Wednesday 17 May: Neath Fair. D.M. cutting, Lloyd carrying clay exceedingly dry, not a drop of water on Coedcae. Betty Matthews gathering stones on vetches.

Thursday 18 May: Revd. N. Thomas called & stayed to tea, he brought back the Pulpit plans.

Thursday 25 May: Harriet Rees from Cwmamman came here at 2/- a week. Her mother brought her & seemed very glad for me to take her.

Tuesday 30 May: Mr. Bagot's sale at Forest Hall near Morristown. I went there by the 10 o'clk. train. Met Mrs. Whittington at the Station. I bought small Pembroke table for Little Kitchen for £1..0..0.

Thursday 1 June: Daniel Jenkins here beginning doing the New Trough for the front. Lloyd to Gellygron for small Pembroke table that I bought at Mr. Bagot's sale. Mr. Morgan brought it in his cart with things he had bought, it was a good deal damaged in coming to Gellygron.

Friday 2 June: Daniel & Samuel here about trough.

Saturday 3 June: Samuel the Carpenter was going to Swansea & brought up medicine for Lizzie.

Whit Sunday 4 June: Pontardawe Welsh School & Choir at Languicke Church. Revds. Jones, Thomas & Williams there, also the 2 Miss Jones' Llangunnor

(Susan & Laura). Lizzie, I, Betty, Lloyd & Harriet there. Collection for singers to go to Carmarthen. I walked to & from Church the first time since 1868.

Thursday 15 June: Grand Circus at Pontardawe. Lloyd drove Lizzie & I to the Post Office where we sat in a bedroom to see the Procession. Mr. & Mrs. A. Gilbertson, the 2 little boys, Fanny, Miss Russel & Miss Ford came up there to us. Lizzie & I went with the A.G.'s to the Circus at 3.30, they asked us to their house to tea but we declined. Mrs. Evans made us take tea which she had quite ready before starting.

Friday 16 June: Lizzie & I went in the carriage to Cwmamman to drink tea at the Vicarage. Most likely for the last time with Mrs. Thomas there. Mrs. Drewry, Willie Hyde, Teddy & Miss Shenton there. They were all very kind & glad to see us & hoped we wd. come & see them to the new house. Revds. D. Jones & N. Thomas came here soon after we left. They were very sorry we were away.

Sunday 18 June: I rode to Church, Lloyd, Betty & Harriet in Church. Lizzie alone in the house. Mrs. Day's baby Christened John Henry. Sacrament.

Monday 19 June: Lloyd drove Lizzie to the Vicarage by 10 a.m. to be examined by Mr. Jones for Confirmation. Evans the Post Office came back with her, had dinner & then went to the sale of the New House (Ynis y Bont at Rhyd-y-fro). I asked him to bid £2 [?] for it for Lizzie as I think it would be a good place for the New Post Office & Evans thinks so too. Lizzie drove with the yarn (3/8) to Mrs. Kirkhouse who gave her a cutting of some pretty shrub with white flowers.

Wednesday 21 June: Llandilo Fair. Dr. & Mrs. Walters & their two sons came here to tea, they had been for a drive & picnic thro Llangyfelach up to Cross Inn & drove here. They seemed to enjoy themselves. The evening was rather dull & cloudy.

Friday 23 June: Lloyd to Pontardawe Brewery for 18 gallons of beer ready for the singers tomorrow evening.

Saturday 24 June: Llewellyn James' son (Charles Davis) brought his Choir up to sing. 14 women & 33 men & boys (48 in all). They sang 19 pieces, most of them very good. I gave them a sovereign also tea & cake & bread & cheese & beer. They were very orderly & left at 9.50. They came here 7.45. Agreed with John Nant-y-Gwin at 3/6 a day & our food to mow the hay.

Sunday 25 June: Lizzie to Church on new mare. Lloyd & Harriet.

Monday 26 June: John Nant-y-Gwin began mowing hay (the Meadow). David Jones a Mason came to assist D.M. about the chimney & see if the leakage can be stopped. Lizzie walked to the Vicarage, called at Gellygron to ask if she might go through the fields there. Mr. Jones said she was ready for the Confirmation.

Tuesday 27 June: Dl. & Samuel painting the trough prior to putting it up. The Mason putting up poles in the Green for scaffolding ready to raise the trough.

Wednesday 28 June: Lewis the Tiler here to strip the slates for putting the trough. Colbren Church near Ystradgynlais re-opened today after its restoration.

Thursday 29 June: The new trough put up this day, 6 men pulled it up by ropes from the Green to the scaffolding & 2 men guiding it, then the 8 men turned it from the scaffold to its place.

Friday 30 June: Lewis the Tiler slating front of house & as it was coming to rain D. Jones the Mason went to help him. We were very lucky in having the slates on before it came to heavy rain. Poor John Harris taken ill in Pontardawe when at Dr. & brought home in Wm. Gellylucka's car. Lloyd to Cwmllynfell to fetch little Mary & the other children as he was in a kind of fit.

Saturday 1 July: D.M. & David Jones put stones round top of little kitchen chimney, laid them in cement. The top looks now very tidy. Lloyd drove me in the Carriage to call at the Gilbertson's, they were out. Drove from there to the Station expecting Lizzie from Bryn Syfi but she did not come.

Sunday 2 July: ***** No one to Church, damp & wet. Lloyd with letters to post. Wm. Lewis here from Church said Revd. N. Thomas told him he was going to leave in Sept.

Monday 3 July: Lloyd to Neath for 4 bushels of Aberthaw lime, he says he paid 4/6. Mrs. Day & the baby went with him to stay until Wednesday.

Tuesday 4 July: Went to Swansea 1st Brecon train & up to Bryn Syfi, where Lizzie had been staying a week. She came with me into Swansea, bought her white kid boots also white kid gloves 3/6, boots 8/6. Ordered a bonnet for myself at Miss Hughes'. Bought Lizzie a ring at Hennesseys 30/- to be a birthday present. Recd. cheque of Mr. Jenkins for £47..11..2. interest of money lent Miss Harris (½ a year due 5th June).

Wednesday 5 July: Lizzie & I took a little pudding to John Harris. We did not see him, he was sleeping.

Friday 7 July: Lizzie's birthday 25 years old. Gave her a ring a mourning one to be engraved on the seal E. J. Lloyd mowing Green. Dl. putting boards instead of the plastering at the top of the table near Dairy door.

Wednesday 12 July: Lizzie & I to Swansea 1st Brecon train. Paid Thomas, Watkins & Jenkins for wood for new front trough & 1 cask of cement by cheque £8..10..0. all paid up to this day. Took back coarse straw bonnet made by Miss Hughes as it was too tight & said I would take a hat again instead. She seemed very sorry & wished to make another bonnet but I was obliged to have one today. Went to Evans' & had a black chip,[1] I do not like it after it is ready but am obliged to have it for the confirmation on Friday. Paid for it £1..1..9. Bought Lizzie a pretty black & white Costume 6/11 cotton. Met Mrs. Morgan of Ashford by Miss Hughes'. She came with us about the bonnet. Asked her up for a day but it was too hot.

Friday 14 July: Confirmation at Pontardawe Church by the Bishop of St. David's (Basil Jones late Archdeacon of York). Lizzie confirmed. Our clergy Revd. D. Jones, N. Thomas, Williams & Jones looked very well. Dr. Walters & the Clydach Vicar there with their Candidates.

Saturday 15 July: Paid David Jones the Mason's son in the presence of Daniel Jenkins Senr. £1..18..6. (7 days @ 5/6). He was the man helping D.M. about cementing the chimnies.

Sunday 16 July: Lizzie rode Polly alone to Church. Harriet to Chapel at 6 p.m.

Thursday 20 July: Lloyd drove Lizzie & I to Swansea. Left here at 2.30 p.m. Went to Baynton's about her tooth. Called on Mr. & Mrs. D. Morgan at 84 Mansel Street. Went to the Annual Meeting of the blind at the Music Hall, bought chair 9/-, cane basket 2/6. Lizzie gave Mrs. Morgan little flower stand

1. Hat made of woven strips of wood.

3/6. Left Swansea 9.40. Lizzie very poorly with her face & all through taken worse in Coed Gwylim & called at Mrs. Lewis for her to lie down. They had gone to bed but I called them up. Saw Williams the Painter & agreed with him to come up on Monday to paint <u>outside</u> woodwork @ 6/6 per day.

Friday 21 July: Lewis the Tiler left this evening after <u>liming</u> the House & doing all about the chimnies to try & make them dry. Used a good deal of new lead.

Paid him 12 days @ 5/-	3 .. 0 .. 0
His Man 3 days @ 3/6, his Son in law 1 day 4/6	15 .. 0
Being all I owe him up to this date	£3 ..15 .. 0

Lewis had been to Cwmllynfell this morning to see what repairs were wanted to Cwmllynfell roof. There is a leakage there. The scaffolding taken down.

Saturday 22 July: Betty limed the Court. The place is now looking very clean & we have been most fortunate in having <u>beautiful fine weather</u>. <u>Very hot</u>.

Sunday 23 July: I rode Polly to Church, Lloyd with me. Lizzie walked, also Betty. Harriet home. Biddy & Wm. here when we came back to see how Lizzie was after being ill on Thursday night.

Monday 24 July: Lloyd to the Station to fetch Williams the Painter & his things, another Painter Wm. came up to work with him. Dl. at Cwmllynfell seeing to some repairs of outhouses.

Tuesday 25 July: Williams had a telegram to say his mother was dead & left midday.

Wednesday 26 July: Commenced raining a little today after a long continuance of dry weather.

Thursday 27 July: Finished carrying Cae front hay. All is now had & in very good condition.

Sunday 30 July: Lizzie rode Polly alone to Church. Harriet to Church. Betty, Lloyd and I home.

Garth

August 5th 1876

Dear Sir,

I am much obliged by your letter. It is indeed a great boon to find that we are to have a Post Office at Rhyd-y-fro, and I am sure you will have much pleasure in thinking you have so greatly assisted in obtaining it.

Respecting a person to keep the Office I think a young woman named Mary Lewis, a Church woman (grand daughter of the late Richard Lewis of Wern ddu formerly I believe a tenant of yours) would be suitable. Her Father David Lewis is Tenant & Land Agent to Mr. Gwyn Jeffreys & keeps the "Travellers Well" at Rhyd-y-fro. If she gets the appointment her Father will immediately build a suitable house in the Village combining Shop & Post Office. Until this is ready a private room can be had close by for the purpose.

I enclose A. Benthall's letter & with thanking you very much for all you have done.

Believe me dear Sir

Yours sincerely,

Margaret Jones

H. Gwyn Esq.

Margaret's draft letter to Howel Gwyn, 5 August 1876.

Sunday 6 August: Lizzie walked to Church. Mr. Thomas walked back with her as far as Saron. Said why he left Pontardawe.

Tuesday 8 August: Intended going to Swansea but could not find Williams the Painter's bill. Revd. N. Thomas called, stayed to tea. He is going to leave. Lent him Farmer's Boy & Mountain Clamberers. He was very disappointed to find I had not gone to Swansea. Met John Morgan on the road & he drove him home "splendid". The Llangadock Saddler left after mending cart and carriage harness.

Wednesday 9 August: Lloyd to Pontardawe, took books to Mr. Thomas, Dr. Syntax, Golden Hours, The Bell, &c. Paid John Jones Crachllwyn Garth Poor Rate &c. by cheque £3..1..8. Paid W. M. Williams (Painter of 84 Western Street Swansea) by cheque £6..1..10. the amount of his bill for painting chimnies, &c. His charge was a great deal too much.

Sunday 13 August: I rode Polly to Church & walked down thro the fields with Lizzie who walked all the way. [Rev.] D.J. said about A.G. [Arthur Gilbertson] finding fault with Thomas' sermon. Lizzie took the Sacrament the first time.

Tuesday 15 August: Lloyd drove me to Neath to meet Mr. Gwyn at the Castle about the appointment of Mary Lewis to the Rhyd-y-fro Post Office. Mrs. Evans came & went with me. She had business in the County Court. I called in returning to see Mrs. Kirkhouse.

Wednesday 16 August: After tea Lloyd drove me to Wm. Lewis to see Sally about my cotton frock & also to tell her to put ribbon on Lizzie's parramatta. Met lots of people on the road, the Budds, the D. Jones, the Lloyds, the Gilbertsons & Revd. N. Thomas. I went up to Ynismeudw to pay Wm. Jones' bill for seed potatoes 11/5. Lizzie to see John Harris & came back with us.

Saturday 19 August: Lizzie & I went to Swansea 1st Brecon train, saw Revd. N. Thomas at the Station, he travelled down with us & walked up to the top of Castle Street with us, he going to Chapman's & we to Baynton's. We called & dined at Bryn Syfi & intended coming home this evening but thunder & very heavy rain came on at 4.45 & we were obliged to stay until Monday.

Monday 21 August: Returned home midday train. Called at Mr. Shepherd's, gave Lizzie medicine for her sickness, & blisters (3) for my back which is very painful, quite at the end of spine.

Tuesday 22 August: Lloyd went home for a week. Wrexham Eisteddfod. Lizzie & I quite intended going there but last week was so hot & such awful thunder & lightning & my being far from well I thought it better to remain at home for us both altho' it was a great disappointment.

Saturday 26 August: Jane Matthews came up at 9.15 driven by Mr. David & Richard who were going to the Colliery. They came here at 4 o'clk. having left the wagonette at the Blacksmith's to repair the axle which broke. They took tea here & left at 6.15. It was pouring with rain, I lent them wraps.

Sunday 27 August: Lizzie & I to Church, each rode part of the way. Lloyd with us. Harriet in Church. My back very bad. When I came home fainted. Wm. Lewis here.

Saturday 2 September: My birthday. Lizzie gave me little basket bought of the blind 20 July & little muslin Neck tie. Lloyd cutting dead branches & ivy off Cae Mawr trees by roadside.

Sunday 3 September: Lizzie & I walked to Church. Lloyd met us with phaeton by Saron. Revd. N. Thomas preached his farewell Sermon at Llanguicke. He walked down with us to Rhyd-y-fro through the fields. "Darlun Lizzie", Betty, Harriet, Annie, Mrs. Day, Mary, Eliza in Church.

Monday 4 September: Lloyd drove Lizzie & I in the carriage to call at Glan-twrch. Mr. & Mrs. Price & Jane seemed very glad to see us & were very kind. Saw the new alterations they were making for Mrs. Hart's coming. Met Dr. Walters & his son in Coed Cilmaengwyn coming from Ystrad & Madeline Gilbertson on horseback.

Thursday 7 September: Poor little Mary Gartheithen died today about one o'clock. I believe she was a good child & that death to her has been a happy release.

Friday 8 September: Revd. N. Thomas came here 11.40 a.m. I had asked him on Sunday to come & dine here some day this week. He left 7.20 p.m. Daniel mending Coed Cae Gwenthey gate, Lloyd mowing Green.

Saturday 9 September: Lizzie & I intended going to Swansea but recd. a letter in Rhyd-y-fro saying Mr. Baynton (Dentist) was from home. We drove on to Pontardawe, to get some hinges &c. from the Ironmongers. Paid E. Jones Butcher. Left some books for Mr. Thomas at the Post Office.

Sunday 10 September: Lizzie rode to Church. Mr. Jones the Curate there. Came with Lizzie over the stile & said he intended coming here to see us. The Vicar stung by a bee & unable to come to Church. Sacrament.

Monday 11 September: Little Mary Gartheithen buried today at Cwmllynfell, funeral passed here 1.30. Lloyd to the funeral, Mrs. Day, Charlie & Webber. Betty staying at Gartheithen with John Harris who was very poorly until they came home. Lizzie to Gartheithen after tea for a few minutes. Daniel put up the Court Doors. I have long wished to have them as I think they will make the house warmer & safer.

Tuesday 12 September: Neath Fair. Lizzie's brother & George Griffiths Maesquarra came here about 8 o'clk. from the fair, they left about 10 o'clk.

Saturday 16 September: Mr. Paddison came here, told him exactly how Day stood, that he was 2 years behind with rent this Sept. 29th inst, & that I must have money. He was astonished. He looked over his stock &c., & advised him either to have a sale at once or sell by private contract. Mrs. Day in Devonshire.

Sunday 17 September: Lizzie to Church on Polly, Lloyd too. A strange clergyman. Betty to Ystalyfera. Harriet in the house with me. Heavy showers.

Monday 18 September: Sent books (Daisy Chain & The Trial) to Revd. N. Thomas. Also 2 Book Markers "May you be Happy" and "No X No Crown". Lloyd took them down with a note from me wishing him much happiness in his new home (Pont Yates) & saying that if he came to the neighbourhood we should be very glad to see him here & could always give him a bed.

Tuesday 19 September: Recd. a letter by post from Revd. N. Thomas thanking us for the nice present sent him yesterday and the good wishes &c.

Wednesday 20 September: Day came to me on the Walk & said he would make a sale.

Thursday 21 September: Revd. N. Thomas came to wish us Good bye. Stayed to tea, left at 9.30. He leaves for Pont Yates on Saturday.

Friday 22 September: Recd. letter from Jane Matthews saying that if convenient Madame Ternon & herself wd. come & spend the day here tomorrow. Lloyd drove me to Swansea, called at Jane's & said I shd. be glad to see them tomorrow & wd. send to meet the 11.30 train. Went to Andrews the Tailor & had Lloyd measured for a greatcoat. Called at Morgan the Paperer's & said I wished to have a room or two papered. Said he wd. send a good man up Oct. 2nd. Called at Post Office saw Mr. Thomas's Gold Watch and framed address which is presented to him on his leaving Pontardawe.

Saturday 23 September: Jane Matthews & Madam Ternon came up by 11.30 train, left last train 7.25. They were very pleasant & seemed pleased with everything. We went for a walk round the front & then on the hill.

Sunday 24 September: No one to Church. Very wet. Harriet to Chapel at 6 p.m.

Monday 25 September: Revd. N. Thomas left Pontardawe for Pont Yates this morning. He has a holiday until Saturday when he goes to his Vicar at Llangendeirne until his house at Pont Yates is ready.

Tuesday 26 September: In cleaning out the White room Lizzie burnt a great many of my dress & jacket patterns, whether purposely or not I do not know. I had laid them all on the washing stand quite separate from all other papers. I told her I was very angry & vexed for they were my best patterns, & said "I wish I were dead out of your way & then you could burn what you liked & my effigy too if you liked".

Wednesday 27 September: Lloyd clearing away on the hill old posts &c. where fern rick used to be. It now looks much tidier. In the afternoon he was with Charlie clearing away old railing by Brick yard, as I am going to put new rails higher up. Lizzie finished cleaning old paper off White room walls, ready to be new papered.

Thursday 28 September: Lizzie gave Day Notice Paper. Daniel mending the Gate by Barn. Harriet washed out the White room, it is now very clean & all ready for papering. I hope no more damp will come in. Wm. Davies Forchegel brought the pot of butter 21 lbs @ 1/6. Paid him £1..10..6. He said John Tynewydd would like to rent this place if Day was going away. I said I wd. do nothing until after Xtmas.

Friday 29 September: Lizzie took letters to post Rhyd-y-fro. Mrs. A.G., the Nurse & two eldest little boys called here in their little pony cart, they had tea. Mrs. G. was very friendly.

Saturday 30 September: Lloyd putting down posts to rail round Brick yard. Dl. & D.M. sawing rails for the same.

Sunday 1 October: Lloyd drove Lizzie & I in the phaeton as far as Morgan Jones' & left the Mare there. My back is too painful to ride to Church. The 1st time I have in the phaeton to Church.

Monday 2 October: Lloyd & Daniel putting all new rails round Brick yard & pointed upright from Barn Pine End to Gate. D.M. making gutter across the road in the yard.

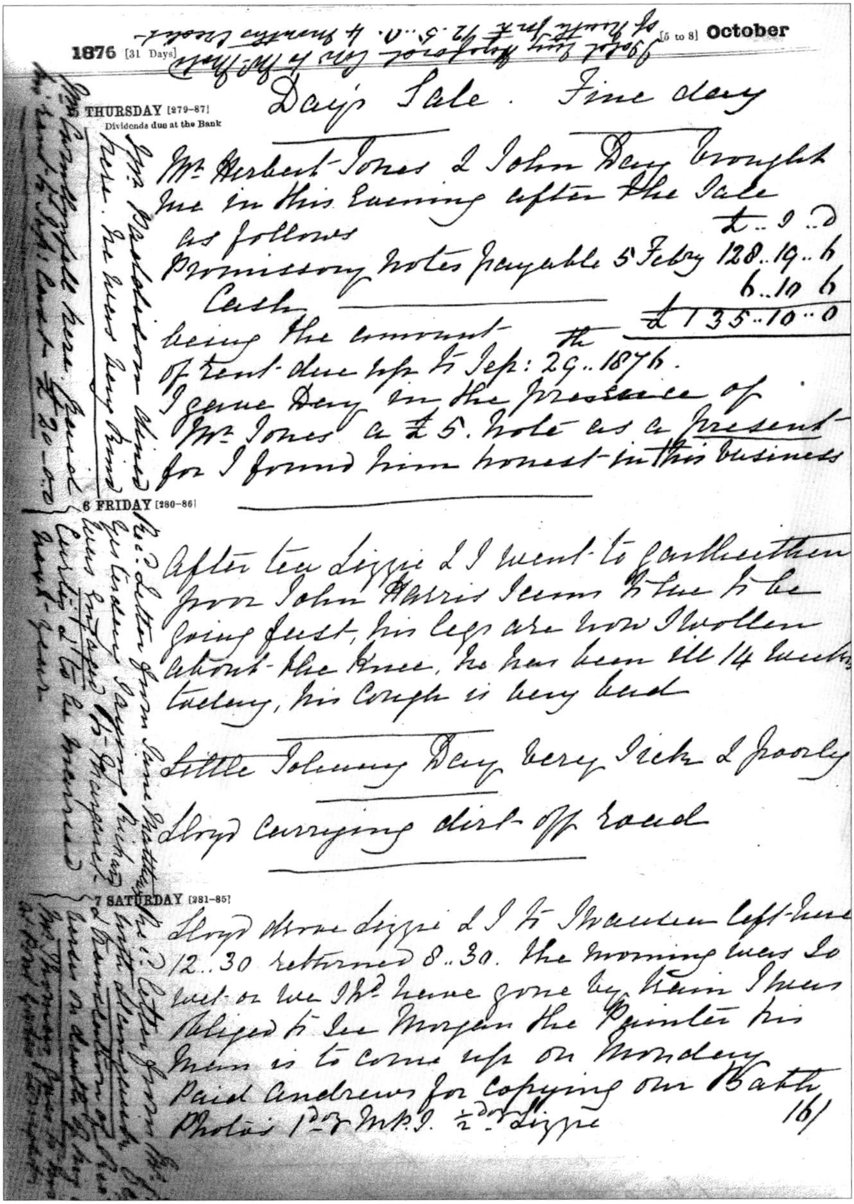

1876 [31 Days] [5 to 8] October

5 THURSDAY [279–87]
Dividends due at the Bank

Day's Sale. Fine day

Mr Herbert Jones & John Day brought me in this Evening after the Sale as follows

	£..s..d
Promissory Notes payable 5 Feby	128..19..6
Cash	6..10..6
being the amount	£135..10..0

of rent due up to Sep: 29th..1876.
I gave Day in the presence of Mr Jones a £5. Note as a present for I found him honest in this business

6 FRIDAY [280–86]

After tea Lizzie & I went to [illegible] poor John Harris seems to me to be going fast, his legs are now swollen about the knee, he has been ill 14 weeks today, his cough is very bad

Little Johnny Day very sick & poorly

Lloyd carrying dirt off road

7 SATURDAY [281–85]

Lloyd drove Lizzie & I to Swansea left here 12..30 returned 8..30. the morning was so wet or we should have gone by train I was obliged to see Morgan the Painter his men is to come up on Monday
Paid Andrews for copying our Bath Photos 1 doz Mr. J. ½ doz Lizzie 16/

Diary entry for sale of Day's stock, 5 October 1876
(Courtesy of Mrs J. Morris)

Tuesday 3 October: Dl. put two pitch pine boards as a shelf for wine &c. above bench in the Pantry. Lizzie went home by 11 o'clk. train & returned by the 7 train. Lloyd took & fetched her. She took quilt home for which Sarah paid me 6/6. Jane sent me black & white neck scarf. Lizzie took pinafore to Margaret's little girl. Harvest meeting at Bettws Church. Dl. put weather boards on Barn roof hill side.

Wednesday 4 October: Very wet a.m. Cleared p.m. Lloyd clearing & cleaning about back of the house a.m. In the afternoon cleaning & raking the front.

Had 3 doz Beer, ½ gal Whiskey.

1 sack of oats from Post Office, ½ bus. beans.

Harvest Thanksgiving at Pontardawe tonight in English. Tomorrow night Welsh. No one from here to either.

Thursday 5 October: Day's sale. Fine day.

Mr. Herbert Jones & John Day brought me in this evening after the sale as follows:

	£ .. s .. d
Promissory Notes payable 5th Febry.	128 .. 19 .. 6
Cash	6 .. 10 .. 6
	£135.. 10 .. 0

being the amount of rent due up to Sep. 29th 1876.

I gave Day in the presence of Mr. Jones a £5 note as a present for I found him honest in this business. Mr. Paddison dined here. He was very kind. Mr. Cwm-llynfell here, paid his rent to Sep. last £20..0..0. I sold my Hereford Cow to Mr. Mold of Neath for £12..5..0, 4 months credit.

Friday 6 October: After tea Lizzie & I went to Gartheithen, poor John Harris seems to me to be going fast, his legs are now swollen about the knee, he has been ill 14 weeks today, his cough is very bad. Little Johnny Day very sick & poorly. Lloyd carrying dirt off road. Recd. letter from Jane Matthews yesterday saying Richard was engaged to Margaret Curtis & to be married next year.

Saturday 7 October: Lloyd drove Lizzie & I to Swansea, left here 12.30 returned 8.30. This morning was so wet or we shd. have gone by train. I was obliged to see Morgan the Painter, his man is to come up on Monday. Paid Andrews for copying our Bath Photos 1 doz. M.P.J., ½ doz. Lizzie 16/-. Recd. letter from Mr. Thomas with Llanguicke verses & translation of Revd. T. Jones' verses on death of his children. Mr. Thomas goes to his own cottage at Pont Yates tonight.

Sunday 8 October: No one to Church. Very wet. Recd. letter from Laura Jones from Mold. She is staying with her brother James.

Monday 9 October: Morgan the Painter of Swansea sent up a man named Hill to do out the White room.

Tuesday 10 October: D. Morgan took out White room grate, the sides are broken. Dl. cut off board & made an open recess for the washing stand in the White room & put skirting at the back, also put heavier weights to two of the front windows upstairs, to make them close tightly at the top, before they are painted.

Wednesday 11 October: Revd. N. Thomas Pont Yates called at 3 p.m. Stayed to tea, left at 8. Lloyd drove him down to his old lodgings at Pontardawe. He came to the Vicarage last night & leaves this Parish tomorrow with all his goods.

Thursday 12 October: Lloyd had his New Great Coat.

Friday 13 October: Lloyd drove Lizzie & I in the Carriage to call at Mr. Gilbertson's & Mr. A.G.'s not in at either house. Jessie Lloyd staying at the A.G.'s. Looked at grates for White room at Davies the Ironmongers. Mrs. Morgan Gellygron a little girl this morning, her 1st child. Sent Lloyd in to ask how she was.

Saturday 14 October: Hill the Painter left after papering & painting the White room & giving one coat of paint to upstairs windows (outside), Porch & large doors. Recd. letter from Revd. N. Thomas Pont Yates asking permission to write to Lizzie.

Sunday 15 October: Lizzie & I in Church. Lloyd drove us in the Phaeton as far as Mr. Jones. Betty & Harriet in Church. Llansamlet Curate.

Monday 16 October: Wrote to Revd. N. Thomas. John Jones Saddler Llangadock came over with Bridles &c. Lloyd drove him in the Phaeton to meet last train at Garnant.

	£ .. s .. d
Lizzie's double reined bridle	1 .. 2 .. 6
" martingale	12 .. 6
Single rein bridle & bit	15 .. 0
Mending straps &c. here	5 .. 0
Paid by cheque	£2 ..15 .. 0

Wednesday 18 October: Dl. made shutter for Court window. Howel Howells (Rachel Gellylucha's nephew) lately come from America called to ask if I knew any thing about Daniel Pentwyn's money. I told him to go to Daniel Bevan (Twyn) or Mr. Kempthorne, that they knew all. D.M. mending Cae front wall under the Green. Lloyd mowing the Green.

Thursday 19 October: Recd. 2nd letter from Revd. N. Thomas asking me to reconsider the subject.

Friday 20 October: Wrote to Revd. N. Thomas saying I could only repeat what I said before that I could not consent to any correspondence. D1. finished putting up new yard gate for Day. He also cut feet of spare bedroom dressing table.

Saturday 21 October: Put up second book shelf in dining room. Recd. letter from Mrs. A. Gilbertson dated 18th which I ought to have had Thursday asking Lizzie & I to lunch with them on that day to meet Jessie Lloyd who is leaving for Duffryn. Wrote to her saying of the delay & enclosing the envelope. I do not at all know how the letter did not come in proper time.

Sunday 22 October: Lizzie to Church on Polly. Harriet & Betty to Church. Lloyd drove Lizzie & I in the Phaeton to Pontardawe Church service 6.30. The 1st time for Lizzie, excellent sermon by Williams, II Tim. Williams preached in both places.

Monday 23 October: Lizzie & I called on Mr. & Mrs. Griffiths Cwmamman Vicarage (the new Clergyman). Saw Mrs. Griffiths, he was out. Miss Shenton called when we were there, she left with us & came with us in the Phaeton to the top of the hill by "The Mountain". She was very glad to see us. Mrs. Thomas is still away. Laying foundation stone of New Carmel we met lots of people, Dr. Rees among the number.

Tuesday 24 October: D.M. finished ditching hedge both sides between Cae Barriwns & Strip.

Wednesday 25 October: Lloyd & D.M. cutting down large trees opposite front door. Lizzie & I put down carpet in my room which is now all clean. John Davies (Tynewydd Forchegel) came to see about renting this place. I told him I would not rent it to any one until after Xtmas, that several had been asking for it but that I had not promised any one.

Thursday 26 October: Lloyd & D.M. finished cutting & taking away 10 large trees opposite front door, the rhododendrons will now have place to grow & more must be planted.

Yesterday Lizzie & I with letters to post called at the Saron Schoolroom to ask if the children could come up here next Saturday to sing & have tea. Rees said he was afraid he cd. not get all so they are to come Saturday fortnight. We turned in to see the new Schoolroom, there is a beautiful view from the house windows.

Friday 27 October: Lizzie put down & mended stair carpet yesterday, the upstairs is now all clean. Mrs. Ford, Miss Ford and M. Gilbertson called yesterday. They walked & had a cup of tea which they seemed to enjoy. They were very pleasant, said Jane Price was engaged to Mr. Benthall & to be married in the Spring. D.M. commenced opening meadow gutters. Lloyd carrying old manure to Cae Barriwns.

Saturday 28 October: Lizzie put braid on my old Linsey skirt. Put braid on her black & white costume, cotton & the bottom trimming after it was washed. The old woman of the Cottage here taking up the geraniums to keep for me in the Winter.

Sunday 29 October: Lizzie & I to Church in the Phaeton. Williams preached. Lizzie had the letter!! Harriet went home.

Tuesday 31 October: Lizzie & I called at Llansamlet Vicarage about 12 o'clk. Dr. Walters at Yniscedwin. Young Gough 21 today. Mrs. Walters came in the Phaeton with us to Swansea to have her photo taken. It was a lovely bright clear day & we enjoyed the drive by Glais & Birchgrove, the view was lovely. We could see Llanguicke Church & Cefn Llan as plain as possible. Called at Bryn Syfi & dined there. Mrs. C. Morgan, Miss Bickly & Miss Prothero called.

Wednesday 1 November: Recd. letter from Revd. N. Thomas asking if I wd. allow him to call here & see Lizzie.

Thursday 2 November: Lizzie & I left here by Garnant train 11.5 a.m. for Shrewsbury where we stayed the night at the Raven Hotel (a hunt ball in the town). Enjoyed the country it looked so rich in its Autumn tints.

Friday 3 November: Left Shrewsbury for Chester.

Saturday 4 November: Lizzie & I went to see Dickson's Gardens, the Market & Cathedral. We stayed to the Service, returned to the Grosvenor Hotel & enjoyed our tea. Revd. Mr. Simpson introduced himself to us & we had a pleasant chat.

Sunday 5 November; Lizzie to St. John's Church Chester a.m. I remained in the House (Grosvenor Hotel). Lizzie & I to the Cathedral at 6 p.m., also the Revd. Mr. Simpson. P.M. we both walked round the City Walls.

Tuesday 7 November: Lizzie & I left the Grosvenor Hotel, Chester at 9 a.m. Took our tickets to Brecon thinking to be home tonight, but we had to wait 3½ hours at Llanidloes which made us too late at Brecon for the Pontardawe train, so we had to sleep at "The Wellington". The day was very fine, bright sunshine which enabled us to have most lovely views of the beautiful country we passed through. Such lovely hills & woods, & the golden tints of Autumn gave such richness to the scene. The first time I was ever in N. Wales & I enjoyed the scenery more than I can describe & Lizzie enjoyed it too.

Wednesday 8 November: Lizzie & I after breakfast went to see the Priory Church (Brecon) & then walked past the Castle Hotel & through the town back to "The Wellington". Left Brecon 11.25 a.m. arrived at Pontardawe about 1 o'clk. & home at 2 after being away a week tomorrow. We had a very pleasant jaunt & enjoyed ourselves very much.

Friday 10 November: Harriet's Mother here. Paid Harriet up to yesterday 24 weeks @ 2/-, £2..8..0.

Saturday 11 November: Rhydyfro School children here singing. They all had tea & cake & the young men bread & cheese & beer. Gave the Schoolmaster 10/-. They all seemed pleased & were much obliged. The day was fine but very cold.

Sunday 12 November: Lizzie & I to Church in the Phaeton. Sacrament Mr. Jones.

Wednesday 15 November: Recd. a letter from Revd. N. Thomas thanking me for mine of the 1st inst. & in allowing him to call here, also saying I had always treated him as a Gentleman.

Thursday 16 November: Lloyd had Gartheithen Mare to help our own to get a Tram of Coal from Ynisderw, 8/6 per tram. Richard Jones cleaned the two clocks & keeps them going one year, paid 5/-.

Friday 17 November: Had 14 lbs of beef from Nant-y-Gasseg at 8d, paid 9/4. Put up the 2 top valance of my curtains after being washed.

Sunday 19 November: Lizzie to Church on Polly. Betty & Harriet to Church, they also went to Tom Tirlan's after tea. Wm. Lewis here showing Biddy's uncle's Will about the bit of land. Mr. Jones at Llanguicke.

Monday 20 November: Lizzie & Harriet helping to sweep the Green after cutting the Fuchsias & forking the beds. Lizzie & I called at Gellygron p.m. the first time since the baby was born. Met Mrs. Ford there.

Paid Daniel Jenkins Carpenter up to this day by cheque

46¾ days @ 5/-	£11..13..9	)
		) 12..10..9
Wheelbarrow	17..0	)

Tuesday 21 November: D.M. cutting Scilp [thatching rods] at Gellyluog. Lloyd cleaning Heol-y-Ty. Lizzie, Harriet & I finished cleaning the Walk.

Wednesday 22 November: Poor John Harris Gartheithen died tonight at 10.30.

Thursday 23 November: Lizzie went home 11 train to tell them poor John Harris was to be buried on Saturday. She returned by the 4 train. Lloyd took

& fetched her. John sent me a nice spare rib & chine. Lizzie bought lamp & benzoline. D.M. after dinner tidied the bottom of Heol-y-Ty, put stones to prevent carts & tidied where road stones had been.

Friday 24 November: Lloyd to Swansea for Reed & Spars to thatch Craig Llanguicke cottage.

28 bundles of reed @ 1/8d.	£2 .. 6 .. 8	
1,200 Spars @ 1/3	15 .. 0	
had of Henry Day (Strand Swansea)	£3 .. 1 .. 8	paid.

Saturday 25 November: Poor John Harris Gartheithen buried today at Cwm-llynfell age 64. John, Lizzie's brother, called here in coming to the funeral. He was very late owing he said to the wet morning. It cleared about 11 a.m. & we had a dry afternoon.

Sunday 26 November: No one to Llanguicke. Lizzie & I to Pontardawe Church at 6 p.m. Had pouring rain in coming home. Sarah Morgan offered to lend us umbrellas, &c. Mr. Williams Jer: 35, 15.

Thursday 30 November: ***** Lizzie & I intended going to Bryn Syfi by the 4.13 train but were too late for it by 5 minutes through my watch being a quarter of an hour too slow. Lloyd drove us to Mrs. Kirkhouse's to wait until the 7 train. She was very glad to see us & we had tea with her. She said she had heard in Swansea last Saturday that Mr. Jenkins was engaged to Miss Wyatt! Gave Mrs. Kirkhouse the little pan of butter I intended taking Miss Walford (about 7 lbs). When we got to Bryn Syfi Miss Jenkins was at Mrs. St. Legers. We went there.

Friday 1 December: Lizzie & I to Swansea, it came on to rain very much & I got my feet very wet. Paid Andrews the Tailor for

Lloyd's great coat & buttons (MPJ)	£5..4.. 0
Paid J. N. Morgan Painter	£4..1..18

Saturday 2 December: Lizzie & I to Swansea, called at Miss Powel's. She was very glad to see us, intended calling on Mrs. John Jones but it came on to rain, called on Jane Matthews, found her in bed very weak & poorly. I sent the Servant for Dr. Padley, he was not in but came late this evening. Went to Mr. Baynton's to stop Lizzie's tooth. Paid him £1..1..0.

Sunday 3 December: Lizzie & I at Bryn Syfi, very wet.

Monday 4 December: Came home from Bryn Syfi midday train.

Wednesday 6 December: Lizzie walked to Llanguicke to fetch the surplice to be washed. She called at Morgan Jones', he was very ill in bed in the parlour, she did not see him. John Thomas Gwernllwyn here, said he wd. buy whatever poles I had to sell. Recd. letter from Mrs. C. Morgan saying they intended erecting a tablet to the memory of the late Revd. T. Thomas Cwmamman & asking me for a subscription. Wrote back & promised a sovereign.

Thursday 7 December: Lloyd to the Station to meet R.P.L. by first train 8.30 a.m. After dinner he walked with me through the yard & cowhouses &c. He said it would take a year's rent to repair them. He thought the land & buildings in a very untidy state & advised my having new tenants. Charles Davies here with 6 of his Choir singing. Gave them 5/-. Gave R.P.L. £1..0..0.

Friday 8 December: R.P.L. left 1st train.

Sunday 10 December: Lizzie & I to Church in the Phaeton, called to ask how Morgan Jones was. He was ill in bed, did not see him. Sacrament Mr. Jones. Mr. Price Llyswel preached.

Monday 11 December: Mr. & Mrs. Griffiths Cwmamman Vicarage called (1st time) in Mr. C. Morgan's Carriage. Mrs. Morgan intended coming back she was not well, they stayed here 1½ hours while the man drove to Pontardawe. They were very pleasant & seemed to wish to be friendly.

Tuesday 12 December: Paid Henry Evans Thatcher for thatching Craig Llanguicke Cottage

7 days @ 4/6	£1 .. 11 .. 6
6 days boy attending @ 1/-	6 .. 0
By cash	£1 .. 17 .. 6

Thursday 14 December: John Davies Nant-y-Gasseg killed our pig, weighed 262 lbs.

Friday 15 December: Lloyd drove Lizzie & I in the Carriage to call on Mrs. Charles Morgan. Met Mrs. Thomas going there. They were in sad trouble, the

Bailiffs being in the house since last Saturday owing to the lawsuit between Morgan & Elford about the Gwain Cae Gurwen Colliery.

Sunday 17 December: No one to Church. Very wet. Betty & Harriet to Tom's after tea.

Monday 18 December: Lloyd drove Lizzie & I to Glan Twrch to wish Jane goodbye before her marriage. Dora Starbuck staying there. Ellen Gilbertson called & was in the Drawing Room when we got there. She had taken Jane an antimacassar. Mr. Price was very kind & friendly. Showed us Jane's presents, the wedding dress & her linen &c. All very nice being good & very neatly made. Returned home by 7.40. When we returned from the Price's, heard that Mr. Charles Morgan had shot himself.[2]

Wednesday 20 December: Sent Lloyd up with a letter of sympathy to Mrs. C. Morgan. Miss Bickley wrote to thank.

Thursday 21 December: Mr. Josiah Rees married to Miss Eliza Harriet Acock at East Teignmouth, Devon.

Sunday 24 December: Lizzie walked to Llanguicke. Lizzie & I to Pontardawe Church at 6.30 p.m. It was prettily decorated.

Monday 25 December: <u>Xtmas Day</u>. Lloyd drove Lizzie & I to Llanguicke Service at 11 a.m. Mr. Jones read the Prayers & Mr. Williams preached. The 3 Curates were to dine with Mr. Jones. I promised Mr. Jones in the Church in the presence of Lizzie & Mr. Williams that I would go <u>bail</u> for the money required for the repairs of Llanguicke Church.

Thursday 28 December: Jane Price Glantwrch married this day at Ystradgynlais Church to Earnest Benthall of London, a very wet day. Poor Morgan Jones Cefnllan buried this afternoon at Llanguicke Church aged 78 years. Lloyd & Betty to funeral.

Friday 29 December: Dl. Howell & 9 of the Church Choir here singing, they

2. Mr. Charles Morgan, Colliery Proprietor, had previously been the plaintiff against Elford regarding the sale of G.C.G. colliery. The case went against Elford but on appeal the initial judgement was reversed with large costs. The decision preyed on Morgan's mind and he could not cope with "the overpowering anxieties". *The Cambrian*, 23 December 1876.

sang a great many pieces & most of them very well. Gave them beer & 10/-. They seemed much pleased. Lizzie was delighted with the singing.

Saturday 30 December: Settled in full with Samuel Jenkins for all work done to this day as follows:

		£ .. s .. d
Samuel	9 days @ 5/6	2 .. 9 .. 6
Thos. Edwards	5 " @ "	1 .. 7 .. 6
Paid by cheque		£3 ..17 .. 0

Sunday 31 December: Lizzie & I in the house all day. Betty & Harriet to Pontardawe Church at 6 p.m.

1877-1879

The diaries for these three years are missing but an insight into facets of Margaret's life during this period may be gained from her letters and other sources.

Mary Jenkins, Bryn Syfi, to Lizzie Jones, 3 January 1877

Dear Lizzie,

Your letter was very welcome. I am glad that your neighbours come & cheer you with a little music this festive season & that you were able to enjoy it but am sorry to hear that Margaret is not well. The weather is certainly anything but cheering, nothing but rain, rain, rain. We cannot have much more I hope. I am pretty well notwithstanding all the little worries I have had. Emily is at home, she is to return when she is better. She declared to the last that there was nothing wrong the matter with her, so in that case she is to come back but at times I feel doubtful as persons so frequently persist in decisions in such cases but however I feel relieved that she is with her Mother.

You have no doubt seen Josiah's marriage in the paper. We had a letter from him but not until we saw the announcement in the paper. I heard from Annie Jevons, she begged me to give her love to Margaret & you when I saw you. She had not heard from you she said but she added she was such a bad correspondent herself that she excused others for being so. She did not name her Uncle's being married so I suppose at that time she did not know. Mrs. Grenfell was saying the last time I saw her that she had fully thought to have written to you but I suppose she forgot. They are now at Maesteg House.

Upon my word you are progressing up your way. What next shall we hear – you are going to have perhaps a Theatre. I saw my cousin Mary on Saturday who said that Jane's wedding went off very well in spite of the bad weather. She had not heard from her on Saturday. It seems almost a pity that Mr. Jones Cefn Llan died worth so much money having only a son so unfit to manage it.

With very much love to dear Margaret & yourself from Uncle John & Aunt Mary.

Yours very affy.

Mary B. Jenkins

William Gilbertson to Margaret Jones, 12 January 1877

Dear Miss Jones

I have received your note of today's date. I am not Vice Chairman of the County Roads Boards but merely a member of it. Mr. J. M. Dalton of Cardiff is Clerk to the Board.

I would recommend your writing to Mr. Dalton telling him what you wish to do and asking what course you should adopt. I expect he will tell you that before anything is done you must get permission from the Board and that you should explain to the Surveyor what you desire so that he may lay the matter before the Board.

I am yours tr[uly]

W. Gilbertson

Death of Dr. William Price, Glan Twrch, 24 March 1877

Memorial from *The Cambrian,* 6 April 1877:

YSTALYFERA. – In our last week's obituary we briefly recorded the death of an old inhabitant of this vale – William Price, Esq., Glantwrch. We feel it due to the memory of this gentleman, that we should this week make more extended reference to him. Mr. Price was a member of an old and very respectable family, well known for many generations in these parts. He was descended from the celebrated Richard Pendrill, whose kindness to King Charles II secured for him a large amount of royal favour. Mr. Price used the arms and motto of his celebrated ancestor. He was a connecting link between the present generation and one that has now few to represent it. His recollections of the events of his early youth, and more mature years, were many, and threw an interesting light on the state of the valley before its solitude was disturbed by scientific operations in mill and forge, in furnace and mine; and before the levelling use of railways was felt in the parish. His large practice gave him an extensive acquaintance with the inhabitants of the district of every class and grade. The name of the good man was one which always commanded respect and esteem, and was truly a house-hold word. He was a thorough Welshman – loved the language of his country, spoke it with great fluency, had treasured up in his memory many of its traditions, and was full of sympathy with the best interests of the Principality. His father was rector of Kilybebill for many years. About thirty years ago Mr. Price married a lady, a member of the family of Jenkins, in the neighbourhood of Swansea. Of their only two children – one is dead, and the other was lately married to an English gentleman. Mr. Price filled many important offices, among others that of County Magistrate. He attended the sessions at Ystradgunlais with great regularity, and administered justice in such a way as to command general confidence. The presence and good deeds of one kind neighbour will be much missed. The day previous to the fatal seizure that suddenly took him at midnight, he had been for hours riding from house to house making provision for the destitute, who are found at this time in large numbers in this locality. His funeral was attended by a large concourse of people – persons of all ranks manifesting a desire to show their respect and affection.

Mary Price, Glan Twrch, to Margaret Jones, 28 June 1877 written on black edged mourning stationery

My dear Margaret,

I have not seen you for a long time & I have been very crippled all the Winter & am now going to ask you a great favour. I am making my will & I hope you will consent to allow me to name you as one of my executors & trustees for Jane & little Dorothy. There is no one for whom I have a greater respect & regard than yourself so I trust you will be as kind to this child of your old friend & kinsman.

Phebe told me that you intended to come & see me the next week. I trust you & your cousin will come & lunch with me on Monday or if wet on Tuesday. What weather we have had, hardly any sunshine.

I hear from Jane that she is pretty well. You know that another little stranger is expected the middle of next month. I am going to send Ruth up for little Dorothy on the 10th.

With kind regards believe me my dear Margaret

Yours very sincerely

Mary

Margaret Jones to John Davies, Land & Mineral Surveyor, 1 September 1877

Mr. Davies, Sir

I have not been well or I should have written sooner. I enclose a cheque for £21 – the amount of your bill. I see you charge immensely high considering how very little I get from the Colliery.

Will you let me know when you will be up next at Cwmllynfell. I am having the Cottage by the "George" thoroughly repaired & I wish you to finally fix the boundary so as for Mr. Bain to put the River in its proper course. He says he will do so at once, as soon as it is fixed. A sudden flood would now do great damage to the Cottage & I am anxious to have it done as soon as possible. The people are desirous of going back on the 29th inst. Is it necessary for Mr. J. O. Jones to meet you again at Cwmllynfell?

Yours obediently,

Margaret Jones

Margaret Jones to Alexander Bain, 1 September 1877

Dear Sir,

I hope that in the course of a week or two Mr. Davies will be up to finally fix the boundary. Meanwhile will you kindly put some barrier to prevent the water going down towards Wm. Rowlands house. I am as you see having the Cottage thoroughly repaired & I hope you will at once kindly have the River put in its proper bed, in case of a sudden flood. Wm. Rowlands' son was here yesterday & he said that his Father & Yourself had been talking on the subject.

Yours obediently,

Margaret Jones

Rev. W. H. A. Walters, Vicar of Llansamlet to Margaret Jones, 4 September 1877

Dear Miss Jones,

We were on the start for Ystradgynlais yesterday when the Post came in. In answer to your letter, Ma desires me to say that you are welcome to have the use of the tea-can any time your man will call for it. Ma finds that the can will hold tea sufficient for one hundred and eighty children. She usually puts one pound and a quarter or half of tea in the can – then when the tea is brewed, pours in five pounds of sugar (which is previously reduced to a liquid state in a basin) and a good quantity of milk. For each child Ma allows three quarters of a pound of cake.

We promise ourselves the pleasure of all calling upon you soon some evening.

With our united kind regards to Miss Lizzie & yourself.

I remain,

Yours sincerely,

W. H. A. Walters

Margaret had written a "*Receipt for a very good cake for general use or for School treats*" which included the method of preparation, ingredients and baking time. She also stated that "*From ½ lb. to ¾ is usually allowed for each child – quantity made for Rhydyfro*

85 lbs flour
8½ " lard
8½ " sugar
30 " currants & raisins
132

All this after baking weighed 152 lbs."

The tea made in the tea-can for an estimated 120 children required:

"*1½ lbs of good tea*
6 qrts of fresh milk almost boiling
8 lbs moist sugar dissolved in 8 qrts. boiling water
14 or 15 gallons of boiling water"

"*This was the tea & cake given to the children of the Rhydyfro Schools Sep. 10th 1877.*"

Margaret Jones to Thomas Jones, 8 October 1878

Dear Mr. Jones,

I am sorry I have not been able to write sooner as I have been very poorly for some weeks. And now to the subject of your letter & before thinking of sanctioning any Engagement between you & Lizzie I must ask what your plans are, where you intend taking her to, and what your income be. I hope you will pardon my being so plain spoken but I only do what I consider my duty, as Lizzie has now no one to look to but myself, & it is well to talk & think over these matters before things go too far.

Lizzie's prospects are these. When she came here I told her Father that I did not expect or wish him to leave her any thing at his death, for that whatever each he would give her sisters, I would give her (not at my death, but whenever she left me). He left the girls £25 a year each, & that is what I shall give Lizzie. The <u>probability</u> is, that at my death she will also have this place settled upon herself & her children. I am very anxious for Lizzie's welfare &

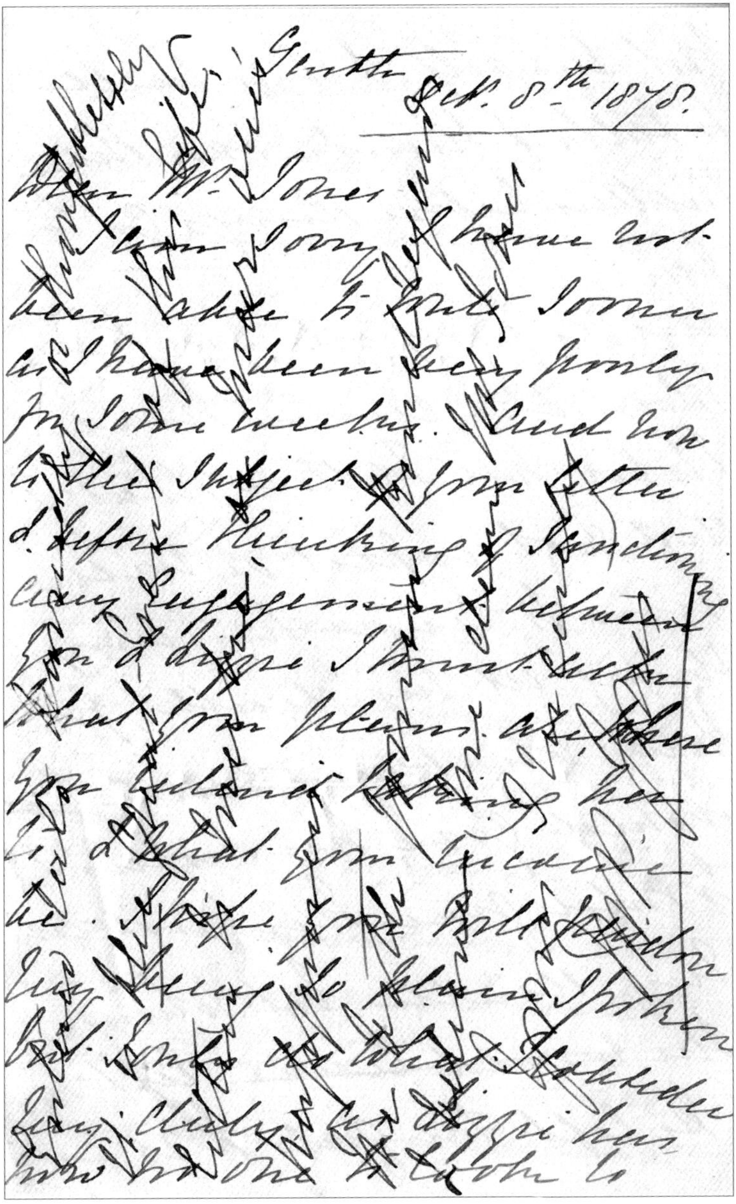

Oct. 8th 1878.

Dear Mr Jones

I am sorry I have not been able to write sooner as I have been very poorly for some weeks. And now to the subject of your letter & before thinking of sanctioning any engagement between you & Maggie I must learn what your plans are, where you intend taking her to & what your income is. [illegible]

Letter from Margaret to Thomas Jones, 8 October 1878
(Courtesy of Mrs J. Morris)

happiness, but please do not for a moment suppose that I am ambitious for her to marry a wealthy man with no other recommendation for I am not – I only want her to have a comfortable home & a kind good Husband. She is not strong & it would never do for her to have much anxiety. You must not think that because I am what people call an "old maid" that I disapprove of marriage, no, I do not, I consider it a very holy & sacred state, & if well matched a very happy one but certainly not one to be entered into hurridly or thoughtlessly. It is <u>the</u> great event of this life, either to make, or mar one's happiness.

We both join in kind regards & believe me dear Mr. Jones

Yours sincerely

M. P. Jones

Margaret Jones to Thomas Jones, 14 October 1878

Dear Mr. Jones,

Your letter of the 11th has a tone of candour in it which I believe, & from the little I know of you I am disposed to think well of you as an honest straight forward man & if I have cause to change my opinion I will let you know.

As a Malster there wd. never be a chance of your having Lizzie for she has such a great dislike to any business connected with Beer or Spirits, & both her Sisters having married in that time is I know a great trouble to her altho' poor girl she seldom speaks of it. As to a farm I am afraid she is very ill suited to be a farmer's wife inasmuch as she is not strong enough to undertake so much care & exertion for you must well know that when a Mistress has often to trust her Dairy & other things to a Servant any hope of much profit is at an end & in these days it requires people to be ever active & watchful for the days are past when Servants were honest in their labour & had a care for their Master's welfare. Dear Mr. Jones don't think me cruel when I write this for <u>now</u> is the time to look at things, not when it is too late, it does not so much matter how <u>near</u> a precipice one may be, not to fall over is the great point.

Perhaps you & Lizzie had better have a talk over things. Neither of you are children & I trust you would both give such an important matter your serious consideration. One thing I ought to say that is that I would never allow Lizzie to marry you or any one else under 12 months. This is Lizzie's home &

you are welcome to come here whenever you like. I shall always be glad to see you. With our united kind regards.

Believe me dear Mr. Jones

Yours sincerely

M. P. Jones

Lizzie Jones to an anonymous suitor, 2 January 1879

Dear Sir,

I am sorry I cannot give a favourable reply to your letter of the 28th ult. I am not at present engaged but must be honest and tell you that it is useless your thinking of me in any other light than that of a friend. I shall always be pleased to think of you as such and hope to see you attend Llanguicke Church as usual.

Wishing you a very happy new year, and with kind regards,

I remain dear Sir

Yours & sincerely

Lizzie Jones

John Davies, Land & Mineral Surveyor, to Margaret Jones, 28 January 1879

Madam,

On the other side you will please find an account of Coal &c. worked under Cwmllynfell during the year 1878 and also other Minerals taken through the same. I have been daily expecting to hear the Cwmllynfell Property has been sold, but I suppose the present position of the Coal & other trade will not induce people to look at Mineral Properties. I should like to know the highest bidding you have received for the place.

I am Madam

Yours faithfully

John Davies

Cwmllynfell

	Tons	cwts		£ .. s .. d
1st Quarter	699 ..	2	Coal @ 6d per ton	17 .. 9 .. 6½
	60 ..	4	Mine " 7d "	1 .. 15 .. 1¼
2nd Quarter	301 ..	16	Coal " 6d "	7 .. 10 ..10½
	26 ..	2	Mine " 7d "	15 .. 2½
3rd Quarter	416 ..	1	Coal " 6d "	10 .. 8
	3 ..	14	Mine " 7d "	2 .. 2
4th Quarter	231 ..	10	Coal " 6d "	5 .. 15 .. 9
	2 ..	1	Mine " 7d "	1 .. 2¼
				£43 .. 17 .. 10

Wayleave on Ystradowen Coal & Mine

				£ .. s .. d
1st Quarter	2985 ..	19	@ ½d per ton	6 .. 4 .. 5
2nd Quarter	1990	7	"	4 .. 2 .. 11
3rd Quarter	4210	2	"	8 .. 15 .. 5
4th Quarter	2455	13	"	5 .. 2 .. 3¾
				24 .. 5 .. 0¾
	Surface Damage			9 .. 0 .. 0
				33 .. 5 .. 0¾

Frances Hariette Lloyd, Kilybebyll, to Margaret Jones, 8 July 1879

Dear Miss Jones,

Will you and yr. Cousin come & lunch with us next Friday at 10? If very wet, I will not expect you, & we must settle another day in that case, instead.

With kind regards to you both.

Believe me

Yours sincerely,

F. H. Lloyd

1880

Margaret's continuing poor health dominated the year. Following a confirmed diagnosis of an ovarian tumour, Margaret suffered from localised peripheral swelling, abdominal distention and painful pressure on adjacent organs. These worrying symptoms prompted sombre memories of her father's oedema prior to his death. For the first quarter of the year she remained largely indoors, receiving a stream of visitors concerned for her wellbeing. Her only outside visit was to Llangiwg Church on Easter Day but her mood remained generally despondent with the expectation of an early death or becoming "a crippled painful invalid". She clung to the reassuring comfort of her "dear home" and not until the early Summer did she start making limited local journeys in her carriage. In November she was forced to take the train to Swansea in response to an urgent appeal to visit John Borlase Jenkins on his deathbed. Throughout the year and despite her poor physical condition she continued to record every incident, visitor and financial transaction in detail. The early references (10, 11 and 13 January) to Tom Jones (T.J.) and the subsequent frequency of his visits to Garth to meet Lizzie suggest a belated acceptance by Margaret of their continuing commitment following his request in September/October 1878 for permission to marry Lizzie.

Thursday 1 January: A little girl of Llwyn-Celyn came with her brothers before daylight to say "Blwyddyn Newydd Dda". I never heard of girls going about before. No good will follow. The Vicar & Mrs. W. R. Lloyd called, they had been to Llanguicke dividing the Charity money & then to J. Bowen Nantmole & were going to the Vicarage to a 5 o'clk. dinner. Little David Forchegel here to tea & supper. They removed some of their furniture &c. to the Maendy today from Cwmscwt.

Friday 2 January: Noticed 1st time a swelling very hard above both my ankles quite a lump on the inside & it is no good sign. Sent for Dr. Rees. Dr. Rees came 5.15, told him I had had a 2nd opinion Mr. Rogers whom I consulted last & that he pronounced it an Ovarian tumour, which in itself was not dangerous but sometimes brought on other diseases. Rees felt my bowels & said it was a tumour. In Oct '78, he thought it wind but it was much altered since then.

Saturday 3 January: Bowels very large & uncomfortable & very puffy all round my waist & hips, the same hard swelling above ankles & cold feet. I am

Fanny Gilbertson, July 1864, aged 20
(Photo: courtesy of Mrs J. Morris)

firmly of opinion the symptoms are those of Dropsy & I told the Dr. so yesterday, they are so like my poor Father's who only lived about 3 months after swelling began.[1] Fanny & M.G. [Madelina Gilbertson] called & Mrs. Richardson. Kate was very nice & seemed so sorry I was so poorly.

Sunday 4 January: Wet, only Evan to Church. I feel my throat, eyes & face swollen & stiff. Dr. Rees came in the afternoon, he said there was slight congestion of the Kidneys, he hoped the swelling would pass off. I do not think it will & I believe my time on earth is very short. Poor dear little Liz: I wish to live for her sake for she will be a lonely little waif without her old Mam & the World is a cold one.

Tuesday 6 January: Dr. Rees called, he thought me smaller in size.

Thursday 8 January: Revd. W. R. Lloyd called about 4 p.m., he had not dined took cold beef &c. & made his dinner when we took our tea, left at 7 in time for Service. Wrote to ask Mr. E. Strick if he could come up tomorrow, sent to say he could.

Saturday 10 January: Lizzie to Swansea 1st train, returned 4.10 train. Lloyd took her each way. She bought present for Tom [Jones] also lamp for me. She took letter to Bryn Syfi from me asking Miss Jenkins to give Mr. Ed. Strick the Deed of Settlement showing how I became possessed of the House at Neath. Lizzie dined at Bryn Syfi. Dr. Rees & the Vicar here when she came back. Lent the Vicar Newton's Sermons on Handel's Oratorio.

Sunday 11 January: No one to church. I am very poorly. T.J's birthday tomorrow (34). Lloyd to post with letter, & little parcel for him, Silver Scarf Pin, & Necktie from Lizzie, little card & Ivory Paper Knife from me. Had fire in my bedroom. Dr. said I must be kept very warm.

Monday 12 January: Margaret Gellyluog brought me oatmeal. Fanny G. called, her 2 Sisters walked up with her to bottom of road, she sent them back & she came & sat 1½ hours with Lizzie & I. She seemed very glad to find me a little better. She said she felt quite anxious after seeing me so ill last Saturday week when they called. I thought it kind in her to come & I felt really grateful, it is so pleasant to be remembered when ill. She wished me to have another

1. Dropsy: An abnormal accumulation of fluid in subcutaneous tissues and/or body cavities, symptomatic of nephritis and heart failure.

Dr's opinion. Said I wd. if I did not soon feel getting better. Harriet came to see how I was, said she would like coming back as servant, said I wd. take her at the rate of £7 a year until May. She is now in the Tin-Works & does not like being there.

Tuesday 13 January: Recd. very nice letter from T.J. acknowledging the little present yesterday.

Wednesday 14 January: Lloyd to Alltycham with letter from Lizzie saying she could not go there today. Lloyd for medicine, brought down belts. Dr. Rees came down in the afternoon, told him I was feeling better, & that as I was not increasing in size I wd. defer having the belts until I could go either to Bath or Bristol, for these do not fit me. He quite approved of it.

Thursday 15 January: Paid D. Morgan Llwynrhidie coal bill up to 31st Decr. last by cheque £2..5..8. He recommended Morgan Walters as carpenter living near Llwynrhidie. Recd. Draft Will from Mr. Ed. Strick.

Saturday 17 January: Had 1 ton of soft coal from Bevan 11/- pd. Lloyd had the Mill Mare with ours 2/6 pd. for loan of her. Daniel Gellyluog went with him but I did not pay him anything. I dare say he expected payment. We begin it next Wednesday.

Sunday 18 January: Evan, Lloyd & Betty to Church. Lizzie in the house with me. John Bowen Nantmole came to see me from Church & stayed to tea, very kind in him.

Monday 19 January: The Alltycham Coachman came to enquire how I was, with Mrs. Lewis's compliments.

Tuesday 20 January: Harriet came here this evening until May at the rate of £7..0..0 a year.

Friday 23 January: Dr. Rees came here, he said I must take the medicine regularly, said my blood was in a very weak state. Lizzie walked to Pontar-dawe, paid Jordan [Chemist] & Davies the Ironmongers. She also put James & Aubrey's cheque for £100 in the Bank at Interest. Ellen G. ran after her to ask how I was.

Sunday 25 January: Lizzie & Harriet to Church. Lizzie sent two of her photos to T.H. by Gwen Walters.

Thursday 29 January: Dr. Rees called this evening in his way from Pontardawe, they had been appointing Master & Matron to the New Workhouse (Mr. & Mrs. Short from New Castle on Tyne). He brought back Dr. Syntax & Family Herald which I had lent his brother.

Friday 30 January: Miss Shenton walked down to see me, came here about 12 o'clk. We all had tea & eggs for dinner as Betty was ill in bed & Harriet had a bad finger. Lloyd took her home in the Phaeton.

Saturday 31 January: Betty very ill. Offered to send Lloyd for Griffiths the Dr., she said no, she could go down herself, & so she did & she came back about 5 o'clk. Sally here, paid £20 on a/c of the note of hand & 6/6 interest to this date thereon, gave her receipt. Paid her 1/- for altering Lizzie's black silk dress being all we owe her. William Cwmllynfell here. Talked to him about John's leaving this farm, said he wd. come down any time if he could help me in any way.

Sunday 1 February: Lizzie walked to Church. T.H. told her he had been to Llandilo, that he saw T.J. Mrs. Harris Gartheithen came up to see me. She took tea with us. Told her how odd & disagreeable Betty was.

Wednesday 4 February: Fanny, Kate & Mrs. Arthur G. called to see me, in the pony carriage. Kate & her 5 children leave for Liverpool tomorrow. Lizzie went to the Kitchen 7.10 p.m. with a penny for Harriet to fetch burum [yeast]. Lloyd in the Dairy scraping off the salt from the flitches of bacon. Lizzie asked who was going to wash it, said she was, Lizzie said you are ill, no one is to touch it until tomorrow, when I will wash it myself.

Thursday 5 February: Lizzie & Lloyd washed the bacon (2nd pig) & floured it all ready for hanging up after dinner.

Sunday 8 February: Lizzie walked to Church, Lloyd & Evan, Harriet to Pontardawe about her finger. She paid Maryanne 1/- for doctoring it. The Vicar Communion.

Tuesday 10 February: Dr. Rees called examined my chest said my cough was from "Dry Bronchitis". Revd. Mr. Lloyd called, he stayed to tea. The Vicar called, John Morgan waiting outside in the Dogcart. Lizzie in the Phaeton to Pontardawe. Put £40 in the Bank (Int. a/c), bought coal riddle, 2 doz. Beer from Fulton (1st this year). Esther back here asking if I would do my best to get her daughter Catherine appointed sewing mistress to Rhydyfro School. Said I wd. speak of her to the Board but that I cd. say nothing of her.

Ash Wednesday 11 February:

			s .. d
Commenced	5½lbs. best Parlour Candles		4 .. 10
"	6½ lbs. Cottage composites		3 .. 3
"	yesterday 1 Gal. Paraffin		1 .. 2
"	27 Janry. 1 Gal. Benzoline		1 .. 4
"	this day 6 boxes N. Lights 7 hours		2 .. 6
		Paid	13 .. 1

Saturday 14 February: Dr. Rees called this afternoon, examined my bowels. Said he was now decided in his opinion that it was an "Ovarian Tumour".

Sunday 15 February: Lloyd to see Mrs. Day at Tarranau Gleison. Evan & Harriet to Church, she took back Mrs. Davies' umbrella lent Lizzie yesterday week. Lizzie at home all day, she finished reading the "Pocket Bible". We were both very pleased with the Tale, it was lent her by Mrs. Price.

Tuesday 17 February: Miss Jenkins came up to see me. Lloyd met her with the Carriage 11.30. I do not remember that she has been here since she came to see Lizzie when she was so ill. Fanny G. called. Mr. Lloyd called on horseback but wd. not stay to tea.

Wednesday 18 February: Miss Jenkins intended returning this evening 5 train but it came on too wet. Recd. letter from Mrs. Bowman saying her brother William, his wife & child returned from India last Novr. on sick leave & that he died 17 Janry. last (at Dublin with his mother-in-law I think). Had from Williams (1st this year) ½ Gal. Gin, ½ Gal. Brandy, ½ Gal. Whisky, 1 doz. Sherry, ½ doz. Marsala, 1 doz. Tarragona. We shall begin all these at once (none in house).

Thursday 19 February: Miss Jenkins left today midday train. Lloyd took her to the Station in the Carriage. She said she enjoyed coming up. John the tenant had heifer calf today for £1 paid.

Friday 20 February: ***** M[argaret]. Evan at Gellyluog cutting Birch for brooms, also sawing some large trees in the hedges that were too much over the Road. Johnny Gellyluog helping him. Put Wine & Spirits had Wednesday in the Pantry. Harriet broke one bot. Tarragona in unpacking the case last night.

Saturday 21 February: Dr. Rees called. Told him I felt much smaller & much more comfortable, the kidneys act better, he told me to go out a little every fine day & that then I might go to Bryn Syfi. How I do hope I shall continue better. He stayed to tea, lanced Harriet's hand. Said Griffith Rees the Mason died about 3 weeks ago. Lloyd fetched load of Birch for Brooms from Gellyluog. Harriet to Pontardawe for meat from Evan Jones.

Sunday 22 February: Lizzie walked to Church. Harriet, Evan & Lloyd. Shani Bryngwina's banns out.

Monday 23 February: I wrote to Miss Jenkins at Glantwrch saying I was better. Lizzie with letters to post, came back by Abraham's. Took his daughter little wine & cake, she is a little better. Lloyd put rhubarb tidy after he had done it up with fresh earth, & Evan had put stones to keep earth up, he replanted rhubarb. I went to the Garden for a few minutes the 1st time this year.

Tuesday 24 February: Mrs. Bowen Nantmole came to see me hearing I was ill. She stayed to tea & left at 7.30. A nice moonlight night. Lloyd & Evan cut down large Scotch Fir overhanging the Wall to the road upper side of front gate. I was sorry to part with the old friend, but Lizzie wished it so much. Walked with Lizzie round the Walks & then Heol-y-Cefn to Iron Gate, the 1st time I had been that way this year. A nice day.

Wednesday 25 February: Lloyd & Evan getting up stump of evergreen oak that we cut down last Spring. The Green will I think look much better without it, it threw out nice young shoots last Summer, but the Winter caused them to wither & die. They put the turf all right after & it looks tidy. I ironed 6 d'oleys & combed the fringe in the parlour. I had begun them yesterday when Mrs. Bowen came. Lizzie recd. a letter from Jane saying she was going to send us a salmon today. Lloyd to the Garnant Station for it. It came in a cheese box beautifully packed & a nice fish 10 lbs.

Thursday 26 February: Paid J. Jones Crachllwyn Garth Poor Rate:

Garth farm	£47 .. 0..0 @ 1/-	£2..7..0	
" cottage	2 .. 0..0 "	2..0	
3 Cots Cwmllynfell	7..10..0 "	7..6	
Smithshop	1..15..0 "	1..9	
	£58.. 5..0		£2..18 .. 3
		less Commission	2 .. 4
			£2..15..11
		land tax	14 .. 7
		House duty	15 .. 0
Garth In. tax on £50 @ 5d.			1 .. 0..10
Cottage " " £2 "			10
		Paid by cheque	£5 .. 7 .. 2

Friday 27 February: Lizzie & Harriet to Llanguicke yesterday to clean up & take down some of the decorations. Mr. Lloyd called at 5 p.m. (yesterday), took tea. Lloyd drove him down to the Church. He brought me some herrings wh. I thought so kind. John Thomas Gwranllwyn here, paid me £10 on a/c of timber had.

Saturday 28 February: Lloyd drove Lizzie to call on the Brynamman Curate, Mr. Morlais Jones & his wife. Had leg of veal from H.W. Thomas Brynamman butcher 11 lbs @ 8½d, 7/9. Very nice meat. Harriet & Lloyd to Rhydyfro Concert 7.30 back 10.40. T.J. came here 8.45 p.m. Walked from Garnant, dry night, roads dirty. Lloyd cleaned heaps away in Heol y Cefn wh. Evan had gathered.

Sunday 29 February: Pastoral Aid collection at Llanguicke. Very wet & showery. Only Evan & Harriet to Church. Sent 2/6 by Harriet for Collection. T.J. & Lizzie singing Hymns a.m. and after tea Belle Mahone.[2] He talked more than usual & made himself very pleasant. He looks delicate.

Monday 1 March: Paid Howell John, Gellyluog In. & Land Tax on the Woodland 1 yr. ending April 1880 1s.5½d. Lloyd to Pontardawe Station for coal had 13 cwt @ 6½d (the first) 7/-. Our own mare brought it up. T.J. left at 7 a.m. in time for 1st train from Garnant. He walked, a dry windy morning.

2. A popular sentimental song written by J. H. McNaughton in 1867 which speaks of grief at the death of "Sweet Belle Mahone" who is asked to "Wait for me at Heaven's gate" by her bereaved lover.

Wednesday 3 March: Lloyd to Llangavelach fair. Wet & windy. A woman from Cwmllynfell (Morgan Morgan's Wife) came to ask if I would let them have the Works Smithshop & the front half of the house Mr. Brock used to occupy. Said I wd. let her know in 9 days or a fortnight. Had 6 doz. Beer, 2 doz. Porter (Williams).

Thursday 4 March: William Williams, Plas y Bryn here paying ½ a year's rent, also £2..0..0 for Rachel Davies. He said his wife had a wish to remove to the house that they used to live in. Lloyd put hooks to hold up the large boarding by Dog's cwb [coop] instead of cord & nails. Dr. Rees called. He had not been here since 21st Feb. Thought I had gone to Bryn Syfi, told him I was not nearly as well since Monday. I am now in much pain in my bowels, hip &c, & getting again much larger.

Friday 5 March: My hip & side of my bowels, & right side of my back indeed the whole of my right side is very painful from my shoulder to my ankle. I did not suffer nearly as much pain before as I do now. I do not think I shall ever be even as well as I was 6 months ago.

Saturday 6 March: Felt great pain in the side of my bowels, when winding the clock this night.

Sunday 7 March: Harriet, Lloyd & Evan to Church. Lizzie, Betty & I in the house. Showers.

Monday 8 March: Wm. Cwmllynfell called to see how I was. Evans the Post Office came up to explain to me about a "Bill of two months" which John my tenant proposed giving me instead of £47 in cash wh. he had promised giving me today. Mr. Evans drew out the bill, wh. I was willing to accept provided John could get either his Brother or Brother-in-law to sign with him. Obliged to have hot flannels put to my back & bowels after going to bed, the pain was so great.

Tuesday 9 March: Dr. Rees called 1.15. Stayed to dinner, left at 4. Told him I was in great pain round my waist & bowels, recommended my wearing a flannel bandage & wished I would go to London to consult a Doctor as soon as the weather came fine. John failed to get any one to sign the bill with him. Told him I thought it wd. be better for him to leave the 25th inst., as I could see but very little prospect in his getting better off. Had 4 doz. Beer from Fulton, 6 doz. Bot. Fulton's beer now in the house including the above had today.

Wednesday 10 March: Harriet & I cleaned out little Kitchen cupboards. Thos. Howells Cefnllan called & stayed to tea the first time I ever saw him here.

Thursday 11 March: Mrs. Thomas & Miss Shenton walked down to see me. Came 2.30 left 7.30. Lloyd drove them up, brought me a seed loaf & night cap for a pattern. Anna Llewellyn (Craig Llanguicke) came to see me, brought oranges, biscuits & peppermint drops.

Friday 12 March: Lizzie to Brynamman for meat. Wrote to Dr. Rees saying I was in great pain at times & that I would wish Dr. Rogers & himself to meet here. Wrote back to say he would write & ask him what day he wd. come.

Monday 15 March: The two Miss Lewis Alltycham called to know how I was. Harriet said I was lying down, so they did not come in. The first time the girls ever called.

Tuesday 16 March: Revd. Mr. & Mrs. Jones, Curate of Brynamman called. Lizzie saw them. I did not. Sorry we could not ask them to stay to tea. Dr. Rees & Dr. Rogers met here at 5 p.m. Rogers is of the same opinion as he was 18 months ago, that it is an Ovarian tumour. Both Drs. agree in their opinions, they say if it does not increase in size I may live for years & that if it does enlarge that its removal wd. be desirable.

Wednesday 17 March: Fanny G. called. The Vicar called but would not stay. Mr. Lloyd came up 5.30 stayed to tea & left 10.30.

Saturday 20 March: Mrs. Kirkhouse came to see me. She drove up at 2.30 in Alltycham Phaeton, she merely took a cup of tea in the Drawing room, said she wd. come up this day 3 weeks. Lloyd finished turfing flower beds and other bad places, planted Deutzia Grasalis opposite front door, & also fuschias.

Palm Sunday 21 March: Lizzie, Lloyd, Harriet [to Church].

Monday 22 March: F. & M. Gilbertson walked up to see me.

Tuesday 23 March: Old Mr. Harris of Pantybettws buried today at Bettws Church aged 66. Lizzie to the funeral (fine day). She went by 11 train & stayed at Margaret's until the funeral came. Came back last train. Young David Forch-egel came to see me. The Vicar called when we were at tea & joined us. Mr.

Jones waited until Lizzie came, & Lloyd drove him as far as Gellygron. He was very friendly. Old Hannah Bryngwina here, told her if they had the cleaning of the Church that they must keep it clean & well dusted.

Thursday 25 March: John Harries of Liverpool came here at 12 o'clk. the first time I saw him, & from the little I saw, I liked him. He seemed a quiet respectable man & I think Sarah has been lucky. He left at 6 o'clk. Lizzie went to send him as far as Cwmgorse.[3]

Good Friday 26 March: Lizzie, Lloyd & Harriet to Llanguicke at 11 a.m. Mr. Lloyd walked with Lizzie as far as Cefn Llan (23 people in Church). Two children were Christened at Llanguicke. Mr. Lloyd asked Lizzie to go down by the Font to respond. I do not at all approve of it & I am not pleased with Lizzie for going for she knew I wd. disapprove of it. Selina came to see Harriet & to know if she wanted a frock. Mrs. Harris Gartheithen came to see me.

Saturday 27 March: Recd. letter from Mrs. Griffiths Cwmllynfell yesterday saying Messrs J. & A. were pulling down some walls about the Colliery & carting the stones to their premises. Today I send copy of his letter to Mr. Ed. Strick as being his Clients I think he ought to know what they are doing. Lizzie to Brynamman to the Butchers.

Easter Day 28 March: Lloyd drove Lizzie & I to Church. The first time for me to be at Llanguicke this year, an excellent congregation & a lovely day, how very dear the old Church is to me & how glad I am to see a good congregation there, all the old attendants seemed so glad to see me for they knew I had been very ill. Sacrament: The Vicar, Harriet, Betty & Evan to Church.

Monday 29 March: Tom Jones came here 11.30 train from Pontardawe, left here 8.30 p.m. & walked all the way to Llandilo getting to "The Walk" about 12 o'clk. The last night he would sleep at "The Walk" as tomorrow his brother removes from there to "Waterloo Villa". I think Tom is sorry to leave the old home. Dr. Rees called, did not stay to tea. Samuel the Carpenter's wife here asking if I could lend them money. Said I could not.

Wednesday 31 March: Paid Harriet for wages up to yesterday & advanced her 7/- to get things.

3. John Harries had married Lizzie's sister Sarah in June 1878.

Monday 12 April: A man from Mr. Marquiss Swansea [*Geo. & S. Marquiss, Painters, 46 Oxford Street*] came up to paper & paint third room & room above dining room. Dr. Walters, his wife & his son Walter drove up here at 12.30.

Thursday 15 April: Evan & Lloyd had some words this evening about an old grocery box that the former was going to make a coal box of. At tea time Evan put himself tidy & went away without saying a word to either Lizzie or myself. I think he behaved shamefully after I had given him work for such a long time & the times so bad, but they are all an ungrateful, runaway family.

Saturday 17 April: Lloyd drove Lizzie to Brynamman 1st train to meet her sister Margaret & her two little girls who were coming to see me before removing to Dowlais. I had not seen Margaret since she was married. She seemed sorry I was so poorly & wished I wd. consult Dr. Lloyd. They left here 4.30 p.m. to meet last train. Edith was a dear little girl, Annie pretty well. Revd. W. R. Lloyd called after they left & stayed till Lizzie returned.

Friday 23 April: The two Miss Salmons & Miss Barbara St. John came here to tea from Glantwrch, the former in the Carriage, the latter on horseback. Mrs. Price sent some nice flowers by them, they were all very friendly & seemed to enjoy the few hours they were here. Sally & her little girl here, Lizzie gave her tatting [knotted lace].

Saturday 24 April: Catherine (John's daughter) came home from Mrs. Richardson's.

Sunday 25 April: Lizzie walked to Church. Harriet to Chapel at 6 p.m. Betty to Ystalyfera, found Evan there. Gave her £1..0..0.

Monday 26 April: The Vicar came here at 5 p.m., stayed to tea, & made himself very friendly. Left 9.15. Mrs. Jones at Ynismeudw. Charlie Day came here to ask if I could lend him £4 for a few weeks to pay for some sheep, said I could not. He said his Mother and Jenny had been to Devonshire & sold the houses for £300, that his Aunt Eliza was to be married shortly & that his Aunt Emma was very ill with cancer.

Wednesday 28 April: Dr. Rees called here 4.10 p.m. on his way home from Rhydyfro School Board meeting. He stayed to tea.

Friday 30 April : Lloyd drove Lizzie 1st train to Garnant. She went to see Ben Jones at Llwyn-yr-Onen, his mother had come up last night to see him. She returns tomorrow & he goes on Monday. He will have been there nearly 3 weeks & is much better for the change.

Monday 3 May: Painter came up 11.30 train, here at 12.45.

Tuesday 4 May: Powell papered staircase, the old paper cleaned off to the bare walls. It looks exceedingly clean & nice now.

Wednesday 5 May: Powell varnished upstairs doors & painted staircase window, the stairs to be all new grained as the steps are so shabby.

Thursday 6 May: R.P.L. came here, he walked from Brynamman, the 1st time he was here this year. I had never written to tell him I was ill. He left last train from Pontardawe. The Vicar & Mr. Lloyd called here in the Dog cart 3 p.m. & took Lizzie for a drive as far as Brynamman, came back 5.15. Mr. Lloyd went on to Pontardawe for Service. The Vicar stayed to tea & went with R.P.L.

Friday 7 May: Lizzie to the Bank with School pence. Met by Gellygron the Vicar, the two Ystalyfera Curates & Dr. Griffiths, they had been to the Rhydyfro School. Mr. Jones drove the two Curates (Jones & Williams) to call here (the first time they ever were here), all stayed to tea & all seemed very friendly. Went to Cae Barriwns to see the potatoes that Lloyd was setting.

Saturday 8 May: Dr. Rees called, stayed to tea. John Gellyluog finished paying his rent to last Sep. The farm was to have been £40 from 1879 March to 1880 March but as he complained of the times I divided the increased £5 making it £37..10 per year. Paid Johnny for helping Evan with wood, 3/-. Lloyd finished setting the potatoes in top of Cae Barriwns where trees had been.

Friday 14 May: Poor Mrs. Budd died here suddenly this day aged 64 years. Her loss will be greatly felt by her Husband, the poor people & indeed everybody for she was so kind & good.[4]

4. Emily Budd (née Rawson) was born in Halifax in 1815. She married James Palmer Budd (1803-83), managing partner of the Ystalyfera Iron and Tinplate Works. They lived in Ynysydarren House, Ystalyfera.

Saturday 15 May: Miss Ford called & brought me lovely flowers, she was very friendly. She is much nicer when alone than with her Cousins the G's [Gilbertsons]. Lizzie went to her Sister Jane's by last train, to stay until Tuesday morning.

Whitsun Day 16 May: Lloyd & Harriet to Llanguicke, Betty & I in the house all day. I am feeling very poorly & often in great pain in my bowels & hips & all round me. I do not expect to see another Whit Sunday on Earth, or if I do, I expect it will be as a crippled & painful invalid. Jenny Day here. Lizzie & Jane to Bettws Church a.m. Lizzie & T.J. to Llandebie Church at 6 p.m.

Monday 17 May: Lizzie & T.J. to Builth. They both enjoyed the day & liked the place very much. They dined at "The Lion" with the M.P. for Radnor. Tom sent me a bottle of eau-de-cologne. Lizzie bought a white chip bonnet for herself.

Tuesday 18 May: Lizzie returned 1st train a.m. Lloyd meeting her at Brynamman. I trimmed Lizzie's bonnet bought yesterday with pretty snowdrop wreath Willy sent from Brighton.

Wednesday 19 May: Confirmation at Cwmamman. Near 200 confirmed of all ages. Lloyd drove Lizzie to Cwmamman. She lunched at the Vicarage with the Bishop of St. David's, Archdeacon James & several others, returned here about 7 p.m. We had both been invited, but I was not well enough to go.

Thursday 20 May: I put up white curtains. Revd. N. Thomas came here 7 p.m. He had taken tea at Sarah Morgan's. I had not seen him since 25 April 1879.

Friday 21 May: Mrs. Thomas & Miss Clark walked down. Lloyd drove them home. Miss Clark seemed to enjoy her evening & liked the place, the 1st she was here. Revd. N. Thomas left by 7.10 p.m. train. He walked to Pontardawe.

Sunday 23 May: Lizzie walked to Church. Lloyd & Harriet, Betty & I in the house.

Wednesday 26 May: Mrs. Kirkhouse walked up to see me, stayed to tea. Lloyd drove her home. It came on very wet about 5 p.m. Rain is much needed. The 2 old women sweeping & cleaning Heol y Cefn, they did it very nicely & Lloyd cleared away the rubbish.

Thursday 27 May: Harriet finished sweeping & cleaning from Cae Barriwns gate to Coach House gate. I never saw all the back so beautifully clean, it gave me <u>great pleasure</u> to walk up from Iron Gate to the house & see all so nice & the afternoon <u>was lovely</u>. Garth & its surroundings are to my mind <u>very pretty</u> when tidy, <u>dear</u> home of my childhood! <u>In thee may I die</u>.

Friday 28 May: Mrs. & Miss Ford called in Pony Carriage. Brought me beautiful flowers, the 1st time <u>Mrs</u> Ford has been here since W.G. [William Gilbertson] turned Lizzie out of the Pew. She was very nice and friendly. They came the Back road which is <u>exceedingly tidy</u> from Iron Gate to the Coach House.

Saturday 29 May: Griffith Evans here. Paid him £3..0..0 for his services in playing the Harmonium at Llanguicke Church from Easter 1879 to Easter 1880. Harriet to Swansea to buy Boots, dress &c. Spent 7/-.

Sunday 30 May: I am feeling <u>very poorly</u>, in bed all day until 5 p.m. Lizzie & Harriet in the house, Betty & Lloyd to Church.

Monday 31 May: Griffiths Cefnllan called to see me (hearing yesterday I was not well) in his way to Brynamman. Lizzie ironed Sarah's 12 towels & tablecloth. Harriet & I cleaned the Silver with "Goddard's Plate Powder" <u>1st time</u>.

Tuesday 1 June: Old Mary Thomas (Mrs. Thomas Cwmamman's sister-in-law) came here under the pretence of coming to see me, but really to ask if I wd. give her something, gave her 2/-. Mrs. Davies Forchegel came to see me hearing I was very poorly, she also came to ask if they should cut the grass in the Church yard for the cows, told her I wd. ask Mr. Jones & let her know again. Had 2 doz. Beer (Fulton) <u>all paid to this day</u>. Lloyd mowing the Green. Harriet, Betty, Old Betty & Lizzie all helping to clean.

Wednesday 2 June: Nanny Cwmllynfell came here to ask for the loan of <u>a sovereign</u> until Septr, lent her £1..0..0. Wm. Lewis came to see me. Lizzie & Harriet cleaning & raking the Walk, picking up all large stones. Lloyd putting long stone post to hold up the earth by side of front gate.

Thursday 3 June: Unpacked Beer & Porter had 3rd March.

6 dozn. Bottles of Beer – Williams
3 " " " Porter – "
6 " " " Beer – Fulton

This makes 17 dozn. of Beer & Porter wh. is <u>all</u> that is in the house.

Wednesday 9 June: Miss Jenkins came up 11.30 train. I went in the carriage to meet her.

Friday 11 June: Miss Jenkins left last train, Lizzie took her to the station in the carriage. Lizzie met young David Forchegel at the Station coming from Oxford, he had had his B.A. & hopes to be ordained in Septr.

Saturday 12 June: Lloyd to Ty Isha Waingurwen for 4 cwt of long hay @ 5/6d. £1..2..0 paid. Sent for Dr. Rees. I am very ill & in great pain this evening. Said he wd. come tomorrow. Mrs. Jones Llwynrhidie ill in scarlet fever.

Sunday 13 June: No one to Church. Dr. Rees came down this evening, saw me in bed, said I was very weak & that he thought the thunder had upset me.

Tuesday 15 June: Margaret Thos y Gove (Jonah Pistill Llwyd's wife) buried today age 34 next August.

Monday 21 June: Dr. Walters called 9.30 a.m. on his way to Llandrindod Wells. Mrs. Walters who is very weak goes by 12 o'clk. train from Swansea to Llanwrtyd where they stay the night. He had heard I was ill & seemed very sorry to see me in bed. He read 2 Cor: V Chap. & gave such a nice prayer. He was very kind & wished much I was well enough to go to the Wells & to share his carriage. Dr. Rees called (thought me rather stronger) walked with him & Liz. round the front. Liz. gave him flower seeds, he stayed to tea. Planted out in Lizzie's bed by front gate 11 carnation cuttings given by Mrs. Thomas Septr. 19th 1879, also 13 cuttings given by Mrs. Kirkhouse last week.

Wednesday 23 June: Had basket of geraniums &c. from Wheeler Glos'ter. Lloyd had Polly shod by Pontardawe Blacksmith 1st time, 3/6 paid.

Thursday 24 June: Betty limed the Court.

Friday 25 June: William cleaning & edging the pebbles in Heol y Cefn which had not been done since poor old D.M.'s death 3 yrs. ago. Betty limed the cow house & washed the doors & flags, it is now clean & the drains all right. Dr. Griffiths & the Vicar called about 6 p.m., they had been for a ride over Gellyonen, Baran & down by Pwll-y-Watkin. Hannah Bryngwina brought me a fowl.

Saturday 26 June: William finished Heol y Cefn & began turning heap behind the stumps. Lloyd carrying off stones & dirt on Heol y Cefn. Harriet & Lizzie finished the Walk, the front is now exceedingly clean & tidy. Betty limed the Dairy.

Sunday 27 June: Lizzie walked to Church. Anne, Harriet's sister here. They both went to Church, also Lloyd, Einon, Catherine & Mary. Betty & I at home. Had a roast fowl for tea. Liz and I enjoyed it.

Monday 28 June: Lizzie wrote to her brother acknowledging his letter & P.O.O. [Post Office Order] of yesterday. Sent a receipt for her money due last March. Fanny G. called, she came home from London last Friday week. She said Mrs. Bowman was much better that some Dr. abroad had done her great good. Revd. W. R. Lloyd called, stayed to tea. He had not been here for 6 or 7 weeks. I don't know why.

Thursday 1 July: William turning heap & putting manure with it inside Cae Barriwns gate. Lloyd opening gutter under the Wall from John's Pistle to little hill gate by our hay house.

Friday 2 July:

In the Pantry

6	bot.	Gin
6	"	Whiskey
6	"	Brandy
25	"	Sherry
6	"	Port
5	"	Tarragona
2	"	Marsala

In the Pantry

Beer **W**		36 bot.
"	Fulton	72 "

In Cupboards

Beer **W**
Porter **W**

No spirits in the house except a little Gin & Brandy in the Stand, & a little Sherry in the Decanter.

Saturday 3 July: Dr. Walters called & took tea in his way from Llandrindod.

Sunday 4 July: Lizzie to Church, Betty & Lloyd. Harriet in the house with me. She went to Chapel at 6 p.m. After tea Lizzie & I walked up to Pen-Cae-Lan, the 1st time I had been on the hill this year, a lovely evening but rather windy. After coming down we went to John's & he showed us the Bible & lent Liz. the Apocrapha.

Monday 5 July: Harriet & I planting daisies under kitchen window a.m. John Halifax called. Harriet & I planted pansy cuttings under Court wall p.m. Miss Shenton & Miss Clark called, stayed to tea. Lloyd drove them to the "Mountain". Wm. Jones began mowing Wain-Hir. Had 18 gal of Beer from Williams.

Tuesday 6 July: Very wet. Lloyd cut down arbutus tree by drawing room window, it was all dying away. I cannot think why, it used to look very nice. Dr. Rees called, stayed a very short time being wet.

Wednesday 7 July: My dear little Lizzie's birthday. I gave her black & white cotton frock. N.T. [Rev. Nathaniel Thomas] gave her Brooch (College Cap shape).

Margaret Jones to (possibly) John Davies, Surveyor, 10 July 1880

Dear Sir,

My tenant William Griffiths was here yesterday & he said he thought you & Mr. Hay would be going to Cwmllynfell some day in next week. I beg you will see that all is done properly & the place given up in safety and according to the Conditions of the Lease. If my memory is correct I think there used to be a bridge or some mode of communication between Cwmllynfell and Ty Newydd &c. That was all very well when the lease was in force but now that has terminated I must beg you will see that all communication between Messrs. James & Aubrey's land and mine ceases, and that all persons & animals from henceforth crossing over my property will be trespassers & treated as such. Wm. Griffiths is in no way authorized by me to give . . . [*last page missing*]

Margaret's Diary entry for 21 July 1880 confirmed the action taken by John Davies.

Sunday 11 July: Lizzie & Harriet walked to Church. At 3 p.m. Lloyd drove me from here to Languicke, thinking to be in time for the Sacrament but I got there just in time for the Sermon. Lloyd waited with Phaeton outside. I think I never was so glad as to see the dear old place, I really cried with joy to be once again in the old Church & the communicants (18) seemed so glad to see me.

Wednesday 14 July: Lizzie & Harriet raking Walk & cleaning up the front. D.W.J. at John's. Mr. & Mrs. Griffiths Cwmamman called & stayed to tea, they were very pleasant & thanked us for our subscriptions for Brynamman New Church. Mr. Griffiths said he had been asked by a Carmel Deacon to build a Church or some place for Church worship between the Star & Wain cae-gurwen. He wanted me to promise £200 towards it & that it should be called St. Margaret's & that the Curate of that place could also officiate at Llanguicke if our Vicar wished. I wish I was rich enough to give the money, but I am not.

Saturday 17 July: Mary the Blacksmith buried today at Baran. Lloyd & Einon to the funeral. Harriet was to have gone but it came on very wet & very heavy & near thunder (age 34 last March). Lizzie received "Beeton's Dictionary", 2 vol. from T.J. a beautiful & useful book & one I hope she will often read. It was to have been a Birthday present but being quite a new edition, there was a delay in getting it.

Sunday 18 July: Lloyd, Harriet & Betty to Church. Lizzie & I in the house. Recd. "Standard" from N.J. showing Gynlais was taken up for theft at St. Bartholomews.

Monday 19 July: Maud Gilbertson 19 years old today.

Wednesday 21 July: Fanny G. & Mrs. Ford called, brought me some nice flowers. Showed them Lizzie's birthday present, they liked the books very much. Heavy thunder after tea. Recd. letter from Mr. Davies saying he had been up to Cwmllynfell & that Mr. Hay had put all the pits &c. safe & that the keys of the vacant cottage had been given Wm. Griffiths. Lloyd cut down branch overhanging closet, and Harriet cleared away some of the stumps.

Thursday 22 July: William commenced cutting Cae Barriwns hay. Finished mowing the Meadow & the Croften yesterday. Very heavy thunder showers. Water flowing over Receiver. Lloyd took the pipes down & put round tin in Receiver to prevent small leaves choking it.

Friday 23 July: Lloyd drove Lizzie to Pontardawe. She put School pence in Bank &c. Had 40 lbs flour & 6d. potatoes.

Sunday 25 July: Lizzie, Lloyd & Harriet to Church. Betty & I in the house. Mr. Lloyd.

Tuesday 27 July: Lizzie wrote to Daniels. Lizzie to Rhyd-y-fro school 2nd time to the sewing. Spoke to John's people about their geese being in the Green yesterday a.m. and this morning, they make such a mess. Recd. letter from Fanny Salmon from Tenby enclosing her two photos. She wishes Liz & I were down with them. They are at 20 Norton with a Miss Williams.

Wednesday 28 July: Dr. Rees called in his way from Rhyd-y-fro School Board, took tea & stayed till 7.30. Said Ted was at home. Lizzie, Lloyd & Harriet in the Phaeton to Pontardawe Church. All the School children (Sunday) there celebrating the Centenary (or 100 years). Dr. Walters addressed the children in Welsh and Revd. Mr. Wolfe (Sailors Home) Swansea in English. Mrs. Walters & Walter there but Lizzie was not near enough to speak to them.

Thursday 29 July: Lizzie & I took a quiet walk up to Cae Cwtta along Heol y Cefn & home round the road, at the bottom of Heol y Ty met Mrs. Whittington & Mrs. Griffiths coming to call & to ask if Lizzie should go with them to the Children's tea on Saturday, said she should. The first time they were ever in the house.

Friday 30 July: Young Walters Llansamlet drove up to see how I was after tea, said they all intended coming up soon. Stayed to supper & left at 9 p.m.

Saturday 31 July: Lizzie walked down to Dr. Griffiths & went with Mrs. Griffiths to the Sunday School tea drinking on Tyn Pant field. Lloyd fetched her at 7 p.m.

Sunday 1 August: Only Lloyd to Church. I was taken suddenly sick at 1 p.m. & Lizzie stayed with me. Betty ill in bed. Harriet to Pontardawe Church, told her she ought to have gone to Saron as I told her & also that she was to come home quickly. She was by 9 but she wd. have been sooner from Rhyd-y-fro.

Tuesday 3 August: Lizzie went down last train to Bryn Syfi. Miss Jenkins had asked her to come & stay there during the Swansea Eisteddfod which begins tomorrow.

Wednesday 4 August: William began mowing Cae Front 10 a.m. Lloyd cutting border under John's house, rather inclined to be impertinent & that he wd. not like to call at Old Betty Matthew's door unless they were up, not even when passing there after 6 a.m. even if I told him to do so. Told him that shd. I require the old woman any time of night or day, that I shd. expect my servant to obey orders, & that if he would not do so, I must find a man that would. He really is getting touchy that there is hardly any managing him.

Thursday 5 August: Recd. letter from Lizzie asking me to send down midday train her opera cloak & my white shawl &c. &c. as she was going to one of the Grand Eisteddfod Concerts. Did so. R.P.L. came by 11.30 train, left the last train. Walked both ways. He is 67 years old today & wonderfully strong & active for his age. Carried the vetches & some of Cae Barriwns hay.

Friday 6 August: I was very poorly all night & in great pain. Got up midday feeling easier. I hemmed Llanguicke White Cloth, it was torn both ends.

Saturday 7 August: Lizzie returned 4 o'clk. train from Bryn Syfi after being there since Tuesday. Miss Jenkins took her to the Mumbles Hill last Wednesday & she enjoyed the view.

Sunday 8 August: Lizzie, Harriet, Lloyd & Betty to Church. Young Walters Llansamlet came with Mr. Jones to Llanguicke, he had done some duty at the Reading Room, Mr. Lloyd having gone for his holiday. Sacrament.

Sunday 15 August: Lloyd drove Lizzie and I to Church gate.

Thursday 19 August: Fanny G. and Miss England called.

Sunday 22 August: Lloyd drove Lizzie and I to Church gate.

Monday 23 August: T.J. came up from the Mumbles 4 o'clk. train.

Tuesday 24 August: T.J. & Lizzie went after dinner for a walk to Gellyonen Mountain, the 1st time Liz. was ever there, they had tea at the "Spa", returned here at 8 o'clk. exactly. Poor Mrs. Whittington died 8.30 p.m. at Bryncelyn, Pontardawe.[5]

5. Mary Prestcott Whittington (aged 66), mother-in-law of Dr. Griffith Griffiths of Bryncelyn, Pontardawe. She was formerly a Postmistress in Wine Street, Neath, widowed early with 3 daughters and 1 son. Her eldest daughter Elizabeth had married Dr. Griffiths in 1865.

Wednesday 25 August: T.J. left 1st train for Swansea thence to the Mumbles where he stays until Friday & then to the Wells. Swansea Agricultural Show today & tomorrow.

Thursday 26 August: Lloyd drove Lizzie and I in the carriage to call on Mr. & Mrs. Morlais Jones Brynamman, they took us to see the New Church which is in building. They promised to come here to tea next Wednesday. Paid H. W. Thomas 8/3d. being all I owe up to this day. Paid Evans the draper 15/6d. the balance of what Harriet owed.

Sunday 29 August: Lizzie, Harriet, Betty & Lloyd to Church. I at home all day (very warm). The Vicar said Revd. N.T. [Nathaniel Thomas] had had Kidwelly.

Monday 30 August: Jane, Lizzie's sister, came here about 3 p.m. Stayed to tea & left 7.30. She rode down, the 1st time I had seen her since she was married (2 yrs. last June). She looked very nice, thinner than when a girl.

Wednesday 1 September: Revd. Mr. Lloyd called 2 p.m. Mr. & Mrs. Morlais Jones Brynamman came down 3.30. All stayed to tea & all very friendly. Lloyd drove Mr. & Mrs. Jones home as far as Wain Gurwen & after drove Mr. Lloyd to his lodgings.

Thursday 2 September: My birthday. R.P.L. came up 11.30 train left 7 train. Lloyd drove him both ways. Lizzie gave me new short nightgown she had made & her bone studs.

Friday 3 September: Lloyd to Black Mountain for a load of lime for mortar.

Monday 6 September: Lloyd cutting branches off oak trees in Cae Mawr hedge. Liz & I on the road with him. Young David Forchegel called, stayed to tea, left at 10 o'clk. He brought back Cassells Magazine I had lent him. He intends going to St. Asaph's this day week in readiness for the Bishop's ordination. Fanny G., Ellen & Alice Drake called.

Sunday 12 September: Lizzie, Harriet & Lloyd to Church. David walked up with Lizzie to wish me goodbye, he leaves tomorrow morning for St. Asaph. Gave him "Heb groes Heb goron" [No cross No crown] and my photo. Sacrament Mr. Williams. Catherine took the Communion 1st time at Llanguicke.

Monday 13 September: Lloyd to the Station with cart sent empty back to Williams, had box containing:

6 bottles	Gin	)	This is the first order had
6 "	Whiskey	)	since June 30th – bill
6 "	Tarragona	)	paid up to that time.

Tuesday 14 September: In the house, not including those of yesterday:

19 bottles	Sherry	Porter	32 bottles		
5 "	Port	Beer	69	"	**W**
2 "	Marsala	Beer	42	"	Fulton
2 "	Tarragona				
12 "	Orange Brandy				
4 "	Brandy				

English Harvest Service Pontardawe Church. Lloyd drove Lizzie there. Revd. Tom Jones Llangunnor preached.

Wednesday 15 September: Returned by train to D. & F. Williams:

15 dozn. & 3 empty bottles
3 Cases
2 Hampers

According to their a/c there are still owing 7 dozn. & 8 empty bottles, 1 Hamper, 1 Case, 1 Jar up to 30th June last.

Welsh Harvest Service at Pontardawe, Revd. Stephen Davies Swansea preached. Very wet, no one from here. Catherine went [to] Mr. Bevan, Cadoxton Brewery as Servant.

Thursday 16 September: Lloyd drove Lizzie to Garnant in the phaeton to fetch the box of apples Jane had sent me. Lloyd called at Dr. Rees for the books we had lent him, "Canwyll y Cymry"[6] & "Quicksands".

6. *Canwyll y Cymru* was a collection of divine poems by "the old vicar" Rhys Pritchard (1579-1644) and first printed during or before 1658 and published as a complete edition in 1681. An English translation *The Welshman's Candle* was published in 1771.

Friday 17 September: Lewis the Tiler & his son-in-law here liming the house. Swept dining room chimney & rose the carpet. James the Mason putting pebbles round Walk under hay house.

Saturday 18 September: Lewis limed the front of the house today again owing to the rain last night. Mr. Jones Llanguicke called 1.15 p.m. on his way to Cwmamman, said he would call again in returning but it was too late. Paid the Int. £20.

Sunday 19 September: Pontardawe Singers at Llanguicke. Collection made for their going to the Llanelly Festival. Fine day. Lizzie, Betty, Harriet & Lloyd to Church. Our Pew so full that Lizzie felt faint & obliged to go out.

Tuesday 21 September: Harriet cleaning upstairs windows outside. Lizzie to Post, met Revd. W. R. Lloyd by Saron coming up, he stayed to tea & until past 10 o'clk. Morgan Walters making geranium box to put by front door. Lewis roofing Closet.

Thursday 23 September: Mrs. A. Gilbertson, her 4 boys & their Governess Miss Bird called in the wagonette.

Saturday 25 September: Samuel Williams brought cask of salt butter, 49 lbs. He sells his casks in January & whatever he then has per lb. I have agreed to pay. It is now 14d per lb.

Sunday 26 September: Lizzie, Harriet & Lloyd to Church. Betty & I in the house. Mr. Lloyd, the Vicar & the Choir at Ystalyfera.

Monday 27 September: Sarah & her Husband came here 11.45. After tea Lizzie & they walked to Pontardawe Church to hear the singing rehearsal conducted by Mr. Radcliffe, the festival is at Llanelly on Wednesday, they enjoyed the singing & returned here 10.15.

Tuesday 28 September: John Harries & Sarah left for Cwmamman soon after breakfast. Lizzie walked with them till near the Brewery. Lloyd drove Liz & I in the carriage to call at Dr. Griffiths. We met their man by the gate who said Mrs. G. was in Leicestershire so we did not go up, gave him our cards. Liz called at the Vicarage with 4/- from me towards the Choir expenses tomorrow. We drove on as far as "The Lamb" then returned calling at P.O. By Gellygron

Gate overtook Revd. & Mrs. Lloyd, & Mr. Turberville going for a walk. They came up with us in the carriage & took tea here.

Wednesday 29 September: Lloyd drove to Lewis the Tiler's to tell him to come down tomorrow if fine. Polly fell under him & cut one knee badly. Lizzie gave John Jones, this tenant [of Garth Farm] the Notice paper in my presence at 5 minutes to 10 o'clk. a.m., he owes me £93 this day. Wm. Owen gave me the 3 keys of the Colliery Cottage & paid me £2..18.

Thursday 30 September: Lewis the Tiler finished liming the house (Kitchen side). He was prevented before by the rain. A nice dry day today. Swept little Kitchen & Drawing room carpet, rose Drawing room carpet. Lizzie wiped down the Paper & I dusted the pictures. Harriet cleaning grate. Paid Lewis up to this day for work, lime, sheets & sand (Work £1..18..3, goods 16/11.) £2..15..2 paid.

Friday 1 October: Lloyd drove Lizzie to Brynamman 11 train. She went to see Mary Jones, Bridgend, who intends going to America in a fortnight. Called at Jane's & left the Sheets &c. packed up for Sarah at the "Railway", called at Margaret's. Lizzie paid up H. W. Thomas Butcher up to this day.

Thursday 7 October: Laid the Foundation stone of Bryn Amman New Church (St. Catherine's) by G.H. Strick. Dr. & Mrs. Walters dined here at 12 o'clk. Lizzie went with them.

Friday 8 October: Lizzie to Bryn Syfi 1st train to see Mr. Jenkins who has been very poorly. She dined there & Mrs. & Miss Higginson called & took tea there. She paid Cambrian Office bill 7/- for advertising Cwmllynfell last year.[7] Paid for Lloyd's chair 15/-. Laura Lewis going down same train.

Monday 11 October: Lizzie walked to Bogelegel to tell them the Llanguicke Harvest Service was postponed until next week. She stayed there to tea & was much pleased with the tidiness of the place. Dr. & Mrs. Griffiths called here in their Dog cart, the first time after Mrs. Whittington's death.

Tuesday 12 October: Mrs. Lewis Brynheulog called. She said she had long been thinking of coming to see me hearing I had been so ill. She was very friendly.

7. Advertisements for the sale by auction of Cwmllynfell Colliery appeared in *The Cambrian* on the 8, 15 and 29 November and 6 December 1878.

Wednesday 13 October: Lloyd drove Lizzie & I in the carriage to Glantwrch. Mrs. Price was better than I expected & seemed very glad to see us. Miss Davies was there, she took us to see the Mill Cottages which have been repaired. We had tea at Glantwrch & it was the first mouthful I had taken from my own home this year & today the longest journey. Morgan Walters finished painting the 4 gates, railing & garden door, also footstools for Llanguicke. Paid him up to this day. Charlie Williams & Mr. W. Player called.[8] Fanny G. and Ellen called, they had walked & came to rest for half an hour.

Thursday 14 October: Miss Shenton came to see us & to say her sister Mrs. Thomas comes home from Glasgow on Saturday next. Miss Morris brought her down in the carriage as far as the Brewery & Lloyd drove her as far as us.

Friday 15 October: A lovely day. Lloyd washing & cleaning in Kitchen Garden. After dinner I went with Lloyd to the Saw Pit, set fire to rubbish. He cut down a dead tree opposite back entrance & some branches of others. The Gate is newly painted & made easy & all looks tidy. Cwmamman Harvest Services.

Sunday 17 October: Lloyd drove Lizzie & I to Church.

Monday 18 October: Had half a ton of soft coal from Evans & Bevan, Neath, our mare alone, 5/6 paid. James the Mason repairing the piece of our Garden Wall that fell some months ago, top part next Hill, he finishes it Wednesday night. The weather is most favourable being so dry & fine.

Tuesday 19 October: James the Mason & Lloyd at Cwmllynfell making the River safe in case of flood by Hay's house.

Wednesday 20 October: Lizzie, Harriet & Lloyd to Llanguicke. Davies dressed the Font & window sills with Ferns & Grasses. Altar sill had "Myfi yw bara y bywyd" [I am the bread of life] in red letters on white ground surrounded with Holly wreath, scarlet geraniums & snow berries, fringe of corn round Altar Posts & small Stwcan [stook or sheaf of corn] in little window. Fringe of corn & flowers round Pulpit & both Desks "Gŵyl Cynhauaf" [Harvest Festival] in Ivy leaves on white board above the Font. I did as much as I could here in putting on letters & tying corn fringe &c, but am not well enough to go to the

8. William John Player, Manufacturing Chemist of Longford House, Cadoxton, Neath.

Church today. Hope to go tomorrow. Our scarlet geraniums were lovely, looking like wax & the Dahlias beautiful, they seemed as if waiting to bloom their best for the dear old Church. God bless them.

Thursday 21 October: Llanguicke Harvest Home. A fine dry day, rather cold. Service at 3 p.m., excellent congregation.

Prayers read by Revd. W.R. Lloyd
Lessons " " The Vicar
Sermon " " Revd. D. Griffiths, Cwmamman Ezek.X Ch. 13V.

The Church very prettily decorated by Lizzie, Davies, Mrs. Bowen & Thos. Howells. All the Saronites & their Pastor, Mr. Jones Carmel, Dr. Griffiths, Mr. Hedley & Mrs. Kirkhouse's pupils in Church. I felt quite happy & proud to see the old Church looking so nice. Revd. and Mrs. Griffiths dined here & went with us in the phaeton, & returned with us to tea.

Friday 22 October: There was a sharp frost Wednesday night which completely killed the dahlia leaves & spoiled the geraniums. It seems as if they only remained in perfection to go to Llanguicke.

Saturday 23 October: Poor Jonah Jones Bryn Brain buried yesterday at Cwmllynfell aged 76 years.

Sunday 24 October: Lloyd drove Lizzie & I in phaeton as far as Cefnllan Cottage. We walked from there to Church.

Monday 25 October: Mrs. Howells Nantmole buried today at Baran Chapel (she was Mrs. Lewis Alltycham's sister). Lloyd mowed the Green. James the Mason putting pebbles round Walk leading up to Hayhouse Walk from front door.

Tuesday 26 October: Rain commenced today after a long period of fine weather. It has been a lovely, dry & mild Autumn.

Saturday 30 October: Lloyd drove Lizzie & I in the phaeton to Cwmllynfell thro' Brynamman & home thro' Ystalyfera. The place looks desolate, all the works being stopped & all the rails & every thing removed & houses empty. John Jones Bookseller lives in front part of Hay's house. House formerly occupied by Mr. Brock, sadly pilfered & stripped of every thing.

Sunday 31 October: Lizzie & I in the house all day. We were tired after yesterday & it is very cold, but dry. Lloyd, Harriet & Betty to Church. The Vicar.

Thursday 4 November: Mrs. Herbert Lloyd a son the 4th boy (11th child).

Sunday 7 November: Lloyd, Harriet & Betty to Church. I in the house all day feeling very poorly, my bowels painful and constipated. Told Betty to tell William Lewis that I begged Sally would be here tomorrow 10 a.m. that I wanted a black dress made. She came, and promised it ready next Wednesday, recd. it at Bryn Syfi.

Monday 8 November: Recd. telegram from Miss Jenkins at 10.30 a.m. saying "John is much worse come down if you possibly can". I went down midday train, Mrs. Nancarrow met me at the Station with a cab. Drs. Hall & Rogers had been up, said there was no hope of poor Mr. Jenkins, he was perfectly conscious to the last, the last hour or two he often said "Good Night", "I am going", Miss Jenkins saying "to sleep my boy". "Yes, yes Good Night" he replied. He died at 8.10 p.m. very quietly Miss Jenkins, Mrs. Morgan, the Servants & myself in the room. A truly moral & innocent man, age 57 years last Sep. 26th. When I arrived & went to his room he looked up & said "Margaret you went away without wishing me good bye". I said "Yes, you were asleep", he looked up saying "Oh well" & gave me a kiss.

Tuesday 9 November: Mrs Price came to Bryn Syfi midday train, having had my letter this morning saying Mr. Jenkins was dead. Poor thing, she is a great cripple. Lizzie in Liverpool & hearing Uncle John was worse, telegraphed to say she wd. come down at once. I telegraphed back to stop her coming tonight. She sent back to say she would come tomorrow.

Wednesday 10 November: Lloyd came down to Bryn Syfi to see how I was, as I was so poorly leaving home on Monday. Sent him to Victoria Station to meet 3.25 train from Liverpool in case Lizzie wd. come by it. She did not. Sent Lloyd with Mr. D. C. Jones to Swansea to get a new hat & necktie, as he is to come to the funeral on Friday. Lizzie returned from Liverpool, left Lime Street 12 o'clk. at Swansea 6.40 p.m., Bryn Syfi 7.45. Mr. David Morgan met her at Station & brought her in a cab to the Lodge. Mrs. Morgan to the funeral. I am not well enough to go.

Friday 12 November: Poor Mr. Jenkins buried today at Llantwit. Funeral left Bryn Syfi at 11 a.m. Miss Jenkins, Mrs. D. Morgan, Lizzie & Charlie Jenkins (aged 11 years) in first Mourning Coach. In the other Mr. Benthall, Richard Matthews, Mr. D. Morgan & Mr. Morgan (Bolgoed). Revd. T. J. Bowen Kilvey buried him as Archdeacon Griffiths was at Llandaff.

Sunday 14 November: A very wet day & stormy. Lizzie & I at Bryn Syfi with poor dear Miss Jenkins, a sad & empty house without poor Uncle John.

Monday 15 November: Lizzie & I returned 11.30 train from Bryn Syfi leaving poor Miss Jenkins very sad & lonely in heart. How she will miss her dear Brother. She gave Lizzie a picture "The death of Nelson", we brought it up safely. We had it very wet from Station, came on to snow p.m. the first this winter. Mr. & Mrs. David Morgan are going this day to stay at Bryn Syfi.

Wednesday 17 November: Revd. W. R. Lloyd called, Lizzie & he went for a walk as far as the Brewery & returned to tea 5.30. Samuel Bogelegel called on his way from Neath to say he would bring the pig here next Tuesday.

Thursday 18 November: A disagreeable snowing morning. Fanny G. & Miss Ford walked up to see us, Fanny said she was going to Liverpool on Monday. Lloyd with our Mare & cart helping Morgan Gartheithen to carry truck of coal from Wain Cae Gurwen (3 loads each).

Saturday 20 November: John Williams, Pentreharn married this day at Llanguicke to Sarah Davies, Nantygasseg (his 2nd wife) banns.

Sunday 21 November: Lizzie & I in Church, left phaeton at Cefnllan Cottage, the roads were so slippery. Dr. & Mrs. Griffiths at Llanguicke sat in our Pew. Very cold & dry. The Vicar.

Monday 22 November: Lloyd opening gutter across Heol-y-Ty below front gate, it had choked with gravel & small roots of trees. Miss Barbara St. John now staying at Glantwrch rode down here about 1 o'clk. She stayed to lunch & left 3.30. I wish we had known she was coming, she was very pleasant.

Tuesday 23 November: Bought Pig of Samuel Williams Bogelegel, he cut it up for me, weighed 219 lbs. @ 10/- a score

		£.. s.. d
he cut it up for me, weighed 219 lbs. @ 10/- a score		5.. 9.. 6
Cask of Salt Butter had from Bogelegel 25th Sept. last 49 lbs. @ 14½		2..19..2½
All paid this day	By cash	£8.. 8..8½
Had 11 cwt. Soft coal from Pontardawe Station	Paid	s.. d 5.. 9

Wednesday 24 November: Had 3 loads Llwynrhidie coal.

Thursday 25 November: John Morgan's things all sold under Bill of Sale at Ynismeudw & they go to lodgings in Pontardawe.

Friday 26 November: Lizzie went down to Bryn Syfi midday train to see poor Miss Jenkins & to stay until Monday.

Sunday 28 November: Lizzie at Bryn Syfi. She went to Kilvey Church a.m. with Mr. David Morgan. Lloyd, Harriet & Betty to Llanguicke. I in the house all day, feeling very poorly & in much pain. The Vicar.

Monday 29 November: Lizzie returned from Bryn Syfi 11.30 train, Lloyd met her, the D. Morgan's staying there, she liked Mrs. Morgan very much.

Tuesday 30 November: Miss Ford called, she brought beautiful chrysanthemums &c.

Thursday 2 December: Lewis the Tiler came here from Cwmllynfell, he had been up to see what repairs were required at the Colliery Cottage. Says there must be new leaden gutter, new slates (those of Engine House will do), new troughs & pipes & many other things, in all not less than £15, expenses £10. Mr. Brock allows towards it.

Friday 3 December: Recd. letter from Miss Jenkins saying Mr. Jevons would be down either tomorrow or Monday. The D. Morgans left Bryn Syfi yesterday. Lloyd to Pontardawe shoeing the Mare & putting leather under shoes, 3/6 paid. Harriet & Lizzie finished raking the Walks & sweeping the Green, all is now tidy.

Saturday 4 December: Mr. Jevons came to Bryn Syfi this evening to see into poor Miss Jenkins affairs. T.J. came here 9 p.m. Lizzie gave him "Jack & I".

Sunday 5 December: Lloyd & Harriet to Llanguicke. T.J. & Lizzie walked to Pontardawe thinking to be in time for Church 6.30 p.m. but the service must have begun at 6 for they were late & did not go in.

Monday 6 December: T.J. left 7.15 a.m. Walked to Garnant. Selina (Harriet's mother) came here. Morgan Walter Carpenter came here for me to tell him about repairs required at the Colliery House Cwmllynfell. He goes up tomorrow. My bowels exceedingly painful all last week, & my hip. I am greatly afraid I shall soon not be able to walk, the pain is much more acute than it was.

Tuesday 7 December: Lizzie & I went to Bryn Syfi midday train to stay a few days. Mr. Jevons there. I consulted him about the Disentailing deeds. He said they were quite right & that I could by making a Will give the land to who I liked. The Vicar & Revd. W. R. Lloyd going with us to Swansea, they were very pleasant.

Friday 10 December: Mr. Jevons left Bryn Syfi for Liverpool 12 o'clk. train. Will come down again in a little time. Mrs. D. W. Morgan & her niece Gwendoline dined at Bryn Syfi. I came home 3.40 train, they & Lizzie saw me off & then went into Swansea.

Monday 13 December: Went by train 11.30 to Cwmllynfell. Lloyd drove me to the Station, put up horse & phaeton at Post Office, & he came up same train. Wm. Griffiths met me with his car at Gwys Station.

Tuesday 14 December: Wrote to the Rhydyfro post master (Richard Lewis) saying that when I called yesterday for my letters 10.30 a.m. I found the doors locked & no one in attendance & that if such a thing again occurred I wd. report his neglect to the G.P.O. London. Letter sent by my servant Harriet Rees.

Saturday 18 December: The Saron Choir (15) came here to sing at 8.30 p.m. They sang twice by front door & the rest in the Kitchen. A lovely moonlight night but showery. They had written to Lizzie to ask if they should come. Gave them 6/-, they were much pleased. Lloyd to Cwmllynfell.

Tuesday 21 December: Recd. from Williams 1 Kilo Burton ale, carriage paid to Pontardawe for 18/-. No. of cask 220893.

Saturday 25 December: Lloyd drove Lizzie & I to Llanguicke service 11 a.m. A lovely bright morning & the dear old Church looking so "serchus" [beloved] with the sun shining in, a good congregation. It quite gladdened my heart to see all so cheerful & bright & so nice. May God bless every hand & heart that in any way helps to keep up dear old Llanguicke. Mrs. & Miss Lewis Alltycham & Mr. Hedley in Church. Mrs. Lewis quite overcome with crying at the Communion. I thought she would faint! Sacrament: The Vicar.

Sunday 26 December: Lloyd drove Lizzie & I to Llanguicke. Betty, Harriet & her sister to Church. Mrs. Bowen came from Llanguicke with us in the phaeton to Rhydyfro. Harriet to Wain Cae Gurwen Eisteddfod yesterday.

Thursday 30 December: Miss Ford called, brought me a nice bouquet of Christmas Roses & Lizzie a little Almanack for 1881. I went to John's house & spoke to him & Esther about the rent, & if he could not give good security for the arrears of rent up to Sept. last I begged him to meet me tomorrow at Mr. Scale's office, Neath. Said he would not come. I told him I wd. at once place the matter in Mr. S's hands. John came after me & begged me to wait until this day week. Said I would.

1881

This was another full and challenging year for Margaret. Her dissatisfaction with the running of Garth Farm, increasing rent arrears and deteriorating personal relations with John Jones culminated in the termination of his four years' tenancy and, after a brief but welcome interlude, his replacement as tenant by David Morgan and his family. Lizzie's friendship with the Rev. Nathaniel Thomas continued but her relationship with Thomas Jones (T.J.) developed to the stage where he became an occasional overnight visitor at Garth and Lizzie's companion on a visit to Liverpool. Despite suffering several debilitating bouts of sickness Margaret's fluency as a diarist, her sometime acerbic opinions and her detailed financial recording continued with few unchronicled days during the year.

The 1881 census recorded the following occupants of the three Garth properties. In *Garth* lived Margaret (aged 46), Lizzie (aged 28 and listed as a landowner), Elizabeth (Betty) Evans, dairy maid (aged 54), Thomas Lloyd, coachman (33) and house-maid Harriet Rees (19). In *Garth Lodge* lived two former servants, Mary Griffiths (78) and Elizabeth Richards (62); both were widows and designated as 'solitaries' (see diary entry 20/4/81). In *Garth Farm* lived John Jones (58), tenant farmer of 160 acres, his wife Esther (47), their two daughters Catherine (27) and Mary (15) and their son Eynon (21).

In addition to the habitual itemisation of "Bills paid up to 31st Decr." of the previous year, Margaret started her 1881 Diary with a priced stock list of "things in the house".

	£ .. s .. d
(5 dozn. Beer **W** @ 4s/3d. 14 bot: Porter @ 4/-	1 .. 8 .. 11
(18 Gal. Cask Beer **W**. just tapped	18 .. 0
3 dozn. Beer Fulton	7 .. 0
(6 bot: Tarragona @ 1/8. 2 bot: Marsala @ 1/8	13 .. 4
(5 bot: Port @ 4s/. 9 bot: Sherry @ 3s/6d	2 .. 11 .. 6
(2 bot: Brandy @ 5/-. 2 bot: Whiskey @ 3s/4d	16 .. 8
(3 bot: Gin @ 2s/5d. 12 bot: Orange Brandy 30s/	1 .. 12 .. 5
	£8 .. 7 .. 10

	£ .. s .. d
(Dry Bacon in the House @ 1s/- per lb.	
(4 Whole Hams 76 lbs. 2 Whole Gammons 49 lbs.	6 .. 5 .. 0
(Piece of Ham & Bacon 10 lbs.	10 .. 0
(8 Pigs cheeks 10s/-. 2 Ox Tongues 3s/-	13 .. 0
(2 Dry flitches (of the Pig had from)	5 .. 10 .. 0
(Bogelegel last Novr. 110 lbs. @ 1s/)	
35 lbs. of Bogelegel salt butter @ 14½d. per lb.	2 .. 2 .. 3½

Sunday 2 January: Lizzie walked to Llanguicke. Lloyd in the house. Drove us both at 6 p.m. to Pontardawe Church. Mr. Lloyd preached. Isai. XL11.16. Mr. Lloyd & the Vicar very pleased to see us, the latter took Liz & I all round to see the decorations wh. were very nice. Margaret Pen-y-Garn came here to dinner. Betty to Ystalyfera. Harriet to Llanguicke & to Saron at 6. Very mild night.

Tuesday 4 January: Lizzie & Harriet raking the Walk. Dr. Rees called in his way from Pontardawe 3 p.m., took some lunch. Said I looked better, he had not been here since Sep. He & his man were going to drive to Cwmllynfell. Fanny G. & her sister Kate called (walked). Kate seemed glad to see me better. Said she wd. come again before leaving. Fanny asked us to come & lunch but I declined. They were both very pleasant to Liz and I. Rev. N. R. Lloyd called, stayed to tea, left at 10. Lent him Dr. Syntax. All of us today talked of Miss Lewis's marriage. She is they say 16 years older than Mr. Hedley!

Wednesday 5 January: Charlie Williams called in his Dog cart to ask for the shooting, told him to go over the land when he liked. He gave me 5/- towards repairing Llanguicke. Lloyd drove Lizzie to call at Dr. Griffiths & to take back the 3 books lent by poor Mrs. Whittington. Lizzie paid the Post Office Book £8..17s. also Jordan [Chemist] 10/-. Then to Bryn Syfi by 5.30 train to stay till Friday with Miss Jenkins.

Thursday 6 January: David Hopkin Nantygwin & Howel Jones Llachart Fawr here making a valuation for John this tenant. John brought me in their valuation £56..0..8½ which I do not consider to be in accordance with the agreement.

Friday 7 January: Sent Lloyd with a note to Trenache [Farm] to beg Mr. Paddison to come here today if possible.[1] He was just starting for Swansea & told Lloyd he would be at Pontardawe 4 p.m. train. Lloyd shoeing mare & met that train. Lizzie & Mr. Paddison came up together.

Sunday 9 January: Lizzie, Lloyd & Betty to Church. Harriet at home with me. She went to Pontardawe Church at 6 p.m. Had fire in my bedroom first time this winter. Very cold frost. Recd. letter from Mr. Scale saying he had seen Mr. Paddison & that the tenant could not claim for manure.

Monday 10 January: Had ½ ton of coal from Neath, paid 5/6, our mare alone, we begin it tomorrow. Harriet took the two myrtles to the old woman to keep during this cold weather. Lizzie & Harriet sweeping up the leaves &c. in the front.

Tuesday 11 January: Einon carrying manure, sent Lizzie to tell him I thought it was better not for them to carry any more. John came in to ask why, I said that if he intended being paid for it, I wd. only do according to the agreement, & that he had better read it over, "I hope the agreement is not going to rob me". I said "You remember I do not order you to carry any". He continued

1. Charles Henry Paddison (51), Solicitor and farmer of 151 acres, Trenache Farm, Neath.

carrying afterwards. Lloyd to Neath for beef & mutton. Hutchins sent a horrid leg of large mutton cut to 6 lbs. altho. I had ordered small.

Wednesday 12 January: Ground covered with snow, a sharp frost. No wind & nice sunshine. Revd. N. Thomas came here 5.30. Walked up from Pontardawe 4.10 train.

Thursday 13 January: Mr. Paddison came here to see John's cattle, said he had seen Mr. Scale & that he said the agreement was not properly stamped but that it could be any time by paying £10.

Friday 14 January: Lizzie and Revd. N. Thomas walked to Llanguicke returned 2.45 to dinner. He left here in time for 7.10 train to Swansea. Snow covering ground and frost.

Sunday 16 January: Lizzie, Lloyd and Harriet to Church. Betty and I in the house. Very cold sharp frost, snow covering the ground, no wind bright sunshine. After tea Lizzie read "Moses the Patriot" from "Sunday Magazine".

Friday 21 January: Llwynrhidie coal 11 cwt. Very deep snow.

Saturday 22 January: Poor Mrs. Harris late of Pant-y-Bettws buried today at Bettws Church. A fine day but very deep snow.

Sunday 23 January: The red heifer a she-calf yesterday.

Tuesday 25 January: Miss Ford and Maud Gilbertson walked up to see me, this is the first time I have seen Maud for many years. She came to tell me that she had been to the Bridgend County & Hunt Balls, & that she was now "out". She was 20 years old.

Wednesday 26 January: John Harries & Sarah came here 11 a.m. left at 5 p.m. Sarah looked very well. We were very glad to see them. They leave tomorrow for Liverpool. The ground covered with snow & very disagreeable. They came in "Amman Inn" Car. Gave Sarah 2 lbs. fresh butter. She gave me black Shetland Shawl to wear in the house. D. Morgan, the Coal, here about renting this farm, his wife & himself would come and see it.

Friday 28 January: The Vicar called in his way to Cwmamman. Paid me ½ year's interest due 30th Dec. last. Took Lizzie with him in the little Dog cart to call on the Griffiths' Cwmamman. It was a most disagreeable afternoon, such a rapid thaw & the roads so wet & full of snow. Came on to rain before their return. Mr. Jones was going out to dinner at 6 p.m. so he had no time to stay long.

Saturday 29 January: Had ½ ton Rhyddyn coal. Lloyd with only our mare. 5/6 paid.

Sunday 30 January: Lloyd and Harriet to Church. Lizzie and Betty in the house. Very damp and wet. Revd. Mr. Lloyd.

Monday 31 January: Lloyd to Cwmllynfell with cheese to change, it was not nice tasted & Thos. said he wd. take it back. Anne, Pwllwatkin came for Red Heifer's calf, one week old, £1..5..0. paid.

Tuesday 1 February: Mrs. Jones of Carmel came here, stayed to tea. She said Samuel Griffiths formerly of Gwrhyd had asked her to speak to me in favour of his having this farm.

Thursday 3 February: Harriet went up to Dr. Rees' to have her tooth taken out. She had her new linsey dress, 3 aprons, 2 twill petticoats which her mother had bought for her. Pouring with rain all day. Lloyd in Smith's shop all the afternoon having cart wheels re-banded as the bands were getting slack. Wrote to Mr. Jevons, sent him Miss Harris' two letters & my replies to her.

Friday 4 February: Llwynrhidie coal 15 cwt. Recd. Hare and Pheasant from Jonah O. Jones. Had 10 lbs. tea @ 2/6. Paid £1..5..0. We owed Mrs. Harris 3 lbs. of it. Had 1 Gal. Gin, 1 Gal. Whiskey, ½ Gal. Brandy, 1 dozen Bottles Sherry. The first order this year.

Saturday 5 February: Lloyd went home for a week. I sent a Cock & Hen, a present to his Parents.

Sunday 6 February: Lizzie, Harriet and Betty to Church. I alone in the house. The Vicar.

Monday 7 February: Recd. letter from Mr. Jevons about extension of Miss Harris' lease. Harriet to Pwllwatkin with Lizzie's cloth jacket for Mary to stitch all round. Very wet all day.

Tuesday 8 February: William Lewis called in his way from Abernant Brewery, said he had promised Daniel the Carpenter to speak to me in favour of his son-in-law Samuel Griffiths, as tenant for this farm.

Wednesday 9 February: Paid J. Jones Crachllwyn, Garth Poor rate &c. as follows:

			£ .. s .. d
Garth Farm	£47 .. 0 .. 0 @ 1/2d		2 .. 14 .. 10
" Cottage	2 .. 0 .. 0 "		2 .. 4
3 Cots. Cwmllynfell	7 .. 10 .. 0 "		8 .. 9
2 " Colliery	7 .. 5 .. 0 "		8 .. 5½
			£3 .. 14 .. 4½
		Less Commission	4 .. 10½
			£3 .. 9 .. 6
Garth Income Tax	£50 @ 6d		£1 .. 5 .. 0
" Cottage "	£4 @ 6d (This is an		2 .. 0
overcharge as the rent is only £2..12..0)			1 .. 7 .. 0
Garth Land Tax			14 .. 7
Garth House Duty on £20 @ 9d.			15 .. 0

Paid J. Jones by cheque £6..6..0 the whole amount.

Thursday 10 February: Revd. W. R. Lloyd called 5 p.m. Stayed to tea, left 11 p.m. A wet showery evening. Mr. & Mrs. Hedley Gellygron returned yesterday after their marriage.[2] They say he is 27 & she 43, 16 years difference in age! Too much.

Friday 11 February: Lizzie & Harriet to Llanguicke p.m. to take down Christmas evergreens & to tidy the texts & Chancel which remain.

Saturday 12 February: Fanny G. called. Said Kate left yesterday. The Vicar called, stayed to tea, rode on to see Morgan Walter (Carpenter) & then at my request attended the Concert at Rhydyfro. He was full of the School Board

2. Ernest Hall Hedley J.P. married Mary Ann Lewis, eldest daughter of Griffith and Margaret Lewis of Alltacham. Griffith Lewis and his brother-in-law John Morgan of Gelligron owned several local mining concerns and, for a decade, the Ynysmeudwy Pottery. E. H. Hedley was a mining engineer and a colliery owner and acquired his father-in-law's mining business on Griffith's death in 1887, *Around Pontardawe 2*, 102.

Election. Concert at Rhydyfro schoolroom. Lloyd drove Liz & I to this Concert in the Phaeton. A lovely moonlit night. Dr. Griffiths, Chairman, the Vicar & ourselves & Mr. Jones Carmel on the Platform. All passed off well. Harriet & Betty there.

Sunday 13 February: Mr. Lloyd. Very wet. Only Lloyd to Church. Harriet to Saron at 6 p.m.

Monday 14 February: I am very poorly all day & in great pain. Went to bed after dinner. David Morgan the Coal & his wife came here 4 p.m. to see the place. Esther was very kind & showed them all the house, dairy &c. & said she was very sorry to leave. D.M.'s wife (Mary) came upstairs to talk to me, said she liked the place, thought every thing very clean & tidy, but thought it small for their family & begged to have a new dairy built, told her I would not promise to build or alter anything.[3]

Tuesday 15 February: Recd. letter from J. Jones Crachllwyn saying "the Rateable value of Garth is the same as it was on the old valuation, that is £47..0..0." John Harries' birthday yesterday, Lizzie sent him a Coventry Book Marker "Hope the Anchor of the Soul".

Wednesday 16 February: Lizzie re-waisted & enlarged my grey linsey petticoat. I trimmed the purple felt hat I bought of Sarah with new black velvet & gave it to Lizzie. She looks very nice in it & wears it tomorrow.

Thursday 17 February: Election of School Board Members. Lloyd drove Lizzie & I to Rhydyfro school to give our Votes. A fine day.

Friday 18 February: Lizzie & Harriet raking & cleaning the Walk, the front is all tidy. Lloyd carrying out heap of earth & manure over lower part of Cae Barriwns. Lizzie went to the Bank with School pence &c. Bought 2 Garden Rakes at Davies'. A lovely day. She enjoyed the walk.

Saturday 19 February: Lloyd carrying out heap of compost from under wall by little gate to top of Cae Barriwns (potato ground) to level alongside of wall, p.m. he swept up about the back. Fanny G. called, all the others gone to Neath. Expected T.J. this evening but he did not come.

3. David and Mary Morgan had previously farmed Cilpentwyn (36 acres).

Sunday 20 February: Lizzie, Lloyd & Betty to Church. Harriet in the house with me, she went to Chapel 6 p.m. I was very poorly in the night & obliged to get up at 5.10 a.m. Harriet was very good & made a nice fire in the Parlour by 5.50 when I came down stairs. It all looked very comfortable but I was in great pain & discomfort. How I wish I was well, to enjoy life.

Wednesday 23 February: R.P.L. walked up from 11.30 train, brought us Apples, Oranges, Almonds, & Shoe Nuts & a tin of Pine apple.

Thursday 24 February: Lizzie & Harriet digging up the Walk between Front Gate & variegated holly. There are so many stones, the ashes won't remain. Fanny, Ellen & Madeline G. called 12.20. The two last went picking water-cresses while Fanny sat a quarter of an hour with me. A lovely day. Dr. Thomas, Miss St. John and Miss Budd called on horseback 1.15. just after the G's left. They did not come in.

Friday 25 February: Harriet & Lizzie finished digging up the Walk midday, it is now ready for ashes. Mrs. Dr. Griffiths called. She had been calling on the Bride (Mrs. Hedley) at Gellygron. She found F. & E. [Fanny & Ellen] Gilbert-son there. Said John Morgan had been taken up for Forgery at Ross. Mr. Jones Llanguicke called 7.45 p.m. on his way from Bryn Amman from Revd. Morlais Jones'.

Saturday 26 February: Betty wheeled ashes to put on the Walk that had been dug up yesterday. Lloyd drove me to Pontardawe. Had new shovel 2/-, lampshade 3d at Davies'. Paid Evan Jones the Butcher's bill 13/9d up to 31st Dec. Asked him to vote for the Vicar's being Chairman of the School Board. He would not promise, told him I was quite astonished at his turning his back upon the Church.

Sunday 27 February: T.J. came here last night, he & Lizzie & Betty in the house all day. Lloyd, Harriet & I to Llanguicke.

Monday 28 February: T.J. left first train from Garnant. D. Morgan (the Coal) & his wife came here. I took them to see the farm house, yard & all the out-buildings. They liked all, but wished very much to have a new dairy & for the present one to be a back kitchen, but I would not promise. They rented the farm at £56 per year, all taxes to be paid by me. I promised to give £5 towards making or repairing the hedge between Coitcae & Wain Fawr, also to put wire fence to divide Cae Mawr. D.M. putting a man at his expense to work with my man & for no charge hereafter to be made for his work. I also said that if the children were good I wd. give £1 between them in the year.

Tuesday 1 March: Lloyd to Llangyfelach fair. Mrs. Thomas & Mrs. Garford came here about 3 p.m. Stayed to tea & were obliged to walk back as Lloyd was away. Gave Mrs. Garford 2/- towards Harmonium. Sent Harriet with letter to D. Morgan at Llwynrhidie Colliery, saying I would not build a new dairy.

Wednesday 2 March: Harriet to P.O. with Butter & Eggs, and a letter to be sent to Miss Gilbertson. Poor old Joseph Morgan buried today at Llanguicke. Lloyd drove Lizzie & I to the Church where we waited until the funeral came. I had never been to a funeral before, but I went today out of respect to the Church & his Calling. He had been Parish Clerk over 40 years (age 79).

(Copy)

Garth March 2nd 1881

Mr. David Morgan

Sir,

I have been looking round this place today, & am more determined than ever that I will not build a New Dairy, nor allow any one else to do so, the accommodation here has satisfied the tenants without complaint or change for the last 14 years & it must continue to do so. I think it only fair that you should know my determination at once, so that you & your wife may not entertain any false hope. I send Harriet up with this so that you may get it this evening.

Yours truly

Margaret Jones

This letter was delivered by my servant Harriet Rees to David Morgan, Cilpentan, at Llwynrhidie Colliery, he has rented this farm & becomes my tenant 25th inst.

Saturday 5 March: Lloyd to Pontardawe shoeing mare. Hopkin John took load of coal to Llanguicke.

Sunday 6 March: Lizzie & I in Church, Lloyd, Betty & Harriet. Damp and small rain. I took cold. Pastoral Aid collection at Llanguicke, 19/6. Revd. T.H. Hughes the Deputation preached.[4] The Vicar read the Prayers.

Tuesday 8 March: Thomas Jones "Tir Eleanor Morgan" came here, he walked from Brynamman. He seems a very nice man. I had never seen him before, and was very agreeably pleased with him. He paid up the Note of £13. I gave him 10/- to give his daughter Sarah. Lloyd drove him to meet last train 5.30. Lloyd met with a cow in coming home, the mare got frightened & broke the harness. I think he was a little tipsy, he said no. Fanny G. & Miss Ford called, brought flowers, patterns of children's clothes for the Bazaar for Lizzie.

Thursday 10 March: Mr. C. H. Paddison & David Hopkin (Nantygwin) came here by appointment 10.30 a.m. to make a Valuation on this place between John Jones, the tenant & myself. After we had all signed & read the Paper appointing the two Valuers & their Umpire in case of any disagreement in the Valuation, John said the Agreement of Tenancy was of no good as I had broken it by giving him notice. I said I did not think so, but that I wd. show it Mr. Scale & he shd. decide.

Friday 11 March: Mrs. A. Gilbertson & her eldest boy called in the wagonette, said they were going to call on the Bride (Mrs. Hedley) Gellygron.

Saturday 12 March: Mr. Paddison & David Hopkin Nantygwin made a valuation here. Mr. Scale said the agreement was not broken but as sound as a lease & by it John could make no claim for manure, but I told Mr. Paddison that I wd. allow what was reasonable for the hauling & spreading & for the manure taken to Wain Pedr Erw, valued £19.

Sunday 13 March: Very wet. Lizzie, I & Betty in the house. Lloyd & Harriet to Church. Lloyd to Pontardawe posting a letter to Mr. Scale saying a valuation was made yesterday.

Monday 14 March: Lizzie went to see Jane 1st train, returned midday. Lent her £10. Lizzie brought little puppy from Jane's "Dash" 2 months old.

4. A Deputation was a process used by Christian missionaries to raise support for their departure to a mission field.

Tuesday 15 March: Griffith Walters Cefnllan called here on his way to & from Brynamman. Told him about John & about the valuation. Mr. Jones the Vicar came here about 7.30 p.m. Counted over the Llanguicke monthly collections, & spoke of the repairs. Told him all about John the tenant & showed him all the Valuation Agreement &c.

Wednesday 16 March: Catherine Rowland here paying 1 year's rent up to 25 of this month, £4..0..0. Richard Lewis here saying he wd. like getting the appointment of "Whipper in" for the Schools.

Friday 18 March: Mr. Scale's cousin came up this morning 8.45 in a dog cart & put a Bailiff in possession of John's cattle, until the rent was paid up to Septr. last, £58..10..5. Lloyd taking up snow berry and one laurel, lower side of Walk, they were injuring other trees.

Saturday 19 March: The Bailiff's left this afternoon, John having paid the money to Mr. Scale.

Sunday 20 March: Lloyd drove Lizzie & I to Church. Harriet & Betty in the house. Esther came in after tea to say she hoped I was not offended with them. I said "Oh no, it is you that wd. most likely be offended with me". She said "No indeed we have always found you a good Mistress & all has been a misunderstanding, for we wd. have paid you every halfpenny before leaving".

Monday 21 March: Recd. a letter from Mr. Martin Scale enclosing a cheque for £58..10..5 the arrears of rent due Sep. last & which was paid him by John Jones last Saturday. John came in to ask if they must leave on the 25th. I said No that they may remain until 8th April. He cried & seemed very penitent & hoped we wd. come & see them at Cilmaengwyn. Daniel Davies came to help Lloyd to cut down 2 large trees between front gate & the old garden. Austen's Panorama at the Rhydyfro Schoolroom 7 p.m. Lloyd drove Lizzie & I there. It was a poor affair. Harriet too.

Tuesday 22 March: Lloyd drove me to Pontardawe. Placed Mr. Scale's cheque of £58..10..5 to my credit in the Bank. Put £10 of Thos. Jones note to my Interest a/c. Paid all the Rhydyfro School pence in my hands to the Llanguicke School Bd. by cheque £26..9..0. Called at the Rhydyfro School, the boys writing, the girls sewing & knitting.

Thursday 24 March: Catherine came home for a holiday (Walsall).

Friday 25 March: Lloyd cut his left hand in cutting bread. David Morgan had possession of this farm from John Jones. D. Davies & Lloyd cutting down 3 trees by closet Walk.

Saturday 26 March: Old Mrs. Williams Pentreham left, said she wd. prefer seeing Esther & her family going to a Cottage than to Cilmaengwyn. Daniel Davies came to finish taking down a tree that got fast in the other branches yesterday owing to the high wind. Lizzie recd. Brecon County Times from "the Deputation".

Sunday 27 March: Lizzie & I to Church, Lloyd & Harriet & Anne & little Mary her sisters. Betty in the house. Mrs. Jones invited Lizzie to tea to the Vicarage next Thursday, & to go to the Sunday School Competitive Meeting.[5]

Monday 28 March: Harriet gathered all the old broken crockery on the hill, about the quarry, & by the ashes in a heap & Lloyd took them in the cart to Parson's Pit on the Bog. Lizzie raking the stones about the Pistle & Cae Barriwns gate. Had 2 loads Llwynrhidie coal. Betty washed Green dining room cloth 1st time.

Tuesday 29 March: Old Betty & Harriet cleaning Back Road, tidying above pebbles & sweeping down the gutter. John's cows make it all so muddy going to the Hill. Commenced covering Lizzie's little white gypsy straw hat with black velvet & silk. Betty washed Sarah's sheets. The blue ran very much, must be washed again.

Wednesday 30 March: Old Betty & Harriet finished cleaning Back Road. Lloyd carried off the dirt. I am in great pain all day until after tea. Lizzie not well. Mrs. Bramah (the Gilbertson's Aunt) married to Mr. Crowe in Pontardawe Church by the Vicar. They are going to live in Norway.[6]

Thursday 31 March: Lloyd drove Lizzie to the Vicarage to tea. She went from there with the Vicar & Mr. Jones the Curate to the Sunday School yearly Musical Meeting at the School room. Gave Harriet & John's people tickets but the latter did not go.

---

5. A Competitive Meeting or *Cyfarfod Cystadleuol* was a form of local eisteddfod with music and verse competitions.
6. Francis Crowe (age 40) of Bloomsbury, son of Sir John Rice Crowe, married Margaret Anne Bramah (42) widow.

Friday 1 April: Lizzie & Harriet to Llanguicke p.m. to take down Christmas wreaths. Lloyd digging up potato ground in top of Cae Barriwns. Old Betty picking up the clods.

Saturday 2 April: Fanny G. called, brought Liz & I a piece of her Aunt's wedding cake. Lizzie finished mending her black & white cotton dress that I gave her last birthday. It washed very well & looks so tidy.

Sunday 3 April: Lizzie walked to Church. Very bright & dry but very windy, Betty, Harriet & Lloyd also. I in the house all day.

Tuesday 5 April: Tom Tirlan came here to open gutter between Plantation & Cae Barriwns. Lloyd carrying earth from Cottage to top of Cae Barriwns. Wm. Lewis came here, took him all round yard & through the cow houses. Said they were very tidy. Talked about Heol Hugh. Dr. Rees called in his way from Board of Guardians. Lizzie & I walked to Cae Barriwns, down Heol y Cefn to Saw Pit, back over the road & to see Heol Hugh. A lovely day but cold.

Wednesday 6 April: Lizzie to Bryn Syfi to see Miss Jenkins. She was having the house painted outside. Lizzie to Swansea, paid Griffiths the Chemist's bill. She bought "Dodd's Discourses" 4 volumes & "The Captive's Daughter" all for 2/6d. secondhand.

Thursday 7 April: Morgan Gartheithen here ploughing top of Cae Barriwns as far as Lloyd had cleared out the stones & roots of the trees. Morgan p.m. hauling out the large trees from Cae front that Lloyd & Daniel Davies had cut down under Hayhouse. D. Morgan (new tenant) called in his way to & from Alltwen fair. Gave him the Agreement to take home to read over.

Thursday 14 April: John & his family removed from this farm to Cilmaengwyn farm. He had been here 4 years & altho. very clean tidy people he proved himself at the last a very disagreeable man and a rogue. I hope I may never meet his like again.

Good Friday 15 April: Lizzie, I, Harriet & Lloyd to Church 11 a.m. Revd. W. R. Lloyd did the duty & came back with us to dinner. Left at 5.45 p.m. in time for Pontardawe Church. Selina (Harriet's mother) here. Gave her 10/- for Harriet to pay for clothes.

Saturday 16 April: David Lewis here putting little kitchen door to hang the other side. John taking away the Hay without coming to settle with me. I stopped Hopkin John's son with the gambo load until I settled with John & he gave me a Note of hand for the balance £3..11..6. David Lewis Rhydyfro witness to the Note. Lizzie to Llanguicke with a very pretty text "Crist Cyfodwyd" [Christ is Risen] in blue letters on white ground & blue vandyked border all round, in Chancel window.

Easter Day 17 April: Lizzie, I, Betty & Lloyd to Church. Harriet in the house alone as we expected T.J. about 4 p.m. & he came. Sacrament. 23 communicants. Gwen Cefnllan 1st time. The farm house Empty! John's people left on Thursday & David Morgan not come. Liz & I like the feeling of privacy very much.

Monday 18 April: T.J. & Lizzie went after dinner for a walk to the Gwrhyd Chapel, a fine day but a cold wind. Gwen Cefnllan came here to see the farm house & buildings, liked them very much. John Thomas Gwernllwyn & another man called in their way from Carmarthenshire to see the trees I had to sell. John said he cd. only give 7d per foot as truck was at a standstill. I used to have 11d. – said he would come for them in 3 weeks.

Tuesday 19 April: David Morgan's wife & several women came down to paper the farm house. Lloyd drove me to call on Mrs. Kirkhouse. She is very poorly, some sort of bronchitis. A cold day & I took cold. Liz poor child not well & did not come. New bucket from P.O.

Wednesday 20 April: Old Betty & Mary left the Cottage. They were two very ungrateful old women, particularly Mary for they wd. never try to pay one penny rent, nor come to sweep or weed, unless it quite suited them & their manners & language very bad.

Thursday 21 April: Bettws Bazaar. Lizzie did not go. David Morgan, Cilpentan, & his family came here to live this day. Lloyd helping to remove their furniture. I hope they will prove good tenants & that we shall get on well.

Friday 22 April: M***** I am very ill in bed all day. Last time Feb. 1st 11 weeks. Ellen G. and her friend Miss Oldham called. Revd. W. R. Lloyd called, stayed to tea. Grand Concert at Pontardawe Long Room. I shd. greatly liked to have gone but I was not well enough.

Saturday 23 April: Lloyd & Lizzie sowing seeds in Kitchen Garden. Parsnips (Jersey), Carrots, Onions, Leeks, Turnips, Lettuce &c. Lizzie & I went over to see the new tenants 7.30 p.m. Mary showed us over the house, all was very tidy, & made us take tea & cake in the Parlour, a very comfortable room & a lovely fire. David not at home.

Sunday 24 April: Lizzie, Harriet and Lloyd to Church. Betty to Ystalyfera. I in the house.

Monday 25 April: Lizzie & Harriet at the Cottage a.m. burning the wallpaper & old rags. Lloyd & Betty set 2 rows peas "Duchess of Edinburgh".

Tuesday 26 April: Lloyd to Station for cask of Beer, 18 gallons. Told David Morgan that he might have the Cottage garden for potatoes this year as Cottage was vacant, he seemed very glad.

Wednesday 27 April: Lizzie & I walked to the Cottage & to see the Garden & hedges, brought up shelves of cupboard. While there Harriet brought us the letters, one a postcard saying Dr. Walters, his wife & son would come up this afternoon, they came to tea. Walter hopes to be ordained in June & to have a Curacy in Liverpool.

Thursday 28 April: Lizzie trimming Ivy under hay house & cropping strong shoots off laurel. Harriet cleaned out the Drawing Room. Lizzie recd. letter from Mrs. Griffiths Cwmamman asking if she would assist at her stall in the Brynamman Bazaar 28th July next. Lloyd to Pontardawe (John Harris) for 2 cwt seed potatoes 4/6 per cwt.

Saturday 30 April: Began 20 lb box of tea today had from Jenkins and Co. London. £2..10..0 paid.

Monday 2 May: Morgan Walter here putting new bottom to Blanket Coffer & putting the boards below the drawers making it 7 inches deeper. Anne Hicks' husband buried today at Carmel, a very large funeral.

Tuesday 3 May: Yesterday Einon this way looking for their sheep. Yesterday Lizzie & Harriet raking the Walk. Lizzie & I walked as far as Cae Cwtta to see Tom turn the heap of earth. We found that someone had cut off the leader of the pretty little Scotch fir tree that we had a few years ago planted by Heol y

Cefn entrance gate. We were both so vexed, especially Lizzie as it had now grown just above the wall.

Wednesday 4 May: Clerical Conference at Carmarthen yesterday & today. Heard yesterday that Mrs. Dr. Griffiths was going to have a baby, about 15 years since the 1st baby was born, it died quite an infant.

Friday 6 May: Morgan Walker here putting new elm footboard to 3rd bedstead, the other had broken. Revd. W. R. Lloyd here to tea.

Saturday 7 May: Lloyd finished cleaning Heol y Ty. I walked down to Heol Hugh gate where David Morgan was ditching & repairing hedge between Coitcae Gwartheg and Wain dan ty. I lined the Blanket Coffer with 3rd room blue curtain. Lizzie walked to see Mrs. Kirkhouse, she came by Llanguicke, past Alltycham saw Mr. Lewis & Laura & they made her come to the house, the 1st time she ever was there. She only stayed a few minutes, they were very kind.

Sunday 8 May: Lloyd drove Lizzie & I to Church. Betty & Harriet. Sacrament. 17 communicants.

Tuesday 10 May: Lloyd mowed the Green 1st time this year. Tom Tirlan repairing Cae Barriwns hedge under the Fir trees. Gwenny cleaning Cae Barriwns, paid her up to this day 6¾ days at 1/-, 6/9.

Wednesday 11 May: Tom Tirlan weeding the old garden & screening the weeds so as not to take away earth.

Thursday 12 May: Mary Smith came up on Horseback from her Aunt's (Mrs. Bowen) to see us. Stayed to dinner & tea. She is quite crippled with rheumatism. Miss James, Lalla Kirkhouse, Dotty & Lucy Biss came here to tea. Paid Jenkins for 20 lbs tea had 30th April last by cash £2..10..0.

Friday 13 May: Harriet cleaned out the Hall & the Drawing room. Lizzie to Evan Jones for meat, had leg of veal 9¾ lbs @ 9d, paid 7/4.

Saturday 14 May: Mrs. Kirkhouse came here to spend the day. Lloyd went for her at 11 a.m. & took her home at 5.30. Richard Matthews called in his way to Swansea, said his wife, the 2 children, servant & himself were going to Dartford next week.

Sunday 15 May: Lizzie, Harriet & Lloyd to Church. Betty & I in the house.

Tuesday 17 May: Dr. Rees came down 12.30. Lizzie wrote to him yesterday saying I was not so well & that my throat was very painful.

Wednesday 18 May: Revd. D. Jones called here on his way to Caegurwen School Board meeting, he returned here to tea.

Thursday 19 May: Harriet washing out spare bedroom above dining room. Mrs. A. Gilbertson & her sister Jessie Lloyd called. I have not seen her for years ('68 I think it was at Glantwrch). She was very nice, kind & friendly. Lizzie was quite pleased with her. Lizzie to Bryn Syfi last train.

Friday 20 May: Put my dear Mother's 4 blankets (C.P.) after Lizzie had turned & bound them all, in the Coffer, which I had lined with old blue chintz to keep them from dust. Also 3 of the thick home made blankets (J) & 1 pair of best shop blankets, these are all clean having been washed last Autumn.

Saturday 21 May: Lizzie returned from Bryn Syfi 4.10 train. Dr. Rees called but wd. not stay to tea. Said my throat was better. Put down spare room carpet after I had mended it, & altered it, clean valance &c., it all looks nice & clean now.

Rogation Sunday 22 May: Lizzie & I in Church. Lloyd, Harriet & Betty. Harriet to Chapel 6 p.m. Mary Smith, Mrs. Bowen the Mill, her daughter & another girl in Church.

Monday 23 May: Griffith Evans here. Paid him £2..2..0 for his services in playing the Harmonium at Llanguicke Church from Easter 1880 to Easter 1881. Told him it was the same sum I could promise him this year. He said his wife would take to the cleaning of the Church instead of Hannah Morgan who gives it up, at the same price £2..2..0 per year. Lizzie paid Griffiths for the "Cyfaill Eglwysig" up to last Easter 1/-.[7]

Tuesday 24 May: Tom Tirlan finished spading the old Garden, it wants more earth especially where the apple trees were. Lloyd harrowing the meadow.

---

7. *Y Cyfaill Eglwysig* was a Church monthly paper, edited at this time by the Rev. William Evans (1823-1900), Vicar of Rhymney and prebendary of Llandaff Cathedral.

Wednesday 25 May: Lloyd mowing the Green. Harriet & Gwenny cropping & sweeping. Revd. D. Jones called in his way from the Caegurwen School Board meeting, said they hoped to lessen the Salaries of the masters & teachers.

Friday 27 May: Lizzie in the phaeton to Pontardawe to buy brushes for Llanguicke p.m. Paid Hannah Morgan Bryngwena up to this day for cleaning Llanguicke Church, 9 months (@ £2..2..0 per yr.), £1..11..6 paid.

Saturday 28 May: Lloyd drove Lizzie & I to Llanguicke 10 a.m. Hannah Morgan gave up the cleaning of Llanguicke Church to Anne, Griffith Evan's wife who recd. from me 1 sweeping Brush, 1 liming brush, 1 scrubbing brush & 1 small black lead brush, all new from Davies the Ironmonger's yesterday, 9/11 paid. Lloyd cleaned & edged Church Walk.

Sunday 29 May: Lizzie, I, Lloyd, Harriet & Betty in Church. Mary John at Llanguicke. She told Harriet that Catherine had left for Manchester last Friday for service. She had been home 9 weeks. Mrs. & Miss Ford called p.m. They returned from Bath &c. last week, they were very friendly, said the garden looked very neat. They saw the owl in Heol y Cefn.

Monday 30 May:

	£
Had 100 Geraniums from Wheeler	1 .. 5 .. 0
Also 1 crimson rose 1/- (3 dahlias gratis)	1
	1 .. 6 .. 0
Basket	5
Garden seeds (Kitchen)	9 .. 8
	£2 .. 0 .. 8
Basket returned & discount	6 .. 3
June 3rd. By cheque paid	£1..14 .. 5
	Paid

Tuesday 31 May: The little boy of Llwyncelyn (David Griffiths) told Lizzie that John the Blacksmith's son George had taken away the young grey Owl from Cae Barriwns fir trees, sent up Harriet & the boy to tell George to bring the Owl back directly or I wd. send Lloyd for a Policeman to make him do so. He brought her back & I told him how wrong it was in him to take what did not belong to him. He seemed very penitent.

Wednesday 1 June: Lizzie & Harriet planting out geraniums in the Green & boxes.

Thursday 2 June: Gwenny cleaning about little hill gate & the Quarry. Tom burnt all the Eithen [gorse] &c. he had cut in the Quarry. It looks much tidier.

Friday 3 June: Lloyd drove me to Mrs. Kirkhouse's to see about the flower pots, they were not ready. She gave me 3 pincushions for the Bazaar. Went to Sally's to ask her to make Lizzie's grey print frock by Thursday. Said she wd., took her also the Velvet Bell Pulls to be new covered, also the black & white print to make us both dresses, bought of her a rem[nant] of light print 5½ yards for Lizzie, either frock or petticoat. After tea Liz and I called at Cwm Vicarage to see Mrs. G. about the Bazaar. She showed us some of her things!! Took the phaeton over the 2 bridges, but not to the house, road not finished. 1st time I had seen the bridges.

Saturday 4 June: Lizzie cleaned & wiped down the 3rd room walls which were much spotted by damp, Harriet washed out the room, it now looks nice & clean. Harriet to Swansea yesterday bought new hat, cotton dress &c, in all 13/6. Bought Water Pitcher instead of one she broke. Lloyd clearing off stones &c. from Heol Cefn.

Whitsunday 5 June: Lizzie, I, Lloyd, Betty & Harriet to Church. Mr. Jones asked Lizzie to go to the Vicarage to tea & then go to Pontardawe Church. She cd. not go owing to having only her house boots on, said she wd. go another evening. Communion: The Vicar.

Whit Monday 6 June: Paid J. Jones Crachllwyn Garth Poor rate &c. as follows:

		£ .. s .. d
Garth farm	£47 .. 0 .. 0 @ 1/4	3 .. 2 .. 8
Cottage	2 .. 0 .. 0	2 .. 8
3 Cots. Cwmllynfell	7 .. 10 .. 0	10 .. 0
2 " Colliery	7 .. 5 .. 0	9 .. 8
	£63 .. 15 .. 0 @ 1/4d	£4 .. 5 .. 0
	Less commission	5 .. 7
		£3 .. 19 .. 5
Garth High way rate £47 @ 5d.		19 .. 7
Caegurwen " 4 cots. 12..5..0 @ 6d.		6 .. 1½
By cheque		£5 .. 5 .. 1½
Pd. in error 2½d. too much, see cheque book		Paid

Lloyd & Harriet to Gellyonen Mountain.

Wednesday 8 June: Lloyd took the calf to grass to Griffith Walters, Cefnllan, at 1/- per week. Betty washed & ironed all the upstairs muslin blinds, & I made new short calico tops, Liz made new green blind for spare room, all the windows now look very clean & tidy.

Thursday 9 June: R.P.L. came here 12.20, walked from Station, Lloyd drove him to meet last train. He brought me lobster, oranges & cherries, also 100 Llanguicke cards from Eynon the Printer for wh. I paid 5/- & 6d for the envelopes had before. Revd. W. R. Lloyd called, stayed to tea. Tom Tirlan finished turning the manure heap on the Hill, very tidy.

Friday 10 June: Mrs. Price had asked Lizzie & I to lunch at Glantwrch (Miss Jenkins there) & we had accepted, but it was too wet for us to go. John Tirlan spreading the ashes after burning the trash by saw pit & making it tidy. Lloyd carrying off stones from Cae Barriwns gate p.m. Shoeing the mare. Recd. the three pinafores for Bazaar from Mrs. Kirkhouse.

Saturday 11 June: Lloyd drove Lizzie to meet last train at Garnant, she goes to Jane's till Monday.

Sunday 12 June: Lloyd & Harriet to Church. Betty & I in the house. My face very painful. M. A. Harris in Church. The Vicar.

Monday 13 June: Lizzie returned. Jane & her husband drove her as far as the Iron Gate but wd. not come to the house 4.30 p.m. Lloyd finished burning old trash in the Quarry, took old crockery &c. to the Bog and swept up the back nicely & cleared all away. Betty limed & washed cowhouse, Harriet raking the Walks & clearing all small firewood from by little gate to pigsty. All is now very tidy, both Back & Front & back road. Tom Tirlan putting up little bridge to Cae Barriwns Wood & clearing away Briars from the Walk old Tom E.J. had made these 20 yrs. ago.

Tuesday 14 June: Miss Rees (Tirbach) & her Brother Johnnie came down to tea (walked), left at 10. The Dr's servant brought the Dog cart for them. Lizzie took them after tea to the top of the Hill & thro' Cae Barriwns wood to see the Owls. Lloyd digging between Cae Barriwns potatoes.

Wednesday 15 June: M*****. Lizzie & I lunched at Glantwrch, Lloyd drove us in the Carriage. Mrs. Price very crippled, but very kind. We walked down to the Hut & to the Well, all round the Gardens & by the old Mill Cottages, all looking very nice & tidy. Tom Tirlan opening gutter in Cae Barriwns wood & putting stones in wet places on the Walk.

Saturday 18 June: Tom Tirlan after having earned here £5..17..6 left, the Tin Works commence Monday.

Sunday 19 June: Lizzie, I & Betty in the house all day. Harriet to Church. Very showery, Lloyd to Tarranau Gleison, Mrs. Day & her husband gone to Swansea to see Charlie who now lives there.

Monday 20 June: Daniel Davies came here to cut & prepare the Post for the wire fencing to be put up in Cae Mawr.

Tuesday 21 June: Barnaby Fair, wet and showery. D. Morgan & his wife to the fair.[8]

Wednesday 22 June: Took Lizzie in the Carriage to within a mile of X Inn (Ystrad Amman) to go to Llwyn-yr-Onen to ask John to alter the P.O.O. he had given her for £2..10. as she had signed her name Elizabeth instead of Lizzie. She walked back over the Hill & met Lloyd by the Cottage going to meet her by last train with the Carriage. Very wet. Lizzie & I called in going this morning 10.30 at Mrs. Thomas's. Tom had come down for a few days. I asked him, his Mother, Miss Shenton & Miss Clarke here to dinner on Saturday, they accepted. Showed the things for Bazaar.

Thursday 23 June: Lizzie sent Jane 5 sovereigns. Lizzie, I & Daniel Davies fixing place for wire fence in Cae Mawr. Lloyd & Daniel took poles to Pontardawe to saw.

Friday 24 June: My face & gums very painful all day. Lizzie very poorly with a severe cold. Mr. Lloyd called 6 p.m. We had taken tea, he wd. take none, had bread & cheese at 8 p.m. a.m. Betty to E. Jones for meat. Forequarter of lamb, 7 lbs. @ 1/-, 7/- paid. Lloyd, Harriet & Betty cleaning the Green.

Saturday 25 June: Fanny G. and Miss Ford called. Expected Mrs. Thomas, Tom, Miss Shenton & Dora Clarke here to dinner but the morning was very

8. A traditional fair celebrating the feast day of St. Barnabus and held in many towns (e.g. in Llandeilo from the 14th century) to promote their commercial life.

wet, it cleared midday thought they might come to tea, but they did not. Daniel to Gas Works for Tar, 18 gal. 4/6.

Sunday 26 June: Lloyd & Betty to Church. Harriet went home. Liz & I at home all day. Lizzie very poorly with a severe cold. After tea we both went for a little walk through Cae Barriwns wood & home [by] Heol y Cefn with Lloyd who was bringing the cows. Betty showed us the shawl, handkerchief & dress Miss Rees gave her.

Monday 27 June: Cut the Ham & Gammon out of the Bogelegel second flitch. Lloyd with a letter to Mrs. Price asking if the Benthalls would come here to lunch either tomorrow or Wednesday. Mrs. Price wrote back saying Mr. Benthall returned to London to-morrow & that Jane & the children would remain at Glantwrch another fortnight or 3 weeks, & that she & the children were going to lunch at Cilybebyll on Wednesday. Returned Revd. W. R. Lloyd's book. He sent back "Cassells Magazine" and "Dr. Syntax", also a few strawberries.

Tuesday 28 June: Recd. letter from Andrews the Tailor saying Lloyd's clothes could be ready by July 12th.

Wednesday 29 June: Lloyd took the phaeton down to Burchell, he was measured by C. J. Andrews for new suit of clothes. Had new carriage sponge 2/6 paid.

Thursday 30 June: Lizzie & I went to Bryn Syfi 5.30 train to stay till Tuesday.

Sunday 3 July: Lizzie went with Mrs. Nancarrow to St. Mary's Swansea a.m. All the Militia Men there. Lizzie went by herself to the Iron Church St. Thomas's at 6.30. Canon Eden preached & Dr. Evans read the lessons. I at home all day with Miss Jenkins.

Monday 4 July: Lizzie & I to Swansea a.m. to be fitted for her new dress at Evans. Lizzie went with Mrs. Nancarrow & her sister Miss Mitchell p.m. to the Mumbles thence on Donkeys to Caswell & Langland bays, returned to Bryn Syfi 8.30. It turned a damp misty afternoon & Liz was tired & a bad headache.

Tuesday 5 July: Lizzie & I returned home last train.

Thursday 7 July: Dear little Lizzie's birthday. R.P.L. & T.J. dined here. Lloyd took Richard to meet last train to Swansea, Tom stayed the night. Miss Jenkins gave Lizzie little ruby brooch, T.J. a gold brooch, N.T. Birthday card, J.H. book marker. Sarah birthday card and I gave her my gold chain for her locket, & little round table. R.P.L. brought her a basket of dessert, strawberries, cherries, plums, pineapple & 2 nice sewin. Poor child she looks very weak & delicate but I hope she will get better & live many years & in happiness.

Friday 8 July: Lloyd took Carriage harness saddle to Davies of Neath to be re-stuffed & repaired, he called at Trenache for the great coat lent Mr. Paddison last March. Dr. Rees called in his way from Swansea to see Lizzie's knee wh. is swollen & painful.

Saturday 9 July: Lloyd with Dl. Davies putting supports to Wire fencing in Cae Mawr & tarring the same. Fanny G. called, showed her Lizzie's new dress wh. she liked. The Workhouse children at A.G's.[9]

Sunday 10 July: Lloyd, Betty & Harriet to Church. Lizzie's knee painful & I could not go as the Phaeton was at Swansea & the Harness at Neath to be mended. Wm. Lewis said Biddy was taken ill yesterday in coming from Swansea, & that they had had a Post Office. Daniel Cilpentan's wife & some others came to see the tenants, she came in to see me. Sacrament.

Monday 11 July: Lloyd and Dl. Davies finished tarring Cae Mawr wire fence 4 p.m. Lloyd to Neath to fetch carriage saddle wh. is new panelled & mended. Came home through Glais to ask how Biddy was. She is much the same (a bad cold it is).

Tuesday 12 July: Dl. Davies & Richard Lewis commenced mowing the meadow this morning. Lloyd to Swansea midday train to fetch his new clothes from Andrews & the whip from Burchell.

Friday 15 July: Lloyd drove Lizzie & I in the Carriage to the opening of Brynamman New Church St. Catherine's consecrated by the Bishop of St. David's. A lovely day. Mrs. Thomas of Skewen there. I had not seen her for more than 24 years, she was very friendly.

9. Arthur Gilbertson of Glanrhyd House inherited the tinplate enterprise of W. Gilbertson & Co. Ltd. in 1882. He was a paternalistic employer, local benefactor and a County Magistrate for the Pontardawe Petty Sessional Division. Pontardawe Workhouse was built in 1879 to accommodate 130 inmates. Fanny Gilbertson was the eldest (37) of Arthur's 4 unmarried sisters.

Saturday 16 July: Elizabeth Bryn Syfi came up here 11.30 train with Mr. Jevons' letter about Miss Harris's money to Miss Jenkins. We were all very busy with the Meadow hay. Harriet walked with her as far as Gellygron. Lizzie's knee painful. Dl. Davies & M. Lewis finished mowing the Meadow about 4 p.m. & then helped to carry the hay, James Harris & Thomas the P.O. helping too.

Sunday 17 July: Lloyd & Harriet to Church. Betty, I and Liz in the house. I cannot go as the phaeton is at Burchells & Lizzie cannot walk on her swollen knee.

Tuesday 26 July: Lloyd took Betty & Mary Shonny in D. Morgan's Car to Ystalyfera this evening. Settled with Betty up to this time.

	£ .. s .. d
7 years wages @ £4..0..0 per yr.	28 .. 0 .. 0
Money had on a/c at various times	12 .. 10 .. 0
Balance due to her	£15 .. 10 .. 0

Paid Betty the above balance in Gold £15..10..0 in the presence of Lizzie & Mary Shonny.

Wednesday 27 July: Dr. Rees called in going to Rhydyfro School meeting, left his horse here & walked down. Had in Cae Barriwns hay. The whole of it carried to-day. James Harris & Hannah Daniel's son with Lloyd. Tom came after tea to help. Hay in good condition. A sunny afternoon brisk wind.

Friday 29 July: Put blister on Lizzie's knee 8 p.m.[10]

Saturday 30 July: Lizzie in bed all day, knee very painful.

Sunday 31 July: Lloyd to Church. Harriet to Chapel at 6 p.m. Lizzie & I at home all day.

Wednesday 3 August: R. Lewis commenced cutting Cae front. Obliged to give [up] at 9.30 a.m. owing to rain. Wrote to Mr. Strick saying Miss Harris'

10. Possibly Margaret applied a blistering plaster or ointment to irritate the skin and produce a blister. See also 29 October and 27 November.

mortgage money was due to be paid the 9th inst. & asking if he had written to Mr. Josiah Rees, & if further trustees were necessary.

Friday 5 August: R.P.L. came up 11.30 train. Lloyd met him at Gellygron with the Carriage. He is 68 this day. He brought up Sewin, Cucumber, Pears, Plums & black Cherries, all very nice. He left last train, Lloyd drove him to the Station & Lizzie too. She drove on to Evan Jones' to see for some meat, had none to suit. R. Lewis finished mowing Cae front 2 days, 6/-paid.

Saturday 6 August: Had leg of lamb from Phillips, 3/11 paid. T.J. came up 8.30 p.m. train from Swansea, here at 10 o'clk exactly. Brought me a lovely bunch of grapes, "Wine in the Cluster".

Sunday 7 August: Lloyd & Harriet to Church. Lizzie & T.J. went up the Hill for a walk after dinner. He left for Llwyn Cwm 8.15. walking over the hill. I in the house all day.

Monday 8 August: A very wet day. Lloyd to Pontardawe to shoe the Mare. He paid John Harris the 1/- owing for ¼ cwt of potatoes had some time ago. Paid Chillcot the Gas man for 18 gall. of Tar had for wire fencing in Cae Mawr, Paid 4/6. Also Phillips Butcher for leg of lamb 3/11 paid. Lloyd said he was sorry he had given me notice to leave & that if I had nothing against him he would like to remain, told him that I was quite willing for him to stay, but that I expected him to keep things tidy, & to be more sober than he had been lately.

Tuesday 9 August: Lloyd finished carrying dirt off the road to Cae Cwtta. Lizzie's eyes very sore & painful.

Wednesday 10 August: ***** M. I am very poorly & my bowels very sore lying on the bed most of the day. L. *****

Harriet baking. Lizzie had a hot lamb's tail & a few potatoes for her supper, said she enjoyed it, poor child. She eats but very little & is very thin.

Thursday 11 August: Lloyd weeding the pavement gutters from the Court doors to the Coach house &c. I wrote to John Harries saying Lizzie's knee had been bad & that I was afraid she could not come to Liverpool.

Friday 12 August: Griffith Walters Cefnllan came to see how we were as we had not been to church for such a long time & brought the Llanguicke offertory of 3rd July,

		7 ..10
added our 1/- each		2 .. 0
	Entered in Book	9 ..10

Griffith said he thought Lizzie looking very thin and ill.

Saturday 13 August: Mrs. Edwin Paddison, her 3 children, Charles, Alice & George, & her brother George's little girl Maud came here unexpectedly to tea yesterday.[11] She had not been here for many years, I shd. think quite 15 & what made them come this very wet afternoon I cannot think. Young Davies Forchegel called but wd. not stay to tea, his feet being wet.

Sunday 14 August: Lizzie to Church on D. Morgan's pony, Lloyd walking with her, her knee painful. Harriet to Church. Young David Davies (Forchegel) preached the first time at Llanguicke, he is a Curate at Chirk. Sacrament: The Vicar.

Monday 15 August: A cheap Excursion to Liverpool, 6/- there & back. Henry Morris, Margaret, John Morris, Hannah Jones & many others went up.

Tuesday 16 August: Revd. D. Jones called midday, paid me £10, ½ year's Int. due last June. He seemed anxious about Lizzie's knee & advised my taking her to London for advice. Altho. she had not been to Church for many Sundays & he knew she was very poorly, he never came to see her until now, when he brought the Int. which I had written for 9 days ago. Revd. W. R. Lloyd went for his Holidays today.

Thursday 18 August: Recd. letter from Mr. Player, Chemical Works, Neath, asking for a truck of Cwmllynfell coal trusses. Dr. Rees & his Sister called 12 o'clk. to see Lizzie. Willy Paddison drove his sister Rosa & Miss Reason here to tea, Ethel & Julia also came. I had not invited the two latter. Finished Cae front, hay greatly injured by long rain.

---

11. Anne Margaretta Paddison (44) wife of Edwin, farmer of 60 acres, Tyrisha, Dulais Lower Neath.

Friday 19 August: Young Davies, Forchegel came here to tea, he leaves tomorrow for Chester where he will preach at St. Peter's, that Vicar going to preach at Chirk instead.

Saturday 20 August: Lloyd went home 11.30 train for a week.

Sunday 21 August: A very wet stormy day. Lizzie & I at home all day. Harriet to Church. Had a nice fire in the Kitchen. Lizzie fetched her little table & read to me from the Sunday Magazine. We both took our tea in the Kitchen 4.30 before Harriet returned & we enjoyed it very much, so clean & comfortable.

Monday 22 August: David, Wm. Harris' son from Rhydyfro brings the letters about 10.30 a.m., stays to clean the stable &c until post time at 4 p.m. when he leaves. He is to come every day until Lloyd's return as we have only Harriet.

Tuesday 23 August: Harriet washed Lloyd's bedclothes, his bed will be nice & clean when he returns, also his room, & Kitchen loft.

Wednesday 24 August: Lizzie invited to tea at Dr. Rees' but could not go, no one to drive her up. Fanny G., Mrs. Lawrence & her little boy Clive called here, stayed an hour & a half. Harriet & I turned out the 2 Coffers on Kitchen loft, put all the Newspapers in one & the other left empty. Had Lloyd's room thoroughly swept out & put tidy & Harriet washed it out clean, it was very dirty.

Thursday 25 August: Harriet & I finished cleaning down Kitchen loft. It is now thoroughly cleaned & scrubbed out, knife board taken down stairs, no knives or boots to be cleaned upstairs again.

Friday 26 August: Harriet washed out the pantry, dairy and kitchen, all very tidy when Lloyd returned this evening 8.45. Lloyd brought me some fine trout.

Saturday 27 August: Had load of Llwynrhidie coal. Lloyd took the screw for tightening wire back to David Smith, Alltwen, wrote a note to him saying we had broken it & that if he wd. kindly get it mended that I would pay the charge.

Sunday 28 August: Lizzie to Church on David Morgan's pony & Lloyd with her. I at home all day. Anne, Harriet's sister & little Mary came down. Harriet in the house all day as her best boots had gone to be tapped & the shoemaker had not sent them back.

Monday 29 August: Churned 5 lbs. of butter, kept 3 lbs. Put other 2 lbs. with 4 lbs. bought of Mary into little pot for Sarah wh. Lizzie will take up if she goes. Lizzie ironed Sarah's bolster & pillow cases. Very wet all day. Lizzie wrote to Sarah, T.J. & Miss Jenkins.

Tuesday 30 August: Mr. Jones the Vicar called. Stayed to tea & then to Clydach, said some of the Church people were leaving for the New Chapel in Pontardawe.

Wednesday 31 August: Lloyd's month's notice up. Lizzie rode D.M.'s pony as far as Gellygron, going to Bryn Syfi 1st train to see Mr. Jevons & Will. On getting there they were going to Glantwrch to spend the day & Lizzie went for a turn to the Mumbles by herself, a fine day. Wore her Bazaar dress & hat. Had phaeton from Burchell after been newly painted & done up. Lloyd went for it this afternoon & Lizzie returned with him, they were here 8.30 p.m. Harriet washed our room.

Thursday 1 September: I have a very bad cold & cough & in bed until 3.30 p.m. Fanny & Ellen G. called.

Friday 2 September: M*****, 48 years old. My Birthday. R.P.L. could not come up as his Aunt Mrs. Griffiths died last Tuesday. Lizzie gave me 2 pretty little cards, pair of cuffs & pen holder. T.J. sent me a note wishing me many happy returns of the day & a nice little scent bag.

Sunday 4 September: Lizzie walked to Church, the first time since her knee was bad. Lloyd & Harriet to Church. I in the house all day, very bad cough & my voice quite gone.

Monday 5 September: Betty came here this evening from Ystalyfera to stay while Lizzie is away in Liverpool.

Paid Wm. Williams Pheasant's Bush	
Poor Rate on Gellyluog Wood @ 10d.)	£ .. s .. d
(2 qrs. due & now paid wood valued @ 30/-))	10 .. 0
High Way rate on same @ 6d.	1 .. 6
	11 .. 6 Paid

Tuesday 6 September: Lizzie left here by 1st train to Swansea thence by train 12.30 to Liverpool. A wet disagreeable day. I intended going to Swansea to see

her off but I was very poorly with violent cough, & today great sickness & very ill. Sent Harriet to see her off.

Wednesday 7 September; Mr. Thomas (a man from near Llandilo) called in his way to Neath fair with a mare for me to see. She is rather heavy but had good action, & he leaves her here on a week's trial. He will take my chestnut mare in exchange with £12 in money. He values his mare at £35 but John Gellyluog says at the present price of horses she is not worth more than £25.

Thursday 8 September: Neath Fair. Lloyd with note to the Vicarage asking if Mr. Jones wd. come up this evening. Dr. Rees called, said I must not go out in case my cough wd. turn to Bronchitis. He did not like the new mare wh. is here on trial, too much of the Carter. The Vicar came up 7.30 p.m., told him W.R.L. [Rev. W. R. Lloyd] said it was all an untruth, & that there was no foundation for it, & to be as usual. The Prince & Princess of Wales & 3 of their daughters in Liverpool. Lizzie saw them.[12]

Friday 9 September: Lloyd & D. Morgan tried the new mare in the Car, they went to the Vicarage. Mr. Jones likes her very much except her hoofs wh. are cracked. They went on to Gwernllwynwyth (to be paid for D.M.'s pony sold yesterday) & she went remarkably well & very quiet.

Sunday 11 September: Lloyd with letters to Post. Betty & Harriet to Church. Mrs. Evans the Post Office rode up to see me, stayed to tea until 10.30. Evans walked up from Church seeing her late. Sacrament.

Tuesday 13 September: Archdeacon James of Carmarthen visited Llanguicke Church. Our Vicar told me he was astonished to see it in such a bad state, that it was hardly better than a Barn. R.P.L., his Brother, Olwen, Mrs. Hadlow & Ithel intended coming up in a Fly to spend the day but I had written saying I was very poorly & that I could only see Olwen & Mrs. Hadlow, but they did not come as I was ill.

Thursday 15 September: St. Paul's Mission Church at Glais opened today. Mr. Davies of Liverpool was one of the Preachers. Revd. W. R. Lloyd called, stayed to tea. Said the house seemed empty without Lizzie. He returned last

---

12. Prince Edward, Princess Alexandra of Denmark and Princesses Louise Victoria (aged 15), Victoria Alexandra (14) and Maud Charlotte (12) to open the Alexandra Dock.

Friday after his holiday up the Rhine. Read to me the speeches in the Liverpool paper of the Royal Visit to that City.

Friday 16 September: I went down midday train to Bryn Syfi. Mr. Jevons his eldest son Will there.

Saturday 17 September: Left Bryn Syfi 3.40 p.m. train. The Vicar travelled in the same carriage with me to Pontardawe, said the Archdeacon was astonished to see Llanguicke Church in such bad repair, &c, &c. At the Station saw Mrs. Kirkhouse & her girls, said her Daughters were going abroad to school next week.

Sunday 18 September: Lloyd and Harriet to Church, Betty & I in the house all day. Harriet to Chapel at 6 o'clk. Very showery.

Tuesday 20 September: Paid J. Jones Crachllwyn Garth Poor rate as follows by cheque:

Garth farm	£47 .. 0 .. 0 @ 1/4d	£3 .. 2 .. 8
" Cottage	2 .. 0 .. 0 "	2 .. 8
3 Cots Cwmllynfell	7 .. 10 .. 0 "	10 .. 0
2 " "	7 .. 5 .. 0 "	9 .. 8
	£63 ..15 .. 0	£4 .. 5 .. 0
	Less Commission	5 .. 7
		£3 ..19 .. 5
Garth Sanitary Rate farm @ 1d		3 ..11
Cottages " " £16..15..0 @ 4d		5 .. 7
		9 .. 6
	Less Com.	1 .. 4
		8 .. 2

Wednesday 21 September: Lizzie came back from Liverpool after being away a fortnight yesterday. She left Liverpool 12 o'clk. midday & was at Garnant 7 p.m. where Lloyd met her with the phaeton. T.J. travelled with her.

Thursday 22 September: Lloyd brought home the Calf from Cefnllan after being there 15 weeks @ 1/-, paid Griffith Walters by his daughter Mary, 15/- paid 26th inst.

Friday 23 September: Took off my dear Mother's ring which she put on this day 24 years & which was never once off my finger during that time. It had now got so thin & worn that I was afraid to wear it any longer in case it wd. drop off & I shd. lose it. Fanny G., Maud & Miss Comer called. Biddy called in her way from Dl. Jenkins.

Saturday 24 September: Harriet gave me a month's notice yesterday.

Sunday 25 September: Lloyd drove Lizzie & I to Llanguicke, the 1st time since the phaeton was done up. The last time I was in Church was Whit Sunday 5 June, I could not go as the phaeton was not safe & gone to Burchell to be done up & repaired. A nice day. Harriet & Betty also to Church.

Monday 26 September: Austin (a painter from Marquiss) came up to finish the stairs. Wm. Cwmllynfell here in his way from Pontardawe fair, said Thos. was married & that he (William) intended going to Dretêg & leave Thos. at Cwmllynfell.

		£ .. s .. d
Little Mary Cefnllan brought a fowl 3 lbs.		3
A Goose 3¾ lbs @ 3/9, 6 wings 6d.		4 .. 3
Grass for calf 15 weeks		15
	Paid	£1 .. 2 .. 3

Tuesday 27 September: Cwmamman Harvest Service.

Afternoon	Prayers	Revd.	Morlais Jones
	Lesson	"	Nathaniel Thomas
	Sermons	"	Bowcott (Llawaden)
Evening	Litany		Revd. Nathaniel Thomas
	Lesson	"	Bowcott
	Sermon	"	Jones (Curate Llansamlet) Joel III. 13
		"	N. Thomas (Carmarthen)

Lloyd drove Lizzie & I to afternoon service 2.30, took tea at the Vicarage & stayed to Evening Service but not to supper.

Wednesday 28 September: Brynamman Harvest Service. Same Clergymen as yesterday. The Vicar called in his way from Wain Caegurwen School Board

Meeting. Did not know of the Services yesterday & today. Austin the Painter left last train, Lloyd took him & all his things to the Station.

Saturday 1 October: Lloyd drove me to Neath to see Mr. Scale about the Bill John Jones (my late tenant) had sent me & to ask him to get the money for the notes of hand John owes me, said he was afraid it must be all put in the County Court. Bought Bird cage for Lizzie, 7/-, Stair brush 2/-, 6 kitchen basins 9d., 3 canvas towels 11d.

Sunday 2 October: Harriet & Lizzie to Llanguicke.

Monday 3 October: Jane Matthews came up 11.30 train to stay until tomorrow. She brought up 3 robes from Evans' for Lizzie to select one for Jane's baby, 8/6 paid.

Tuesday 4 October: Lizzie & Jane after dinner went to see the Children at Rhydyfro Schools. Picked beautiful mountain ash berries in coming back. Jane left last train. Lizzie took her to the Station.

Thursday 6 October: Had tomorrow 70 lbs of cheese from Cwm @ 3d, 17/6 paid. Told Thos. of the £1 mistake, too much rent was paid & that I kept it for the repairs of Llanguicke.

Friday 7 October: Lizzie & I to Cwmllynfell 11.30 train from Pontardawe, walked up from the Station thro' the fields, into the road leading to the Barn. William & his wife had gone to Dretêg farm. They are going there to live, & leave Thos. & his wife in Cwmllynfell & we went up today to wish them good bye at Cwmllynfell where William & Margaret have lived [blank] years last March but they are to continue my tenants & not Thos. although they live in Dretêg. Called at Robert's house, it was very nicely done up. Called also in the other cottages, all glad to see us.

Saturday 8 October: Recd. a letter saying Jane was not so well. Lizzie went to see her 5.30 train from Brynamman. Met Mr. Griffiths at the Station & he came with me to Cwmamman to meet Liz by the 7.10 train.

Sunday 9 October: Lizzie, I, Lloyd, Betty & Harriet in Church. Sacrament.

Wednesday 12 October: Lloyd took Lizzie & Harriet to Llanguicke in D.M.'s car with flowers &c. to decorate the Church for Harvest Service tomorrow. They walked home. I was not well enough to go, & Lizzie too felt poorly.

Thursday 13 October: Llanguicke Harvest Service.

Prayers	Revd. D. Jones Curate
Lessons	" Williams "
Sermon	" Jones, Abercrave
	Revd. Tudor Thomas, Llanwrtyd

The Vicar, Revd. W. R. Lloyd & Revd. Mr. Rees (Garth) also in Church but did no duty.

Mr. & Mrs. Jones (Carmel), Dr. Griffiths & a very good congregation.

Sunday 16 October: Lloyd drove Lizzie & I to Church. Betty & Harriet to Church. Heavy rain coming home. The Vicar.

Saturday 22 October: Saw in the "Llanelly Guardian" of last Thursday (20th inst) the appointment of the Revd. N. Thomas to Llanddarog Vicarage. He had been Curate of St. David's Carmarthen about 4 years.

Sunday 23 October: Lloyd drove Lizzie & I to Church. Betty & Harriet to Church. Mary John there. Revd. W. R. Lloyd.

Wednesday 26 October: Fanny G. called, said she should never cease regretting she was not in Swansea 18th inst.[13] Harvest Service at Pontardawe, English 7.30 p.m. Revd. D. Jones (Curate) intoned the Service. Revds. Williams & Lloyd read the Lessons. Revd. J. C. Llewellyn Pontypool preached Acts 14-17. Lloyd drove me down, Lizzie not well & stayed at home with the 2 girls. Wrote to Dr. Rees saying Lizzie was ill & for him to come down. Lloyd shoeing mare.

Friday 28 October: Lloyd drove me to Pontardawe Bank. Saw Mr. Walker about Cwmllynfell Colliery & showed him Map copied from Tithe Map & gave him particulars & the price of the farm & minerals £7,000. It is the Ex-

13. The new East or 'Prince of Wales' Dock was opened by the Prince and Princess of Wales. Their arrival and progress through Swansea, the enthusiastic welcome of the crowds, the decorations of flags, motto banners, Venetian masts, triumphal arches and gas illuminations lining the royal route, the presentations, tributes, loyal addresses, toasts and responses, the fireworks, bonfires and choral greetings, the formal naming and opening of Alexandra Road and the Dock, the lists of eminent guests to the Royal Luncheon Pavilion and the Royal Ball (starting at 10 p.m. and "concluded for want of dancers at about 4 a.m."), were all recorded in great detail in *The Cambrian* on 19 October 1881.

Mayor of Colchester enquiries are for. Lizzie sent Revd. N. T. Twine bag & ball for his birthday tomorrow which I posted.[14]

Saturday 29 October: Put a blister to Lizzie's side last night which rose nicely this morning.

Sunday 30 October: Lloyd, Betty & Harriet to Church. Lizzie & I in the house both not well.

Monday 31 October: Fanny G. called, said she was going to stay near Cardiff on Saturday & from there to other friends until near Xmas.

Wednesday 2 November: Dr. Rees called, stayed to tea.

Friday 4 November: Had 19 lbs of Beef from Gotregarth 12/6 paid. Goose from Gorsellydan 4/6 paid.

Sunday 6 November: Lizzie walked to Church. Harriet, Betty & Lloyd. I at home all day not well. My bowels so very constipated. Expected T.J. last night but it was very damp & disagreeable after all the rain & he did not come.

Tuesday 8 November: Went to Glantwrch by 11.30 train, found Mrs. Price much better. Said she thought Jane would be moving into her New house this day week. Saw patterns of Jane's paper for the rooms. Mr. Herbert Lloyd & Mr. George Strick called at Glantwrch. Returned 5.30 train. Lizzie sent little Ben two pint bottles of Cod Liver oil had yesterday from Bell & Co.

Thursday 10 November: Morgan Walters commenced repairing the Barn doors. Duke of Edinburgh [Prince Alfred Ernest Albert] came to Swansea (1st time) to inspect Naval Volunteers, he only stayed a few hours. He goes on a tour of Inspection on Welsh Coast.

Sunday 13 November: Lloyd drove Lizzie & I to Church, Harriet & Betty. Evan in Church, said he would come here next Saturday. Sacrament: The Vicar.

---

14. A decorative knitted or crocheted twine bag was a popular and useful Victorian gift. It was made of coloured open-work stitches, finished with ribbons and filled with a ball of coloured twine which could be drawn out for cutting.

Tuesday 15 November: David Thomas the Carpenter called here to see old carriage springs &c., did not see us, his offer of 12/6 was much too little & he was well aware of it too. He was going up to Llanguicke to meet the Vicar. A Committee held at Llanguicke Church to decide whether it had better be re-roofed now or in the Spring, the decision was to postpone the work. Grey heifer to Nantygasseg bull.

Thursday 17 November: Lloyd taking up the 3 old stumps in piece under Hay house. Bought 15 lbs Beef of Gwen Gotregarth @ 8d, 10/- paid.

Friday 18 November: Lloyd took the Cwmllynfell plans of the Big & the Brass Veins to Mr. Walker of the Bank (Pontardawe). He has now in his charge the two plans of today, 2 Maps & 1 newspaper cutting (giving account of J. & A.'s coal at the Portsmouth Dockyard), in all 5 things. Mr. & Mrs. Griffiths Cwmamman & their niece Lizzie Lewis walked down, stayed to tea & supper. Lloyd drove them at 9 p.m. as far as the Mountain. A damp & wet afternoon.

Saturday 19 November: Evan came down to see the road (Heol Hugh). Measured it with Morgan Walters, told Evan, John Jones & I were likely to go to law about it & that he wd. be called as witness to my verbal agreement with John. Ellen G. called on horseback, did not come in. Sally here, paid £6..10. Int. on £130, also 2/9 for 22 lbs newspapers had some months ago. I paid her as per her bill for all work done to this date, 16/3d.

Sunday 20 November: T.J. came here last night. Lizzie very poorly with pain in her side & pit of stomach. She did not go out of the house. T.J. & I to Pontardawe Church 6.30 p.m. (Mr. Lloyd). Harriet to Llanguicke & to Chapel at 6 o'clk.

Monday 21 November: T.J. left 10.55 train from Garnant. Samuel Bogelegel here offering a pig, said he had taken Cathulus farm & wd. be going there next Sep. 1882.

Tuesday 22 November: Morgan Walters finished repairing the Barn doors, the two lower small doors are both all new wood. Morgan Harris Gartheithen bought Llwyncelyn Cottage (sold by Auction to-morrow) for £59. It is rather over ½ an acre of freehold land, the Cottage is in poor repair. Isaac Jones Glynmeirch buried today.

Wednesday 23 November: Revd. W. R. Lloyd called 2.20, had lunch (cold turkey) & stayed to tea. He was sorry to see poor Lizzie so ill on the sofa. Ellen G. called on horseback & sat an hour, she was sorry to see Liz ill. Dr. Rees called at 5 p.m., said he thought Lizzie's Liver better & that the pain in the pit of her stomach was Neuralgia. Commenced the brown pot of butter for Parlour about 18 lbs.

Thursday 24 November: Morgan Walters putting up new weather boards to the pine ends of the Barn. Lewis the Tiler re-laying the Barn crests & fastening some loose slates, 4/- paid. Morgan Walters repaired the Dog's cwb & put new rail by D.M.'s pistle.

Friday 25 November: Went down to Gartheithen to meet Benjamin Daniel Llwynpryred to talk about the mare he had heard of likely to suit me. He had not seen her, her owner is Meredith Davies Lamb & Flag Inn Glyn Neath price £30. I will write to him to-morrow about her. Harriet took things had from Shoolbred home to be made.

Saturday 26 November: Mrs. Harris Nantrickets here with a Tongue, 2/- paid. Very wet all day. Begun the bread of a sack of flour (had 31st ult.) this evening. Lizzie went to bed 12.20 in great pain.

Sunday 27 November: A terrible storm of wind & rain last night. Wind very high today. Lloyd & Harriet to Church. Lizzie in bed all day, put on blister last night. Mrs. Harris came up to see her, brought nice wheaten loaf.

Wednesday 30 November: Dr Rees called in his way from Rhydyfro School Board meeting. Very wet day.

Thursday 1 December: Ellen G. called & brought some books for Lizzie to read. Lent her some Young Ladies' journals (6). Lent 1 year of Temple Bar (1865). Mr. Lloyd called, stayed to tea.

Friday 2 December: Morgan Walters repairing our Stable. Bogelegel daughter brought me half a pig, 106 lbs @ 10/6 per score: £2..15..6 paid. Recd. letter from Mr. Scale saying that the disputed case between John Jones & myself would be heard on Thursday next 6th inst. Lent Morgan Harris Gartheithen £6..0..0 paid.

Saturday 3 December: Lloyd drove me to Neath thinking to see Mr. Scale, he had gone to Aberdare. Evan brought me 3 brooms, he slept at Gartheithen. Betty salted the ½ pig had yesterday. Bought some nice soles in Neath. Liz enjoyed them.

Sunday 4 December: Lloyd, Harriet & Betty to Church, Mary & Einon there. Lizzie & I at home all day. Lizzie has been in less pain all day.

Friday 9 December: Tapped cask of beer yesterday.

Sunday 11 December: A sharp frost. Lloyd drove me to Church as far as Cefnllan, the new Glyn Neath mare the 1st time, she went very quiet. Betty to Church. Lizzie in the house not well. Harriet to Chapel 6 p.m.

Tuesday 13 December: Mrs. Ford called in pony carriage. W.G. not well, all the girls away except Miss Ford. Gwen Cefnllan came to see Lizzie & brought her a nice fowl. Lloyd sifting ashes for Walks. Lizzie went over to D.M.'s for a few minutes, she had not been there since August (about 4 months!). When Liz and I were sitting in the Drawing room after dinner a little bird flew & pecked to each of the lower panes of window next the fire. We both remarked it.

Friday 16 December: Had 16 lbs of beef from Goetregarth @ 8d, 10/8 and a tongue 2/6. Paid 13/2.

Saturday 17 December: Rhydyfro Singers here, gave them 3/-. Mended my grey Carmalite frock & made it short dress.

Sunday 18 December: Lloyd & Harriet to Church. Lizzie, I & Betty in the house.

Monday 19 December: Paid J. Jones Crachllwyn Garth Poor rate as follows:

Garth Farm	£47..0..0	@ 1/6d	£3 .. 10 .. 6
2 Cots Cwmllynfell	5..0..0	"	7 .. 6
2 " " Colliery	7..5..0	"	10 .. 10½
	£59..5..0	"	£4 .. 8 .. 10½
J. Jones' son David			Paid by Cheque

No Commission allowed.
2 Cots vacant.

Mrs. Arthur Gilbertson called & her little boy Cecil, she was very sorry to hear Lizzie was so poorly, said her sister Mary was coming to see her 9th Janry. Begun 10 lbs of tea today.

Tuesday 20 December: Revd. D. Jones called midday to ask if we were going to decorate Llanguicke for Xmas. I said No excepting a text on the Chancel Window, as the Windows were so broken, & if all had been in good repair Lizzie poor girl is too poorly to cut out the letters or exert herself in any way. A terrible wind last night 3.30 a.m. which lasted about 3 minutes. I never heard anything so awful, it did no harm here except to a few branches. Liz was quite frightened. Bought 1 cwt potatoes "German Reds" of Reed Ystalyfera 4/6d.

Tuesday 27 December: Pontardawe Church Choir (5) came here to sing. I gave them 5/-, Lizzie gave 1/-. They had bread & cheese & beer & cake in Kitchen. Lloyd to Pontardawe, re-moved the Glyn Neath mare's shoes, the 1st time she was at the Blacksmith's.

Wednesday 28 December: Daniel Morgan fetched us 18 cwt of lump coal from Garnant @ 4½d, 6/9, Haulage 3/-. Gate two horses 8d. Begun this day. Lloyd sifting ashes. D.M. killed two pigs.

Thursday 29 December: Lizzie recd. a letter & Xmas card from Lizzie Lewis from Cherbourg. I recd. letter from Jane Benthall saying they cd. not come here to lunch to-morrow asking us up on Monday & saying they were returning to London on Tuesday.

1882

Underlying Margaret's daily routines, social interactions and financial transactions lurked her continuing uncertainty about Tom Jones's eligibility as a potential husband for Lizzie. Having lodged at Garth over the New Year until 3 January, T.J. was not mentioned again in this diary until 8 April. A week later Margaret wrote to him and declared her belief that he and Lizzie were unsuited for marriage on account of their many incompatibilities including Lizzie's fondness for "refined society", from which he was presumably excluded. Nevertheless she reluctantly gave her consent, but only after a six months' engagement to allow them time for "serious consideration of the future". T.J.'s visits continued but were infrequent and brief. Towards the end of the year Lizzie's attention was diverted to caring for her sister Sarah whose deteriorating condition led to her postpartum death. This was a tragic reminder of the cruel mutability of life whose transience Margaret expressed in her final entry: "The last day of this year 1882 God alone knows who will see this day twelve months."

Sunday 1 January: Very wet, no one to Church, cleared about 4 p.m. T.J. and Liz went for a turn down Heol y Cefn, brought me bunch of Holly. Harriet to Chapel 6 p.m. Lloyd went home yesterday. Liz & I had several cards. Fire in drawing room.

Tuesday 3 January: T.J. left 1st train from Garnant. He thought of going yesterday but it was so wet & there was no particular necessity.

Monday 9 January: Poor old Mrs. Saunders died at Swansea aged 80 years, buried at Cilycwm near Llandovery.

Thursday 12 January: Revd. W. R. Lloyd here to tea. Lizzie taken very poorly & in great pain at 11 p.m., just as we were going upstairs to bed. Sent Lloyd for the Dr. who came at 1.45. Said there was nothing serious but I am uneasy and we have decided to have Dr. Thomas for consultation.

Saturday 14 January: Dr. Thomas, Ystalyfera came here 4 p.m. to see & examine Lizzie who is suffering such severe pain in the Pit of her Stomach, sides & back. Dr. Rees here also. Dr. Thomas said he saw no serious symptoms at present & was hopeful of her recovery. It is her naturally weak & delicate constitution that makes us fearful of what may occur.

Sunday 15 January: Harriet, Lloyd & Betty to Church. Mr. Jones Llansamlet Curate officiated. Recd. Rhydyfro Concert tickets & Posters. John Bowen here from Church. Old Evan here.

Friday 20 January: Ellen, Madeline & Frank Gilbertson called, they walked. Revd. D. Jones called, said that some of the School Board members expressed themselves not pleased at the Finance Meeting on Wednesday that Concert Placards were issued without asking the sanction of the Board, said I wd. write to Mr. Turberville tomorrow.

The Garth
Jan 20th 1882

Dear Sir,

I write to apologise & express my regret for having issued the Placards announcing a Concert at the Rhydyfro Schoolroom without first having obtained the Sanction of the Board.

I beg you will explain to them that it was quite an oversight on my part and no want of respect to them. I also wish thoroughly to exonerate our Vicar & his Curate Rev. W. R. Lloyd from any implication in this matter, as the fault lies entirely on me, and in conclusion I ask if you will kindly give us the use of the Schoolroom gratuitously for the purpose

I remain dear Sir

Yours very truly

Margaret Jones

D. B. Turberville Esq.

Margaret's letter elicited an immediate & satisfactory reply from D. B. Turberville in his capacity as Clerk to the School Board.

Saturday 21 January: Sent Lloyd with a note to Mr. Turberville apologising for issuing Concert Placards without first having the sanction of the Board to use the Rhydyfro School room, said all the blame was on me & not on the Vicar or Revd. W. R. Lloyd.

Sunday 22 January: Lloyd, Harriet & Betty to Church. Einon [Jones] in Church, went to Gartheithen & then came here, 1st time since they left. Lizzie & I at home all day. Liz went for a walk as far as the Stone on the Hill, away only 20 minutes.

Wednesday 25 January: Recd. from Miss Rees Tirbach Llanguicke Church card having collected 10/- paid. When Lloyd was tying the cows the little spotted heifer (Betsey) went up stone steps & on the stable roof which she broke very much, the slates falling through into cowhouse & stable. She jumped down into the yard, apparently she is not injured but I fear there may be something internal.

Friday 27 January: The Vicar & Mr. Lloyd here to tea, arranging Rhydyfro Concert Programme. After tea we 4 had a game of "Old Maid" and "Whist". Spent a very pleasant evening.

Saturday 28 January: Lizzie had her Ulster from Evans' Brynamman. Lloyd went for it, he sold 6 Concert tickets on his way 1/- each.

Sunday 29 January: Only Lloyd to Church. Harriet to Chapel 6 p.m. John Bowen here to tea, paid 10/- for Concert Tickets. Lizzie read "Hannah the Matron" & "Samuel" from Sunday Magazine. Lizzie recd. letter from N.T. [Rev. Nathanial Thomas] "Peacemaking".

Thursday 2 February: Miss Shenton walked down, stayed to tea. Lloyd drove her part of the way back. Had load of Pontardawe coal by Morgan Harris, 3s.6d. paid. He spoke to me about Catherine. Mr. Lloyd brought up Concert Programmes.

Friday 3 February: A concert held at the Rhydyfro Schoolroom in aid of the restoration of Llanguicke Church. It was very well attended & all passed off nicely. Mr. H. N. Miers, Mr. Jones (the Clydach Curate), all the Turbervilles & Mrs. Kirkhouse's School there. Revd. Morlais & Mrs. Jones, Mrs. Evans, 2 Miss Rees' Tirbach, Miss Thomas, Mrs. Kirkhouse, the Vicar & Revd. W. R. Lloyd took tea here & we all walked down. The Jones' & Liz walked up here & I walked up alone after receiving the money had at the doors. Harriet, Betty & Lloyd there. A fine mild light night.

Saturday 4 February: Richard Matthews came down from Garnant, stayed to tea & Lloyd drove him to the Station. I went as far as the Post Office to ask Mrs. Evans if she knew of a dressmaker. Poor Mr. Gilbertson died midday 72 years.

Sunday 5 February: Lizzie & I in Church, the 1st time for Lizzie since Nov 13th & the 1st time for her to Llanguicke with her new mare. I spoke to Griffith about the fire, that it ought to be lighted a.m. & not only just in time for the Service. Liz wore Ulster first time.

Tuesday 7 February: Lloyd commenced carrying old manure to Cae Barriwns.

Wednesday 8 February: Lloyd carrying manure to Cae Barriwns. Wm. Howells (William Penlan's nephew) here asking for my support as he is trying for the post of "Whipper in" or Attendance Officer to the Languicke Schools. Said I wd. do what I could.

Thursday 9 February: Poor Mr. Gilbertson buried today at 12 o'clk. at Pont-ardawe Church age 72. A small private funeral. Lizzie intended going to tea to Tirbach but it came on wet wh. prevented her. Mended & re-trimmed sleeves of her black silk dress.

Fanny Gilbertson to Margaret Jones, *c.* 9 February 1882

[n.d.]

My dear Miss Jones,

Very many thanks to yourself and cousin for your kind sympathy. My dear father's end was very peaceful, but the shock to me is dreadful. I am quite well thank you. As soon as I go any where I shall come and see you.

All are well and join in love and thanks to you and your cousin. I have not been able to get black edged paper yet.

Yours very affectly.,

Fanny Gilbertson

[Note Margaret's comments in her diary on 14 and 17 February implying the need to observe the proprieties of bereavement protocol].

Friday 10 February: R.P.L. & Olwen came up 1st train, returned the last. They had been to Pontardulais yesterday & are sleeping at the Westbourne Hotel Swansea. R.P.L. put his name down on Lizzie's card for £5 towards repairing Llanguicke Church. Wrote to Mrs. F. H. Perkins saying I should be glad to see her on Tuesday. Wm. Davies Forchegel here asking for my aid, he is trying for the post of "Whipper in" to the Schools, said I had promised another.

Sunday 12 February: Lizzie rode the new mare 1st time to Church. Lloyd walked with her. I am very poorly today & in bed till 5 p.m. Betty in the house with me. Harriet went home to see her Mother.

Tuesday 14 February: Lloyd met 11.30 train from Swansea. Mrs. Perkins came to spend the day on her way to Mrs. Thomas'. Lloyd took her up. She seemed very pleased to see Liz & I, told me of a celebrated London doctor for women, Dr. Priestly & hoped I could go up to consult him. She was very kind & Liz liked her so much. Ellen G & her sister Kate called, the latter & her children leave for Liverpool tomorrow. She came to say Goodbye. I was quite surprised to see them so soon, the Father buried only last Thursday. Mr. Paddison called in his way from Bogelegel.

Thursday 16 February: Lloyd took Fashion book back to Sally. Cut out 2 chemises & a nightgown of unbleached calico for Lizzie (Shoolbred 7d a yard yesterday).

Friday 17 February: Fanny G. called here on Horseback, her Father was only buried yesterday week. I was quite surprised that she called here before we had called upon them. She was very kind & friendly. Lloyd getting up stumps by privet hedge by old garden. Lloyd after tea to Bogelegel asking Samuel if he cd. come here. I want to talk to him about our hedges, ditches & gates.

Saturday 18 February: John Thomas late of Cwrt-y-Bariwns buried today in Carmel, he died of cancer.

Sunday 19 February: Lizzie rode to Church & Lloyd walked with her. Betty & Harriet to Church. I at home not feeling well.

Monday 20 February: Harriet doing up carnation bed, lots of them have rotted away. We have now put many cuttings, but I am afraid it is not the proper time. Mrs. Jenkins (old Sherborne's grand-daughter) here asking if I wd. recommend her daughter Elizabeth as Mistress to Rhydyfro School. Said I know nothing of the girl. (Cut out 2 chemises & 1 nightgown for Liz. No, it was last Thursday I did so).

Tuesday 21 February: Miss Ford walked up alone to see us, the younger G's had gone to Neath.

Wednesday 22 February: Recd. patterns of carpets from Shoolbred's. Lloyd finished carrying out manure to Cae Barriwns, there is some left in the dung hill which was not rotten enough & wh. he has turned into a tidy heap.

Thursday 23 February: John Thomas took away a load of timber from by the front Gate, 4 large trees that had been cut down from by privet hedge between old garden & the Walk. I put a top & Lizzie put a band to my old white flannel petticoat. Lloyd took little Heifer “Betsey” to Nant Rickets Bull, the Nant y gasseg one too large as she is so small. Lloyd finished spreading the manure on Cae Barriwns. It covers about 3 parts of the field, all we had rotten enough.

Friday 24 February: Lloyd cleaning Heol y ty after the wood had been there wh. was taken away yesterday, it now looks tolerably tidy. Harriet p.m. sweeping grass lower side of Walk & tidying a little. Nice day. Recd. letter from Mr. Scale saying John Jones (my late tenant) had paid the money ordered by the County Court, Dec. 6th.

Saturday 25 February: Very wet. Lizzie intended going to stay a few days with Jane but was prevented by wind & rain. Lloyd repairing flower boxes for the Green.

Sunday 26 February: Lizzie & I at home all day. No one to Llanguicke. Very wet. Harriet to Chapel 6 p.m. Lloyd to Pontardawe Church 6 p.m.

Tuesday 28 February: Lizzie went to stay a few days with her sister Jane. Lloyd drove us in the phaeton all the way to Bettws Church, it was the first time I had ever been there. Lizzie crossed the River to Cross Inn & Lloyd drove me home. We had it very wet all the way back. It was fine going. Harriet washed the kitchen loft & killed the Cat, she had become so dirty in her habits.

Wednesday 1 March: Commenced cleaning kitchen cupboard. Lizzie had a letter from Jane Matthews saying she was sorry to hear from Richard that she had been ill & hoped she was better. Jane too had not been well.

Thursday 2 March: Finished cleaning out the kitchen cupboard, had all the ware & glasses washed & the shelves too. Took the Dragon ware out of the hamper, had them all boiled & put loosely back in the hamper. They are all new & for dear little Lizzie when she has a house of her own.

Friday 3 March: John Thomas came for the larch wood by the saw pit, some of them were getting rotten they had been lying there so long. John Griffiths the Timber Merchant came here. Paid him his bill for boards &c. up to Dec. 31st, £5..3..0 cheque. Nothing owing up to this date. A lovely day. Lizzie took tea at Llwyncwm. Had sack of oats & 40 lbs. of flour from Post Office. Old Evan brought me 5 brooms, paid 1/-.

Saturday 4 March: Lizzie returned from staying at Jane's 4 p.m. train. I found her at Garnant House with Miss Shenton, Mrs. Drury there. We wd. not stay to tea. Pd. Dl. Jenkins the "Prince Albert Inn" 9/- what I owed for leg of veal. Lloyd swept down leaden gutters &c. Betty limed a little in the Court, it was so dirty.

Sunday 5 March: Lizzie walked to Church, the first time she has walked since last Nov. 6th. It came on very heavy rain in about quarter of an hour after leaving here but she went on, her Ulster kept her pretty dry but I wd. much prefer her having turned back. Lloyd & Betty to Church. Revd. T. H. Hughes the Deputation expected but he was not well & stayed in the Vicarage.

Monday 6 March: Fanny G. called, told us they intended leaving Pontardawe in September next & going abroad for a year or two. She was very nice & friendly & I am very sorry they leave. Ellen sent Liz her photo. Showed Fanny the carpet patterns. Harriet went yesterday to see her cousin John who lives at Craig Trebanos. Lloyd cutting the ivy.

Tuesday 7 March: Harriet to Llangavelach fair, it was 11.35 p.m. when she came back. She said the girl that was with her lost her shawl & they walked back a long way but did not find it. Very wet. Recd. box of music from R.P.L., they are comic songs wh. he lends me. Lloyd p.m. at Gellyluog cut a bundle of birch for brooms.

Wednesday 8 March: Wrote to Mrs. Perkins to thank her for her two kind letters with the addresses of the 2 London Drs. & the lodgings. Dr. Priestley, 17 Hartford Street, May Fair. Dr. Playfair, 2 Hanover Square. Lodgings, 4 Clarges Street, Piccadilly, very comfortable but very dear. Lloyd to Llangavelach fair, he too did not come back until 11.35. I told him to be home at 10 o'clk. Saw him tomorrow morning & merely said that if he could not return in proper time, he could not expect to go again.

Thursday 9 March: Lizzie unpicked my green silk dress wh. I intend giving her for a dress. Lloyd edging by the line from D.M.'s gate to the pistle & scraping away all the weed & grass under Hall window, opened gutter by the wall.

Friday 10 March: Very wet all day. Lizzie recd. letter from her sister Margaret with 10/- for Llanguicke Church repairs. Lloyd p.m. shoeing the mare, 3s.6d pd.

Saturday 11 March:

Paid Garth Poor rate as follows

		£ .. s .. d
Garth Farm	£47..0..0 @ 1/4d	3.. 2 .. 8
2 Cots Cwmllynfell	£ 5..0..0 "	6 .. 8
1 " T.J.R.	£ 3..0..0	4 .. 0
	£55..0..0 @ 1/4d	£3..13.. 4

Paid by cheque

Monday 13 March: Lizzie & I called at the Gilbertsons, the first time after the Father's death, only Mrs. and Miss Ford in the house. Maude in bed with a cold, Ellen in Liverpool, Fanny & Madeline in Swansea. We called at Glan-rhyd, Mrs. Moore, her two children & another lady there. Saw Mrs. A.G.'s little girls (3) first time. Mrs. G. lent Lizzie "Cornhill Magazine". We called at Dr. Griffiths, Mrs. Griffiths not in. Called at Mrs. Kirkhouse's, had a cup of tea there. In coming home near the Reading Room the hind spring of the phaeton broke, Lizzie sat in front with me & Lloyd walked.

Tuesday 14 March: Harriet went last night to Gartheithen for Barm [yeast] & Rachel Morgan too, in coming back they were greatly frightened by Rachel the Servant's appearing under Cae Mawr with something white over her. I went over to D.M.'s & said I was very much displeased at their maid's having played such a trick.

Wednesday 15 March: Daniel Davies came here to trim the hedges &c. I went with D. Morgan to see about his clearing top of Wain Daniel to plant potatoes, told him that whether he left this farm in 12 months or more I would not allow him anything for clearing the piece, he said he did not expect to be paid.

Friday 17 March: Lloyd fetched with our mare alone from Thomas o'r Cwm by Caegurwen Arms

2 loads Nut coal 24 cwt @ 3d.	6 .. 0
1 load small " 10 " " 1½d	1 .. 3
We were quite out of hard coal, this is the first had this year.	7 .. 3 paid

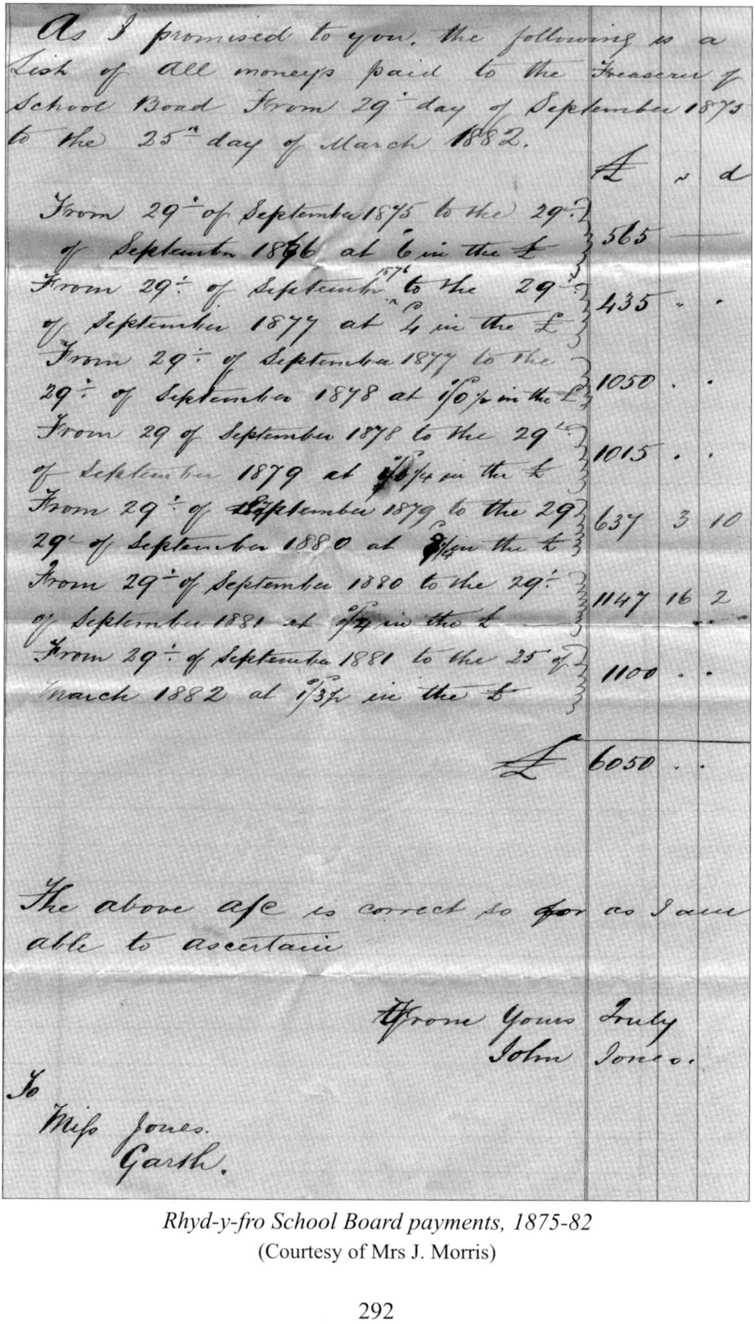

As I promised to you, the following is a List of All moneys paid to the Treasurer of School Board from 29th day of September 1875 to the 25th day of March 1882.

	£	s	d
From 29th of September 1875 to the 29th of September 1876 at 6d in the £	565	—	
From 29th of September 1876 to the 29th of September 1877 at 4d in the £	435	.	.
From 29th of September 1877 to the 29th of September 1878 at 1/0½ in the £	1050	.	.
From 29 of September 1878 to the 29th of September 1879 at 10¼ in the £	1015	.	.
From 29th of September 1879 to the 29th of September 1880 at 8¼ in the £	637	3	10
From 29th of September 1880 to the 29th of September 1881 at 9¼ in the £	1147	16	2
From 29th of September 1881 to the 25 of March 1882 at 1/3½ in the £	1100	.	.
£	6050	.	.

The above a/c is correct so far as I am able to ascertain

From Yours Truly
John Jones.

To
Miss Jones.
Garth.

Rhyd-y-fro School Board payments, 1875-82
(Courtesy of Mrs J. Morris)

Saturday 18 March: ***** M. Wm. Harris brought 4 apple trees & planted them in old garden, paid him 8/- paid. Rhydyfro Eisteddfod. Liz & I walked down to the Concert at 7 o'clk. Eos Rhydyfro, Blodwen Myrddin, Llinos Morganwg, Eos Danyrallt, Llew Cynlais & Asaph Glan Dyfi sang. Harriet & Lloyd to the Concert, Betty in the house. Home at 10.35.

Sunday 19 March: Lizzie walked to Llanguicke. Harriet home to see her Mother & the baby. I in bed all day in great pain in my back & all through me. Lloyd to Church. Betty in the house.

Monday 20 March: Evan commenced trimming the road side hedges. Daniel Davies digging & picking up stones & turf in old garden. Lloyd carrying earth from Cae Cwtta heap to level it. Lizzie put piece on feather bed. Madeline & Maude G. called. Had books. Lizzie had bath & put on new chemise & flannel waistcoat that I had mended.

Friday 24 March: Wm. the Tailor came here to cut out the Brussels carpet for dining room. His thumb is bad & cannot sew it until next week. Recd. letter from Mr. Edmondes, Gwaencaegurwen saying Selina Rees (Harriet's Mother) had had a relapse & wd. be glad if Harriet could come home for a week. I sent her home after dinner.

Sunday 26 March: A great storm of wind last night & today. Lloyd to Church. Lizzie, Betty & I in the house.

Tuesday 28 March: Gwenny Llwynmeudw buried today. Lizzie & I went to stay a few days at Glantwrch, went by 4.10 train.

Thursday 30 March: My throat & neck very painful. Dr. Thomas said it was rheumatism of the muscles. Lizzie went to Pontardawe by the 5.20 train to go to the Competitive Concert in the Schoolroom and then home. Rachel Morgan & Wm. went with her in the phaeton. Harriet returned from staying at home.

Friday 31 March: Lizzie came up 11.30 train. Mr. & Mrs. Glanteg & Mr. Jones the Curate lunched at Glantwrch, Dr. Thomas declined. Mrs. Hedley (Mary Anne Lewis) a son, stillborn at Alltycham.

Palm Sunday 2 April: Lizzie, Miss Davies & I went in the carriage to Ystalyfera Church 11 a.m. & to Ystrad[gynlais] at 3 p.m., took 2 wreaths. The first time Lizzie had been to either of the churches on a Sunday.

Good Friday 7 April: Lizzie, Harriet & Lloyd to Llanguicke 11 a.m. Evan & Dl. Davies in old garden.

Saturday 8 April: T.J. came here this morning through Swansea.

Easter Day 9 April: Lizzie and T.J. to Llanguicke, Betty & Lloyd, Harriet & I in the house. Harriet to Chapel at 6.30. How much pleasanter it was last Easter with Farm House vacant, so much more private & quiet.

Monday 10 April: Lizzie and T.J. walked to Baran after dinner. Fanny G. called, said she & her two youngest sisters were going to Worcester on Wednesday & that she was going on to London, wd. not be home until end of May. David Phillips brought me 1 hun[dred] cabbage plants 1/-, gave him 6d, 1/6 paid.

Paid Griffith Evans his salary as Choir leader	£2..2..0
Mrs. Evans cleaning Church	£2..2..0
being all the money due to them this day	£4..4..0

Tuesday 11 April: Betty & Harriet begun spading in the garden. Lloyd hauling earth to old garden.

Wednesday 12 April: Betty & Harriet setting the plants had on Monday. Lloyd hauling earth from the hill to fill up old garden.

Thursday 13 April: Miss Ford called, said her Mama had a cold & cd. not come, that they were quite alone & wd. be glad if we came down some evening to tea, came on a little rain, lent her my cloak. She brought some nice flowers. Betty & Harriet setting early potatoes in the garden, they have dug the ground well. Lloyd hauling earth to old garden.

Friday 14 April: ***** M. Lloyd shoeing the mare, 3/6 paid. Evan finished steeping Wain Daniel roadside hedge at 4 p.m. Evan planted lilac tree on the side of Walk to hide D.M.'s dairy.

Saturday 15 April: Concert at Rhydyfro, Esther the Queen, a very poor attendance Lloyd said.

Draft of a letter written by Margaret Jones to Thomas Jones

April 15th 1882

Dear Mr. Jones,

I received your letter yesterday. I wish you had spoken to me for then I could have explained myself clearer than on paper. You must be aware that as a friend I think very well of you believing you to be honest, moral & in every respect a steady well conducted man but I can never believe that you & Lizzie are suited to be man & wife & the more I see of you together the more thoroughly I am confirmed in my opinion & I think that after 12 months of wedded life you wd. both find I was right. You are extremely reserved, quiet, silent & un ambitious. Lizzie on the contrary is frank, cheerful, fond of refined society & with good conversational powers at which I am often surprised for her early youth as you well know was much neglected & had not even the ordinary care of a Mother but her attention, quickness of observation & ambition to improve has made her what she is. If however you & Lizzie are bent upon being married I have only to say that I give my consent on the condition of a six months engagement which will give you both time to a serious consideration of the future. I have just asked Lizzie what your salary is, she says you have never told her & that she has never asked you. I am greatly surprised that if you think of her as a wife you do not treat her with more confidence in your private affairs, for childlike & little as she is I never receive or pay any money without telling her & making her clearly acquainted with all my affairs & I have never found her betray the trust. And now in conclusion I as her guardian ask what will be your salary as a married man? & shall expect a plain answer. I think I told you before that during my life Lizzie will have £25 a year the same as her Father left her Sisters & that at my death it will be increased.

With kind regards

Yours sincerely

M. P. Jones

Not a correct copy but as well as I can remember.

Sunday 16 April: Lizzie walked to Church, Betty, Harriet & Lloyd. I at home all day. Recd. the "Child's Reins" we had lent Mrs. Perkins for a pattern & a letter and flowers from her.

Tuesday 18 April: Old Hannah Gotregarth buried today at Saron, aged 85 years. Betty to the funeral. Biddy came up at 2 p.m. stayed an hour & went with Betty to funeral.

Lloyd fetched with our mare from Thos o'r Cwm (Mountain Colliery)

2 Loads Nut coal 23½ cwt.	@ 3d		5 .. 11½
1 Load small " 9 "	1½d		1 .. 1½
We were quite out of coal, this is the 2nd had this year.			7 .. 1

After tea 6.30 p.m. Lizzie & I went to Gartheithen to see Mrs. Harris, the house was so clean, they had been to the funeral. Mrs. Harris Nantrickets there. Evan planted sycamores on the Coed Cae.

Friday 21 April: Lizzie walked to Pontardawe, put School money in the Bank &c.

Sunday 23 April: Lizzie rode to Church. Lloyd & Harriet, Betty & I in the house. Cwmcoy flitch of Bacon fell down, the cords gave way.

Monday 24 April: Evan mending gutter in Cae front by front Gate & putting it tidy. Had 2 cwt long hay of D. M. Lloyd cleaning out Hayhouse & making place to put old white cow there as she is near calving & so stiff to get up. John Evans the P.O. came up after tea to see me, he is now in Llampeter. He seems a nice unassuming boy, stayed to supper. Showed him Church & Concert a/cs.

Thursday 27 April: Fine day. Prince Leopold, Duke of Albany, married this day at Windsor to the Princess Helen, 4th daughter of the Reigning Prince of Waldeck & Pyrmont. Harriet & Lloyd digging in kitchen garden. Betty until 4 p.m. picking stone in Cae front.

Friday 28 April: Dr. George Lamson hung this morning at Wandsworth Jail for giving poison to his brother-in-law Percy John (a schoolboy) in Dec. last. Lloyd mowed the Green with scythe first time this year.

Saturday 29 April: A terrible storm of wind & rain. Lloyd mending wooden post in Court. Evan went through Gellyluog wood, several trees cut he was there before.

Sunday 30 April: Harriet & Lloyd to Llanguicke. Lizzie, I & Betty in the house.

Monday 1 May: Cut out 3rd room Bed curtain and Lizzie began sewing it (12 yds. @ 5d, Shoolbred). A very cold showery & windy day, most unlike May.

Wednesday 3 May: R.P.L., Olwen & Ithel came up 11.30 train. Lloyd met them at Gellygron, & drove them down to meet 7 train. The first time Ithel was here. After they arrived it came on a terrible storm of thunder & rain. After dinner it cleared very nicely when Lizzie, Olwen & Ithel went for a walk up by Pwll-y-Watkin & down through Rhydyfro. R.P.L. gave Lizzie £5..0..0. towards repairing Llanguicke Church.

Friday 5 May: Wm. Williams Plas y bryn here paying his rent 1 year due last March, £3..0..0. Paid him 5/- for boarding up the windows of Hay's house [Colliery Manager] with old boards, carrying slates from Weighing house by the Works &c. 5/- paid. Lloyd & I sowing seeds in Kitchen Garden, parsnips (Jersey), carrots, leeks (St. David's), onions & turnips. Mary Jones a son, Trevelian.

Saturday 6 May: Lloyd & Betty in Garden setting peas, beans & kidney beans, parsley, lettuce, &c.

Friday 12 May: Morgan Harries ploughing top of Cae Barriwns for potatoes, 7/- paid. Betty went for Daniel Gotregarth who brought their pulleys, to get the poor old white cow up.

Saturday 13 May: The old white cow brought a Bull Calf in the Hay house where she had been removed to from cow house some weeks as she was so weak & crippled & unable to get up without help. She is 19 years old.

Rogation Sunday 14 May: Lizzie, Harriet & Betty to Church. Lloyd in the house all day feeling sick. Liz went & came back over the Hill. I went to meet her returning as far as the big stone. A very clear bright afternoon but with cold east wind. Sacrament: the Vicar.

Sunday 21 May: Lizzie & I in Church, Lloyd & Harriet, Mr. Rees Cwmllynfell in Church.

Thursday 25 May: Lloyd fetched with our mare from Mountain Colliery 28 cwt coal @ 2d, 4/8 paid. This is the 3rd had this year.

Saturday 27 May: I put up the new print curtain that Lizzie made for 3rd bed[room]. I had it washed & it looks very nice, the room is now very tidy & T.J. sleeps there tonight. Put there a new little Birch looking glass, 6/10d.

Whit Sunday 28 May: Lizzie walked to Church. T.J. went with her part of the way over the hill & then returned to me. At 5 we both went to meet her as far as the Stone. Harriet, Lloyd & Betty in Church. Sacrament: Mr. Lloyd.

Whit Monday 29 May: Bazaar at Maesllwch Castle near Glasbury. Saron Sunday School children had tea & cake in the Rhydyfro Schoolroom. They had invited Liz & I to go there. I went & called for Mrs. Harris on my way & enjoyed it very well. A nice evening. Harriet to see her Mother after dinner. Lloyd to Swansea & Mumbles. Lizzie & T.J. for a walk to the River.

Tuesday 30 May: T.J. left 1st train for Swansea.

Thursday 1 June: Archdeacon Griffiths Rector of Neath married in London by the Bishop of Llandaff to Miss Janet Matilda Morgan, youngest daughter of the late Rees Morgan, Draper of Neath. Lloyd drove me up to Glantwrch to see Jane, Mrs. Price's hand in a sling. The two little girls are nice children. I lunched there. Lizzie in the house not very well.

Friday 2 June: Paid D. Jones Crachllwyn Garth poor rate as follows:

Garth farm	£47..0..0 @ 1/-	£2.. 7..0
2 Cots Cwmllynfell	5..0..0 "	5..0
1 " T.J.R.	3..0..0 "	3..0
	£55..0..0 by cheque	£2..15..0

This rate made April 21st 1882.

Saturday 3 June: Mrs. Kirkhouse came here to dinner, Lloyd fetched her. Her boarders, two Miss Briss's, two Miss James's & Miss Williams came up to tea at 4 o'clk. They all walked home together. They had been very good in collecting for the repairs of Llanguicke Church.

Mrs. K.	£4.. 8.. 0
Mrs. K's pupils	£3..12..10
	£8.. 0..10

Evan finished sowing grass seed (Wheelers) in the old Garden.

Sunday 4 June: Lizzie rode to Church. Lloyd & Harriet, Betty & I in the house. My hip bone very painful. Mr. Lloyd.

Tuesday 6 June: Lizzie to Swansea with Mrs. Kirkhouse, went to Andrews with Habit body, it is not a good fit. Liz intended staying a night or two at Bryn Syfi but Miss Jenkins was at Glantwrch.

Wednesday 7 June: Fanny G. called on horseback. David James Rhydyfro met with severe accident in coming from Neath, Chemical Wagon getting into collision with his trap.

Thursday 8 June: Betty in bed nearly all day with toothache. John Thomas Gwernllwyn gave me a cheque for £11..9, recd. some [time] ago £10: £21..9..0 being all money due to me for timber up to this day. He gave me oak for roller in exchange for Gellyluog Chemical wood.

Sunday 11 June: Lizzie walked to Church, Harriet, Lloyd & Betty. I at home all day. The Vicar published Vestry for Tuesday about having Church repaired & hoped I wd. attend.

Tuesday 13 June: Recd. letter from Revd. David Jones asking me to attend the Vestry today 12 o'clk at Llanguicke about the repairs, it was 11.10 when I had it. Lloyd drove Liz & I up where we arrived as they were starting off, we being late. The Vicar, Mr. Russel Lloyd, Dr. Griffiths, G. Walters Cefnllan & Wm. Lewis were the only persons who attend. We went into the Church when the Vicar said, the Roof & Windows were to be immediately done & the Pews & other repairs according to the money collected. I named having a Vestry built.

Wednesday 14 June: Lizzie wrote to Sarah who is 33 tomorrow. Had ½ bushel (25 lbs) of linseed for calf, 5/-. Betty liming ceiling of Lloyd's room with whitening. It was so black & dirty that I made her wash it first with soap & water, limed the wall & Harriet scrubbed the floor well.

Thursday 15 June: Griffith Walters Cefnllan here, lent him £20 for which he gave me a note of hand. Lizzie witness to it. Had 10 lbs tea, begun it this day. I owe Mrs. Harris 1 lb and Mary ½ lb.

Friday 16 June: Lizzie & I called at the Gilbertsons. Mrs. G. Llewellyn there. They were all very pleasant. Went on to Sally's about a frock for Lizzie, they showed us the house. Sally had papered the bedrooms & passage very nicely and painted too. They have one very good bedroom. In returning called at Mr. Turberville's office & said I resigned being treasurer of the Rhydyfro School & gave a cheque for £8..13..4, the balance of School pence due from me to the Llanguicke School Board to this date. Finished cleaning kitchen loft. It is now quite clean & all tidy. Dr. & Mrs. Griffiths, nurse & baby called. Evan who was about the Walk said we were not at home.

Monday 19 June: Harriet cropping & thinning London Pride under D.M.'s house, it was getting too much into the Walk, Lloyd screening ashes and digging up Walk from Cow house to Parlour window & filling it up level. Evan finished putting steps by front Walk. Mr. & Mrs. Griffiths Cwmamman & Julia Lewis came here at 5 p.m. Stayed to tea & Lloyd drove them to "the Mountain", left here 9.15 p.m. They found us all busy in the garden. Gave £2 towards Llanguicke. Asked us up to a lecture at their Schoolroom on Friday next on Greece & Italy by Joe Thomas. Promised to go.

Wednesday 21 June: Barnaby Fair. Very wet & cold in the morning, cleared about 3 p.m. Harriet cleaned the Drawing room. Fanny G. & Miss England called at 5 p.m. in Pony carriage.

Thursday 22 June: Lloyd fetched with our mare from Mountain Colliery 3 loads of coal:

	s .. d
2 Loads 28 cwt @ 2½d	5 ..10
1 " 14 cwt @ 2d	2 .. 4
	8 .. 2 paid

Morgan Walters finished making Store Room window, putting the glass, mended the door frame.

Friday 23 June: Recd. tel[egram] from Lizzie 5 p.m. saying Fanny Salmon & herself wd. come up tomorrow. Harriet cleared spare room & 3rd room. Intended going to Mr. Joe Thomas' lecture on "Travels in Greece & Italy" at Cwmamman Schoolroom & to take tea at the Vicarage, but it came on heavy showers & looked like thunder. Lloyd finished putting ashes on little Walk from Drawing Room window to "the Steps", it is well done being 1st dug up. Betty cleaned & limed Cheese loft.

Saturday 24 June: Lloyd to Pontardawe for 2 squares of flooring & 2 rafters. Lizzie returned last train 8.30 from Bryn Syfi. Fanny Salmon came with her. Betty cleaned & limed the Dairy.

Sunday 25 June: Lloyd drove Fanny Salmon, Lizzie & I to Pontardawe Church 11 a.m. Lizzie walked to Llanguicke, Harriet to Chapel 6 p.m. Betty in the house.

Tuesday 27 June: Lizzie & Fanny S. went to Cwmamman Vicarage to tea. Lloyd took them as far as "Mountain" & left here for them at 8.30. I was very sick & could not go.

Wednesday 28 June: After dinner Lizzie & Fanny S. went for a walk to Llanguicke Church & home by Cefnllan Isha & through Rhydyfro. Harriet sweeping & raking up the leaves in the front. Miss Ford called & brought flowers. Liz & Fanny met her returning by Ffynnon Amman.

Thursday 29 June: Lizzie went to the Kitchen after dinner to tell Betty to go & weed the coltsfoot out of the grass seed in the old garden, found all the silver forks & spoons thrown carelessly on the table among the steel knives & forks & everything in a very untidy state. She spoke about [it] before both girls and Harriet was impudent & rude saying one Mistress was enough. When Lizzie told me I soon went & spoke to Harriet saying Lizzie's duty was to see that all was properly done & cared for & that her orders were to be obeyed except when altered by me &c.

Friday 30 June: Julia Lewis & Mr. Joe Thomas walked down here to tea, Lizzie walked home with them as far as Brewery. Fanny & I returned after going a little beyond the Blacksmith's. At 12 o'clk Miss Fanny & myself drove down to Pontardawe.

	£.. s..d
Paid Post Office book to this day	11..16..0
" Jordan " "	7..0
" Phillips (Butcher) " "	10..5

Harriet gave a month's notice to leave. She told Liz she was very sorry for what she had said & hoped she wd. forgive her.

Saturday 1 July: Fanny Salmon returned to Bryn Syfi 5.30 train. Lizzie went with her to the Station. She took a basket of ferns.

Sunday 2 July: Lizzie & I to Llanguicke, Lloyd, Betty & Harriet. After tea Liz & I went to sit an hour with Mary Morgan next door. John Bowen Nantmole gave Liz his photo.

Monday 3 July: Lloyd mowing the lawn. Evan screening ashes. Harriet washing. D.M. commenced mowing his hay.

Tuesday 4 July: Lloyd cut up 2nd flitch of Cwmcoy Bacon. After dinner Betty & I took everything out of the Pantry & she limed it. Harriet washed the shelves & boards. It is all now nice & clean.

Wednesday 5 July: Cleaned Pantry, under the stairs. Lloyd carrying ashes rubbish to Cae Cwtta heap. Evan screening ashes (finished it). Lizzie took letters to post, met Herbert Lloyd in returning. He & his wife are at Cilybebyll for a week, he had been to Bryn Amman & was walking home.

Friday 7 July: Dear little Lizzie's birthday. R.P.L. could not come owing to a School Meeting. T.J. came 11.30 train & stayed the night. He sent her in a letter a little birthday bookmarker. N.T. a Book, Welsh & English Poetry. I gave her material for a dress & lining (Black alpaca). Julia Lewis, Jane Matthews (from Paris) & Sarah birthday cards, & some one "A bard in distress" some verses of Welsh poetry. Lizzie heard John's wife (Hannah) had miscarried.

Saturday 8 July: T.J. left 10 a.m. for Garnant train. D. Morgan paid half a year's rent last night to last March. I gave Daniel & Rees 5/- each. Lizzie wrote to thank N.T. for the book. Lloyd to Swansea for himself midday train.

Sunday 9 July: Harriet went home, returned in very good time 9.40. Lizzie & I in Church, Lloyd & Betty. Recd. letter from Mrs. Kirkhouse who is now in London staying with her son George. Sacrament: 20 communicants. The Vicar. Samuel Jenkins in Church, Mary & Einon.

Monday 10 July: Morgan Walters putting down posts for boarding by the coal. Evan & Lloyd helping him. Lizzie wore her Habit first time. Called at the Vicarage taking back the specification of Llanguicke repairs that Mr. Jones lent me yesterday. She said Mr. Jones said she looked "uncommonly well". She came back here to tea & then went to call on Mrs. Thomas. She & Mrs. Drury had gone to Cefnforest to tea. Betty & Harriet for a couple of hours weeding the grass seed in old garden.

Tuesday 11 July: Very wet & showery. Went with Lizzie to Sally's to have her fitted on for Alpaca dress.

Wednesday 12 July: Morgan Walters finished the boarding by the coal, it is now quite closed in & looks very tidy.

Thursday 13 July: Some woman from Cwmllynfell came here to wish to rent Plas y bryn (Railway side) for her son who is lately married. She wanted some repairs & alterations, said I would go up & see before I wd. promise anything but a stepladder.

Friday 14 July: Harriet & I cleaned out under the stairs, quite clean, dusted all the bottles & replaced them in hamper yesterday afternoon. Evan & Lloyd removed Poplar roots that were by coal to the Green, put firewood into Pig-stye, & stakes for use in a heap by the wall, cut rushes &c. above wall, quarry & all round wh. with the new boarding by coal makes it very tidy. Evan & Lloyd cleaned all up & swept from D.M.'s pistle gate to our pistle road gate. The back is now very clean & tidy.

Saturday 15 July: Brynamman Church consecrated this day twelve month. Anniversary Service held there today at 7 p.m. Lloyd drove Liz & I there in the phaeton. The Vicar of Llandilo, Revd. Lewis Price preached, his curate Mr. Jones read the Prayers.

Sunday 16 July: Lloyd & Harriet to Church (very showery). Lizzie, Betty & I in the house. After tea Mrs. Evans the Post Office came up on horseback.

Monday 17 July: Evan & Tom Tirlan begun mowing the meadow, the wet weather has prevented our commencing sooner & now it looks very threatening for more rain.

Wednesday 19 July: Rain prevents our mowing so Evan & Tom begin to open quarry for stones to rebuild garden hill wall &c.

Friday 21 July: Miss Ford, E & Maude G. called & brought lovely flowers & came with Fanny's love to ask Lizzie & myself to dine at 1.30 any day next week, said we would on Thursday if fine.

Saturday 22 July: John the Blacksmith's bidding & tea at the Old Star. Harriet & Lloyd went. Spoke to Harriet saying her month would be up next Friday, but if it wd. not inconvenience her as she had not had a place & if she was willing to stay another month or two or until we had had the Hay, I should be glad as it wd. suit me better than having a new girl in now. She seemed very pleased & said she was quite willing.

Sunday 23 July: Lizzie walked to Church, Harriet, Lloyd & Betty. Heavy showers. Thos. Howells walked back with Lizzie, stayed to tea & left at 9.30.

Monday 24 July: Free delivery of letters to this House begins this day. Post girl here at 8.30 a.m. Tom Tirlan p.m. gathering fern to put under short hay. Had 2 gambo loads of meadow hay. Betty washed Lizzie's lemon coloured dress skirt, polonaise & lace.

Thursday 27 July: a.m. carried 2 loads as much as was fit of the meadow hay. At 1 o'clk Lloyd drove Lizzie & I to lunch with the Gilbertsons. Mrs. & Miss Ford, Fanny, Ellen & Maude at home, Madeline in London. They were all very kind & pleased to see us. Ellen gave Liz carnation cuttings. I wore violet silk, Lizzie enlarged the waist 7 inches. Lizzie wore her light dress, washed last Monday & looked very nice.

Friday 28 July: Tom Tirlan commenced cutting Front field. Lizzie rode to Cross Inn to see Jane & Margaret, called at the Vicarage. Mrs. Hughes was pleased to see her & said the mare was a "lovely creature". The first time she wore her Habit to X Inn.

Saturday 29 July: Finished carrying the meadow hay all in excellent condition.

Sunday 30 July: Lloyd only to Church. Very showery. Harriet toothache a.m. to Chapel at 6 p.m. Lizzie, Betty & I in house all day.

Monday 31 July: Evan & Tom finished mowing Cae front & commenced Cae Barriwns. Fanny G. called, showed her the 1/10d Shetland shawl.

Tuesday 1 August: Betty churned 3 lbs of butter. Looked very like rain, which made us carry a few loads of Cae front hay. It was not in good harvest but better we thought than if it had rain.

1 Dozn.	Port		½ Gal.	Gin
1 "	Sherry		½ "	Whiskey
½ "	Tarragona			

The first from Williams since I paid his bill up to 30th June last.

Wednesday 2 August: Finished carrying the Front field, rain came on just as the last load was put in the Hay house.

Thursday 3 August: Evan mowing hay at Gartheithen.

Friday 4 August: Carried half Cae Barriwns hay. A lovely day of sun & wind.

Saturday 5 August: Finished carrying Cae Barriwns hay. All of it in good condition & good crop.

Sunday 6 August: Lloyd drove Lizzie & I to Church. Betty, Harriet & her sister Anne to Church. Harriet to Saron & then to send Anne home. Lloyd drove Lizzie & I to Pontardawe 6.30 p.m. John Evans P.O. played the organ beautifully I thought.

Bank Holiday Monday 7 August: Lloyd a few hours helping D.M. with hay. After tea he carried the little bit of hay off the vetches & off the Croften & the rusks off meadow & Cae Cwtta. A picnic from Pontardawe to Carreg Cenen castle in a wagonette & 4 horses. They went at 9 a.m. returned 11 p.m.

Tuesday 8 August: Tom Tirlan cutting Cae front ditches & raking the trash into heaps. Finished cleaning up the lawn & Walks, it looks now pretty tidy into the Walk wh. is bare of ashes. Lloyd set fire to rubbish heap in Quarry. T.J. came here 8.40 p.m. to go to Llandaff tomorrow.

Wednesday 9 August: Llandaff Choral Festival (Welsh). Lloyd drove Lizzie & T.J. to Neath to go to Llandaff leaving here 5.45 a.m. to meet 7.25 train. Lloyd left phaeton in Neath & rode back here 9.55. He left here again at 6 p.m. to meet 8 o'clk train & they returned here at 10.40 p.m. A lovely day but very hot. They met R.P.L & Party at Bridgend & went with them to the Festival & dined with them at the Queens Hotel, Cardiff. Lizzie brought me "Views of Cardiff".

Thursday 10 August: T.J. left here 7 p.m. & walked to Llandilo.

Friday 11 August: Lloyd fetched 2 Loads of coal with our Mare, the first after paying Morgan & Thomas up to 30th June last. We are quite out of coal.

15 cwt at 1½d.	1..10½)	s..d
15 " " 3d.	3.. 9)	5..7½

Saturday 12 August: Harriet to Swansea to buy dress 1st train. Rees Jenkins (Gwenny's husband) came here with 2 letters he had had from John Harries saying Sarah was very poorly & begging for Susan to go up to her, she cannot go, so we settled for Lizzie to go up Monday. Poor child I am not half willing for her to have such a journey.

Sunday 13 August: Lloyd, Betty & Harriet to Church. Liz & I in the house as we partly expected Jane. She came about 3.30. She was quite willing to go with Lizzie tomorrow to Liverpool. T.J. came here about 4 p.m. offering to go to Liverpool but we declined as Jane was going. He drove from Swansea to Pontardawe & walked up here. Jane's husband came for her.

Tuesday 15 August: Harriet & I dug up carnation bed & planted cuttings. I hope some will grow. Lloyd took Williams' empties to Station, 2 cases, 1 cask direct to Brewery. All empties returned to this date.

Wednesday 16 August: "Eos Rhydyfro's" farewell meeting in the School-room. Dr. Griffiths Chairman, Revd. E. Edmunds of Swansea & several others on the Platform. "Eos Dyfed" R.M.A. & Dan Protheroe sang.

Saturday 19 August: Fanny G. called on horseback, promised to lunch there on Tuesday. Harriet brought her horse as Lloyd had gone to Swansea for his watch.

Sunday 20 August: Harriet, Lloyd & I to Church, had heavy rain in returning.

Tuesday 22 August: Lunched at the Gilbertsons. Came on to heavy rain, they wished me to stay the night or return in their close carriage but I preferred returning in our phaeton. Harriet in the middle of washing out the little kitchen when I came back. Such an uncomfortable place in the pouring rain. Betty was so kind & so vexed she had a lovely fire in the kitchen.

Wednesday 23 August: Jane Matthews & little Borlase came up 11.30 train & returned 7 train.

Thursday 24 August: Jane & her two children, Susan & David, came here. I met them at Bryn Amman Station 12.30 train & took them to Garnant to meet 5.30 train. When I returned young Davies Forchegel was here, he had taken tea, stayed to supper & left 9.15.

Friday 25 August: Harriet cleaning Dish Covers. Mrs. Jones of Carmel came here to tea, Mr. Jones came for her. Mrs. Harris, Gartheithen came here to ask if I could lend them £25 by end of Sept, said I could.

Saturday 26 August: Dusted little kitchen walls & cleaned it all out clean. Harriet swept out the 4 bedrooms, rose the stair carpet & put it down. Upstairs all tidy against Lizzie comes home on Monday.

Sunday 27 August: Betty, Harriet, Lloyd & I in Church. Williams the new Curate at Ystalyfera read the Prayers. Young David preached a very good Sermon Matt XV.28. the 1st. time I heard him. What a happy day for his old Father & Mother to see their youngest son a fully ordained Clergyman preaching in the old Parish Church. An excellent congregation & good singing. Fine day.

Monday 4 September: Lizzie rode to Pontardawe, cashed John's P.O.Os £15. Came home & had tea & rode to "The Prince" Cwmamman to ask Dl. Jenkins if he wd. buy the calf.

Tuesday 5 September: Paid Betty £4..0..0 being one year's wages due to her this day. Finished mending grey Carmalite dress after Betty washed it, put on new flounce & repaired the sleeves, &c.

Sunday 17 September: Lloyd drove me to Church, Harriet also. Lizzie in the house & Betty, both not well.

Monday 18 September: Davies Aberavon called here about 7 p.m. on his way from Bryn Wyth. He was tipsy & boasted of his money or at least that his children wd. be rich. He promised £5 towards Llanguicke if Lizzie would go down for it.

Wednesday 20 September: Lloyd fetched 3 Loads of "Mountain" coal with our mare. We were quite out of coal.

	s .. d)	
16 cwt @ 3d	4 .. 0)	s .. d
15 cwt @ 2d	2 .. 6)	8 .. 4½
15 cwt @ 1½d	1 .. 10½)	

Friday 22 September: Lent Morgan Harris Gartheithen £25 on note of hand. Lizzie witnessed.

Monday 25 September: Lloyd shoeing mare. Jane Matthews came up 11.30 train. She had written Saturday but we only had her letter today at 9.45 a.m. It was very wet & we feared Lloyd wd. not be back in time to go & meet her, but he was. Lloyd drove Lizzie to the Cwmamman Harvest Service. Came very wet. They left here 6 p.m. & returned 11.10 p.m. Jane remained at home with me. The Evening preachers were Mr. Jones Llanvihangel and Mr. Roderic of Cocket. I had a very bad cold & cough.

Tuesday 26 September: Jane left 11.30 train for Glantwrch. I was very poorly in bed & Lloyd sent telegram for Dr. Rees from Pontardawe. He came down about 6.30 & examined my chest. Said there was no inflammation at present but that I must be very careful now & all through the Winter. Lizzie put on her Habit for Jane to see & mounted Polly. She had never seen her on horseback & thought she looked very nice.

Friday 29 September: Gotregarth Sale. John James is leaving the place in wh. he has lived since his marriage & where all his children were born. Ellen G. called to wish us Goodbye. She leaves for London on Monday to join her Sisters. The two Miss Purdons are staying with her at A.G.'s.[1] They went on a little in the pony cart & called here for her on their way back.

Saturday 30 September: Expected T.J. but it came on wet. Lloyd went home for a week.

Sunday 1 October: No service at dear old Llanguicke owing to repairing. New roof & windows. Lizzie, Betty & I in the house all day. Harriet to Chapel at 6 p.m. Very wet & windy. Lloyd gone home. Evan sleeps here now he is away.

Wednesday 4 October: Liz recd. paper from N.T. saying the Llanddarog Harvest Service would be Oct. 25th.

---

1. "The two Miss Purdons" would have been related by marriage to the Lloyd family of Plâs Cilybebyll. The sisters Frances Hariette Purdon and Georgina Margaret Purdon married Herbert and Francis Elliot Lloyd respectively. Frances bore 7 daughters and Georgina 1 daughter, any two of these may have been referred to by their mothers' maiden name to distinguish them from the many Lloyd and Gilbertson children. If that is the case Ellen Gilbertson would have been their Aunt.

Thursday 5 October: The 2 Miss Purdon's called. Lizzie was going to Post & met them under Cae Mawr & returned with them. Nina goes to Corston to Mary Leach tomorrow.[2] I received a nice letter from Madeline G. enclosing her photo. They are all four girls & Frank in lodgings, 7 Bulstrode Street, Cavendish Square, London. The girls leave for France on Tuesday next. Liz recd. letter from Jane saying she had found a maid for Sarah to go in Nov.

Friday 6 October: Mrs. Turberville called to ask for a subscription to Clydach Church Vestry Room. They are going to build a new one to cost about £130, gave her 5/-.

Saturday 7 October: The Vicar & Dr. Griffiths called. Gave Mr. Jones the following money for Llanguicke Church repairs:

Rhydyfro Concert Money	£10..17..4	)	
Money collected by Mrs. Kirkhouse &c.	10.. 0..0	)	£ .. s .. d
My own subscription	5.. 0..0	)	25..17.. 4

Mr. Jones gave me stamped receipt for each of these sums.

Sunday 8 October: No service at Llanguicke. Harriet & Lloyd to Pontardawe 6.30 p.m.

Monday 9 October: T.J. left at 7 a.m. thinking to get 1st train from Garnant but he was too late as the train is altered this month 45 minutes earlier. Lizzie recd. letter from John Harries saying Sarah wished to come down. She rode up immediately to X Inn to ask if Jane or Margaret would take her in, both said they wd. & that she cd. come any day. Lizzie wrote to J.H. telling him to bring her down at once. Lizzie was back at 4 o'clk. Lloyd drove her down to meet the 5.30 for Swansea. She is going to stay until Friday with Mrs. Nancarrow.

Tuesday 10 October: The Gilbertsons were to leave London for France.

Wednesday 11 October: A letter came for Lizzie from John Harries saying Sarah intended coming down on Friday next & that he had written to tell Jane.

2. Mary Leach (née Lloyd) (1836-1922) was the daughter of Francis Edwardes Lloyd of Plâs Cilybebyll and a sister of Ellen Gilbertson. In 1867 Mary married her fifth cousin Henry Leach and lived at Corston in Monkton parish, Pembrokeshire.

Thursday 12 October: The Post girl brought the letters 10.15 a.m., in about 20 minutes afterdays Mr. Owen sent up one of the school boys with the Standard Newspaper & a note saying it had been found on the road by one of the children who brought it to him.

Friday 13 October: Lizzie returned 11.30 train from Swansea. She had been staying with Mrs. Nancarrow since Monday evening.

Saturday 14 October: Lizzie went to Cross Inn 5.30 train to be Godmother to Margaret's baby tomorrow, who will be christened Augusta Elizabeth by Revd. Morgan Hughes. John Thomas the Star [Inn] putting sheet iron behind & all round spare bedroom grate.

Sunday 15 October: Very wet morning. Lloyd to post, had letter from Mrs. Price saying Jane & her family came down Friday & wd. leave the 24th asking us up to see them. Betty & I in the house all day. Harriet to Chapel 6 p.m. Margaret's baby Christened Augusta Elizabeth. Dr. Walters preached Harvest Service at St. David's Liverpool. John Harries & Sarah there, the last for her.

Tuesday 17 October: Mrs. Evans the Post Office drove Mrs. Horace Walker & baby up to see me, the first time Mrs. W. was here. Recd. a letter from Sarah this morning. She wrote it & posted it herself yesterday.

Wednesday 18 October: Mrs. Harris Gartheithen here 7 p.m. saying that if John wd. be leaving Gellyluog in March that her son-in-law Charles wd. like to have the offer of it.

Thursday 19 October: Sarah went to Walton 8 p.m.

Saturday 21 October: Sarah went to Whittingham.

Tuesday 24 October: Recd. letter from John Harries saying Sarah had gone. Lizzie rode to Llwynyronen to see John. Put down spare room carpets after the curtains had been washed & floor scrubbed, all is now clean & tidy. Lizzie altered & mended the white curtains, they now look very improved.

Thursday 26 October: Lizzie & I left here 1st train to Swansea thence by 12.30 train from Victoria Station to Liverpool. Stayed the night at North Western Hotel.

Friday 27 October: Lizzie & I went by tram car to 38 Wyatt Street. There at 9.20 a.m. J.H. in the house, had a cup of tea at Mrs. Davies' & took J.H. with us to the Dr. at Pembroke Place, talked with him & went by next train 1 o'clk. to Preston thence by cab to see Sarah. Both Liz & I felt happier after seeing her & finding her comfortable. Returned to Liverpool & stayed at 38 until next Thursday, sleeping at Mrs. Davies'.

Saturday 28 October: Lizzie sent N.T. the Liverpool Views as birthday present.

Sunday 29 October: J.H. to Church. On his return Liz & I went with him to Stanley Park for an hour before dinner. Nice fine day.

Monday 30 October: Went to New Brighton this afternoon. Came on heavy rain.

Thursday 2 November: Lizzie & I left Liverpool 12 train for Swansea. We drove up here in a Fly & pair from Bullins as we had heavy luggage.

Saturday 4 November: Morgan Harris Gartheithen paid 1 year's Interest on £25, due last month

		£1.. 5..0
He paid me for loads of stones to Road.		
I settled with him up to this date	Veal	6..9
1 day Ploughing in May 7/- fetching soft coal	Feb. 3/6	10..6
		Paid 17..3

2 loads Mountain Coal 30 cwt @ 3d 7/6d

Tuesday 7 November: Paid D. Jones Crachllwyn Garth poor rate & road rate as follows:

Garth farm	£47..0..0 @ 1/-	£2.. 7..0
2 Cots Cwmllynfell	5..0..0	5..0
1 " T.J.R.	3..0..0	3..0
	£55..0..0	£2..15..0
Garth road rate (Blaenegel) £47 @ 4d		15..8
Cwm " " (Caegurwen) 8 @ 6d		4..0
	By cheque	£3..14..8

Tuesday 28 November: Lloyd fetched loads of Mountain Coal

1 Load 14 cwt @ 3d	3..6
1 " 15 " " "	3..9

Wednesday 29 November: Betsey brought a she calf which we rear, it is her 1st calf.

Monday 4 December: My darling Lizzie left here 7.15 a.m. to meet 1st train at Garnant for Cross Inn. Stays an hour at Jane's & then to Pantyffynon to meet the 11 train for Liverpool, due there 5 p.m. The weather is very cold. Recd. a telegram by Lloyd 7.30 from little Liz saying she had a safe journey.

Wednesday 6 December: Recd. letter from Lizzie saying she & J.H. intended going to see Sarah today. Went to Bryn Syfi 1st train. Recd. a telegram from J.H. re-telegraphed by Z.E. [Zephania Evans] at 11.30 saying Sarah had a Son, also a letter midday from Dr. Wallis saying she was confined yesterday.

Friday 8 December: Harriet washed out all the lower cupboards in little kitchen. She had washed out the upper ones last Wednesday. They now smell sweetly, of mice before. The Vicar called about 5 o'clk. on his way from Llanguicke, stayed to tea, showed me John Griffiths bill for repairs of the Church wh. I think high. Said service wd. be re-commenced at Llanguicke next Sunday, closed since 1st Oct. owing to repairs. 10 Sundays.

Saturday 9 December: No letter from my darling Liz by either post wh. makes me uneasy & anxious in case she is ill after such a cold & dreadful journey on Wednesday

Sunday 10 December: Lizzie in Liverpool, I in the house all day. Service re-commenced at Llanguicke. Betty, Lloyd & Harriet to Church.

Monday 11 December: Recd. telegram from Lizzie 38 Wyatt Street at 5.30 p.m. saying "Sarah is sinking fast, the Dr. has no hope, I think you better come up". Telegraphed back "Message just had, shall be up tomorrow without fail".

Tuesday 19 December: Poor Sarah buried today 3 p.m. at Bettws by the new Vicar Revd. Evan Lloyd. A large & respectable funeral. The little baby christened at Jane's after the funeral by the same clergyman, Evan John the name Sarah had chosen.

Wednesday 20 December: Lizzie returned 12.30. I & Lloyd met her at Brynamman.

Thursday 21 December: Lloyd fetched 3 loads Mountain Coal.

15 cwt @ 3d	3 .. 9
15 " " "	3 .. 9
15 " " 1½d	1 ..10½

Friday 22 December: Lloyd fetched 10 cwt of coal from Ynisderw, 4/3d. We were almost out of soft coal.

Saturday 23 December: T.J. came here last train from Garnant. A mild night. Lloyd to Swansea midday for pleasure.

Sunday 24 December: I, Betty & Lloyd to Church. The 1st time I was at Llanguicke since it was repaired. I liked the new roof & windows & wish much to have the inside done, new seats, pulpit, &c. Harriet to Chapel 6 p.m. Lizzie & T.J. in the house all day. The Vicar was surprised & sorry to hear Sarah was dead.

Monday 25 December: Xmas Day. A wet morning, only Lloyd to Llanguicke at 11 o'clk. T.J. & I intended going to Pontardawe Church at 7 p.m. but it was too wet, & he, Lizzie & I were in the house all day. Played whist p.m. Lloyd & Harriet to Wain Caegurwen Concert at 6 p.m., home at 11 p.m. I felt faint & poorly & went to bed before the others.

Tuesday 26 December: T.J. intended leaving 9.40 train but I asked him to stay until midday. He decided upon walking home after tea, but it came on too wet & he waited until tomorrow morning. We played whist after dinner & after tea.

Wednesday 27 December: Paid D. Jones Crachllwyn Garth Poor rate as follows:

Garth Farm	£47 .. 0 .. 0	@ 10d	£1 ..19 .. 2
3 Cots Cwmllynfell	7 ..10 .. 0	"	6 .. 3
1 " T.J.R.	3 .. 0 .. 0	"	2 .. 6
1 " Thos. Williams	2 .. 0 .. 0		1 .. 8
By cheque	£59 ..10 .. 0	paid	£2 .. 9 .. 7

T.J. left this morning 6.40 a.m. in time for Garnant train at 8 a.m., thick small rain. Liz & I recd. cards & kind letters from N.T.

Friday 29 December: John Bowen, Nantmole, here saying he had been through Gellyluog wood & that he considered the piece alongside the River alone worth £500
the rest 200
in all £700
excepting the trees in the hedges and those are not included in this sum. All the cutting, haulage, & every expense to be upon the Purchaser. John Bowen told me in Lizzie's presence that he gave this valuation believing it to be right & as if he valued his own Timber.

Saturday 30 December: Evan went through Gellyluog wood yesterday & singular to say he too considered the piece alongside the River worth £500.

Sunday 31 December: Lizzie, Betty and I in the house all day. Heavy showers & very damp & misty. Lloyd & Harriet to Church. The last day of this year 1882 God alone knows who will see this day twelve months. I wrote letters to N.T., Miss Ford, Mrs. Walters, T.J. and John Harries. Lloyd to post.

1883-1887

The diaries for these years are unaccountably missing. A selection of some of the letters written by and to Margaret during this period follows:

1883

W. R. Lloyd to Margaret Jones, 16 January 1883

Dear Miss Jones,

It will give me great pleasure to join you at dinner on Friday next. Thank you very much for the pretty card sent me – it is indeed unique "Cymru am byth". I hope the weather will be fine as it considerably enhances the enjoyment of the delightful walk up to Garth. With kind regards to you both and "Blwydyn newyd da" as well.

I remain

Yours truly

W. R. Lloyd

Thomas Jones to Margaret Jones, 17 February 1883

Tir Eleanor Morgan

17th Feb. 1883

Dear Miss Jones,

Having been from Home the later end of this week, your letter came to hand too late for this evening's Post. We shall start from Cross Inn for Bryn-amman Station next Monday morning by the 9 a.m. Train where, if you will kindly send to meet us, we shall be able to be at our work early.

I am much gratified by Miss Lizzie's good opinion of me, if she [section missing] of a friend, she shall find, the [missing] circumstances, I shall always make all endeavours to prove myself worthy of the confidence she reposes in me.

Far indeed be it from her to be in any trouble – so long as she gets you for her good, kind friend, and benefactress (with God's blessing) her prospects are cheeringly, and I do believe she does appreciate her good fortune, and feel exceedingly thankful for your kindness. May she always continue worthy of your love, is the earnest wish of, with kindest regard for you both,

Dear Miss Jones

Yours faithfully

Thomas Jones

N.B. If raining, we shall come over the next first fine day.

Ellen Gilbertson, Ynysderw, to Margaret Jones, 18 March 1883

My dear Miss Jones,

I am so sorry I have not been able to get up to see you for so long, but I have been away & since baby came have also been very busy. Can you & your Cousin come & lunch with us any day after this week. If you send me a line to say what day would be most convenient to you we should be so glad to see you.

Believe me

Sincerely yours

E. Gilbertson

The baby mentioned was possibly Ellen's eighth child, Winifred.

Margaret Jones to the Pontardawe Magistrates

(Copy) *The Garth 20th April 1883*

Gentlemen

A summons was served here last Monday for the straying of cattle. I desire to express my regret that my cattle (2 Cows & a Bull calf 11 months old, the whole of my stock save one horse which is never out of the Stable except when in use) should have trespassed. My Gates are continually opened by some mischievous persons and left so, & often taken off their hinges & thrown aside, last Saturday night at 10.30 every gate was closed & by Sunday morning one had been taken free and placed on the middle of the road. I should be glad if the Police were to exercise a little activity to bring these miscreants before your bench as it is almost impossible to keep any animals within bounds when ways are opened for them to stray. Hoping you will deal leniently with this my first offence.

I remain Gentlemen

Yours obediently

Margaret Jones

To Messrs. The Magistrates

At Pontardawe

20th April 1883 Police Court

Georgina Nancarrow to Margaret Jones, 6 May 1883

1 Mackworth Villas

Sunday May 6 1883

My dear Miss Jones,

I found dear Miss Jenkins in bed very weak, the pain had left her, also the faintness. R. Hall said she was to take one pill, instead of two, from that, I think the pain caused the faintness, dear soul, she said "I feel as if I were going so cold, the perspiration on my face, I am better again". She was quite warm and comfortable when I left her last night at 9 p.m. I told the girls if there was the least change to come for me, if dear Miss J. was going on well they need not come down this morning. I should go up after dinner, stay with her two or three hours. Mr. Hall is coming over this morning.

I will send you a few lines again tomorrow. I do not think you had better say I have written, as in a few days she may be just as usual, she told me with such a smile of pleasure Lizzie had come to see her – if Lizzie walks in one day it will be nothing to be surprised at. My dear Miss Jones I hope I have not frightened you or dear Lizzie.

With warm love to you both

Your affectionate friend

Georgina Nancarrow

Fanny Gilbertson, 6 Esplanade, Tenby, to Margaret Jones, 29 August 1883

My dear Miss Jones,

Very many thanks for your kind letter of this morning. As I learn from it, you will be at home this week. I am going to take the liberty of proposing coming to you on Friday next, instead of Monday. It would suit my friends arrangements here, better for me to leave on Friday, as more friends are expected this week. I should not reach Pontardawe till the train a little before 7 o'clock, as of course I shall have to go through Swansea. If it will not be quite convenient to you to see me on Friday evening, will you be so kind as to send me a telegram to this address tomorrow, and I will remain here till Monday, but if I do not receive one, I shall conclude Friday will suit you. I shall be so delighted to see you, and hope your face will be better. It was always such a pleasure to come to Garth to see you and Miss Lizzie. We have had a most enjoyable time here, & even the childrens enjoyment has not been spoilt, though they have a slight attack of chicken pox, for they are so well they go about as usual. We have all been sailing a good deal, trying to catch fish, but have not been very successful. With much love & hoping to see you soon.

Believe me

Yours very affectly,

Fanny Gilbertson

Margaret to Lizzie

The Garth

Decr. 31st 1883

My precious Lizzie,

This day brings another year to its close. For nearly 17 years we have lived happily together & by your presence this little home has been wonderfully cheered & brightened in every way, and your absence will cause a blank & space that can never be filled. By to-morrow a new year will have dawned upon us & God alone knows our destiny in its future, it will like all others bring its crosses. May yours dear child be light & easy with a bright crown at the last the reward of a good girlhood.

My best love and my best wishes to you, my own dear & affectionately loved little girl from your sincere & faithful cousin,

M. P. Jones.

1884

On 10 January Lizzie (aged 32) and Thomas Jones (37), a Farmer of Llwyn-cwm, were married in Llangiwg Church. The first letter anticipated Margaret's ambivalence in "looking forward to Lizzie's leaving for her new home".

Thomas and Lizzie Jones
(Photo: courtesy of Mrs J. Morris)

Mary Mackenzie to Margaret Jones, 1 January 1884

13 Bennett St.,
Bath.

My dear Margaret,

I was very glad to receive your kind letter, thank you also for the pretty card of good wishes, so sweetly expressed. I intended sending you a greeting for today, but have so little time over & above my little daily duties that my good intention was not fulfilled – but I cannot delay telling you how extremely sorry Aunt and I are to hear of your being so unwell & suffering, dear Margaret, it is indeed sad tidings of you, & I wish you were within reach, that I might go & sit with you some times, or contribute in some way to your comfort – but as that cannot be at present I can only assure you of my affectionate regret, & frequent thought – I have often wondered how you were – you do not say, but I hope there is prospect of ultimate recovery? It is sad for you looking forward to Lizzie's leaving for her new home (please offer her kind congratulations from me) but try not to dwell on that, or any future sad expectation, something pleasant & unexpected may take place before. What a blessing it is that we "know not what a day may bring forth" is it not! The last two years have been nothing but sickness & trouble to us. I forgot if I have told you of the fall my dear Aunt had, nearly two years ago, in the bedroom? She fell in rising from the sofa, & has been more & more of an invalid ever since – she is not paralysed, but from weakness has lost all use of her limbs, & can not read, work, or do any thing, & is done for like a baby, & being very stout & heavy, it is a most trying, difficult thing to manage. We never leave her, & have a day & a night nurse. So as I am the only responsible person to see to everything, it takes nearly all my time, & is an anxious, lonely life.

My Aunt's general health is wonderfully good considering her age, 84 – & she retains her colour & mind, but nearly all her cheerfulness & animation are gone. Mrs. Mackenzie is pretty well, but cannot leave the sofa, so they do not meet.

I am well, thank you. I have had so much to go through, in various ways, that I feel specially thankful to be so now – at times I get "down" a little. With our best love and most affectionate good wishes, ever believe me,

Yours affectionately,

Mary Mackenzie

List of Linen sent Mrs Thomas Jones, 22nd March 1884

1 pair fine twilled sheets
1 large pr. Barnsley sheets
1 small pr. " "
2 prs. Servants cotton sheets
1 fine linen bolster case
2 " " pillows
1 Barnsley bolster case
2 " pillows
1 small linen bolster case
2 Servants calico bolster cases

---

1 pr. Twilled sheets) Lent in change with Barnsley
1 bolster case 2 pillow cases) for yr. bed
4 toilet cloths folded long ways) Lent
2 side board cloths 1 tray cloth)
These things are lent until your new ones arrive.

2 Toilet cloths
1 double damask Table cloth
1 single " " "
1 unbleached damask Table cloth
2 dinner napkins
2 Kitchen Table cloths
12 Diaper towels
4 Servants bedroom towels
2 coloured bedroom towels
6 linen check glass cloths
5 Kitchen towels
2 " Rollers
2 Market cloths
4 Calico dusters
2 Pudding cloths
1 Ironing calico cloth
1 Slop pail cloth
1 Bedroom Apron
1 old Blanket for floor cloths

List of <u>Electro</u> plate & <u>Silver</u> sent Mrs. Thos. Jones, 22 March 1884

6 Electro Table forks)
6 " dessert forks) from Miss Jenkins
6 " Fish Knives)

---

4 Electro Table spoons)
1 " Sauce ladle)
1 " Mustard spoon) from M. P. Jones
2 " Salt ")
3 " Egg ")

---

6 Silver dessert spoons)
6 " Tea ") from Miss Jenkins

---

1 Butter Knife <u>silver</u>)
1 Sugar tongs ") from M.P.J.

The Silver sugar tongs is <u>lent</u> until yours comes.

---

6 White handle dessert knives
3 black " knives & forks
1 " " Cooks knife & fork
1 Wooden spoon
1 Iron "
3 Kitchen dessert spoons
4 " tea "
4 Wings
1 box plate powder
1 Chamois leather
3 dinner mats)
3 napkin rings) Lent until you arrive
1 Teapot Cosy

I <u>lend</u> you 4 Antimacassars in case Miss Grueber has not left you any.

Mary Price, Glan Twrch, to Margaret Jones, 29 March 1884

My dear Margaret,

At last I have received the tea set which I had ordered so long ago as a Wedding present for Lizzie, the same as I gave Mrs. Dale but it seems it had to be made which accounts for the delay. There is also a little Tea Table, a remembrance from Janie. Now do you think my dear you will be likely to drive up to see me on Monday or Tuesday & stay a few days. I shall expect you, let me know. The weather is nice & dry now & I am all alone. Miss Price left me this day week & I am certainly better than when last you saw me though this East wind prevents my getting quite rid of Bronchitis.

My cousin Mary with Mrs. Jevons & her son & Miss David Morgan came up for a few hours on Tuesday last. I think my cousin Mary is looking better & more cheerful the last twice I have seen her. I think Mrs. Jevons a very sweet looking woman & not as delicate as I expected.

Is Lizzie staying with you now, if so maybe she would come up with you & waive ceremony for she knows I cannot call upon her. Failing your being able to come up shall I send Hamper & package down by train with Phebe on Wednesday morning next to Pontardawe.

With my kind love to you & Lizzie believe me my dear Margaret.

Your affectionately

Mary Price

Mary B. Jenkins, Glan Twrch, to Margaret Jones, 15 October 1884

Dearest Margaret,

Mrs. Price wishes me to write to say she would be very glad if you would come up to see her now when I am here & stay a few days. She would be very glad to talk a little with us as she cannot read much or work – so for my sake as well I wish you could come. We saw Miss Gilbertson yesterday, she thought you were a little better for your visit to Ilfracombe.

Mrs. Price encloses some papers that she received from Jane respecting your enquiry about a Musical Box. Mrs. Benthall says the music of that one is a continual expense but she encloses another that is not such a continual expense. Mrs. Price's eyes are still very bad but I think they are a little better but indeed they still look very inflamed & are very painful.

Now do be good natured & strain a point & come to see two poor old ladies.

With our united love ever dear Margaret

Yours affectionately,

Mary B. Jenkins

Mary Price, Glan Twrch, to Margaret Jones, 30 December 1884

My dear Margaret,

Where do you get those pretty Welsh cards? Thank you for your kind good wishes. We have been expecting every day to see you up for the happy visit is now soon drawing to a close & my children leave me on Friday! I expect my cousin Miss Jenkins Brynsyfi up this evening to see them. Now do try & come up tomorrow & with kind love stay until New Year's Day in which all unite to Lizzie & yourself.

Believe me

Yours affectionately

Mary Price

My cousin goes back tomorrow. I shall be left all alone Friday. Nine o'clock.

1885

Margaret Jones to Elizabeth Jones **n.d. [May 1885?]**

I had your letter yesterday, also another from one of your late Mistresses in reply to further inquiries.

Your stay at both your situations has been short. If you come to me you <u>must</u> <u>make</u> up your mind to be a <u>good</u>, <u>steady</u>, <u>industrious</u> girl and to be happy *in a quiet country place, an early riser, down stairs by 6 o'clock a.m. and in every thing a clean, useful, willing maid & careful of all put under your charge.*

You should go to Chapel once every Sunday, either morning or evening & must be in at 9 p.m. and as I said before you must often go to Church. The way here is by train from Aberdare to Neath where I will send a car to meet you & shall require you on Tuesday week the 8th of June.

Please write & let me know if you agree to what I have named.

You will find me a strict Mistress & a kind one if I find you a good girl.

Yours truly

M. P. Jones

In May 1885 Margaret had roughly drafted the following notice on a scrap of paper:

"Wanted as General Servant an active
Steady girl with good Character.
Apply by letter
Miss Jones
The Garth Pontardawe"

1886

Only one page of the diary for 1886 has survived. The two entries refer to the death of Lizzie's first child.

Tuesday 4 May: Dear little Othniel died this morning at 1 o'clk at 2 Glenview Villas Llandilo aged 10 months from Bronchitis, poor little darling he suffered very much from shortness of breath. I came home last train from Llandilo.

Wednesday 5 May: Lloyd drove me up to Llanguicke to meet Griffith Evans at 9 a.m. to select a resting place for little Othniel. Went to Llandilo by last train from Garnant.

1887

There is no diary for this year. On 28 February Lizzie gave birth at Glenview Villa, Llandeilo, to a son who was named Alfred Ynyr Douglas. He was baptised at Llangiwg Church on 31 May. Tom's occupation was listed as 'Clerk'.

1888

Margaret made 142 diary entries during this year, with only 17 after 10 August. The lack of narrative commentary between 26 August and 26 November and the brief statements on 10 and 12 October suggest that she was staying with Lizzie's family in Llandeilo throughout this period and also from 2 to 16 December. Apart from her frightening "coldness round my heart" on 4 March Margaret's health appeared to be good until 20 July when she confessed to feeling "very poorly for many weeks", which prompted visits from Lizzie, Douglas and T.J. A persistent concern for most of the year was Margaret's financial relationship with her tenants at Crachlwyn Farm, their desperate attempts to pay off their debt and their eventual bankruptcy.

Wednesday 11 January: Evan & Lloyd cut down the last fir tree lower side of closet walk, 5 trees were left standing from last year. I feel so sorry after them, they were like friends of my childhood, planted by R.P.L. 55 years next March.

Saturday 14 January: John Bowen Nantmole[1] here stayed to tea, talked over "The Crachllwyn business that it would be better to get 10/- in the £ than nothing".

Sunday 15 January: Betty to Llanguicke. Elizabeth to Cwmgorse after dinner, did not return. Showed me at dinner the old silver fork, she broke it in the strongest part of the handle by cleaning it last Friday. I told her I was vexed & angry.

Monday 16 January: Lloyd fetched 1 load of through coal from Cwmgorse, 2d per cwt (13½ cwt) 2/3d paid. Lloyd had 5 cwt of soft coal at the Station (the Gnoll coal) 8d per cwt. 3/4d paid. The ½ ton had of the same man Nov. 17th '87 cost only 5/3d, a little over 6d per cwt. Why such a difference?

1. John Bowen, farmer of Nant-moel Isaf, Rhyndwyclydach.

Tuesday 17 January: Elizabeth came back at 5 p.m., said she had been very sick & ill, but was now much better.

Thursday 19 January: Sent to ask Daniel to come to me, told him that I was not pleased that their ponies were always on my fields & that they must keep them off. Promised to turn them to the Hill. Morgan Harries brought 7¾ lbs of beef from his sister Jane @ 7d, 4/6 paid. It was too dear. Xmas beef from Phillips was only 7½d & good beef too. Betty washed my stripe petticoat.

Friday 20 January: 1 load of small coal (Cwmgorse) 1/- paid. Evan repairing Hill fence from Heol-y-Cefn gate to the Meadow. Yesterday Lloyd turned heap in Cae Cwtta.

Monday 23 January: John Thomas came up for the trees, they are the last large trees lower side of little Walk, they were placed in March 1833 by R.P.L. six months before I was born. I feel so sorry after them, more especially as my dear Mother liked them so much.

Wednesday 8 February: Morgan Gartheithen's little girl born, the first child (Margaret).

Monday 20 February: I returned from Llandilo midday. Lloyd met me at Garnant.

Tuesday 21 February: Margaret Jane Jones from Pontardawe came here as maid at the rate of £8..0..0 a year or 3/1d per week. Her mother brought her up which I was glad of, as then she could see the place.

Saturday 25 February: John Bowen Nantmole came here asked if he wd. see Mrs. [Esther] Jones of Crachllwyn & say from me that if any of the family would like to buy my interest in it they could have it for £1,820 & whatever dividend came from the Bankruptcy Court wd. be returned them as I only wanted my due which stands thus:

Price of farm at sale	£1675	
J. Jones debt & Int: to me	141	
G. J. Evans bill say	4	£1820..0..0

This offer is made before any Deeds are made. Mr. Bowen said he would make them the offer and let me know the result this day week.

Monday 27 February: Paid Dd. Jones Garth Poor rate

			£.. s.. d	
The Garth	£17..10..0 @ 2/6		2.. 3..9	
Garth farm	37..15..0	"	4..14..4½	
3 Cots. Cwm[llynfell]	7..10..0	"	18..9	
1 " D. Williams	3..10..0	"	8..9	
1 " Noah Jones	3.. 0..0	"	7..6	
1 " Thos. Davies	3.. 0..0	"	7..6	
Pd. by cheque				£9..0..7½

This rate is 2 quarters & made Nov. 25th '87 and clears all taxes up to March 25th '88.

Dd. Jones is now paid

£100 for collecting poor rate
£ 20 " " Jan. rate
£ 20 " " Highway rate
£140 in all

Tuesday 28 February: Little Douglas' birthday, he is one year old today. I gave him a case with fork & spoon, not real silver. May God bless him & his Parents through life. Sent Lizzie yesterday "The old Black Ox" (her 1st five pounds from her father) thinking she may like to give it her little boy.[2]

Wednesday 29 February: D.M. killed the Bull, had a round of 14 lbs @ 7d (8/2d paid). Mr. Jones Llanguicke & Mr. Davies called, stayed to tea & left at 6 p.m. in time for Service at 7.30.

Thursday 1 March: Jane came to my room about 7 a.m., said her chest was very painful & that there was a thickness of snow on the ground, at 7.35 Betty came to my room and said Jane had put on her things to go home, & was then going through the Gate. Betty asked her if she had told me she was going, she said No, but that she had said her chest was painful. The Post boy said he had met her in Rhydyfro. I sent Lloyd down about 10 o'clk to tell her Mother she

2. The Black Ox Bank was established by farmer's son and drover David Jones in Llandovery in 1799. Branches were set up along the drovers' routes where drovers and others could deposit cash and transact business. The Bank printed its own banknotes depicting the Welsh Black Ox. The Llandeilo branch of the Black Ox Bank was established by 1842.

had gone home without telling me a word. Her Mother came up in the afternoon & said her side was painful & that she was delicate having "grown so rich", being so tall & only 17 years & that she felt a kind [of] "Gwaelder"[3] in the morning after only bread & cheese for supper that it remained a kind of lump in her chest. I asked her what she expected to have, said she wd. have liked a cup of tea with it. I said the tin with tea was on the mantelpiece & that she could have taken a cup, or she could have come & asked me & that it was not likely I should have refused such a simple request.

Saturday 3 March: Jane's sister & brother came up for her clothes. I paid the little girl the one week's wages due to Jane 3/1d. Lloyd took her box down in the cart after tea. Had ½ sack of leather tie flour, 1 sack Blk oats @ 2/2d per bus.

Sunday 4 March: Lloyd to Church. Betty in great pain with her leg. I feel a great coldness round my heart, which rather frightens me.

Monday 5 March: John Bowen Nantmole came here, said he had seen some of the Crachllwyn people & that they declined either purchasing or renting the place. He thinks they are poor.

Tuesday 6 March: Had 2 doz. beer (paid) 17 bot. in house.

Wednesday 7 March: Gomer Evans came up, told him to offer Beynon the Crachllwyn for what I gave, £1,675.

Thursday 8 March: Lloyd drove me to Pontardawe. Mr. Evans the P.O. and his son Gomer signed my Will, dated this day. Called at Mrs. Kirkhouse's.

Tuesday 13 March: David Rees of Llanelly Hung today at Carmarthen for the murder of Thos. Davies at Llanelly Nov. 12/87.

Sunday 18 March: Evans P.O. came up with Policy & Title Papers. Poor Roger Williams, Tiler, Pontardawe, died of Bronchitis.

Monday 19 March: Wrote to Beynon. Noah Jones' wife & Thos. Davies' wife here paying the rent.

---

3. Welsh *gwaelder*: feeling unwell, wretched, low.

Tuesday 20 March: Daniel (Cilpentan) buried.

Wednesday 21 March: Roger Williams buried at St. Peters.

Thursday 22 March: David (John Thomas' nephew) came up to pollard the poplars, cut them 10 ft. from the ground, in Heol y Ty. Mrs. Evans P.O. here saying Gomer could not come up as he had to go to Swansea.

Friday 23 March: William Griffiths Cwmllynfell here, paid half a year's rent up to this 25th March. He came now thinking I wd. like to have money as I had bought the Crachllwyn. They now live at Ystradowen. Morgan Harries' Wife & baby came up to say Wm. Price declined the farm.

Easter Sunday 1 April: Betty & I to Church. Only Lizzie & Douglas in the house, on our return they came to the bottom of the road, & we drove up as far as Wain Hir, & back up Heol y Cefn.

Wednesday 4 April: Received a decided reply from Mr. Gomer Evans that he wd. not purchase Crachllwyn. Wrote by post boy to tell him that I should go to Swansea by midday train to have Mr. Strick's opinion on the matter of deeds, as I consider G.E. young & inexperienced for this complicated affair.

Thursday 5 April: Lizzie went to see John Jones the Railway by 11.15 train & also to see Mrs. Jones Llwyncwm. Douglas & I went to Garnant, & met her again by 4.30 train. Mrs. Jones the Crachllwyn came here in a few minutes after I returned. The purport of her coming was to ask if I wd. let them remain there, & if I wd. buy her life Interest in the farm. She said she thought she ought to have £400 for it. I told her that was an unreasonable price, said I would give £100. Took her in the phaeton as far as David's house, on my way to the Station, she asked me to come & see the Crachllwyn & I promised to go either Saturday or Monday.

Saturday 7 April: Lloyd drove Lizzie & I, after an early dinner up to Crachllwyn. Mrs. Jones received us kindly and took us over the farm. She asked if I wd. give £200 for her life interest. I said No only £100.

Sunday 8 April: T.J. & Lizzie walked to Church. Douglas stayed with me.

Monday 9 April: Hopkin Jones Bogelegel came here to see me about the rent of Crachllwyn & he thought it would be better for his Mother to sell her interest & so complete every thing. Arranged for them both to come here.

Friday 13 April: Saw the Vicar at the Post Office.

Sunday 15 April: Lizzie & I in Church. Margaret brought Douglas as far as Cefnllan & stayed there until we returned. It came on wet. I told Griffith he could have his money (£4..4..0) whenever he liked to come up. Said he wd. not come, that he was paid for services done at Llanguicke Ch. & there on Easter Monday, he ought to be paid.

Tuesday 17 April: Lizzie & Douglas left for Llandilo by 11.15 train from Garnant. Mrs. Jones the Crachllwyn came here to say that her son Hopkin had gone to Devynoc & Trecastle fairs & found they could not go to Neath to see Mr. Cuthbertson tomorrow.

Thursday 19 April: Mrs. Jones the Crachllwyn came here on her way from Neath. She had seen Mr. Cuthbertson, & he said he would deliver the Marriage Settlement to Mr. Strick when required.

Saturday 21 April: Betty washed the stairs & put down the stair carpet. She said she had not rubbed the paint with beeswax for years!!! – I am greatly mistaken if she did not do so last year, when the new carpet was put down.

Sunday 22 April: I went to Church also Betty. The Vicar.

Wednesday 25 April: Lloyd set small seeds in Kitchen garden. Evan finished by the little gate & dug up the Walk as far as the pool.

Thursday 26 April: Pontardawe Competitive Meeting.

Friday 27 April: Evan commenced putting down posts at saw pit for wire fencing along road side. Lloyd setting potatoes in the Green. Margaret & I planted daisies opposite the front door.

Sunday 29 April: No one to Church. Thick small rain. Margaret to Chapel 6 p.m.

Monday 30 April: Richard Jones, Pontardawe cleaned the Clock for which I paid him 2/6d & he is to keep it right for one year. Evan came by Cwmllynfell today, said that some of the hedges had been cut & some of the wood used for shutting. He saw Thomas, who said nothing about leaving.

Tuesday 1 May: Lloyd swept Dining room chimney. We took up the carpet yesterday.

Thursday 3 May: Wm. Jones Ynismeudw called here about the Barb wire for fencing by saw pit.

Friday 4 May: Lloyd & I put down Dining Room carpet, & Margaret cleaned the furniture. The room now looks nice & clean.

Sunday 6 May: Only Lloyd to Church. Morgan Harris & W. Price were at Llandilo yesterday. Lizzie sent me K[idney] Beans and Newspapers by Morgan, wh. Lloyd had in coming from Church today.

Sunday 13 May: All 4 of us in Church. Margaret to Chapel at 6 p.m. Sacrament, Jones (Curate). I did not take charge of Collection.

Tuesday 15 May: David the Mill came here to paint the Gates. Some 3 men from Cwmgorse went to Nantygwin to cut some kidney bean sticks & brought them to the road through this land between Entrance Gate & Cottage, had loan of Abernant brewery dray to take them up. David Hopkin the tenant informed Mr. Kempthorne & they are to be summoned. This D.M. went up on the dray with them, but he never mentioned a word to me, until Whitsun-day.

Wednesday 16 May: Came on to rain wh. prevented David the Mill coming up to paint. Mrs. Kirkhouse went to Bath today, 20 Charles Street. Asked me to go with her, but I could not.

Whitsun Day 20 May: Only Lloyd to Church, took a beautiful bunch of flowers for dear little Othniel. Betty & I in the house, Margaret gone home. [Rev. T. E.] Davies.

Whit Monday 21 May: Received letter from Mr. Strick saying Mr. Turberville had written to say that John Jones would not sign the necessary deed for the Sale to me of his Wife's life interest in Crachllwyn Ucha. Sent Lloyd to Bogelegel, Hopkin gone to some fair.

Tuesday 22 May: Hopkin Jones came here this morning, told him about his Father refusing to sign. Said he would see him, & bring me an answer. Hopkin Jones after been to Crachllwyn came here about 9 p.m. with a letter signed by his Father saying he was willing to come at any time to sign in the necessary conveyance of his Wife's life interest, that his refusal was through a misunderstanding with Mr. Turberville.

Saturday 26 May: David the Mill putting new cross bars to railing between us & D.M.'s pistle. Poor old Hannah Twmi buried at Llanguicke.[4] Betty to the funeral.

Sunday 27 May: I went to Church, also Margaret. Thought a great deal of my poor Father who has been lying at Llanguicke 24 years tomorrow. Williams.

Thursday 31 May: Mr. Aubrey Lewis the Road Surveyor here, he quite approves of the posts put for railing by the saw pit and now the wire will be put on them next week.

Trinity Sunday 3 June: Only Betty to Church. Margaret to Chapel 6 p.m. Lloyd took letter to Post, & came back fearing he wd. be late for Llanguicke. The Vicar.

Tuesday 19 June: Paid Dd. Jones Garth Poor & High Way rate. This rate is for 2 quarters from March 25th '88 to Septr. 29th '88. Poor rate made May 25th '88, High Way rate made 8th June '88.

				£ .. s .. d
The Garth		£17..10..0	@ 1/8d.	1 .. 9.. 2
Garth farm		37..15..0	"	3 .. 2..11
3 Cots. Cwm.		7..10..0	"	12.. 6
1 "	D. Williams	3..10..0	"	5..10
1 "	Noah Jones	3.. 0..0	"	5.. 0
1 "	Thos. Davies	3.. 0..0	"	5.. 0
				6 .. 0.. 5
Garth High Way rate on		£55..5..0	@ 2d.	9.. 2½
Cwm. Cots "	" "	17..0..0	"	2..10
		By cheque		£6..12.. 5½

Sunday 24 June: Dear little Othniel's birthday, had he lived he wd. have been 3 yrs. old today. We all went to Church. The first time for Douglas, just before

4. Hannah Morgan of Gwrhyd aged 74.

the Sermon, he squeaked, pretending to frighten some little girls & Margaret took him out.[5]

Monday 2 July: Swansea Wool Fair. Johnny Gellyluog married to Mary Forchegel at Ystalyfera Church.[6] (Very wet).

Friday 6 July: Lizzie & I in Swansea. Lizzie bought the Gold & White tea things for their general use (10/-) also

Hat for herself 17s. 9d.
Hat for Douglas 4s.11d.

Saturday 7 July: Dear Lizzie's birthday. Gave her the pale cream Rose for her bonnet bought yesterday, only 6¾d.

Sunday 8 July: We all went to Llanguicke but Margaret & Douglas did not come into Church. Poor Douglas' bowels very relaxed after we got home. Sacrament: Williams, this day 6 years he preached his 1st. sermon, he said so publicly.

Tuesday 10 July: Lizzie & Douglas left by 11 train from Garnant after been here one month to-morrow. Lizzie intended going yesterday but it was too wet.

Sunday 15 July: Brynamman Anniversary Service. Dr. Walters to preach there at 2 p.m., dined here on his way there. T.J., Lizzie & Douglas came over in Dog cart to dinner. We all 3 went up with Dr. Walters in his carriage, & Lloyd & Margaret brought Douglas & Dog cart to "Farmers" 7.30 for them to start back from there. Dr. W. put M. & myself down bottom of road. Lloyd walked home.

Tuesday 17 July: Received a letter from Dr. Walters asking me to come down, that Mrs. Walters wd. be so glad to see me. Wrote to say I wd. come to-morrow.

Wednesday 18 July: A dull misty morning & a little rain but it cleared off at 12 o'clk & Lloyd drove me to Llansamlet, got there just as they were going to

5. The first time since his baptism in Llangiwg Church on 31 May 1887.
6. John Williams (aged 24) Farmer of Rhyd-y-fro to Mary Davies (23) Spinster of Forchegel Farm at Holy Trinity Chapel, Ystalyfera.

dinner. Poor Mrs. Walters seemed delighted to see me. Poor thing it is quite sad to see her so changed only a frame of skin & bone & unable to bring out her words, she is perfectly sensible but can't speak. We had tea at 5 o'clk and I left at 5.30. They were all very kind & showed me all the alterations made in the house wh. are a great improvement. Had two or three sorts of cabbage plants. Called at John Thomas & at Biddy's.

Friday 20 July: In great pain in bowels & back the whole of last night. Had a nice warm bath in little Kitchen at 9 a.m. which greatly relieved. I remained in bed all day perspiring freely. I have felt in great heat & very poorly for many weeks, perhaps it is now coming to some crisis.

Sunday 22 July: No one to Church. I in bed very poorly, got up to tea. Margaret went home after early dinner, comes back to-morrow. Mary Morgan came in to see me.

Monday 23 July: Morgan Harris & William Price here. Rented Cwmllynfell to Wm. Price for £45..0..0 a year, he is to have possession 25th March 1889. I have promised to give him 6 new gates & gate posts, and 10 tons of lime for the farm.

Wednesday 25 July: I am very poorly mostly in bed since Thursday. Dr. Rees said I suffered from dry Bronchitis & ordered mustard poultice to be put to my left side, back & front. This is the first time Dr. Rees has attended since I paid his bill up to Dec.87.

Saturday 28 July: Lizzie & Douglas came 1st train to Garnant. She was anxious to see me as I was ill.

Sunday 29 July: Dr. Rees to see me. No one to Church. Margaret to Chapel. D.M. & Mary came to see me, also Mrs. Harries Gartheithen.

Tuesday 31 July: John Jones Crachllwyn here saying the deed could be signed at Mr. Turberville's office Pontardawe. I did not see him being in bed.

Wednesday 1 August: Dr. Rees called, his brother Alfred & his Wife were outside in the carriage but did not come in. Lizzie was making red currant jelly, & I was not equal to seeing them.

Thursday 2 August: Lizzie & Douglas left 11 train for Llandilo. She wanted to see some things before the Eisteddfod on Monday. Said she wd. come again end of next week.

Friday 3 August: Had fire last night in my bedroom & this morning had a nice wash & clean clothes, which was a pleasant & wholesome change after all the poultices, oil, &c. I have used and so much perspiration.

Sunday 5 August: Dr. Rees called, thought me rather better, said "You must be very careful of yourself". Margaret went home after dinner. No one to Church. R.P.L. 75 years old this day.

Monday 6 August: Llandilo Eisteddfod.

	£..s..d
Had 1 Load thro' coal 13 cwt.	2..2
1 Load small	1..0
Paid	3..2

Thursday 9 August: Dr. Alfred Rees came to see me, said he wd. give me some pills which he thought wd. allay the cough & promote expectoration. He is much improved since I saw him & has a nice quiet manner & seems kind & gentle. His brother Howel is gone to the Medical Assocation at Glasgow. His wife was in the Dog cart, but did not come in. Recd. letter from Mr. Strick saying John Jones the Crachllwyn had signed for the sale of his wife's marriage settlement.

Friday 10 August: Finished carrying the Vetches, and some of Cae front. A cloudly dull day.

Sunday 19 August: No one to Church.

Tuesday 21 August: This is the day appointed for paying John Jones of Crachllwyn's dividend in Bankruptcy of 3s/5½d in the £.

Wednesday 22 August: Mr. & Mrs. Griffiths Cwmamman took tea here. Lloyd took them part of the way home. Dd. Thomas "New Star's" son William returned to America.

Sunday 25 August: Miss Baxter & Dr. Griffiths little girl called to ask how I was, they saw Douglas. Dr. Rees called, told him that as I continued so ill

I should like to call in Dr. Thomas Ystalyfera. Carried 3 loads short hay to Hay house.

Wednesday 10 October: Lizzie left Llandilo for Garth 11 train to see how things were getting on as I have been away some time at Llandilo.

Thursday 11 October: Sally's little boy buried at Llanguicke.[7] Betty to funeral.

Friday 12 October: Lizzie returned last train. Douglas was a very good boy during the time she was away. She said all was right at Garth & that she enjoyed her little visit.

Sunday 11 November: T.J., Lizzie, Douglas & I went for a walk to the Park after dinner. It was a lovely afternoon, the last time I was in the Park was on my way from Llanwrtyd with Miss Jenkins in 1864 over 24 yrs ago. What a change those years have made in me!! Met Mr. & Mrs. Williams the Chemist in the Park & walked with them. A number of shows in New Road ready for fair to-morrow.

Tuesday 27 November: Paid David Jones Garth Poor rate. This rate is for 2 qrs. from Sep. 29th '88 to March 25th '89.

The Garth	£17..10..0	@ 1/8d	£1.. 9.. 2	This poor
Garth Farm	37..15..0	"	3.. 2..11	rate made
3 Cots. Cwm.	7..10..0	"	12.. 6	23rd Nov. 88
1 Cot D. Williams	3..10..0	"	5..10	
1 " Noah Jones	3.. 0..0	"	5.. 0	
1 " Thos. Davies	3.. 0..0	"	5.. 0	
	£72.. 5..0	@ 1/8 in £	£6 .. 0 .. 5	
Paid by Cheque				

Hopkin Jones' name is on the Rate book as tenant or Occupier of Crachllwyn.

Wednesday 28 November: Hopkin Jones brought me the Map of Crachllwyn Mawr as he had promised.

Friday 30 November: Margaret Evans came here to-day. She was home during my stay at Llandilo. Lloyd put shelf in middle cupboard.

7. David Davies aged 2 months of Pheasant Bush, Pontardawe.

Saturday 1 December: ***** Evan came here to settle with me. D.M. & Evan measured Cae front wall as follows:

Wall under the lawn 97 yds.@ 1/-	£4..17..0 paid
Roadside Wall from Cae front to Cae Barriwns gate	
21½ yds. @ 1/6d.	£1..12..3 paid

Evan had money on a/c as he required & now every thing is settled & paid up to this day between us. He left here end of Sep. last as I had no work for him, especially as I cd. not go out after my attack of Bronchitis. He is now breaking stones on this road by Gellygron & walks to Ystalyfera every night!

Monday 17 December: Margaret Anne came up to finish covering the easy chair. Dl. Morgan killed my pig.

Tuesday 18 December: Daniel cut up the pig, it weighed 220 lbs (11 score exactly after eating 4 cwt of Barley meal). Richd. Lewis here showing D.M. & myself a letter from John Phillips the Cross Inn postman, saying the letter of which R.L. is accused of opening was in a torn state when it left there, & that he J.P. quite exon[erated].

Tuesday 25 December: Margaret went home early this morning thinking to go to the Morriston Eisteddfod, but she was too late for the train. Lloyd drove Lizzie & T.J. to Llanguicke service at 11 a.m. Betty, Douglas and I at home. There were no decorations at all. Mr. Jones Ystalyfera officiated, the Vicar not well.

Wednesday 26 December: Wm. Price (who has rented Cwmllynfell) came here, told him I wd. not allow Thos. Griffiths to use the Falda Bach as a road way to the Coal pit he had opened, nor wd. I allow him to keep powder in the Powder house he had erected on one of Cwm[llynfell] fields. T.J. left, Lloyd drove him, Lizzie & Douglas as far as Cwmgrose Church & he walked to meet last train.

Thursday 27 December: Expected the Benthall's here to lunch but it was too wet for them to come. Lloyd to Pontardawe shoeing the mare.

ADDENDUM

Entered on the first page of the diary was the following valuation of "Gross & Rateable Value & Acreage of Farms & Cottages" owned by Margaret and copied from the Llanguicke Rate Book, 27 November 1888:

		Gross	Rateable
	(The Garth	£20..0..0	£17..10..0
141 acres	(Garth Farm	£40..0..0	£37..15..0
	(" Cottage	£ 3..0..0	£ 2..10..0
84 acres	Cwmllynfell Farm	£40..0..0	£38.. 0..0
	Colliery Houses	£ 4..0..0 each	£ 3.. 0..0 each
	Llynfell Cottage	£ 4..0..0	£ 3..10..0
	W.R. & Plas y Bryn	£ 3..0..0 each	£ 2..10..0 each
71 acres	Crachllwyn	£50..0..0	£47.. 0..0
75 acres	Gellyluog		

1889

Margaret's diary entries for the year totalled 152. She made no entries in January and only 4 in February owing to her commitment to caring for Lizzie's young son Douglas (Ducca) in Garth and, following the delivery of Lizzie's still-born daughter, to caring for Lizzie in Llandeilo until 12 March. There were to be many more days spent in Lizzie's Llandeilo home during the year and these too were not recorded. Her other concerns were mainly associated with the viability of her various properties, particularly the ongoing problem with the Gelliluog tenancy, the general tardiness of rental payments and her difficulty in finding reliable replacement tenants. Her comments clearly show the hardships faced by upland tenant farmers and their families.

Saturday 9 February: Concert at Carmel Chapel in aid of Jacky Shone's grandson who is crippled. Margaret went with the D.Ms.

Sunday 10 February: George Kent, landlord of the Glos'ter Arms Swansea & late Butler to Mr. T. J. D. Llewellyn Penllergare murdered by a Zulu named Tom Allen who had hidden himself under the Bed.[1]

1. See Bernard Lewis, 2009, 147-154, for an account of the crime and subsequent trial.

Sunday 17 February: Poor Lizzie – a little girl – still born, a very pretty child with beautifully formed hands & feet.

Monday 18 February: Recd. a letter at 9 a.m. from T.J. saying Lizzie had given birth to a still born little girl yesterday 1.30 p.m. & that he wd. bring the little Coffin over in a Fly today. They were here at 10.45 left for Llanguicke at 1.30 & back at 2.45. After a cup of tea T.J., Douglas & I returned in the Fly leaving here 4.30 & getting to Llandilo 6.40. Poor Lizzie was anxiously expecting us & so glad to see Ducca who is now quite well. Dr. Davies said he looked in perfect health. Day was dry but roads very heavy. Douglas had been here without his Mother since 9th Jan: nearly six weeks.

Tuesday 12 March: Returned home from Llandilo 12.30 train after been there 3 weeks yesterday, brought back cheese, 27 lbs @ 3d, 6/9, 2 cwts potatoes 10/0. Called at Mrs. Thomas', Mrs. Drury there. I thought Miss Shenton aged, their servant had gone home ill before Xmas and they were badly off for help. Ted's wife was confined of an 8 months child 3 weeks tomorrow, it died in 2 days.

Saturday 16 March: Pontardawe fair. Betty, Lloyd & Margaret to the fair. B. came back 7.30, L. 10.50 and M. 11.30. I did not say a cross word but was as pleasant as if it had been good time. Wm. Griffiths here paying the rent up to Sep. '88. Told him Wm. Price wd. take possession of the land the 25th inst. Wm. Price here, told him to take possession of Cwm[llynfell Farm] on the 25th inst.

Wednesday 20 March: I walked down to Cae Mawr gate to see D. Morgan putting stakes down for the wire he is going to put on top of the ditch to prevent sheep to the road. Walked with him up to saw pit, & told him he was to keep his Animals out of the old saw pit, & use the road only, said he would.

Thursday 21 March: John Thomas the Gwernllwyn here, told him John Gellyluog would be leaving in another [blank] & to find me a tenant. John's wife is very ill in bed or he shd. leave now, as he is so backward with rent. John Gellyluog here this morning said he wd. bring me £10 next week.

Friday 22 March: Margaret finished covering the smallest old green quilt with my old figured black alpaca skirt.

Sunday 24 March: Lloyd with letters to Post & then to Church. Margaret to Carmel 6 p.m.

Tuesday 26 March: Sent Lizzie 15 lbs salt butter.

Friday 29 March: Lloyd shoeing the mare. Had 5 bus. oats 3/6 paid. M.A.E. came here to finish my grey skirt. She also mended old black jacket. Paid M.A.E. all I owed her up to this day, 23 days £1..3..0 Cotton &c 11d. £1..3..11 paid. She intends going to Pontardulais tomorrow for a fortnight.

Saturday 30 March: Julia a He Calf. Margaret intended leaving today as her Mother is not well, but promised to stay until after Easter.

Sunday 31 March: Lloyd to Church. Margaret at home.

Wednesday 4 April: Finished putting up the White Curtains after washing them. I do not think they will bear another putting up, they are old.

Thursday 5 April: Finished putting the carpet down in spare bedroom, the room has been thoroughly washed by Margaret. Betty when making butter this morning & without any provocation suddenly accused me of sending to tell them at the Post Office last Summer that our butter was not good or not nice. I never spoke to them about the butter, a likely thing that I shd. speak ill of what I had to sell without being asked. I cannot think what made her invent such a lie & I told her so.

Sunday 7 April: Lloyd to Church. Margaret to see poor Rachel Troedyrhiw after tea. She was very weak.

Monday 8 April: Morgan Harris took Julia's calf one week old last Saturday, £1..0..0 paid. Heard that David Jones Crachllwyn intended resigning the Collectorship owing to some mistakes in the Accounts. Rose Drawing room carpet.

Wednesday 10 April: Lloyd put down Drawing room carpet & Margaret & Betty cleaned the furniture.

Thursday 11 April: Thos. Griffiths left Cwmllynfell (where he was born) for Ystradowen.

Friday 12 April: Lloyd brought the 5 cwt soft coal from Station, paid 5/-. Lloyd took 4 cases containing 5½ dozn. empty bottles to Station for Messrs Williams & Co. John Bowen Nantmole called & took tea here. Betty cleaned out the Pantry.

Saturday 13 April: Old Nanny Penrheol buried today at Carmel. Betty to funeral. Grey cow brought He Calf. Cleaned & washed out the Hall.

Palm Sunday 14 April: No one to Church. Margaret went home after dinner.

Tuesday 16 April: John Thomas Gwernllwyn called late this evening saying he had told Mr. Miers that Gellyluog would suit A.G. and that he knew of a tenant if John leaves. Recd. letter from Jane Benthall saying they intended coming here tomorrow afternoon.

Wednesday 17 April: Mr. Benthall, Jane & the 2 little girls came here 2.30 p.m., had tea at 4 and left at 5 o'clk. They were very friendly & pleasant. Jane said the A.G.'s [Arthur Gilbertson's family] were going to Tenby & that Jessie Lloyd had been to Canada to see her Brother Frank & his Wife. Had 1 Gal. Brandy, 1 Gal. Whiskey, ½ Gal. Gin, 6 bottles of Sherry & 6 of Port from Williams, the 1st this year.

Thursday 18 April: Lloyd set Vetches in Cottage garden (½ bus. vetches & ½ bus. oats).

Friday 19 April: Primrose day. Lloyd & Margaret to Llanguicke. Lloyd after dinner went to see the Days.

Saturday 20 April: Lloyd to Biddy's for 2 cwt of potatoes Scotch Rocks for setting, 9/6. Felt very poorly all day & became very sick about 6 o'clk.

Easter Sunday 21 April: Betty & Lloyd to Church. Margaret to Carmel at 6 p.m. Sent £1..0..0 in an envelope for Betty to put on the plate from me as I cd. not go to Church. Sacrament: T. E. Davies [Curate].

Tuesday 23 April: Lizzie & Douglas came here 2 o'clk. train from Llandilo, the first time since the little girl was born.

Wednesday 24 April: Poor Rachel Troedyrhiw buried today at Saron. Betty & Margaret to the funeral. Lloyd for coal.

Saturday 27 April: Sold grey cow's calf to Beynon Gotregarth to go away on Monday, 2 weeks old today. Paid £1..10..0.

Sunday 28 April: Only Lloyd to Church. Too showery for Lizzie to go.

Monday 29 April: Recd. a bill yesterday by Lloyd from G. Evans for the "Cyfaill" (2 years) & a lock for the Church-yard gate. Sent him the money today by Lloyd. 2s..7d. paid.

Thursday 2 May: Lizzie walked to Cefnllan to ask Gwen about a servant.

Sunday 5 May: No one to Church. Showery & thunder. Margaret to Carmel.

Sunday 12 May: Lloyd drove Lizzie, Douglas and Margaret to Church. Betty & I in the house. Sacrament: T.E.D.

Monday 13 May: M.A.E. came to make Douglas' White (oatmeal) sailor suit.

Tuesday 14 May: David Jones Crachllwyn came here to say that his Mother had asked the Tilers that were at the Pant to come & repair the Cowhouse roof which had been injured by the storm, & to ask if I would come up & see the place today. Lizzie & I went from here at 4 p.m. leaving Ducca here with Margaret. The Crachllwyn outhouses are in a bad state (roofs & walls & wood-work). I told John James, the Tiler, to repair the roofs as well as he could & with as little expense as he could.

Wednesday 15 May: Neath Fair. The little boy of Pwll Watkin set fire to the Furze between Wain Vawr & Wain Hir & injured some of the oak trees. Sent Lloyd over to say what was done. Daniel said he had cautioned the child & that he did not think he would do any mischief again. Lloyd cleaning & digging the piece before front door & planting Sweet William by little gate &c.

Thursday 16 May: Lizzie & I intended going to see Mrs. Price but it came on to rain by Gellygron so we went to see Mrs. Kirkhouse instead. Lloyd put up the mare for an hour & a half at the X Inn while we took tea with Mrs. K. We then drove down to see Biddy & to get some buttons for Lizzie's buff cotton dress &c. Heard that poor Mr. Jones the Ystalyfera Curate was dead, died last Monday.

Friday 17 May: Revd. John Jones, Curate of Ystalyfera buried today at Ystalyfera Church, aged 40. A very nice, quiet man, beloved by all classes.

Sunday 19 May: T.J. & Mr. Stone drove over from Llandilo here at 11.20 a.m., left 7.30 p.m. after dinner. They went for a drive as far as Ynismeudw & Douglas too, this mare in the dog cart. Mrs. Day came here at dinner time left at 6.30 p.m.

Tuesday 21 May: Lloyd drove Lizzie, Douglas & I to Glantwrch. Mrs. Price seemed very glad to see us. Mrs. Dr. Thomas, Dora Stradling & her niece Gwladys Griffiths of Milford there. Showed us the alterations that had been made.

Friday 24 May: Lizzie & Douglas left for Llandilo 11 a.m. train after been here a month last Tuesday. Gave her 3 lbs of butter.

Saturday 25 May: Margaret washed out 3rd room & stairs. I rose & put down stair carpet. Wm. Price Cwmllynfell & his little boy here. Said 4 gates had come & that he wd. be glad to have the Posts. Said Evan should come up to see about cutting them on Friday. Lloyd to Glantwrch with 3 ducks from Jane Gartheithen 4/6 paid.

Sunday 26 May: Lloyd to Church. David Phillip & his son-in-law came up to tea. They were going to Saron at 6, funeral sermon after poor Rachel Troedy-rhiw. Mary & several others were at Rhydyfro having come in Car[riage] to Pontardawe.

Monday 27 May: After tea went to Gartheithen to pay 4/6d for Mrs. Price's ducks, heard there that D. Jones the Collector was not at the Audit today & had most likely gone off as his Parish Accounts are in a mess. Bought 10 lbs cheese of Mary D.M. Rachel papering their large bedroom.

Tuesday 28 May: Margaret washed down Kitchen loft.

Wednesday 29 May: Betty & Margaret cleaning out Dairy.

Friday 31 May: Evan who is now working at Llwynhen went to Cwmllynfell to cut 12 gate posts with Wm. Price for the 6 new gates. Evan will be there today & tomorrow. Margaret cleaned the Kitchen.

Saturday 1 June: Margaret Evans (Ystalyfera) left here this evening. She had been here since November 30th 88. Paid her to this day at the rate of £8..0..0 a year.

Sunday 2 June: Lloyd to Church. I am very sick & a dreadful headache, in the bed all day.

Monday 3 June: The Vicar and T.E.D. to Llandilo. Mr. Jones merely called at the door on his return 9.5 p.m. with the newspaper from Lizzie & saying they had tea there & that they were all well. I cleaned out all the little Kitchen cupboards & swept under oilcloth.

Tuesday 4 June: Sarah Anne Howells from "Pen-y-Bank Seven Sisters" came here today as maid at the rate of £7 a year, recommended by Mrs. Walters Cefnllan. Lloyd filling up the ruts in Heol-y-Cefn. Wm. Harris & Thos. Morgan the Mill came here collecting money for school children's tea at Rhydyfro on Whit Monday, gave 4/-.

Wednesday 5 June: Sarah cleaned out the Pool. Lloyd earthing potatoes in Kitchen garden.

Thursday 6 June: Betty & Sarah liming the Court. Lloyd planted cuttings of Geraniums in box by front door & the remainder of the Geraniums that used to be in the boxes planted in bed under Court wall. Put out Nasturtiums.

Friday 7 June: Betty & Sarah finished cleaning the Court. Heard from Mrs. Price that Dr. George Rees of London was dead.

Saturday 8 June: Lloyd sweeping & cleaning up the front & back. Evan called on his way to Ystalyfera. Paid him for the days at Cwmllynfell about Gate Posts & cleaning the Graves at Llanguicke, in all 4 days. Paid him 10/-. Lloyd took the Ducks to Glantwrch in D.M.'s Car. Mrs. Price sent me 6 geraniums, a cucumber & some cut roses.

Whit Sunday 9 June: I intended going to Church but it came on heavy rain at 1 o'clk which prevented. No one to Church. Sarah to Chapel 6 p.m. I went to D.M.'s for an hour after tea. They were very pleasant.

Wednesday 12 June: Lloyd planted 1 pint of K. beans in the front, the ones in Kitchen garden having failed or eaten up by slugs.

Thursday 13 June: After dinner Betty & Sarah limed & cleaned out the Stable. Llangadock Church re-opened. Lizzie went there with Miss Sarah Lewis & Miss Davies. She saw Dr. Walters & Mrs. Griffiths there & spoke to them.

Friday 14 June: Lloyd went home for a week by 11 train today.

Saturday 15 June: Ted Thomas & his family left Garnant. Lizzie went to Llandilo Station to see the children, & Miss Shenton went back with her, also to buy a bonnet.

Sunday 16 June: Sarah to Church, told her she may go to Cefnllan to tea, then to Chapel which she did & here 9.20.

Monday 17 June: John Thomas (Gwernllwyn) here speaking about J.W. [John Williams] Gellyluog and saying he wd. advise his giving up the farm in Sep. instead of March, also said that Jordan the Auctioneer intended coming to see about the Sale & to be responsible for a year's rent. Told T.J. of the money Z.E. [Zephania Evans] owed me, he owes him £85 – poor prospects I fear.

Friday 21 June: Llandilo fair. Eynon called to see Lizzie. Lloyd returned through Llandilo but did not call at Lizzie's. Betty & Sarah finished cleaning the Kitchen loft.

Sunday 23 June: Lloyd drove me to Church, the last time I was in Church was July 8th '88 with Lizzie & Douglas, one year into a fortnight I have been so ill after the attack of Bronchitis. I was at Bryn Amman Church July 15th '88 & then got very ill on July 20th '88. Betty & Sarah in Church, T.E.D. Owen's child Christened. Dear little Othniel's birthday tomorrow, took up nice flowers.

Monday 24 June: Lloyd & William Davies (Molecatcher) commenced cutting my hay (Vetches). Thos. Davies Cwmllynfell & his brother-in-law W. H. Morgan here, the former to pay his rent, the latter to know if I wd. lease the Colliery house & buildings to him for a Woollen Factory for 21 years or longer. Said he would be glad of my answer this day three weeks. Said he shd. have it then.

Wednesday 26 June: Carried the Vetches hay. Nant-y-gwin little boy died suddenly on the field.

Saturday 29 June: Nant-y-gwin little boy buried at Baran. Sarah's father came here to say her Sister was worse, she went home with him (Joan died at 9 p.m. tonight).

Sunday 30 June: Lloyd to Church. I very sick & ill all day, had mustard poultice at 7 a.m. on my chest. Gave Mary D.M. flowers to take to Coitcae Mawr.

Monday 1 July: Finished carrying Cae Barriwns hay & all of it without one drop of rain. Morgan Gartheithen helping us a few hours in the afternoon with horse & car.

Tuesday 2 July: Carried the Croften hay. All our long hay has been had in, in excellent condition (no rain). I hope we shall be fortunate in having the meadow. Wm. begins it today. The Woman of Coitcae Mawr buried today at Alltwen. Lloyd to funeral.

Thursday 4 July: Mrs. Jones the Crachllwyn here paying ½ yrs rent due last March £25..0..0. She had John James the Tiler's receipt for repairing roof &c. but I did not pay her that bill, until I had seen the work. The amount is £3..11..0. I think I dated the receipt I gave her for the rent the 5th instead of the 4th wh. was an error. She said she was anxious to have the farm either in her own name or her's & Owen's instead of as now in Hopkins'. Told her I wd. see Mr. Strick about it.

Saturday 6 July: Finished carrying the meadow without a drop of rain, made a rick of the hay on the meadow, one Gambo load only to hay house. All our hay is now in & in excellent condition not having any rain. T.J. drove Lizzie & Ducca here, 9.40 when they arrived.

Sunday 7 July: Lizzie's birthday. Lloyd drove Lizzie & Betty to Llanguicke. T.J., Ducca & I in the house. Sarah at home. Lloyd drove T.J. & Lizzie to Pontardawe Church at 6.30 (T.E.D.).

Monday 8 July: T.J. returned to Llandilo. Lizzie and Douglas went with him in the Dog cart as far as Wain Fawr.

Thursday 11 July: Lizzie went to Llandilo 11 train. Douglas & I went with her to Garnant, & afterwards called at Mrs. Thomas'.

Friday 12 July: Lloyd drove Lizzie, Douglas & I to Cwmamman thinking to see Mr. Brodie but he was attending the County Court in Llandilo.

Saturday 13 July: Lloyd drove Lizzie, Douglas & I to Cwm[llynfell] to see the Colliery house &c., promised to let Noah Jones know this day month if I should require him to leave in Sep. Went to Cwm. House the 1st time since Thos. Griffiths left. Liz. liked the back Kitchen. Had rain coming home.

Sunday 14 July: Lizzie, Douglas, Betty & Sarah to Church. Mary Phillip was in Church & she came here in the phaeton with Lizzie & returned to Ystalyfera after tea. She came to see if she cd. hear anything of Evan, he is at Llwynhên & has not been home for 3 weeks, being busy haymaking. I was dressed to go to Church but did not feel well enough. T. E. Davies.

Saturday 20 July: T.J. came last train. Lloyd met him at Garnant, brought gooseberries & raspberries.

Sunday 21 July: No one to Church. Margaret came down to see Douglas.

Monday 22 July: T.J., Lizzie & Douglas left here to meet 11 train for Llandilo. Wrote to Sarah's mother to say she was not feeling well & wd. come home 4 p.m. train tomorrow to see the Doctor.

Tuesday 23 July: Sarah went home saying she wd. come back tomorrow.

Wednesday 24 July: Lloyd cleaned the Candlesticks on Dining room sideboard.

Thursday 25 July: Lloyd fetched small load of Clay.

Friday 26 July: Lloyd drove me to Pontardawe. Saw Mrs. Evans P.O., told her I asked her for the last time if she had the money to pay. She said No & that she begged me to wait until tomorrow fortnight (August 10th). I told her if I did not get the £140 – then, I would take proceedings to recover them at once.

Saturday 27 July: Lloyd took down the top of the meadow rick as it had got wet in all the heavy rain & after drying put it back & some fern on it.

Sunday 28 July: Lloyd to Church. Betty & I in the house.

Tuesday 30 July: Mended my little umbrella & darned my umbrella. Went with Betty after tea to Ffynnon Bryn Cam for water.

Friday 2 August: Sarah's Mother & Aunt came here for her clothes saying she was not well enough to come back to service. She came here 4th June left 23rd July, 7 weeks 1 of wh. she was at home when her Sister died. Pd. 6 weeks @ 2/8½, 16/3 paid. Mr. Illtud Thomas Glanmor near Swansea died.[2]

Saturday 3 August: Went to Llandilo to stay a few weeks. Lloyd drove me to Garnant thinking to be in time for 2 o'clk. train, but lost it. Went to Mrs. Thomas to stay until last train, had tea there. Mrs. Thomas & Mrs. Drury took me to the Station. Douglas & his Father met me at Llandilo. Brought 3 padlocks at Rees Davies' for Hay house & the lower gate, 1/6 paid.

Monday 5 August: Llandilo Eisteddfod. Lizzie & T.J. to the Concert.

Monday 12 August: Evans the Post Office called at Llandilo. Told him I wd. not wait much longer for the money. William Cwmbryn & his brother-in-law Charles called at Llandilo to see me about Gellyluog.

Saturday 24 August: Had 15 cwt stone coal lumps @ 5/10, 4/4½ paid.

Wednesday 28 August: Madame Patti-Nicolini at the Brecon Eisteddfod.

Thursday 29 August: Anne Anthony left Glenview. She had been with Lizzie 1 year & 9 months & is shortly going to be married.

Sunday 1 September: Morgan Harris Gartheithen's Wife a son born today, the 2nd child.

Monday 2 September: My birthday, the first ever spent at Llandilo.

Friday 6 September: Lizzie & Douglas went to Garth by 11 train to see how they are getting on. A lovely day.

Saturday 7 September: Lizzie & Douglas returned last train having enjoyed their little jaunt.

2. Illtud Thomas (1813-89) was a substantial landowner in Swansea, Gower and the Swansea Valley and was the father of Isabel Frances de Winton Thomas who married Frank Gilbertson on 24 April 1896. See P. W. Jackson, 2001, 42-46.

Thursday 12 September: Returned home last train from Llandilo after staying there nearly 6 weeks. Liz, T.J. & Ducca came to see me off.

Monday 16 September: Mrs. Evans P.O. came up to beg I wd. wait until the 1st week in Oct. that she wd. then try & square up the £40 & that John wd. join in the note for £100. Fanny Gilbertson called, she came to Glanrhyd last Saturday from Mrs. Price's where she had been staying a week. It is 5 yrs. since she was down. Anne the Mill asking if they shd. have Gellyluog. I said 2 other parties were before her.

Friday 20 September: Went up to Cwmllynfell. Noah Jones leaves his House this 29th & I have rented it to Thos. T. Thomas Blacksmith at Hendreforgan Works for £4..10..0 a year, the tenant to pay all taxes. Went to Tynewydd to see Shani who gave me a warm welcome & very nice tea & cake. She goes to Llandilo tomorrow & will call to see Lizzie. Wm. Griffiths came to meet me at Cwm, told him I wished to have all a/c's settled between us. Said he wd. come down soon. Had heavy rain in coming home, here at 8.20 p.m.

Sunday 22 September: Farewell sermon by the Revd. T. E. Manning at the Unitarian Chapel Swansea. He goes to Sheffield.

Monday 23 September: John Thomas paid me as follows:

	£ .. s .. d
365 solid feet of Scotch fir & Poplar trees at 6d. per foot)	9 .. 2 .. 6
1 large Oak tree on Gellyluog	1 .. 0 .. 0
	£10 .. 2 .. 6
Paid J. Thomas 2 days for his nephew David cutting Poplar trees 22nd March 88)	7 .. 6
Recd. a cheque of John Thomas For £9..15..0 which settles all money matters between us up to this day.	£9 .. 15 .. 0 Paid

Saturday 28 September: Fanny G. called to wish me goodbye. She intends leaving Glanrhyd for Mrs. Pritchard's on Friday. Perhaps we may never meet again.

Sunday 29 September: Margaret came to see us, stayed the night. It was after dinner she left Ystalyfera. Lloyd to Llanguicke.

Saturday 5 October: Sent Douglas a Duck & 2 Puddings & the only 2 apples that we had off the trees.

Sunday 6 October: Lloyd to Church T.E.D[avies].

Monday 7 October: Mr. Stone (The Brewer) leaves Llandilo today.

Tuesday 8 October: Anne the Mill here saying how glad she wd. be to have Gellyluog. Wm. Davies Forchegel here saying Johnny & Mary wd. like to have Gellyluog.

Wednesday 9 October: Beynon Gotregarth applied for Gellyluog, said several others were before him. Harvest Services at Cwmgorse. Lloyd, Betty & I went at 6.30. Mr. Jones, Curate of Llansamlet and Mr. Davies of Old St. John's Swansea were the Preachers. Both very good, the first the best. Mr. & Mrs. Griffiths were very anxious that I should come to their Services tomorrow & lunch with them, but I could not go.

Thursday 10 October: Jordan the Auctioneer & John Williams Gellyluog here. John's sale is this day week, told them I must be paid the 12 months rent due last Sep. & have a note of hand from Jordan for the half year's rent due next March to be payable on May 1st '90 before I wd. allow the sale to take place. Jordan said he wd. bring me the year's rent (£37..10..0) this day week before he went to the sale & also give me his note of hand for the ½ year due March. I also promised to give John Williams the 1st May £5..0..0 as compensation for surface damage to the farm in hauling timber out, sold to John Thomas.

Friday 11 October: Went to the Bank & when at the P.O. Mrs. Leach & her sister Jessie Lloyd who are staying at Glanrhyd & on their way to lunch at Cilybebyll, finding I was at the P.O. came in & we had about 20 minutes chat together in the Parlour, both Mary & Jessie were very friendly & both looked very well & so active, so different to me, & so little difference in age, Jessie being 55 and Mary 54 & I 56.

Sunday 13 October: Lloyd drove me to Church. Betty also. The new Curate at Ystalyfera (Revd N. Thomas' brother) officiated first time at Llanguicke.

13 years ago N.T. [Rev. Nathaniel Thomas] left this parish for Pontyates near Kidwelly

Tuesday 15 October: Jordan the Auctioneer, John Thomas & John Williams Gellyluog came here at 6.30 p.m. to settle matters before the Sale.

	£ .. s .. d
Jordan paid me one year's rent due Sep. 89 for Gellyluog	37 .. 10 .. 0
I paid John Williams for damage done to the farm in hauling Timber	5 .. 0 .. 0
John Thomas paid John Williams for damage to land by drying the Bank &c.	2 .. 10 .. 0

J.W. asked me if I would take up the farm last Sept. instead of next March the end of his year, as he cd. sell all & thereby have a better sale. Said I would.

Wednesday 16 October: Lewis Walters Craig Trebannos & his Wife (people recommended to me by John Thomas the Timber Merchant) came up to see me about Gellyluog. Rented the farm to them from 29th Sep. '89 as yearly tenants @ £40 a year.

Thursday 17 October: Sir Daniel Gooch Chairman of the G.W.R. Co. died last Tuesday.

Wednesday 23 October: Returned from Llandilo 12.30 train. Called at Cwm. Vicarage. Both Mr. & Mrs. Griffiths seemed very glad to see me. Asked Mr. G. if he knew something about the law of Springs & Rivers relative to the proposed Reservoir & Pipe track at Cwmllynfell. Said he did not. Called at Garnant House. Mrs. Thomas not at home & Miss Shenton out.

Thursday 24 October: Sold the Old Fountain, several pots & saucepans & other old iron to the Rag Man about 112 lbs 1 .. 1
7 lbs of tea @ ½d per lb. 3½
1 .. 4½

Mary Phillips here, said Margaret had gone to the Tin Works! since last Monday. The son of Ddafadfa brought me half a cheese 17 lbs @ 2½d. (3/6d), 2 lbs Honey (1/-), Bees Wax 1 lb. (1/-) 5 .. 6 paid

His Mother on the road with Gambo. I took her some biscuits & wine, she wd. not come up as they were in a hurry to go to Morriston with their load of cheese, butter & poultry. John Bowen Nantmole here saying he knew of a tenant for Gellyluog, told him the farm was rented to Lewis Walters.

Saturday 26 October: John Morgan the Surveyor here about the Cwmtwrch Water Supply. Asked him if they had a right to take the Ystradowen Spring which now emptied itself into the Llynfell, as by that means the River wd. become very dry in case a Water Wheel or other Machinery wd. be required again at Cwmllynfell. Said he wd. speak to Mr. Herbert Lloyd about it & let me know.

Sunday 27 October: Wet & Windy. No one to Church. I became very sick soon after breakfast & very poorly all day in & on the bed. Lloyd's banns out at St. Peter's 1st time.

Monday 28 October: Had load of ball coal, it is now 1/6 instead of 5d the load, 1/6 paid.

Friday 1 November: Sent Douglas a taper for his little candlestick.

Sunday 3 November: Wet all day. No one to Church.

Monday 4 November: Had 15 cwt stone coal lumps @ 4d per cwt, 5/- paid. Had small load of Clay. The load had 24th August has lasted 10 weeks. We begin this load today.

Thursday 7 November: Harvest Service at Llanguicke.

Sunday 10 November: All of us in Church. The Church was decorated after the Harvest Service & looked very well & a good Congregation. Sacrament: T.E.D.

Monday 11 November: Had ½ sack of flour from Biddy,

Paid Daniel Davies for the flour	17 .. 0
also 2½ cwt Potatoes had last Spring	11 .. 9
He paid me £6 – 1 yrs Int. on £120, due last month.	£1 .. 8 .. 9 paid

Wednesday 13 November: Begun eating the bread of Biddy's flour had last Monday (140 lbs).

Friday 15 November: Sent Lizzie little Pan of Salt Butter by train, 21 lbs. Had 1 load of ball coal, 1/6 paid.

Saturday 16 November: Lloyd putting earth with the lime inside Cae Barriwns gate. Mr. Jones Gellygron called & stayed to tea, said he thought he knew of a man near Brecon who wd. like to buy Crachllwyn.

Sunday 17 November: Lloyd's birthday, 42 today. Lloyd to Llanguicke. Betty & I in the house.

Wednesday 20 November: I went to Swansea 9.40 train & returned 4.10. Called at Mr. Strick's Office to see him about the Ystradowen Well, the water of which they want a pipe track & easement through Cwmllynfell land. The Vicar & Miss Jenkins coming up in the same carriage with me, Miss Jenkins going to Glantwrch. Heard Mr. Josiah Rees was in London (he is Chief Justice of Bermuda). Called at Mr. Glynne Price's Office to enquire about Quarry. Said he was about letting it to Mr. Hedley & Revd. Selby Jones. He had promised it me some years ago.

Saturday 23 November: Lloyd married at St. Peter's by the Vicar Revd. D. Jones.[3]

Monday 25 November: Benjamin Daniel Llwynpryved called here in his way from Bettws fair to say he had seen Mr. Kempthorne in Swansea who asked if he knew of land to be sold, told him of Crachllwyn.

Tuesday 26 November: I wrote to Mr. Kempthorne saying Crachllwyn was for sale. Wrote to Mr. Strick saying I wanted £100 at once & that Revd. David Jones promised to be ready with £50 on Friday & that I begged him to get £50 from Mrs. Jones to meet that.

Friday 29 November: Poor old William Penlan buried today at Llanguicke aged 75.[4]

---

3. Thomas Lloyd (40) Garth Coachman married Elizabeth Thomas (24), spinster of Cwmgors. Margaret's wedding gift was a Bible whose inscription read: "This Bible is presented to Thomas Lloyd on his marriage Nov. 23rd 1889 by Miss Jones of Garth in whose service he had been the last 16 years".
4. William Jones of Penlan Cottage, Rhyd-y-fro.

Saturday 30 November: From Biddy had:

	s .. d
1 bag barley meal	12 .. 6
½ cwt. salt, ¼ onions 1/8d, candles 10d.	3 .. 10
	16 .. 4 paid

David took 62 lbs. old newspapers @ 1½d. per lb. for which he paid 7/9d. Wrote to Mr. Strick saying I must have the money £100 from D. Jones on or before the 7th Decr. or that I shd. take proceedings to get it.

Monday 2 December: Miss Hopkins Ynismeudw & her Cousin Miss Prosser called to ask me for Margaret Evans Ystalyfera's character. Mrs. Hopkins had some idea of taking her as a servant. Had 2 loads of ball coal 3/- paid.

Tuesday 3 December: Lloyd put R.P.L.'s potatoes in the Oats cask in Store room, & took all the green potatoes from hayhouse to storeroom.

Wednesday 4 December: Lloyd carrying the Wood & fern from Cottage to hayhouse. I walked down to the Cottage. Harry Lewis, Brynheulog married to Victoria Ellen Worthington, of Norton, Cheshire.[5]

Thursday 5 December: Lloyd finished cleaning the Cottage & fetched a small load of coal for himself to light fire there.

Friday 6 December: Lloyd carrying up leaf mould from Cottage.

Sunday 8 December: No one in Church. Very wet afternoon. Mrs. Kyle whose daughters are or were assistants at Evan's died at 127 Gorse Lane Swansea to be buried at St. David's Carmarthen on Wednesday, age 71 years.

Sunday 15 December: Very wet, no one to Church.

Monday 16 December: Daniel killed our pig.

Tuesday 17 December: Lloyd to Pontardawe shoeing Polly. Had parcel from Taylor. Lloyd said Moses had left Glanrhyd & was keeping a shop near Ynis-

---

5. Lewis Harry Lewis (1860-1943) was the eldest son of Lewis Griffith Lewis (1830-1920), owner of Pontardawe Chemical Works. A selection of photographs with a brief descriptive commentary of 'The Lewises of Brynheulog' appears in *Around Pontardawe: The Second Selection*, 1999, 51-58.

gelynen, that a Coachman from Penllergare had come to Mr. Gilbertson's. Daniel cut up our pig, it weighed 247 lbs (12 score 7 lbs).

Wednesday 18 December: Sent Douglas 4 Plum Puddings, spare rib, pork pie & little plate & 2 tea cakes. Had 15½ cwt stone coal lumps @ 4½ per cwt, 5/9½d. The load of lumps had Nov. 4th would last until next Monday (7 weeks).

1890

Margaret completed only a third of the year's diary, partly owing to her absence from Garth when staying with Lizzie's family in Llandeilo and when looking after young Douglas at Garth, especially during the five weeks prior to the birth of Lizzie's son Godfrey in October. Margaret's affection for Douglas, who she referred to as 'Ducca ba', is revealed in her tenderly expressed letter to him on his third birthday. As in previous years Margaret endured many days when she was "altogether quite out of health", and fretted over a number of painful symptoms, hinted at an accident in late May and later suffered from an acute skin infection which led to her complaint of medical neglect. Recurrent problems with the tenancies of Gelliluog and Crachlwyn were further stressful frustrations.

Wednesday 1 January: Mr. T. J. D. Llewelyn Penllergare is made a Baronet.

Thursday 2 January: My finger very painful (3rd on right hand) sent Lloyd for Dr. Rees he lanced it.

Friday 3 January: Had ½ ton soft coal 6/9 paid. T.J. came last train, sent Daniel with their car to meet him as Lloyd had gone for coal.

Saturday 4 January: T.J. left by 11 train from Garnant.

Sunday 5 January: Dr. Rees here. My finger very painful & all up & under my arm, he said my blood was in a bad state.

Tuesday 7 January: Lizzie & Douglas left for Llandilo by 11 train from Garnant. Dr. Rees here, thought my finger better.

Wednesday 8 January: Mrs. Jones of Crachllwyn here paying half a year's rent to Sep. 89. My finger too painful to give her a receipt.

Thursday 9 January: 1 load of small coal 1/6 paid.

Friday 10 January: Sent Lloyd to Ystalyfera, to see if Margaret Evans could go to Lizzie until she could get a maid. She could not, as she was going this day on a month's trial to the Hopkins's of Ynismeudw.

Wednesday 15 January: Lloyd & his Wife went to the Cottage to live. I pay him 18/- a week wages and he is to pay me 1/3d per week for Cottage.

Wednesday 22 January: 13 cwt of Large hard coal 5/- paid.

Tuesday 28 January: Rebe [Rebecca] the new Servant came to Lizzie on a month's trial. I hope she will suit.

Thursday 30 January: Gwen Bryn Maen came here to sew.

Saturday 1 February: Gwen went home this evening & did not come again till 11th inst. Said she was not well.

Sunday 2 February: Lloyd to Church. Willie Paddison & his Aunt Anne came here about 5 p.m., had tea and left at 7.15 for Trenache. Willie brought me 6 pretty little Muslin Neck ties (hand worked). Willie only came down Thursday & leaves again for Brighton tomorrow, he has 4 children.

Wednesday 5 February: Wrote to Mr. Hopkins Ynismeudw House saying the late Dr. G. Owen Rees was one of the Gellygron family & that his brother the Hon. Josiah Rees was now in London & wd. give all necessary information.[1] Sent for Dr. Rees, as I have such sore pimples about both ears, & some small ones all through my hair, he said my blood was in a very poor & bad state & that I was altogether quite out of health.

Thursday 6 February: Lloyd carrying ashes to Cae Barriwns.

Friday 7 February: Lloyd finished carrying out all the ashes to furthest end of Cae Barriwns. I went to the Cowhouse about 11 a.m. when he was letting out the cows. Saw it had not been cleaned out in the morning, told him so, & that I

1. "Josiah Rees Chief Justice of Bermuda is now in London, 20 Bloomsbury street, W.C." was written by Margaret in the diary's 'Memoranda of Reference, &c.'.

expected it to be cleaned out every morning as usual before breakfast. Lloyd is getting very negligent & takes advantage of my not being able to look after things.

Saturday 8 February: Recd. letter from Lizzie, she was not well since Thursday.

Wednesday 12 February: Gwen Bryn Maen left after making my black skirt, 2 slip bodices, an apron & hemming old grey skirt (5 days) & making a pocket 5/- paid.

Thursday 13 February: Sent Douglas an Antimacassar & Pigeon's Wing as a Valentine. Had ½ ton of soft coal from Pwll bach 6/10.

Sunday 16 February: Very wet afternoon. No one to Church.

Wednesday 19 February: Sent Lloyd for Dr. Rees my leg being swollen & inflamed – he came & said I must not walk but keep quiet in case it wd. get into a wound my blood being in such an impure state.

Friday 21 February: Poor Daniel Harris (Nant Rickets) buried today at Saron age 82 years. Lloyd went to the funeral from here to Nant Rickets & came here on their way down, for Betty to go from here to Saron as I was not well & could not be here alone.

Monday 24 February: Sold Julia's calf to Beynon Gotregarth for £1..0..0 he comes for it Thursday night, it will then be 9 days old.

27th Feb. 1890

My dear Ducca ba,

Tomorrow is your birthday. I am very sorry I cannot come over to spend it with you, but I am not well enough to leave home, and the weather is too cold for you to come here.

With my kind love and best wishes I send you a little present – A Sovereign – (the price of Julia's calf) & on Saturday I shall picture you & Mam-ma taking it to the Bank. You are now 3 years old, just beginning to know right from wrong, so that I hope you will do your best to be a good boy, always truthful, and obedient to your Parents and doing at once what they wish. You have a very kind Dadda & Mam-ma, who have nursed you up tenderly and in return, you must be a kind, loving son to them.

May the blessing of God rest upon you through life dear little Douglas, enabling you to withstand all sinful temptations, & to grow up an honest, sober and industrious man, leading in all ways a good and spotless life, which in the end will bring you a rich reward.

With my kind love and every kind wish to you, & your dear Father and Mother, and hoping you may all live long together in health and happiness.

I am my dear Ducca ba
Yours affectionately
Nanna

Friday 28 February: Dear little Ducca ba's birthday 3 years old. I had hoped to have gone to Llandilo to have spent it with them but I am too poorly having such sore little boils above my ears & on my legs. Wrote to Douglas yesterday & sent him in Reg[istered] letter a Sovereign which I said was Julia's calf turned into gold. I hope he will grow up to be a good man.

Saturday 1 March: Poor old Mr. Samuel of Dan-yr-allt Pontardawe died aged 82 years.

Sunday 2 March: No one to Church. Betty's nephew David came to see her, he has five children & lives near Swansea.

Monday 3 March: Llewellyn Bevan of Clydach Factory buried at Baran. Lloyd fetched 2 loads of small coal & 1 tomorrow, 1/1d each, 3/3 paid.

Tuesday 4 March: Llangavelach fair. Betty went to Ystalyfera. Evan had been ill 8 weeks with his arms & legs & is now on the Club.[2] Lloyd cutting the Kitchen Ivy after dinner. Mary came in & sat 2 hours with me after tea knowing I was by myself. The Forth Bridge, near Edinburgh, opened today by the Prince of Wales. I feel interested in it as Benjamen Baker was one of the Chief Engineers. B.B. was the son of Mrs. Baker of Cheltenham & Mr. Coke had him put in the Neath Abbey Works to learn Engineering.

Wednesday 5 March: Had 16 cwt of Stone Coal, 6/- paid.

Thursday 6 March: In bed all day feeling very poorly & the boils above my ears so very sore. Lloyd harrowing the manure on front field & the ashes on Cae Barriwns.

2. A colloquialism for claiming monetary aid from a contributory insurance scheme run by a benefit club or friendly society.

Saturday 8 March: Lloyd had a letter saying his Mother died at 6 p.m. last Wednesday & to be buried next Tuesday. Wrote to Mr. Strick about J.W. Gellyluog.

Sunday 9 March: No one to Church. Mary came & sat an hour with me after tea. I am a little better today.

Monday 10 March: Great explosion at the Morfa Colliery near Port Talbot.[3]

Friday 14 March: Willy Jevon's wife a son, 1st child at Duncton near Petworth.

Monday 17 March: Pontardawe fair. Betty to the fair.

Tuesday 18 March: Bettws Ploughing Match on Llwyn-yr-Onen field.

Wednesday 26 March: Lizzie, T.J. & Douglas left 11 train for Llandilo. Gave Lizzie piece of Ham about 11 lbs.

Friday 28 March: The Grey Cow brought a she-calf.

Sunday 30 March: Lloyd to Church.

Monday 31 March: Benjamin Daniel called here on his way to Llandilo Fair at 6 a.m. & took Lizzie's cloak wh. she had forgotten. Said he had seen the man of Cwmbryn yesterday. W. Williams Cwmbryn came here about 7 p.m., said he wd. take Gellyluog as it was for £30 a year (House and outbuilding repairs to be done by me). Told him L.W. agreed to give £40.

Wednesday 2 April: Lloyd to meet T. Jones at Garnant first train here at 10 a.m. He drove me to Gellyluog to meet the new tenant & his wife about the repairs & to give them possession of the farm at a rent of £40 a year. Lewis Walters to pay all taxes, except the Income tax. T.J. left for Llandilo last train. Hopkin Charles Britonferry died.

---

3. The explosion claimed the lives of 87 colliers, 68 of whom were married, 3 were widowers and the remaining 16 were single. The number of children left fatherless by the disaster was 178, of whom 121 were under 13 years of age. Only 43 bodies were recovered. The Morfa colliery had been worked by Messrs. Vivian & Sons since c. 1840 and there had been two previous tragic explosions in 1863 and 1870 when 30 and 38 men respectively had been killed. *The Times* 13 March 1890.

Good Friday 4 April: Lloyd to Llanguicke 11 a.m. Service. Lloyd p.m. planting the little bluebells in old sieve hoop by the Yew tree. Feeling very poorly all day with great giddiness & headache & most of the day on the bed. Poor Mrs. Walters Llansamlet Vicarage died this morning.

Saturday 5 April: Betty finished liming the Court. Shani Tynewydd called on her way to Gartheithen.

Easter Sunday 6 April: Lloyd to Llanguicke. Sent an envelope with a sovereign in it for him to put on the plate from me. Betty went as far as Saron & returned thinking she would be too late altho′ she left here 2.10 p.m. Williams.

Monday 7 April: D.M. took Grey Cow's calf one week old last Friday, £1..10..0 paid. Rees Jones the Carpenter here about Gellyluog repairs.

Tuesday 8 April: Borrowed Gartheithen Car to go over to Gellyluog to meet Rees Jones Alltwen, the carpenter to see what repairs were required. Lewis Walters also there. Called at Gotregarth to see the pig.

Wednesday 9 April: Poor Mrs. Walters buried today at Llansamlet, public funeral 2.30 p.m. She had been an invalid & helpless about (…) years.

Thursday 10 April: Lloyd carrying out the small heap of lime & earth by Cae Barriwns gate to the top of that field. The Woman of Cwmbryn & her daughter Esther brought me a fowl, the first time I ever saw the woman. She is only 43, & has been blind 13 years.

Friday 11 April: Lloyd set Biddy's potatoes in the garden (Nant-y-Gwin piece). Bought a small pig of Beynon Gotregarth (I think it too dear) £1..14..6 paid.

Saturday 12 April: Paid Mrs. Harris Gartheithen all I owe, 3/2. Paid Shani (by her) for duck had long ago, 3/3.

Sunday 13 April: Lloyd & Betty to Church. Thomas.

Wednesday 16 April: Lloyd took front Wheel of Phaeton to John Hopkin to be re-banded. Mr. Day & his brother-in-law Mr. White called here about the Cwm[llynfell] siding. D.M. told me that he had heard there was some talk of erecting a Brick Works near the Old Pit at Cwmllynfell & that in that case the land wd. be worth £4 an acre, that was about the price his brother had for the Brick Works land at Cross Keys. Lloyd finished setting potatoes in the front under Hay house – White Elephants, Black Kidney & R.P.L.'s.

Tuesday 22 April: Lloyd harrowing Cae front p.m.

Wednesday 23 April: a.m. Lloyd harrowing Cae Barriwns & Vetches.

			s .. d
p.m. Lloyd for coal	13 cwt 1 qr of small		1 .. 8
	14 cwt 2 qrs lumps		5 .. 5½
		Paid	7 .. 1½

Saturday 26 April: P.J. Charles Solicitor Neath died at Tenby aged 38 years.

Sunday 27 April: Lloyd to Church. Mary Phillip & her daughter in Llan-guicke, both came here from Church & left 9.30. I was in bed until 4.30. Very sick & ill. Told Mary to ask Margaret to come down for a week or two.

Monday 28 April: Lizzie & Ducca ba[ch] came here at 4.45. Lloyd met them at Garnant.

Saturday 3 May: Lizzie & Douglas left for Llandilo. Drove them to Duffryn Station to meet the 3.15 train. I waited to see them off. Gave Lizzie 5 lbs butter & some potatoes. In returning overtook Mrs. Thomas & Miss Shenton by the "Raven Inn". They had been to Llandilo.

Tuesday 6 May: Called at Rees Jones to see him about the troughs for Cwm-llynfell. Called at Mrs. Kirkhouse's, said Lalla had gone to a situation in Lincolnshire. Saw Mrs. Evans the P.O., said she wd. pay me the money in 12 months. Lloyd rode [to] Cwm to measure the eaves. Mary Phillip here, paid 15/- int. from her son.

Friday 9 May: Recd. P.O. from John Jones Llwyn-yr-Onen value £9..0..0. Paid Davies & Co. Pontardawe £4..7..0 by cheque as per bill to this day.

Saturday 10 May: Selby Jones here about the Quarry. Lloyd cleaning hedge cuttings on the road side. Called at the Cottage, had rhubarb cake. Wrote to ask Mr. Kempthorne if he had any intention of buying the Crachllwyn.

Sunday 11 May: Lloyd & Betty to Church. Heavy distant thunder a.m. T.E.D.

Monday 12 May: Lloyd finished cleaning up hedge cuttings & burnt the rubbish in Cae Cwtta. I dusted down the Dining room walls & pictures & swept under the sideboard. Lloyd begun mowing the Green, first time this year.

Tuesday 13 May: Recd. letter from Mr. Kempthorne saying he intended coming up to Nant-y-Gwin next week, & would call here. Confirmation at Llandilo.

Friday 16 May: Mr. Kempthorne & Mr. J. O. Jones called here, about 3.15 p.m., they had been to Pwll Watkin. Mr. K. said he would go & see Crachllwyn & let me know again. Recd. letter from Lloyd's sister (Mrs. Winstone) saying she had seen my advertisement for a maid, & that she wd. like my taking her daughter on trial.

Thursday 5 June: Lizzie intended going to Llandilo last train, but Mr. & Mrs. Griffiths Cwmamman came here at 4 p.m. wh. prevented her. They had heard of the accident last Saturday & came to see how I was. They stayed to tea. They came in the "Farmers" wagonette.

Friday 6 June: Lizzie & Douglas left 11 train from Garnant. I took them to the Station in the Carriage, the first time it has been used since Lizzie's marriage. Recd. a letter from Mrs. Winstone saying her daughter went to Cheltenham as Kitchen Maid yesterday, not hearing from me she thought I had engaged the girl from Builth.

Saturday 7 June: Betty washed out the 3rd room.

Sunday 8 June: Very wet. No one to Church.

Tuesday 17 June: Went to Llandilo 11 train. Liz & Ducca ba met me at Station.

Saturday 21 June: Barnaby fair. Lloyd & his Wife in fair, had breakfast & tea at 2 Glenview Villas, Llandilo. Mrs. Day called at Glenview about 10 a.m. She was delighted with the place, had come in a Brake from Ystalyfera.

Friday 4 July: Mr. & Mrs. Matthews called at Glenview & had tea, they had been to Laugharne & Pendine, seeing if they could get nice lodgings to take the children, they came up from Carmarthen & returned to Swansea by the 9 o'clk. train.

Friday 11 July: Lizzie went home by 2 o'clk. train to see how they were getting on. Lloyd met her at Garnant.

Saturday 12 July: Lizzie came back last train. Douglas a very good boy while she was away, but had a bad cold.

Sunday 13 July: Anniversary services at Bryn Amman Church.

Wednesday 16 July: Poor Lewis Walters Gellyluog died this morning.

Saturday 19 July: Poor Lewis Walters Gellyluog buried today at Alltwen.

Wednesday 23 July: Alice a she calf like herself in colour.

Saturday 2 August: Lizzie, T.J. & Douglas went for a drive after tea & when near Llandafan the horse fell & they were all 3 thrown out. Only poor Liz was injured, her left arm on elbow severely bruised. She was altogether very much shaken & frightened & in her state within about 2 months of her confinement the consequences may be serious. God grant she get over it safely.

Monday 4 August: Llandilo Eisteddfod, lovely day. Lizzie & I sitting in back dressing room to see, & hear. Poor Liz very poorly & in her dressing gown. Douglas all day at No. 3 [Home of widow Mary Anne Evans].

Monday 11 August: Returned home from Llandilo last train after been there 8 weeks tomorrow. Left poor Lizzie very poorly after the accident & her arm very painful.

Tuesday 12 August: Margaret Winstone from Dowlais (Lloyd's niece) came here as Maid at the rate of £8..0..0 a year. Lloyd met her at Neath with Garth-eithen car. Lovely afternoon.

Thursday 21 August: Poor Miss Thomas Cae-glas (Llandilo) died after great suffering.

Wednesday 3 September: Wrote to ask Dr. Thomas if he wd. come down tomorrow that I felt very poorly & wd. be glad of his advice.

Thursday 4 September: Dr. Thomas came 3 p.m., said these boils & carbuncles proceeded from an unhealthy state of the scalp & that the heat & itching of my head, ears & neck proceeded from the same cause, said he wd. write to Dr. Rees. Paid him £1..1..0 for this visit. Mr. Benthall drove him down, but did not come in.

Sunday 7 September: Sent Lloyd to Post. Had letter saying T.J. could come on Wednesday. Sent Lloyd with a note to Cwmbryn asking if W.W. could meet T.J. at 11.30 on Wed. at Gellyluog. Said he could. Margaret to St. Peter's a.m., Cwmgorse p.m. D. Phillips Jnr. & his little girl came here p.m. Margaret Evans & some girl from Ystalyfera came here from Llanguicke. M. is in Tinworks.

Monday 8 September: Mrs. Wm. Price Cwmllynfell called in her way to Gartheithen, said her husband begged I would give him a few tons more lime for the farm. Said "No, I wd. not, that I had given him 13 tons which was 3 more than I had promised".

Wednesday 10 September: T.J. came first train from Llandilo. Lloyd met him with Gartheithen Car. He went over to Gellyluog to meet Williams Cwmbryn & to walk over the Farm. T.J. said he wd. not be afraid to give £40 a year. W. offered £30 or £32. Wrote to Dr. Thomas saying Dr. Rees had never appeared & that I thought my case a much neglected one. Dr. Rees came, called at 8.15 when I was going to bed, told him I thought it very neglectful in him not to come before & that I had sent for Dr. Thomas. I gave him my mind pretty freely, his excuse was that "I don't like coming too often to run up a long bill". Told him there was a difference between "too often & positive neglect".

Friday 12 September: Jones Ddafadfa & James Glynllydan came here to see about Gellyluog. They are to give an answer this day week. Mrs. Williams Cwmbryn came to offer £35 for Gellyluog. £30 W. offered before. Some Wm. Lewis from Neath came to ask about Gellyluog. Dr. Rees here, told him I had had a letter from Dr. Thomas this morning saying he had gone to Bryn Amman yesterday on the receipt of my letter. Rees said "he telegraphed for me to meet him there & I sent a tel. to say I wd.," so he is pitched into on all sides.

Sunday 14 September: My hair & head in a dreadful state.

Tuesday 16 September: Lloyd to Neath for Aberthaw lime, 2 bus 2/4. New Bucket for milking 1/9. New Shovel.

Thursday 18 September: Figgures came here to paper my bedroom (fern leaved paper), painted wash stand, dressing table, 3 chairs, window & shutters, & skirting, & fire board, all one coat. Cleaned paper off ceiling & had it whitened.

Friday 19 September: James Glynllydan & his son here about Gellyluog. He offered £35 for 3 years then £40. I offered it at £37..10..0 & then £40.

	s .. d
Paid Figgures 2 days	10 .. 0
3 lbs. paint 1/3, glue 4d, paper border 1/-	2 .. 7
glass for picture frame	4
	12 ..11
8 pieces paper (Swansea) @ 10d.	6 .. 8
	19 .. 7

Saturday 20 September: Margaret scoured out my room.

Sunday 21 September: Margaret to St. Peter's at 11 & Cwmgorse at 6 p.m.

Monday 22 September: Went back to my own room. I do not like the paper nearly as well as the old one put on 7 years ago.

Tuesday 23 September: Old Wm. Rees Gellylucka buried today at Llanguicke.

Wednesday 24 September: Lloyd to clean Walks & at Llanguicke.

Friday 26 September: Pontardawe fair. Betty to the fair. Mary Shonny sent by her a very pretty tea cup & saucer for Douglas. Betty bought him a pretty mug "Think of Me". Dr. Rees here, said my thigh looked better. Lloyd for ½ ton of soft coal 7/6.

Saturday 27 September: Mary Phillip's (Betty's niece) furniture passed this way to Duffryn where she is going to live, her husband working in new Tinworks. She & her mother went by train. Margaret Winston went to Swansea midday to buy boots, caps, &c., returned 7 train. I told her to come by the 4 train.

Sunday 28 September: Margaret to All Saints at 6 p.m. Lloyd to Saron 6 p.m.

Monday 29 September: Mrs. Walters paid half year's rent for Gellyluog due this day £20..0..0. Paid her for 2 grates Lewis had ordered for me to put at Gellyluog 8/2.

Saturday 4 October: I came to lodgings in Swansea 10 St. Helen's Crescent recommended by Mrs. Evans Llandilo. Margaret Winstone came with me as maid as I was so poorly having had so many carbuncles, especially in my hair.

Sunday 5 October: Jane Matthews called on me. I was perfectly astonished to see her, thinking she was in London, as she has had an operation performed in Guy's Hospital not many weeks ago. She looks very well & is getting on nicely & is much relieved.

Tuesday 7 October: Mrs. Matthews called & sat an hour or two with me & had tea. Recd. a tel. from Llandilo at 7.40 p.m. saying Lizzie was confined of a little boy.

Wednesday 8 October: Went to see Lizzie by the 8 a.m. train, found her better than I expected. She had a very hard time and the child born under the influence of chloroform.

Thursday 9 October: Returned from Llandilo by the 5.20 p.m. train & Douglas with me.

Saturday 1 November: Lloyd finished carrying out all the old manure to Cae Barriwns.

Sunday 2 November: Poor Ducca ba very sick & poorly. Wrote to tell his mother so.

Thursday 6 November: Llanguicke Harvest Service. Very wet only Lloyd to Church.

Sunday 9 November: Margaret Evans came here to see Douglas, brought him Grapes & an Orange. He gave her a little pocket hand[kerchief] with embroidered flower on the corner.

Tuesday 11 November: Mrs. Winstone came here & was very sorry Margaret was leaving & that if she had been impertinent that she should fully apologise to me, told her that M. was very untruthful & had when with me in Swansea told Miss Salmon that I had desired her to open my letters the day & night I spent at Llandilo, which was an untruth. Told Mrs. W. that M. told me this morning that she was going direct from here to a situation in London & with her knowledge. The mother said she knew nothing of her leaving here until she had my letter yesterday & that she shd. not go to London but send the P.O.O. for 15/- back wh. were for travelling expenses. She had answered some advertisement when in Swansea. Mrs. Winstone seemed very vexed at her conduct.

Thursday 13 November: Margaret Winstone left after been here 13 weeks last Tuesday. Lloyd took her to Neath in Gartheithen car. Paid her £2..0..0.

Saturday 15 November: Went to Llandilo by 2 o'clk. train. Took Douglas back, after been with me 5 weeks last Thursday. He was a very good boy the whole time & they all thought him looking very well & grown. Gave Lizzie pot of butter 37 lbs.

Sunday 16 November: Douglas to Llanddufeusant Church 3 p.m. with his Father & was a good boy all through the Service.

Wednesday 19 November: Mr. Powell Carregcennen near Llandilo died, suddenly, although he had not been well of late.

Saturday 22 November: Wm. Price Cwmllynfell here. I had written to ask him to come. He said the Blacksmith living in the Colliery House was a quarrelsome man, & that Thos. Davies had been accused of sheep stealing. Price had a very wet night to go home.

Sunday 23 November: Wet day. No one to Church.

Wednesday 26 November: Lloyd & Daniel opening the gutter under chestnut tree in Cae front, it had been choked for some time. Some one last night took several of our gates off their hinges, & the little Iron one. John Williams Cwmtwrch Foundry & his son (my tenant) came here. I told the son he had done wrong in taking people & their furniture into his house, without consulting me, & that I wished him to leave at once, if he could get a house, or as soon as he could otherwise I shd. give him Notice in March to leave in Sept. Said he wd. go, as soon as he cd. get a house.

Saturday 29 November: Mended & put braid to my old silk petticoat. M. A. Price Cwmllynfell & John Harries Ty Newydd's two daughters came from Gartheithen to D.M.'s & Mary brought them in to see me. Gave them biscuits & wine in Dining room.

Monday 15 December: Mrs. Curre (Annie King) died at Caerau to where she had removed from Itton Court Chepstow when her son married.

Thursday 18 December: Mrs. J. H. Rowland of Neath died aged 67, to be buried at Cadoxton. She was Mr. Christopher James' youngest daughter.

1891

There were 114 entries in Margaret's diary during the year, with only one in January and two in February. She did not recommence writing until 6 May when she was occupied in looking after Douglas for an indeterminate period and again for six weeks from 20 July. There were occasional visits to Llandeilo thereafter. While family responsibilities predominated, Margaret was still mindful of the need to manage her assets efficiently. Her diary entries show that her control over her income sources was not only personal, informal and direct, but also fallible in its sensitivity to her tenants' and debtors' ability to pay their dues. During the year, and without the help of an estate manager or professional advice, she was required to make decisions respecting the lease of Cwmllynfell property, the sale of Gelliluog trees, a wayleave charge, a boundary issue and damage to her land from river tipping. At the same time she was obliged to maintain her properties and attend to storm damage. It was a heavy responsibility for a solitary woman whose health was invariably fragile. The death of her cousin, the Rev. Richard Pendrill Llewelyn (R.P.L.), on 22 October was a grievous family loss.

The 1891 census, taken on 5 April, required respondents in Wales to show 'Language Spoken' and the enumerators' returns confirm that Margaret, Betty and Thomas Lloyd spoke both English and Welsh whilst Elizabeth Lloyd seemingly spoke only Welsh, as did all David Morgan's family in Garth Farm. At Lizzie's Llandeilo home all the occupants were bilingual.[1]

Friday 2 January: Josiah Rees, Chief Justice of Bermuda is Knighted. He is now Sir Josiah, it is announced in this day's Western Mail.

Thursday 19 February: Paid James Hinkin Garth Poor Rate.

The Garth	£17 .. 10 .. 0 @ 1/8d.		£1 .. 9 .. 2
Garth Farm	37 .. 15 .. 0	"	3 .. 2 ..11
3 Cots Cwm.	7 .. 10 .. 0	"	12 .. 6
1 " Dd. Williams	3 .. 5 .. 0	"	5 .. 5
1 " Thos. Davies	3 .. 0 .. 0	"	5 .. 0

1. Llangiwg PRO RG12/4468 and Llandeilo PRO RG12/4511. See also G. Parry & M. A. Williams (1999) for a discussion of the ambiguous question 'Language Spoken', its various interpretations, the debate over the validity of the returns and an analysis of the linguistic evidence for the community of Pontardawe; also C. P. Bateson (2001) for an examination of population change in Pontardawe 1851-91.

1	"	Thos. Thomas	3 .. 0 .. 0	"	5 .. 0
1	"	Thos. Lloyd	2 .. 10 .. 0	"	4 .. 2
			£74 .. 10 .. 0 @ 1/8d		£6 .. 4 .. 2
Special Expenses on £19..5..0 (Cots) @ 6d.					9 .. 7½
					£6 ..13 .. 9½
Less Commission on Cots.					10 .. 3½
					£6 .. 3 .. 5½

In. & Land Tax on Cwm. Cottages 9/4d.

Garth Special rate @ 6d. on 1. 4th of £55..5..0 — 6 ..11½

All paid by Cheque

Friday 20 February: Mrs. James Tamblyn (Polly Rees) Glan Llynvi Maesteg a daughter, her 1st child.

Wednesday 6 May: Douglas & I intended going to Swansea by the 9.40 a.m. train but lost it by 2 minutes so we drove to Morriston to meet the tram car as I wanted to see Mr. Strick about the piece of land I have promised to sell Griffith Lewis at Cwmllynfell. Called at Miss Salmon's. She & her Cousin had gone to Bryn Syfi. Called on Mrs. Evans, 10 St. Helen's Crescent, Miss Gabb there. Douglas & I had a walk in the Park & on the sands & then to Llandilo from S. Bay by 6 p.m. train. Paid Pearse & Brown *[22 Wind Street]* for binding "Sturm's Reflections" 2 volumes 4/-. Bought Ducca two Vests & paid all I owed at Evans. Bought pair of Kid House boots at Randalls *[Thomas Randles, 15 Castle Street]*, 5/6 paid.

Thursday 7 May: Douglas & I left Llandilo 11 train. Lloyd met us at Bryn Amman with the Carriage.

Saturday 9 May: Rachel Morgan Walters the Carpenter's Wife buried at Baran. Lloyd to funeral.

Wednesday 20 May: Mr. Davies the new Curate at Cwmgorse called about 5.30 p.m. to say the Annual Services were tomorrow. Evan left midday intending to go to the Turkish Baths tomorrow. Paid him all I owed 22 days on our food at a 1/-, £1..2..0. He has put barbed wire fence under Cae Barriwns Wood, assisted Thos. to put Gate Post at Gellyluog for the 6 new gates from Llandilo & the one new gate from Rees Jones, he also cleaned the Walks at Llanguicke & shut a little Iron Gate to the Cottage & mended Garden Wall.

Thursday 21 May: Lloyd mowing the Green 1st time this year. Cwmgorse Annual Services. Lloyd went 6.30 p.m. Griffith Lewis from Cwmllynfell here, told him I hoped to be able to come up on Tuesday.

Tuesday 26 May: Lloyd drove me up to Cwmllynfell in D.M.'s car. Douglas stayed with Betty.

Friday 29 May: Douglas & I in the carriage to meet Lizzie & Godfrey at Bryn Amman 12.10 train.

Saturday 30 May: T.J. came here last train un-expectedly.

Wednesday 3 June: Betty ill in bed. Lizzie washed the Kitchen. Mary made the Butter.

Thursday 4 June: Rebe [Rebecca], Lizzie's maid came here 4 p.m. Douglas & I and Rebe carrying Godfrey went to Gartheithen after tea to buy a Pig, £1..4..0. paid. Betty slept in Kitchen loft as she was ill & not with Rebe in 3rd room. Little Doddy [Godfrey] not well. I went to call Mary D.M. at 12 o'clk. (midnight). She thought there was nothing serious the matter.

Monday 8 June: Lizzie, T.J., Douglas, Doddy & Rebe left at 10 o'clk. Lloyd drove them in the carriage to meet 11 train at Garnant. Lloyd to Ystalyfera p.m. to say Betty was ill & for Mary to come down tomorrow.

Tuesday 9 June: Mary came here at 11.30 a.m. Arranged for her to come down on Thursday to fetch Betty & take up her clothes.

Friday 12 June: Mary came down today, and Lloyd took up Betty's chest of drawers in the cart & Mary too. Gave her a basin of butter about 3 lbs. Betty said she felt a little better & that if I liked that she wd. stay a week or two longer to see if I could hire of a maid, not for me to be in the house alone & I ill. Said I should be very glad if she would.

Saturday 13 June: I am feeling very ill. Sent Lloyd for Dr. Rees. He said I had Bronchitis & a touch of Influenza, & that Betty had Influenza.

Sunday 14 June: Lloyd to the Dr's. for medicine for Betty & I. M. A. Price Cwm. & another girl called in their way to Gartheithen.

Monday 15 June: Lloyd for coal.

	s .. d
1 Load lumps 14½ cwt @ 6d	7 .. 3
1 " small for balls 15 cwt @ 1d	1 .. 3
	8 .. 6 paid

Tuesday 16 June: John Thomas Gwernllwyn here about Gellyluog wood. Dr. Rees here.

Wednesday 17 June: Mr. Day Hendreforgan here about the Cwm[llynfell] houses, told him I was partly in treaty with the Gwinfe Factory people about them, & that if I did not settle with them, that I wd. write to him, that my price was £25 a year for the houses occupied by Thos. Davies & Thos. Thomas, blacksmith, & the vacant building known as "the Office", "sawpit" & "carpenter's shop".

Thursday 18 June: Hannah Thomas late of "The Crown" Cwmtwrch here, said she had heard I was in the Influenza & had come to see how I was, but I think her chief business was to know what I would take for Wm. Rowland's house & garden, told her I had not quite made up my mind to sell it, but when I did that W.R. shd. have first offer. Lewis Williams here mending the crack in leaden gutter, sent by John Griffiths Pontardawe. It took him about 1½ hours, a boy came with him. Elizabeth returned from her Mother's.

Friday 19 June: Lloyd mowing the Green. Dr Rees called on his way from Pontardawe, said Betty was much better, that I was weak. Lloyd up for medicine for me.

Saturday 20 June: Revd. John Griffiths Rector of Bedwas (formerly of Kilvey Swansea) died aged 68 years.

Monday 22 June: Lloyd to Llandilo fair. Elizabeth here washing 3 pairs of sheets &c. Little boy not well so she was only a few hours. Mr. J. M. Sinnett Solicitor Llandovery, died suddenly, he was married to Sophy Griffiths whose Father died last Saturday.

Tuesday 23 June: Gwen Cefnllan called to see how I was in her way from Bryn Amman, where she had been trying to buy young geese, but they were too dear. Said they intended re-seating Llanguicke Church &c. Rachel Morgan not well, gave her a bottle of Tarragona. They had made & churned the butter twice for me & washed my black shirt.

Thursday 25 June: Lloyd earthing Green Potatoes. Evan putting barbed wire above Pistle. Lloyd cut down privet bush on top of Cae front wall by front gate.

Friday 26 June: Lloyd earthing potatoes kitchen garden. Cut the bacon into hams & gammons.

Saturday 27 June: Lloyd p.m. clearing away the gorse from little gate to dunghill that Evan had cropped, & cleaning about the stones that holds up the earth from the road to the Gorse. Evan finished putting the barbed wire above the Pistle & put Iron Pins in rails to hill & dunghill to prevent the cattle rubbing them down.

Monday 29 June:

	s .. d
5 Bus. oats	15 .. 0
1 Cwt. Bran	6 .. 3
30 lbs flour @ 1/7/10	4 .. 3 from Dd. Lewis P'dawe
	£1 .. 5 .. 6 paid

Friday 3 July: Betty Isaac buried today at Saron. Betty to funeral.

Friday 10 July: Mrs. [Magdalen] Daniel Llwynpryved buried today at Llanguicke age 72. Lloyd to funeral.

Saturday 11 July: Lloyd cut down the Portugal laurel in the old garden that we had removed from lower side of Walk in the Spring. It looked quite dead but I fancy there is life at the root & that it will bud out again.

Sunday 12 July: Betty to Llanguicke, came home by Cwm Scwt. Lost her purse on the Hill, after tea she went to look for it & found it by Pen Caer Lan gate, 14/7d in it.

Monday 13 July: Began mowing hay (the Meadow). Daniel is to cut all mine with their mowing machine @ 4/6 per chain acre (on their own food). Hannah Dl. Sair [*Saer*: Carpenter] cleaned some of the Kitchen tins until dinner & then to the meadow. John Harris Nant Rickets won the trial in London about his

Father's will & Howell his brother lost his claim. Mr. Morgan (late lay reader at Cwmgorse) now at Lampeter called & stayed to tea. He is staying a few days at his old lodgings at Cwmgorse. He was also at D.M.'s.

Wednesday 15 July: Samuel Williams (late of Bogelegel) called in his way from Neath, said he would be very glad if I would come over soon & see Cathelas his present farm, that the Crops are looking beautiful, said I would come some day this Summer. He had tea here.

Thursday 16 July: Dl. finished cutting meadow & then the Croften.

Friday 17 July: Finished carrying the meadow hay in excellent condition, not a drop of rain.

Saturday 18 July: Lloyd mowed vetches piece. Finished carrying Croften, hay in good harvest. Evan tarred the little gate at "the Pool" which he made this week. Lewis Morgan Bryn Carnau near Cilybebyll buried today at Alltwen age 76, the late J. Morgan Gellygron's brother.

Monday 20 July: Met Douglas at Duffryn Station last train. Left here in Carriage 3.30, arrived there 5 o'clk, train in 5.45. Left Duffryn 6 & here at 8 o'clk. Called on Mrs. Thomas in returning & stayed 15 minutes. Wet day.

Wednesday 22 July: The Woman of Bethany buried at Gwryd Chapel.

Thursday 23 July: Daniel cut half Cae front hay with Machine. Carried lower part of "The Strip".

Saturday 25 July: Carried top half of Cae front. Dl. cut lower half.

Tuesday 28 July: Hopkin with Machine mowing Cae Barriwns. Lizzie, little Godfrey & Rebe went to Swansea, to spend the day with Mrs. Evans at 10 St. Helen's Crescent 11 train from Llandilo & returned by the 6 train, they enjoyed their day. Phillips Taylor man here with grocery, said they could not deliver goods here, as the journey was too far.

Wednesday 29 July: Mr. Day & Mr. Arundel (the New Manager) Hendreforgan here, said I would grant a lease of 7 years to the Company on the 2 Houses by the Colliery & the Office at a rent of £25 a year.

Saturday 1 August: Carried about half of Cae Barriwns.

Monday 3 August: Lloyd fetched 2 loads small coal, 26 cwt @ 1d, 2/2 paid. Lloyd took Box with 4 doz. empty ½ pint bottles (due to Mr. W. Jones, Canton, Llandilo) to "the Caegurwen Arms" to be left there till called for.

Wednesday 5 August: Carried a few car loads of Cae Barriwns hay, very cloudy afternoon. Lloyd to Gellyluog a.m. for the two poles Evan cut yesterday for Cae Barriwns field opposite little gate.

Saturday 8 August: Evan & Lloyd finished carrying Cae Barriwns hay at 3 p.m. yesterday. Lloyd then took little car back to Coed Cae Mawr & stayed to help them with the hay. All my hay housed in good order. Lloyd today mowing hay at Gartheithen.

Monday 10 August: Lloyd after dinner cutting hay.

Friday 14 August: Jane Tynewydd called on her way to Gartheithen. Made some barm for me. Sold Alice's calf to D.M. 92 lbs @ 7d, 5 weeks old last Tuesday. £2..13..8 paid. Sent the money to Lizzie as the calf came on her birthday (July 7th).

Saturday 15 August: T.J. came here last train to see Douglas.

Sunday 16 August: After dinner T.J., Douglas & I walked down Heol Hugh thinking to go through Cae Cwm to the River, but the corn prevented us & we returned through Wain pedr Erw, & up the steps opposite Heol y Ty. Douglas & his Father on the Hill in the morning. Fine day.

Tuesday 18 August: The National Eisteddfod opened at Victoria Park, Swansea today. Sir J. T. D. Llewelyn Mayor of Swansea President.

Wednesday 19 August: Mr. Day & Mr. White here. The Prince of Battenburg[2] at the Swansea Eisteddfod.

Friday 21 August: Prince Henry of Battenburg guest of Mr. Graham Vivian at Clyne Castle & party lunched at Craig y Nos Castle with Madame Patti.

2. Prince Henry of Battenburg married Queen Victoria's daughter Princess Beatrice, 23 July 1885.

Monday 24 August: Fanny Gilbertson called at 11.30. She leaves Glanrhyd on Saturday for Llanwrtyd to see Mrs. Price who is there, & on Monday goes back to London, & on Wednesday Sept. 2nd meets Madelina at Edinburgh where they remain a week. She said Kate's Husband had left her two yrs. last March & that no one knew where he was. Fanny said they were going to give up their house in London (where they had been 7 years) & going abroad for a year or two.[3]

Tuesday 25 August: The Right Honble. Henry Cecil Raikes Postmaster General died yesterday at his Flintshire residence.

Thursday 27 August: John Thomas Gwernllwyn here, he said he had reckoned all the Gellyluog trees last Tuesday & that they numbered 1,220 in all (280 trees above the road, 940 below). He offered to give me £150 for the whole & to clear them off by Sept. '92. I think I ought to get £200. Revd. D. Jones, Bangor Teify (Jones one arm) found his servant girl dead & hanging to a beam in the cowshed age 33 years. Verdict, death through hanging, she being at the time insane.

Friday 28 August: Paid James Hinkin Garth Poor rate: half year ending Sept. 29th '91.

The Garth	£17..10..0 @ 1/10d	£1..12.. 1
Garth Farm	37..15..0 "	3.. 9.. 2½
3 Cots Cwm.	7..10..0	13.. 9
1 Dd. Williams	3.. 5..0	5..11½
1 Thos. Davies	3.. 0..0	5.. 6
1 Thos. Thomas	3.. 0..0	5.. 6
1 Thos. Lloyd	2.. 0..0	3.. 8
	£74.. 0..0 @ 1/10	£6..15.. 8
Less Commission on Cots		8.. 7
Paid by cheque		£6.. 7.. 1

Madame Patti's Concert in Swansea.

3. Fanny (1844-1937), Kate (1845-1933) and Madelina (1856-1936) were daughters of William and Eliza Gilbertson. Kate had married W. F. Richardson at St. Peter's Church, Pontardawe, on 2 August 1871 (see Diary entry). Fanny remained a spinster and died on 2 November 1937 aged 93 in the Hotel Grande Bretagne, Athens, leaving £14,973 to her spinster sister Emily Maude Gilbertson (1862-1940).

Saturday 29 August: Mrs. Jones Crachllwyn here paying ½ year's rent due last March.

Tuesday 1 September: Took dear little Douglas to Llandilo last train after staying with me 6 weeks yesterday, & a good boy. We called at the Vicarage 4.20 & there found Revd. Nathaniel Thomas & his Wife at tea, they had come to see the place as he has had the offer of it, Mr. Griffiths having accepted Llanarthney. Mrs. Thomas disliked the place very much. N's uncle was there too, & we all travelled first class to Pantyffynon, the uncle went to Aberdare, they came on to Ffairfach, & then to Llandilo bridge for Llanarthney, thence by their carriage to Llanddarog. Mrs. T. was very kind to Douglas, & he was a good boy.

Wednesday 2 September: My birthday spent at Llandilo. Lizzie, Douglas, Godfrey, Rebe and I went for a walk through the Park to Llandyfeisant Church & home by Horeb. I had never seen the Church before. We sheltered in the Porch from a shower of rain.

Sunday 6 September: Lizzie, T.J. & Douglas to Church a.m. Lizzie & I to Church at 6 p.m.

Tuesday 8 September: Returned home last train from Llandilo. Mr. Griffiths Cwmamman travelled with me from Cross Inn, he was rather perplexed not being able to get a house at Llanarthney, & had not heard whether "Nat" wd. accept Cwmamman. Met Mrs. Thomas, Miss Shenton & the new comers to Garnant House all going to Church.

Thursday 10 September:

	£..s..d
Had 14 cwt. stone coal @ 6d	7..0
" 12 " small " " 1d	1..0
yesterday by Lloyd.	8..0 Paid

Monday 14 September: Wrote to Williams, Swansea telling him to send
6 bot Port
4 " Sherry
1 " Whiskey
1 " Gin to Mrs. Jones Llandilo

Tuesday 15 September: Lloyd drove me to Cwmllynfell in Gartheithen Car.

Wednesday 16 September: Lloyd drove me to Crachllwyn. Lloyd carrying dirt off road a.m.

Thursday 17 September: Lloyd putting up the Hay in Hay house to make place for Fern.

Friday 18 September: John Walters, the Underground Manager at Hendreforgan here to ask if he should have the House formerly occupied by Noah Jones at Cwm Works. Told him I had promised it to Thos. Jones (Mr. Pugh's old workman). Lloyd took load of manure to mix with earth by Cottage & finished carrying the dirt off road. Swept up the back.

Wednesday 23 September: My dear Mother's birthday. Told John Thomas all the remainder of Gellyluog Wood excepting the 2 trees in Cae dan ty by the House for £155..0..0 to be paid 1st Dec. '91. The timber, bark, &c. all to be cleared away by Sept. 29th 1892. I cannot help thinking that the timber is worth £200 – but he would not give more than £155 – & if I did not sell them, a great deal would be stolen this Winter, there was such havoc last Winter. John Thomas has promised to give me 10 larch poles 8 foot long for cow posts for Crachllwyn, & one rail 13 ft long for Garth. Also birch for brooms.

Thursday 24 September: Lloyd cutting off Ivy shoots on Hay house, & digging up the Walk under it, to put quarry stuff & ashes. Thos. Coed Cae Mawr put Iron in pig's nose.

Friday 25 September: Went to Swansea 1st train, Mrs. Griffiths & her little girl travelled with me, told me about [Rev.] T.E.D.'s getting drunk & that he must keep back from the Communion or be reported to the Bishop. Went up to Bryn Syfi, found poor Miss Jenkins in bed with a bilious attack. Went to Swansea at 1 o'clk., bought Ironing Blanket 2¼ yards 4 .. 5
Silk gloves 1/11½, 3 Pocket Hanks 9d MPJ 2 .. 8½
Went to Llandilo by 6 train. Douglas & his Father met me. Susan at Glenview.

		s .. d
Gave Lizzie	1 teapot	1 .. 4
	5 yds. Oilcloth 36 in. wide	5 .. 0
	5 " " 27 " "	3 .. 4
	2 vests @ 5/11 3 P. Hanks @ 9d	6 .. 8
	½ dozn. large ½ dozn. small tea things)	
	½ " " " " plates)	10.. 11
	Basin, Jug, Egg Cups, 2 large plates)	1 .. 7 .. 3

Sunday 27 September: Lizzie & Susan to Church a.m. T.J. & I to Church at 6 p.m.

Monday 28 September: Llandilo fair. I took Douglas to School and went for him. Douglas & I called in on old Mrs. James. She is very poorly.

Thursday 1 October: Lizzie, Susan & Mary Jones to some entertainment at the Drill Hall, & Douglas! He enjoyed it poor little dear, & so they all did. Datta [T.J.], Doddy [Godfrey] & I in the house, no maid. I washed the White & Gold tea things I had brought Lizzie, & Datta carried them to the Attic.

Friday 2 October: Susan left Glenview after been there a fortnight last Wednesday. Jane Davies came to Lizzie until Nov. as Rebe had left.

Thursday 8 October: Lizzie went with Mrs. Jones Canton in the Dog cart to Capel to see poor Georgina who is very ill. They had it fine to go but very wet & windy coming home.

Monday 12 October: I returned home from Llandilo after been there 2 wks. last Friday, during my stay had a severe cold or rather an attack of Bronchitis. Datta & Douglas to the Station with me. Lloyd met me 4 o'clk. train Garnant.

Saturday 17 October: W. Price Cwmllynfell & Dd. Williams Llynfell Cottage here asking about the Boundary between Cwm Farm & the Bryn Common &c. by Falda bach.

Monday 19 October: Had 5 bus. oats, 1 cwt B. meal, 50 lbs flour, 4 lbs sugar from Biddy & paid all I owed. Lloyd took Cart Wheel to Morgan Walters to be repaired (2 new Curbs) paid.

Thursday 22 October: Poor R.P.L. died today at Llangynwyd Vicarage aged 78 years.

Friday 23 October: Lloyd to shoe Polly & brought up 10 cwt soft coal, 7s.6d paid.

Saturday 24 October: Shani Ty Newydd & her nephew John Harris here, he wanted to know if I wd. give him permission to bring coal over Falda bach from Level y bryn & at what charge, said I must see the place first. He said he felt inclined to make a road over Ty Newydd which farm he had lately bought of late James & Aubrey.

Sunday 25 October: Elizabeth & the little boy came up to see me. Finished cleaning out the Pantry yesterday.

Tuesday 27 October: Poor R.P.L. buried today at Llangynwyd, he had been Vicar of the Parish 50 years to this month. I feel his death very much, he was always so ready to help me.

Sunday 1 November: Harriet & her Sister Mary came here 3.30 & left at 6. Harriet was as pleasant as ever.

Monday 2 November: Tied the cows. Rose my bedroom carpet & Betty washed the room out.

Tuesday 3 November: Recd. letter from Lizzie saying that poor Georgina was dead & to be buried on Thursday at Llanarthney.

Wednesday 4 November: Cleaned out spare room. Lloyd carrying manure to Cae front. Lloyd had the mare to go for a load of coal for himself, he left here 5.30 p.m. returned 8.20 (not 3 hours) & took his tea.

Friday 6 November: Mr. & Mrs. Morlais Jones called, took a cup of tea. They were begging for the Bryn Amman Church Endowment so as to enable him to get about £175 salary. Gave them £1..0..0 with which they were very pleased, they intended going on to Alltycham to ask Mr. Hedley. Lloyd fetched 10 cwt stone coal from Llwynrhidie (no lumps here) 5/- paid.

Saturday 7 November: Went to Llandilo 11 train from Garnant. Took Duck & basin Blancmange, tin ginger nuts for Ducca & 1 doz. night lights for Doddy, also a piece of Cloth to make clothes for Douglas bought in London many years ago.

Monday 9 November: Lizzie & Douglas to Swansea 11 train, they returned 7 train having had a wet & dirty day. Doddy a good boy with me. Mrs. Jones Pentre Par called at Glenview & engaged Jane Davies to go to her as Nurse at £11 a year. I think she is glad to get the girl as she has been with Lizzie.

Tuesday 10 November: Came home 2 train from Llandilo. Lloyd met me at Garnant 3.45 and drove me to the Vicarage to wish them Good bye before they leave for Llanarthney. Mrs. Griffiths made me stay to tea, for the last time at Cwmamman with them. Mr. Griffiths was out, I met him near the "Raven" when coming home.

Wednesday 11 November: Lloyd & I cleaned out Kitchen cupboard, washed all the Glass & Ware, the top shelf was done some weeks ago. A wet stormy day.

Monday 16 November: Betty & I cleaned out Drawing room. Lloyd sweeping the Green.

Tuesday 17 November: Lalla Kirkhouse married at Cilybebyll Church to Mr. Charles Belcher of Lincolnshire.[4] Gwen Cefnllan here.

Friday 20 November: Griffith Lewis Cwmtwrch here saying the Hendreforgan Co. were tipping into the River & injuring my property. Lloyd to meet Rachel Jones my new servant 12.30 train at Brynamman in Garthcithen Car, recd. a tel. from Llandilo saying she wd. come by the 3.30 train, some delay about her boxes, so Lloyd waited & put the Horse at the "Farmer's Arms", they came here 5.10 p.m.

Wednesday 25 November: Lloyd drove me to Cwmllynfell in Gartheithen Car to meet Mr. Hay & Griffith Lewis about the Boundary between Cwm. & Hendreforgan by Wm. Rowland's house. The Co. tip into the River which injures my property. Gave the map to Mr. Hay & desired him to see Mr. White & to finally mark out the Boundary, as I intend selling Wm. Rowland's house &c. Had tea at Cwm & dried my clothes for I had heavy rain going up, fine to return.

Wednesday 2 December: Went to Llandilo 11 train from Garnant. Douglas, Godfrey & Winifred met me at Station. Took Lizzie pot of butter about 36 lbs & the boys a bottle of sweets. Old Mrs. Dr. Protheroe got into the train at Llandebie.

---

4. Charles Belcher (25) farmer of Fulbeck to Harriet Hughes Kirkhouse (25) of Alltwen.

Friday 4 December: Returned from Llandilo 2 train. I could not stay longer as I did not know how Rachel wd. get on here. I have a great loss after Betty in leaving home as she was careful of everything.

Saturday 5 December: Rachel turned to me in the Court & stamped her foot on the ground saying "I will not fetch water after night & I must finish my work by dinner time on Saturday". I told her I was astonished at her behaviour that I was not going to put up with it, that no man or woman had ever stamped their foot at me before.

Sunday 6 December: Mrs. Harris paid me the £5 lent her. I told her of Rachel's behaviour. She was astonished.

Wednesday 9 December: Wm. Price & Thos. Davies here paying their rent up to Sept. last. Allowed Thos. Davies for new door 10/-.

Friday 11 December: Sarah, Rachel's married sister, from Gorseinon came up to see her. Took her round the back & front & told her how Rachel complained of the work & also of how she had behaved to me. Sarah left to meet 7 train at Pontardawe & R. went with her to Station. Fine day. Rachel showed me a letter (English) from her Mother saying she hoped she was "doing her best to oblige & was obedient". Lizzie began using pot of butter.

Sunday 13 December: A terrible storm of Wind & Rain the water pouring in through all the front Windows, blew Ivy off garden wall & the pine end of D.M.'s house, uprooted 3 trees in Cae Barriwns wood & 4 under hay house.

Monday 14 December: David Jones Nantmelyn (Carpenter) came here to see what work I wanted done, & promised to come here tomorrow.

Tuesday 15 December: David Jones and D.M. propping up the Barn side of shed & making it safe. Lloyd to shoe Polly, ordered John Hopkin to make new hinges for my cowhouse door, to open out.

Wednesday 16 December: Lloyd to Pontardawe for 4 flooring boards, to make weather boards for pine end of D.M.'s house. Had hinges ordered yesterday. Owen the Crachllwyn here saying the roof of House & Barn had been a good deal injured by the storm on Sunday. Lloyd went up to Bryn Amman to see if John James the Tiler could go to Crachllwyn tomorrow. He could not, nor could he go for a fortnight if then.

Thursday 17 December: David Jones finished putting up D.M.'s weather boards, & my cowhouse door, the frame was ready having been made by John Davies (Dynevor) in Nov. '85. Paid D.J. 3 days @ 3/6 on his own food, 10/6 paid. Told him to go to Crachllwyn tomorrow to do the repairs required after the storm on Sunday.

Saturday 19 December: Sent Lloyd to Crachllwyn to see what damage the storm had done. He said the front troughs were all broken, about 60 slates & a good deal of repairing work.

Sunday 20 December: Rachel to Saron 10 a.m. & 6 p.m. Lloyd to Cwmgorse Church 6 p.m. I in the house with a lovely fire in dining room.

Thursday 24 December: I went to Llandilo 2 train from Garnant to spend my Xmas with Lizzie. Weather too cold for her to bring the children here, & there is so much illness about. Datta met me at the Station.

1892

There was a marked reduction in the number of Margaret's diary entries after 22 March, averaging six per month from April to November (inc.) and none in December. Her poor health continued to cause her concern, but her awareness of financial affairs remained keen. She pursued a debt owed to her by the estate of the lately deceased Vicar of Llangiwg and recorded all sales of butter, bacon, livestock, land and her Poor Rate payments. The death of her old friend and cousin Mary Price of Glan Twrch in July and the departure of her long serving and compliant servant Thomas Lloyd at the end of August presaged Margaret's departure to Swansea for six weeks in the forlorn hope that a change of location would improve her health. The birth of Lizzie's third son on 28 November provided a motive for Margaret's departure from Garth to Llandeilo for the whole of December and most of the first half of 1893.

Saturday 2 January: Returned home from Llandilo 11 train. Douglas carried the new Carriage Whip & walked with me to the Station, Lizzie went to Lockyer's [*Joseph Lockyer, Bookseller & Stationer, Rhosmaen St.*] & then came by Bus with my luggage. Douglas & Lizzie returned to Glenview after seeing me off.

Sunday 3 January: Lloyd to Cwmgorse Church 6 p.m. Rachel to Saron 6 p.m. I in the house alone & no one at D.M.'s but I did not know that till Rachel told me on her return.

Monday 4 January: Daniel killed my pig down in their yard.

Tuesday 5 January: Pig weighed 225 lbs.

Thursday 7 January: Sent Lizzie Spare rib, Chine & 2 Pies. Rachel & Lloyd salted the pig.

Wednesday 13 January: Revd. David Jones, for 32 years Vicar of Llanguicke died rather suddenly this morning altho' he had been in failing health for a long time, age 68 years next month.

Tuesday 19 January: Revd. David Jones Vicar of Llanguicke buried in St. Peter's Churchyard at Pontardawe. Public funeral. Lloyd to the funeral.

Wednesday 20 January: Rachel Jones left this morning to meet first train at Garnant. Lloyd had taken her box last night. She had been a maid at Carreg Cennen but was a worthless & impudent girl.

Friday 22 January: Rachel D.M. & Anne came in after dinner to clean up a bit. Rachel swept upstairs & the Hall, Anne washed out the Kitchen & cleaned the Grate, Rachel had left the Kitchen in a very greasy, dirty state after melting the lard on Tuesday afternoon. Gave Rachel & Anne 1/- each.

Saturday 23 January: T.J. walked here last train from Garnant.

Monday 25 January: T.J. walked to Garnant to meet 11 train, going to call at Rebe's to ask if she would come here for a bit as I had no servant.

Tuesday 26 January: Recd. a letter from Rebe's Mother saying Rebe should come here for about a fortnight as I was without a maid. Lloyd went up in D.M.'s car for her & they came here 5.15 p.m. Lloyd's wife came after break-fast to blue the few things she washed yesterday. Rebe ironed them after tea. Julia brought a He calf.

Wednesday 27 January: After dinner Rebe & Lloyd rose the pig out of the salt.

Thursday 28 January: After dinner Rebe washed out the Dairy, & after tea Lloyd & Rebe cleaned the tins. Sent Lloyd to Yniswen to ask if the girl that had been at Bogelegel should come here as a maid, or until I could hear of a servant, the Mother said she was <u>not at home now</u>, but I think that was only an excuse.

Friday 29 January: Rebe cleaned out the Kitchen. She washed the floor with <u>hot</u> water, soda & black soap & scrubbed it well to get out the grease.

Sunday 31 January: Lloyd to Cwmgorse Church 6 p.m. Rebe to Carmel with the D.M.'s 6 p.m. Mary [Morgan] came in to sit with me.

Monday 1 February: Rebe cleaned out Dining room, fire in Drawing room.

Tuesday 2 February: Lloyd drove me in the Carriage to call at the Vicarage on Laura Jones, after her brother's death. Mr. James Jones & Mr. Jones Llangunnor there, all was in preparation for the <u>Sale</u> on Thursday. Rebe washing, she had got the <u>Kitchen</u> <u>so nicely</u> cleaned out when I returned & the clothes in the flask ready for drying tomorrow if fine. I left 2.10 p.m. back 4.50.

Thursday 4 February: Sale at Llanguicke Vicarage.

Friday 5 February: Rebe cleaned out Spare bedroom, fire had been there 2 days, every thing so damp. Put new muslin blinds to the 3 front Windows upstairs.

Saturday 6 February: Rebe cleaned Hall & <u>washed</u> the oil cloth. She did it <u>very nicely</u> & the Kitchen nicely cleaned by 5.30. She is a <u>quick</u>, <u>willing</u> girl & gets over her work <u>with pleasure</u>.

Monday 8 February: Lloyd churned a.m. & Rebe made the <u>butter</u>, 2 lbs under my direction. Lloyd p.m. putting <u>ashes</u> on closet walk, after digging it up on Saturday. Rebe washed a.m. & ironed after tea fearing she wd. be obliged to go tomorrow.

Tuesday 9 February: Price Cwmllynfell & his Wife came here for the <u>Grey</u> cow's <u>she</u> calf, 3 weeks old next Thursday <u>value £1..10..0</u> but I gave it them for 15/- as Price is kind & helps me about the Cottages & tenants. They seemed <u>very pleased</u> & <u>said so</u>. I went to Llandilo last train & took Rebe home after been here a fortnight, gave her 10/- for the 2 weeks & 5/- a present for her readiness to come when I had no servant. Lloyd sleeps here tonight.

Thursday 11 February: Poor Miss Powell 12 Picton Place Swansea died aged 74.

Saturday 13 February: John the Blacksmith here putting little Clock right after Rachel let it fall.

Monday 15 February: A very bad head & face ache. Gwen Cefnllan here about the £100 owed her by our late Vicar.[1]

Monday 22 February: Lloyd churned, Rachel Morgan came in to make the butter. 4 lbs 14 ozs. Lloyd went in D.M.'s car to meet Winefred to Garnant 3.30 train who comes here as maid from Lizzie.

Tuesday 23 February: Lloyd for a little clay. Had 11 cwt stone coal, 5/6. Lloyd took 4½ lbs fresh butter to Dd. Lewis, the first sold this year 1s.4d.

Wednesday 24 February: Lloyd began repairing the turf alongside the Walk from Holly to front gate.

Thursday 25 February: Directly I came down this morning 8.45, a sudden stupor & giddiness came on, & when the post came I failed to make any sense of Lizzie's letter (which was faultless in all ways) until 11 o'clk. & then it was not quite clear to me, I did not get to feel as usual until 1 o'clk. I never had such a feeling before & I dread a return of it.

Saturday 27 February: Recd. a nice letter from dear Ducca ba, he writes very well for so young a child. Sent Douglas a Reg. letter with half a sovereign to buy a pair of boots & a pair of stockings as a birthday present tomorrow.

Sunday 28 February: Douglas 5 years old today. Lloyd & Winefred to Cwm-gorse Church.

---

1. Margaret does not record the death on this day of the late Vicar's friend and curate the Rev. T. E. Davies, age 42. The reredos in St. Peter's Church Pontardawe was erected in their memory. Williams, 1996, 20.

Monday 29 February: Winefred cleaned the Windows. Mary Cefnllan here saying they had had no reply from the late Vicar's brother about the money. She had heard that the Sister at Llanelly (Mary Jones) was dead. Mr. Davies Cwmgorse Curate here. Lloyd carrying the small heap by the Cottage to Cae front.

Wednesday 2 March: Wrote to Mr. Strick asking for the Int[erest] due from the late Vicar & Mrs. Jones to Dec. 31st '91, also saying I held a bond signed by both Mr. & Mrs. Jones, & that I concluded Mrs. Jones was now the person I was to apply to for payment.

Thursday 3 March: Dd. James "Royal Oak" here to see bacon, bought middle of flitch, 16 lbs @ 7½d, 10/- paid. Bought a pig of D.M. about 4 months old I think, £1..10..0 paid. It is <u>dear</u> as pigs are cheap. D.M. says it weighs 60 lbs now but I don't think it does.

Sunday 6 March: Thos. Coedcaemawr came here about 3 p.m. Said Dd. Thomas the Mason said he would come as soon as frost was over.

Monday 7 March: Mrs. Thomas the New Star buried today at Carmel aged 70 years. Lloyd to the funeral.

Tuesday 8 March: County Council election. I did <u>not</u> go & vote. D.M. set fire to Coedcae. Lloyd set fire to our Meadow.

Friday 11 March: Julia's calf to D.M. 6 weeks old last Tuesday, weighed 97 lbs @ 7½d per lb, £3..0..7½. Mr. John Morgan of Bolgoed died aged 57 years. Griffith Lewis Cwmllynfell here. Mr. Davies Cwmgorse Curate here. Hannah Dl. Sair here, paid her 1 day owing since last summer. Sally ½ day, paid 1/6.

Saturday 12 March: Recd. letter from Laura Jones, saying her sister Mary died 17th Feb. at Llanelly. Laura is now at Llangunnor near Carmarthen. Said she thought there wd. be sufficient funds to meet the late Vicar's liabilities. The solicitor is Mr. C. Morris Carmarthen.

Sunday 13 March: Lloyd to Llanguicke, Betty to Church. Lloyd did not speak to her, it was <u>Communion</u> & he did not wait. Williams.

Monday 14 March: Gwen Cefnllan here, said Betty had been fetching her bed from Mary Tom y Crydd when she met her 12 Feb. Lloyd to Gellyluog for a load of Birch for Brooms.

Wednesday 16 March: Pontardawe Fair. Winefred went with the D.M.'s 5 p.m. returned 11 p.m. Lloyd went 5.30 p.m. returned 11 p.m. I was here all alone from 5.30 until 8 when D.M. & Mary came back. Mary saw Betty in the fair. She sent me 2 nice apples.

Thursday 17 March: Paid James Hinkin Garth Poor Rate as follows, half year ending 25 March '92.

The Garth	£17..10..0	@ 1/10d.	1 ..12 .. 1
Garth Farm	37..15..0	"	3 .. 9 .. 2½
3 Cots. Cwm.	7..10..0	"	13 .. 9
1 " Dd. Williams	3.. 5..0	"	5..11½
1 " Thos. Davies	3.. 0..0	"	5.. 6
1 " Thos. Jones	3.. 0..0	"	5.. 6
1 " Thos. Lloyd	2.. 0..0		5.. 8
	£74.. 0..0	@ 1/10d.	£6..15 .. 8
	Less Commission on Cots.		8 .. 7
	(Cheque given for £8..17..7)		£6.. 7 .. 1 paid

	s .. d	
In. & Land Tax on Cwm. Cots	9 ..10	
Special rate on £16..15..0 (Cots.) @ 6d less commission	7 .. 0½	
Garth special rate @ 6d on 1.4th of £55..5..0	6..11½	paid

Cwm. In. tax £1..2..6 Land tax 4/2d.

Saturday 19 March: Wm. Rowland Cwmllynfell came down to pay his rent due on the 25th inst. He had not been here for many years.

Monday 21 March: Dear little Liz. came here un-expectedly about 1 o'clk. She had walked all the way from Duffryn Colliery calling at Carreg amman. Took her back to Duffryn in the Carriage to meet last Llandilo train 6.30. Gave her the money for Julia's calf wh. came 26th Jan. £3..0..7½. Gave her old

Gammon 26 lbs, bottle of cream & pair of stockings for Datta. I hope Ducca & Doddy will be all right when she returns.

Friday 25 March: Sent Lizzie 6 lbs. butter in Yellow Basin from Garnant (Rachel D.M. made it).

Saturday 26 March: Lloyd fetched a load of clay.

Sunday 27 March: Winefred a bad face ache did not go to Chapel.

Thursday 31 March: Lloyd to Neath for 2 bus. Aberthaw lime & 5 cwt soft coal from Pwll Bach.

Thursday 7 April: Sent Lloyd with my subscription of £1..1..0 towards the memorial Window to be created in memory of the late Vicar (Revd. David Jones).

Palm Sunday 10 April: Winny to Church, back 9.55 p.m. D.M.'s sow brought little pigs.

Saturday 16 April: Had Tels from Lizzie at 12 o'clk. saying they were all 4 coming over in a Fly & wd. be here between 4 & 5 o'clk. to tea. When they arrived, they found I had <u>fainted</u> in little Kitchen & did not come to myself for <u>some time</u>.

Monday 25 April: Recd. a letter from Phebe Williams, Step Inn Llanginning St. Clears saying she wd. prefer a place without cows if she could get it. She was recommended to me by Laura Jones. I think she had been a maid with Mrs. Jones Llangunnor.

Wednesday 27 April: I signed the Conveyance prepared by Messrs. Strick & Bellingham of a piece of land 3 Roods 12 Perches to Griffith Lewis, Gwyr Cottage, part of Cwmllynfell Farm near the "George Inn" for Thirty Pounds. Witnessed by Lizzie.

Friday 29 April: Lizzie to Swansea 9.40 train, walked to Station. I took Douglas & Doddy in the Carriage to meet her 4 o'clk. train. We then called at Mrs. Kirkhouse's only. Polly & Lucy at home, Mrs. K. staying with Lalla (Mrs. Belcher) in Lincolnshire.

Sunday 1 May: Lizzie & Douglas walked to Llanguicke, the first time for Douglas to walk. Godfrey at home with me. Winefred's foot very painful, but she walked to Cwmgorse, wh. made it worse.

Thursday 5 May: Mr. Davies Cwmgorse Curate called 3.15. Mr. James the new Curate at St. Peter's & Mr. Teague called at 4. They all stayed to tea & left at 6.15.

Saturday 7 May: Gomer Evans buried today at St. Peter's aged 30.

Sunday 8 May: Douglas & I in the House. W. to Saron 6 p.m., back 9.20.

Whitsunday 15 May: Dr. Wm. Thomas from America (Dd. Thomas the Star's son) preached at Cwmgorse Church, he was a Dissenting Preacher but is now of the Episcopal Church of America. Winefred to Cwmgorse 6 p.m. back 9.20.

Wednesday 18 May: Winefred Ashton 20 years old today.

Tuesday 24 May: Rachel D.M. made butter, gave her half a sovereign to buy a silk umbrella, a present from me for making my butter & what she had done for me when without a maid. She seemed very pleased.

Wednesday 25 May: Rachel D.M. 25 years old today.

Sunday 29 May: Winefred to Cwmgorse 6 p.m., told her to come back straight from Church as I was poorly. D.M. & Mary came in to see me. Douglas a little toothache. Anne D.M. to Cwmllynfell.

Monday 30 May: Cows to Cae Cwtta first time this year.

Tuesday 31 May: Rees Jones Carpenter Alltwen came here, said he had finished at Gellyluog, told him I must see what he had done before paying him, & that I wd. pay him before 1st of July. Lloyd mowing the Green with the machine.

Whit Monday 6 June: Winefred, Lloyd & all the D.M. children to Swansea to the Royal Agricultural Show. Lloyd's wife with me & Douglas. Mr. Griffiths the new Vicar called on horseback at 12 o'clk. Rees Morgan took his horse. Rees & his mother were the only ones in the house. The first time I saw the Vicar.

Monday 13 June: Mrs. Price Glantwrch 81 years old this day.

Friday 8 July: Rebe came here for a fortnight or 3 weeks.

Sunday 10 July: Rebe & Winefred to Carmel 6 p.m.

Thursday 14 July: Winefred Ashton left. Here 5 months last Monday. Lloyd drove Lizzie, Doddy & Winefred in the Carriage to the Station to meet 11 train at Garnant. Douglas also went to Garnant but returned with Lloyd sitting on the box. Lizzie was obliged to go as Winefred's clothes were at Glenview.

Friday 15 July: Poor Mrs. Price Glantwrch died this day age 81 years. I think it was 47 years today she was married at Llansamlet Church. She had been a Widow 15 years. Lizzie & Doddy came back bringing Anne George with them. Lloyd met them at Bryn Amman with the Carriage.

Sunday 17 July: Rebe and Anne George to Saron 6 p.m.

Monday 18 July: Saw Mrs. Price's death in the Western Mail when at breakfast & that was the first we knew of it. Sent Lloyd with a letter to Jane Benthall.

Tuesday 19 July: Poor Mrs. Price buried today in Ystrad Churchyard. She was a very kind, hospitable woman & will be missed by rich & poor. My Mother & herself were great friends.

Monday 1 August: Perry, a man from near Llandeilo came to see this place, as Lloyd is leaving.[2]

Wednesday 3 August: Recd. a tel. from T.J. saying Perry had decided to go to Port Talbot, that his wife had been there yesterday.

Wednesday 31 August: Elizabeth [Lloyd] came up to pay the rent & to ask if they should remain another week in the Cottage as their house was not vacant of Mr. Turberville. I said No, that I had the offer of a tenant for the Cottage & that I should be glad for them to leave tomorrow.

2. Margaret's will made provision for bequests of £5 each to Thomas Lloyd and Evan Evans "if in my service at the time of my decease".

Thursday 1 September: Lloyd removed his furniture from the Cottage to Pontardawe.

Friday 2 September: John Davies working at Waingurwen Colliery took Lloyd's house at 6/- per month of 4 weeks. Elizabeth Lloyd brought me the key of the Cottage & I sent it by Daniel Morgan to John Davies, I went down with Dl to see the Cottage, it was all left clean & tidy. Elizabeth drawing the Potatoes in the Garden.

Tuesday 6 September: Mrs. Jones of Crachllwyn here paid me £28..10..0 as follows:

Balance of rent £5.. 0.. 0 due Sep. 91
On a/c of rent £23..10..0 " March 92
Balance of £1..10..0 of rent due March 25th 92 and £2..0..3 Tithe due then which she promised to bring me soon.

Rees Morgan took Polly to be shod. Hopkin swept leaden gutter.

Wednesday 7 September: Went to 10 St. Helen's Crescent, Swansea. Douglas & his Father came up in a Fly for me. Douglas stayed with me a fortnight & Datta went to Llandilo by 7 p.m. train from Swansea Bay Station. I hope change will do me good for I am very poorly & my head so giddy and such stupor. Evan [Evans] & Betty take care of house.

Monday 12 September: Douglas & I called at the Matthews, they seemed glad to see us & made us stay to tea. Poor little Douglas was taken very sick in going to the Dining room & had to lie down on the sofa. The servant (Annie) carried him home & Richard came with us, he called again at 10 o'clk. He was asleep & better. Douglas had been riding on the Rocking horse with Trevor & I think that had made him sick.

Friday 16 September: Douglas & I went by tram to Mount Street & then walked to Bryn Syfi. Miss Jenkins was very glad to see us & wanted us to stay the night, but we left at 5.45. Sent grapes to Lizzie by Mr. Williams from Victoria Station.

Tuesday 4 October: Paid James Hinkin Garth Poor Rate half year ending 29th Sept. 92 as follows:

			£ .. s .. d
The Garth	£17..10..0 @ 1/10d.		1.. 12.. 1
Garth Farm	37..15..0	"	3.. 9.. 2½
3 Cots Cwm.	7..10..0	"	13.. 9
1 " D. Williams	3.. 5..0	"	5..11½
1 " Thos. Davies	3.. 0..0	"	5.. 6
1 " Thos. Jones	3.. 0..0	"	5.. 6
1 " John Davies	2.. 0..0	"	3.. 8
			£6.. 15.. 8
Less Commission on Cots.			8.. 7
	By cheque		£6 .. 7.. 1

Friday 7 October: Fanny Salmon returned from Cardiff & Exmouth where she had been staying some weeks.

Tuesday 11 October: Paid D. C. Jones for Glenview Dining room Linoleum 9 yds. square @ 3/6, had last week, which I gave Lizzie. £1..11..6 paid.

Friday 14 October: Fanny Salmon & I went to Bryn Syfi, stayed to tea. Mrs. G. Nancarrow was there when we arrived saying the Grenfells Copper Works were to be stopped & the men (600) to be paid off to-morrow. Poor Miss Jenkins seemed very sorry, her Father & Grandfather had managed the Works under the Grenfells & then they paid well but of late trade has been bad.

Monday 17 October: Fanny Salmon & I took tea and supper at the Matthews.

Wednesday 19 October: Returned home in a Fly from 10 St. Helen's Crescent, Swansea after been away 6 weeks. Fanny Salmon came with us as far as Morriston & returned by Train Car. I do not feel better than when I went away this day six weeks.

Monday 24 October: Rebe came here for her petticoat & body [bodice], said she was going [as] a maid to Lizzie tomorrow week which I am very glad of.

Monday 7 November: Had from Biddy by Thos. Howells

1 bag of Barley meal	12 .. 3
1 " " Bran	5 .. 6
½ sack of flour	16 .. 3

6 lbs Crystal Sugar	1 .. 1½
1 gal. Petroleum	10
	£1..15..11½

Sent to the Station by Thos. Howells
11 lbs. of Butter in little white pan for Mrs. Matthews.

Tuesday 8 November: Rebe went a maid to Lizzie today at £13 a year or 5/- a week instead of Anne George who leaves.

Thursday 10 November: Price Cwmllynfell here paying half a year's rent due Sep. 92. Benjamin Daniel Llwynprevid here, lent him £20 on Note of hand. Recd. letter from Mrs. Matthews thanking me for the butter, & returning the Hamper & pan with many lbs. of Grapes wh. the Capt. of either the Abertawe or Abermaid had brought from Spain. They were much inferior to English grapes but still very nice. Rees went down today for Hamper & brought up a brace of Pheasants from the Station sent me by Mr. Gough.

Friday 11 November: Evan to the Bank for me.

Saturday 12 November: Llandilo fair. Sent Lizzie some of the Grapes I had from Mrs. Matthews by Ben Daniel.

Wednesday 16 November: Neath Fair. Dd. Williams Cwm. here paying his rent, also his father's & son-in-law's. Recd. a letter from Mr. Samuel Morgan Timber Merchant Ystradgynlais, saying his friend sees my price for Crach-llwyn Farm too dear.

Monday 28 November: Recd. a letter from dear Lizzie saying "I feel very ill" by post, at 10 o'clk. had a tel. from Llandilo saying "Little boy this morning tolerably well". I feel so thankful she is confined & hope all will go on well. She expected Baby to be born middle of Octr. (Colin)

Tuesday 29 November: Recd. letter from T.J. saying dear Lizzie was as well as could be expected. Dl. killed our pig. Thos. Davies here paying his own & Thos. Jones' rent, 1 year each to Sept. 92.

Wednesday 30 November: Recd. a letter from Bridget Lewis, Step Hall Pendine, Carmarthen asking if I wanted a Servant that she wd. be happy to come, that she had lived in service with Revd. Albert Jordan, brother to Mr. Jordan the Chemist Pontardawe. Said I did not at present. Betty is now here & will take charge of every thing while I am in Llandilo.

Grey Cow to Bull, Feb. 25th 1892
Julia " " " May 30th "
Alice " " " Aug. 20th "

1893

Margaret remained in Llandeilo until June and during these months made only sixteen diary entries, two of which implied her semi-invalid condition (13 and 20 May). On her return to Garth she had the company of little Godfrey (Doddy) from the end of June and young Douglas (Ducca) from early August, both staying until late November and providing the family affection she craved. Margaret's account of 'Money Received 1893', mainly from rents and interest, contained no reference to a negotiated charge for the planned piping of water through her Cwmllynfell land to Cwmtwrch (24 June and 4 July).

Saturday 11 February: T.J. went to see how they were getting on at Garth.

Wednesday 1 March: Betty sent a pan of salt butter about 20 lbs to Llandilo, very nice butter, we all enjoy it.

Sunday 12 March: Julia brought a He calf.

Thursday 16 March: Pontardawe fair. Mrs. Price Cwmllynfell bought a Pig for me in the fair & brought it up here on her way home, price £1..19..4 paid. I was in Llandilo, Betty here [in Garth].

Saturday 6 May: Price Cwmllynfell called to see me at Llandilo. Paid me £4..0..0 for stones of the old Smithy by the Colliery.

Monday 8 May: M. A. Lloyd, Sister to the woman at Pentre Parr Lodge came as maid to Lizzie.

Saturday 13 May: Price Cwmllynfell & Wm. Williams Plas-y-bryn called at 2 Glenview Villas, also John Davies Garth Cottage who paid his rent up to April 13th 93. All saw me in bed.

Monday 15 May: Llandilo fair. Anne Jones from Cwmllynfell came to see me in coming to the fair. J.J. Llwyn-yr-onen came to pay Lizzie her £5..0..0 annuity & to ask if £5..0..0 had come into this house from Cross Inn wh. meant a P.O.O. for me on a/c of Int. due. He began making such a noise & cursing & swearing that I went into the room & desired him to leave the House or that I wd. send for a Policeman to put him out. He was very reluctant to, but at last when at the door some man who knew him begged him to go, & so he did. I told him never to come to this house while Tom Jones & Lizzie lived here nor to my house. His noisy behaviour had made Lizzie all of a flutter & I desired her not to give a receipt & he kept the money. I told him I wanted my money paid in 3 months.

Saturday 20 May: Shani Tynewydd called to see me at Llandilo. She saw me in bed.

Thursday 1 June: Leet Court at Caegurwen Arms.

Monday 5 June: The Llandilo Church & Baptist Chapel Schools went to the Mumbles. Douglas was to have gone but the morning was damp & looked so like rain, that we thought it safer for him not to go, altho' Miss Price the Vicarage had promised to take care of him. He bore his disappointment so well, & was so pleasant, that as the afternoon was fine we all went for a drive.

Monday 26 June: Recd. a letter from Dr. Rees which had been sent to Llandilo saying that he (as an Ex officio Guardian), one of the Guardians & the Surveyor were deputed to see me respecting the proposed Water supply from Ystradown Well for Cwmtwrch as they think of laying the Pipes through Cwmllynfell land, & wished to know what day next week I could see them. Recd. letter from Lizzie saying they got home very comfortably Friday night at 9.10 p.m. Colin slept all the way.

Tuesday 27 June: Recd. a letter from Lizzie saying Mrs. Williams' baby was Christened yesterday (Annie Mary) & that they had all been in having a glass of Wine.

Wednesday 28 June: Mrs. Harris Gartheithen came to see me, said she was glad to see me come back.

Thursday 29 June: Got poorly & fainted when trying to write to Lizzie, got better about 1 o'clk.

Friday 30 June: Lizzie went to Swansea to see Dr. Griffiths about Colin's face, took Hannah, Colin & Douglas from Llandilo. Doddy at Garth with me. Very hot.

Monday 3 July: John Davies the Cottage shot poor old Dash this evening & Thomas Daniel Sair & Evan buried her on the Hill under the Wire fence not far from Heol y Cefn Entrance Gate. Poor thing. Lizzie brought her here from X Inn in a Hamper many years ago.

Tuesday 4 July: The Deputation (Dr. Rees, Mr. Beynon & Mr. Morgan) came here at 4 p.m. about the Water from Ystradowen Well to Cwmtwrch through Cwmllynfell land. I told them they must put one water tap near Cwmllynfell Farm house & another by the Colliery Houses & pay me £5..0..0 a year. They were agreeable to the Taps, & to paying £3..0..0 a year. I said that if Wm. Griffiths had £10 a year for the Water that I thought they shd. give me ½ for land to convey it. So I suppose they will now find some other way to convey it down.[1]

Wednesday 5 July: Evan had bought during my absence

Hames 3/6d 2 Rakes 1 Pike 4/-	7 .. 6
Halter 6d 2 bus. Aber. lime 2/4	2 ..10
Evan's train to Llandilo 3 times	4 .. 2
	14 .. 6 paid

Thursday 6 July: The Duke of York married to-day to Princess May of Teck. A General Holiday.

1. A letter addressed to Lizzie from Swansea solicitors Strick, Bellingham & Hanson dated 2 November 1900 referred to a letter written by Margaret on 20 April 1894 which "stated her terms" and which appeared to have been £5..5..0 p.a. Pontardawe District Council was prepared to offer that amount "from 29 Sept. 1896 when . . . the Water Works were completed or at an earlier date". The solicitors advised that "the Council ought to pay from the time they entered the land".

Friday 7 July: Dear Lizzie's birthday. Doddy here with me.

Sunday 9 July: T.J. & Douglas came here 12.30 in a Dogcart. Lizzie & the Baby intended coming too, but the morning was showery & prevented them. They left here for Llandilo at 6.55 p.m. Doddy was delighted to see them. Betty took him out a little before they left & when he came back he merely said "Are they gone in the Carriage?" & was quite happy & merry.

Wednesday 12 July: The Revd. James Griffiths (the new Vicar) & his Wife called here, said they were glad to see me home again. The 1st time Mrs. G. was in the House.

Thursday 13 July: Rosa Paddison (Mrs. Rees) & a Mrs. Jordan called here at 12 o'clk. on their way to Cwmamman to see Mrs. Jenkins the Ironmonger who is a sister of Mrs. Jordan & who are Cousins or some relations of Rosa's husband. She has 3 children & is going back to Australia in Sep., her husband who is a Chemist was obliged to return sooner owing to some Bank failure. Rosa is a pretty looking woman & nice quiet manners age 30.

Monday 24 July: David Morgan paid ½ a year's rent for this farm due last March. He asked for abatement. I told him the rent had been lowered a good deal. In 1867 the Day's took it £72..0..0 & now it is only £56..0..0 a yr. all taxes in both cases paid by me & I also give D.M.'s children a present of £1..0..0 a yr. between them.

Friday 4 August: Mr. Benthall, Jane, Dorothy & Mary came here to tea, the first time I had seen them since Mrs. Price's death.

Saturday 5 August: T.J. brought Douglas here to spend his holidays with Doddy who has been here 6 weeks yesterday.

Sunday 6 August: T.J. returned to Llandilo after tea leaving the 2 boys here.

Wednesday 9 August: Poor little Doddy very sick.

Thursday 10 August: Douglas' nose bled.

Saturday 19 August: T.J., Lizzie & little Colin came here in a 4 wheel dog cart.

Sunday 20 August: T.J. left here for Llandilo 6.45 p.m. Poor Mr. W. D. Llewellyn Penllergare staying at Dynevor Castle & [died] in Llandilo Church 11 a.m. this morning.

Sunday 27 August: The Dead March played in Llandilo Church. Poor Mr. Llewellyn was one of the Congregation this day week & a Corpse today. How sad!

Monday 28 August: Douglas took letters to Rhydyfro Post Office for the first time, he is 6½ years old this day. He walked back & fore in 50 minutes.

Tuesday 29 August: David Thomas (Betty's husband) buried at Zoar.

Friday 1 September: Paid James Hinkin Garth Poor Rate as follows, half year ending 29th Sep. 93.

		£.. s.. d
The Garth	£17..10..0 @ 3/-	2..12.. 6
Garth Farm	37..15..0 "	5..13.. 3
3 Cots. Cwm.	7..10..0 "	1.. 2.. 6
1 Dd. Williams	3.. 5..0 "	9.. 9
1 Thos. Davies	3.. 0..0 "	9.. 0
1 Thos. Jones	3.. 0..0 "	9.. 0
1 John Davies	2.. 0..0 "	6.. 0
		£11.. 2.. 0
Less Commission on Cots.		14.. 1
By Cheque		£10.. 7..11 Paid

Had 6 bottles Sherry, 6 of Port
1 gal. Gin, 1 gal. Whiskey
1 gal Brandy. F.E.W.'s man brought them up from Swansea.
Returned bottle of Champagne Brandy & 19 empty bottles & 1 Case.

Saturday 9 September: T.J. came here. Walked from Garnant.

Sunday 10 September: Lizzie & Douglas walked to Llanguicke. Sacrament the Vicar Mr. Griffiths officiated, the 1st time Lizzie heard him do the duty.

Monday 11 September: Evan took T.J. in D.M.'s car to meet 1st train at Garnant, Douglas went to Station. Not having a letter to say when Rosa wd.

come, Evan took Lizzie & Colin in D.M.'s car to meet 2 o'clk. train at Bryn Amman for Llandilo.

Wednesday 13 September: T.J. went to Llanwrtyd Wells.

Friday 15 September: Mary Philip & her little girl (Mary Anna aged 10 yrs. last Feb.) came to see me, they are now staying at Ystalyfera a few days with her mother who is not well.

Saturday 16 September: Poor old Wm. Williams Plas-y-bryn (Wm. Ddolgarn) buried to-day at Cwmllynfell. This day 18 weeks he came to Glenview to pay me his rent. He looked very well then & so tidy. He was only ill 7 days.

Wednesday 20 September: T.J. came here from Llanwrtyd Wells, his hand is better.

Thursday 21 September: Mrs. Jones of Crachllwyn here. She asked Lizzie & T.J. to come up tomorrow to see the place before the Sale.

Friday 22 September: Lizzie & T.J. walked after dinner to Crachllwyn, they said all looked very clean & tidy.

Saturday 23 September: Crachllwyn Sale of Crop & Cattle.

Monday 25 September: T.J. to Swansea 9.40 train, took my small Kitchen clock to Ganz [*Watch & Clock Maker, High* Street] to be cleaned or repaired. He went down to the Mumbles & back here last train.

Tuesday 26 September: T.J. left to meet last train for Llandilo. Walked to Station.

Wednesday 4 October: Rosa Paddison (Mrs. Rees), her little boy Fred, & her two step-sisters (Ethel & Dotty) here to tea. Rosa leaves Trenache this day week for London & sails on the 29th inst. for Australia where her Husband is. Lizzie & her 3 boys were here too.

Thursday 5 October: Llanguicke Harvest Service. Betty & Evan there. I did not feel well enough for Lizzie & Douglas to go. There were no decorations. Evan had cleaned the Walks &c.

Friday 6 October: Mrs. Harris Nantrickets here with Goose & Giblets, 6/6 paid.

Thursday 12 October: Thos. Davies & Anne Jones here paying their rent up to last Sep. I got very poorly when writing out receipts & obliged to lie on the Sofa but not quite unconscious. Paid Thos. Davies 8/- for putting up the Wire fence by Falde bach & 15/8 for the Wire.

Thursday 19 October: Evan fetched ½ ton of soft coal from Pwll bach, 7/- paid.

Monday 6 November: The Vicar (Mr. Griffiths) called, gave me the Holy Communion. Douglas in the room during the time & behaved very nicely.

Tuesday 7 November: Wrote to ask Margaret Evans if she could come here for a month as Rebe was leaving on Saturday & Douglas & Doddy were here.

Wednesday 8 November: Sent Evan to Caegurwen Arms to fetch little Ottoman which little Colin sent me by Wm. Davies.

Friday 10 November: Recd. letter from Margaret saying she could not come as her Mother had sprained her foot.

Saturday 11 November: Evan took Rebe's boxes home after dinner, & she went after tea. Rebe had been here 5 months yesterday. Paid her in full at the rate of £13 per year or 5/- a week.

Friday 24 November: Lizzie, Datta & Colin came in a covered Wagonnette for the 2 boys. Doddy had been here 5 months & a fortnight today, & Douglas 16 weeks tomorrow, dear little fellows, the house will appear very empty after them, they have been quite contented & very happy all the time & very good too. They left 5 o'clk. p.m. & got safely to Llandilo ¼ to 8. Ada the Cottage here. Poor old Mr. James, Dirleton Terrace died today aged 89 years.

Tuesday 28 November: Lizzie's little boy Colin one year old today, sent him a Sovereign yesterday in a letter.

Tuesday 5 December: Alice Paddison married to Mr. Ben W. Davies, Draper, Neath at Crynant Church.

Wednesday 6 December: Paid Thos. Davies (Blacksmith) by Evan as per bill to this day, 5/2 paid.

Friday 8 December: Evan took Polly to be shod, 2/6 paid. Wrote to Douglas.

Thursday 14 December: Doddy very sick & ill getting into scarlet fever. Douglas at Miss Lewis Party, holidays begin.

Monday 18 December: Douglas in bed sickening for scarlet fever.

Wednesday 20 December: Poor Douglas very ill in scarlet fever & not able to swallow any thing.

Thursday 21 December: Intended going to Llandilo today to stay over Christmas but I am afraid as the children are in the scarlet fever.

Saturday 30 December: Mr. Griffiths the Vicar called 4 p.m. thinking to give me the Communion but I was not well enough to see him.

Money Received

1893

1893			£ .. s .. d
Feb.	13th	Garth ½ year due Sep. 92	28 .. 0 .. 0
March	25th	Wm. Rowland 1 yrs. Rent due this day	4 .. 0 .. 0
May	6th	Wm. Price for the stones of the Colliery Smithshop	4 .. 0 .. 0
May	13th	Wm. Williams Plas-y-bryn ½ a yrs. rent due March 93	1 ..10 .. 0
	"	Wm. Morgan Plas-y-bryn ½ a yrs. rent due March 93	1 ..10 .. 0
	"	Dd. Williams Llynfell Cottage ½ yrs. rent due March 93	2 .. 0 .. 0
	"	Gellyluog (Thos. Jones) ½ a year's rent due Sep. 92	17 ..10 .. 0
	"	J. Jones Int. on £160 – on a/c	5 .. 0 .. 0
	"	T. Jones Int. on £400 due Oct. 92	12 .. 0 .. 0
	"	T. Jones " " £100 " Feb. 93	4 .. 0 .. 0
	24th	Crachllwyn	22 .. 0 .. 0
	29th	Cwmllynfell (Wm. Price) ½ a year's rent due March 93	22 ..10 .. 0
June	30th	Fresh butter sold in lbs. from Jan. to June	5 .. 8 .. 8½
July	24th	Garth (D. Morgan) ½ a year's rent due March 93	28 .. 0 .. 0
			£157 .. 8 .. 8½

Sep.	21st	Crachllwyn	25 .. 0 .. 0
	25th	Hannah Williams Plas-y-bryn ½ a year's rent due Sep. 29th 93	1 ..10 .. 0
	"	Wm. Morgan Plas-y-bryn " " "	1 ..10 .. 0
	"	Dd. Williams Llynfell Cottage " " "	2 .. 0 .. 0
Oct.	12th	Thos. Davies Colliery House 1 year's rent to Sep. 93	4 ..10 .. 0
	"	Thos. Jones ditto ditto	4 ..10 .. 0
Decr.	15th	Gellyluog (Thos. Jones) ½ a yrs. rent to March 93	17 ..10 .. 0
	16th	Bridget Lewis 1 year's Int. on £120 – due Oct. 93	6 .. 0 .. 0
	23rd	Cottage John Davies 1 year's rent	3 ..18 .. 0
Jan.	19th	Grey Cow's calf to Dl. Morgan	2 ..12 .. 0
		Julia's calf 86 lbs. @ 7d. "	2 ..10 .. 0
July		Alice's calf 98 lbs. @ 6d. "	2 .. 9 .. 0
			£231 .. 7 .. 8½

1894

Margaret produced a much reduced record of her year owing to her withdrawal from Garth to Llandeilo from 26 February to late November. Over these months there were many pristine pages in her diary with only infrequent comments on matters of interest to her. Despite her long and restful absence she continued to record the details of her income sources and expenditure.

Bills paid to 31st Decr. 1893 entered in 1st leaf of this book. M. P. Jones Garth 1894.

Bills paid up to 31st Decr. 1893

			£ .. s .. d
	Dr. Rees, Tirbach.	Cheque	12 ..10 .. 6
Decr. 16th/93	Bridget Lewis	"	10 .. 7 .. 0
"	F. E. Williams & Co. Swansea	"	17 .. 0 .. 0
Decr. 19th "	Taylor & Co. "	"	5 .. 9 .. 9
Jan. 2nd/94	D. Smith, Alltwen (Tithe)	"	5 ..18 .. 0
" "	J. Griffiths, Pontardawe	"	2 .. 6 .. 8
Jan. 13th "	J. Thomas, Haverfordwest (Tithe)	"	2 .. 4 ..10
Feb. 17th "	Davies & Co. Pontardawe	"	2 .. 2 .. 6
Jan. 11th 94	Betty (Wages)	Cash	6 .. 0 .. 0

" 11th "	Evan "	"	11 .. 0 .. 0
" 10th "	J. Hall, Swansea	"	15 .. 0
" 25th "	Glyn Price (Duke's rent 5 yrs. to Sep. 93)	"	10 .. 0
Dec. 14th 93	M. Harris Gartheithen	"	16 .. 9
Jan. 12th 94	Mary Morgan Garth Farm	"	11 .. 0
Decr. 6th 93	T. Davies Blacksmith	"	5 .. 2
Jan. 25th 94	Late Morgan Walters Sons (Carpenters)	"	13 .. 0

Thursday 4 January: Daniel killed my Pig in their yard. Evan helping.

Friday 5 January: Dl. cut up the Pig, it weighed 323 lbs by their scales, 16 score 3 lbs @ 9/-, £7..5..0. Gave Hopkin & Rees 1/- each for their trouble in cleaning up &c.

Saturday 6 January: Lizzie began the pan of butter I sent her with the Plum Puddings at Christmas about 23 lbs. Recd. letter from Mrs. Thomas saying poor Mr. Burton Day died some months ago.

Sunday 7 January: Mrs. Williams St. Donat's Vicarage (Miss Clarke) died, buried next Thursday 11th inst.

Tuesday 9 January: Sent Lizzie by train from Bryn Amman 3 chines, spare rib, pie & a few steaks. 13 cwt stone coal 4/4 paid.

Wednesday 10 January: ½ ton of soft coal by Evan 7/0 paid.

Thursday 11 January: Paid Evan wages due up to 31st Decr. 93 being 7/- a week or £18 a year. £11..0..0 paid. Paid Betty wages due up to 31st Decr. 93 at the rate of £12 a year. £6..0..0 paid.

Saturday 13 January: Evan went to Ystalyfera after dinner brought Betty 2 aprons.

Tuesday 16 January: Benjamin Daniel called here saying he had been speaking to Mr. Thomas Court Herbert about Crachllwyn & that he wished to know the price &c. so I promised to write this week.

Sunday 21 January: Poor George Kirkhouse age 33 died. He was a Surgeon at Minchinhampton & buried there. His Mother & his Sister Polly lived with him, only ill 2 days. Dr. Rees' father died at Garn llwyd Maesteg.

Monday 22 January: Wrote to Mr. John Thomas Court Herbert saying Crach-llwyn was 71 acres, rent £50 a year, price of Surface & Minerals £3,000.

Wednesday 24 January: Poor George Kirkhouse buried today at Minchin-hampton near Stroud Gloucestershire age 33. Dr. Rees Tirbach's father buried today in Llangynwyd Churchyard.

Tuesday 30 January: Had hay from Thos. Jones Coedcaemawr.

Saturday 3 February: Lent Philip Rees the Postman £1..0..0 to be re-paid me in 2 months. Sent T.J. the stockings that J. Davies' wife footed.

Monday 5 February: Shani Tynewydd called here on her way to Gartheithen. Said Price Cwm. met with an accident last Friday & had injured his left wrist very badly. Had from Biddy

	£ .. s .. d
5 bus. White Oats @ 2/9	13 .. 9
2 cwt. Barley Meal	11 .. 0
½ Sack flour	14 .. 0
28 lbs. Crystal Sugar 5/- Salt 6d	5 .. 6
	£2 .. 4 .. 3

First goods had this year.

Tuesday 6 February: Ada here making pink pinnie for Colin & 2 night gowns for Douglas.

Wednesday 7 February: Mr. Jones Ty'n Coedcae's daughter-in-law buried age 32.

Thursday 8 February: John Davies removed from the Cottage to a House near the Brewery. A fine day.

Saturday 10 February: 12½ cwt coal by Evan, 2s..1d. paid. John Jones came to the Cottage to live at 1/6d per week.

Monday 12 February: Recd. a letter from Lizzie saying she had no letter from me yesterday & was uncomfortable in case I was ill, asked Philip what he had done with Saturday's letters, told Betty he had forgotten to post them but had done so now. T.J. came here at 1.30 from Garnant fearing I was ill as there was no letter to-day, he left here 4.30 to be back last train. I was very sick all the morning. The roof of this Barn a little injured by the Storm & Wind of yesterday & last night.

Tuesday 13 February: Mr. Griffiths called & gave me the Communion. Mrs. Griffiths & Miss Andrews the Post Office in the Carriage on the road. I went as far as front gate & Mrs. G. came up to speak to me. George Thomas hung at Carmarthen for murdering his Sweetheart Mary Jane Jones on the 19th of November last.

Wednesday 14 February: Ada mended sleeves of my crepe cloth dress, the last Sally made.

Friday 16 February: David Nantymelyn Carpenter came here to see what repairs were wanted to the Barn after the Storm on Sunday night.

Monday 19 February: David Nantymelyn here repairing roof of the Barn & other slates that had been loosened by the Storm a week yesterday. He was here 6 hours & charged 7d an hour, 3/6 paid. D.M. came in to show me the Plans &c. of the proposed Railway from Pontardawe to Neath.

Wednesday 21 February: Thos. Coedcaemawr (the son) came here to help Evan to cart out the heap of earth to Cae Barriwns (Heol y Cefn scrapings wh. Evan had carried months ago inside Cae Barriwns gate).

Thursday 22 February: Thos. Coedcaemawr here. Mary John Williams here. I had not seen her for many years, gave her 2/-. She buried her Husband & is a Widow.

Monday 26 February: T.J., Douglas & Doddy came to fetch me in a closed carriage from Cawdor Arms. Ada Davies the Dressmaker returned with me. Lizzie wanted her to sew a little for her. Betty & Evan will take charge of all here & my mind will be happy as I know they are careful & honest.

Wednesday 28 February: Douglas 7 years old to-day. I gave him £21..0..0 which will be placed in the Bank.

Monday 12 March: Miss Mary Grenfell, Maesteg House died at Saville Row London age 58 yrs. of Cancer, an operation had been performed a week ago & it was thought successfully, but sickness came on & she could take no food.[1]

Thursday 15 March: Mrs. Arthur Gilbertson died.[2]

Saturday 14 April: Mrs. Isaac Rees of Aberdare died.

Wednesday 18 April: Mrs. Isaac Rees of Aberdare (formerly Mrs. Williams of Waterloo Villa Llandilo) buried to-day at Llandilo.

Saturday 21 April: Poor Thos. Davis Cwmllynfell buried this afternoon. Lizzie washed my hair & bathed my head which gave me great relief.

Saturday 28 April: Mr. & Mrs. Griffiths Llanarthney called here, they did not stay to tea. Esther took Douglas & Doddy to tea to her Mother's near "The College", it is her brother's birthday.

Wednesday 9 May: Recd. a letter from Rachel Morgan saying Tom Tirlan (Betty's brother) was to be buried <u>to-day</u> at Llanguicke.[3]

Saturday 12 May: Mrs. Thomas, Dora Thomas & Mr. & Mrs. Davies Cwm-amman Vicarage called at Glenview & stayed to tea. Mrs. Thomas said Miss Shenton was now with her sister Mrs. Hyde, if she gets well enough she is to return to her. Dora said she had been married 12 years, her youngest child is 7 years.

Tuesday 24 July: Choral Festival at Llandilo. Mrs. Thomas of Garnant & Mrs. Evans Garnant House called at Glenview & took tea with us. Revd. W. R. Lloyd & his little boy Gilbert called & they also stayed to tea. Mr. Lloyd is

1. *The Cambrian* (16/3/1894) recorded that her death was an "irreparable loss" which was mourned by the entire community of St. Thomas, among whose inhabitants she had led "so vigorous, so devoted and so self-sacrificing a life". Her Christian belief found practical expression in funding and actively participating in many charitable provisions for local dock and rail workers. She was a popular and respected figure and her coffin passed through crowded streets and was followed by a large cortege to Dan-y-Graig Cemetery. Barton, 2009/10, 22-39, and Chamberlain, 1973, 123-42.
2. Ellen Gilbertson aged 43 was buried on 19 March in All Saint's Churchyard, Pontardawe. She was the daughter of Francis Edwardes Lloyd of Plâs Cilybebyll and "died at the birth of her fourteenth child" (Lloyd, 1990,19). See also Jackson (2001), 14-16, 284, 412-3.
3. Thomas Evans aged 75 of Pantywalddu, Neath.

now at Burry Port & asked us to come & spend a day with them. Poor Miss Shenton is in a good deal of pain & is not left alone night or day. She is with Mrs. Hyde, they fear there is some internal Cancer, she is very resigned they say.

Thursday 3 October: 10 cwt soft coal (Pwllbach) 6..0 paid.

Monday 7 October: Godfrey 4 years old today, gave him £12..0..0 which will be placed in the Bank.

Friday 23 November: Elizabeth the Cottage here making balls[4] &c., settled with her (verbal) 30 days, cleaning fields, weeding & with the

Hay @ 1/3d		£1..17..6
	1½ days on our food @ 1/-	1..6

Prizes presented to the Llandilo Volunteers in the Drill Hall by the Honble. Misses Rice. Douglas & his Father attended the Ceremony.

Tuesday 27 November: Mrs. Jones Crachllwyn here, paid £20 on a/c of rent.

Wednesday 28 November: Colin's birthday, 2 yrs. old today. Gave him £6..0..0, also case with fork & spoon. Lord Swansea (H. Hussey Vivian) died this day at Singleton age 73 yrs. His Father (Mr. J. H. Vivian) died Feb. 10th 1855, his Mother (Mrs. Vivian) September 8th '86 age 88 years. Mr. Stone called at Glenview on his way to Pembroke. Lizzie, Colin and Doddy here.

Thursday 29 November: I walked with Lizzie & Doddy as far as Heol y Cefn gate, she carried Colin.

Friday 30 November: Thos. Jones' Wife & Henry Stephen's Wife Colliery House Cwmllynfell here. Thos. Jones paid 1 year's rent, £5..0..0 due Sep. 29th 1894. Henry Stephens 1 year's rent house & stable to Sep. 29th 1894 £5..10..0.

Monday 3 December: Had 4 dozn. beer from Fulton. Returned 7 dozn. & 9 bottles (empties) to Fulton, by his a/c we owe 8 dozn. & 10 bottles. Lord Swansea buried to-day at Sketty. Public funeral. Fine day. T.J. & Douglas left here 1.30 in time for the 2 o'clk. to Llandilo. Took clock to be cleaned.

---

4. A mixture of small coal and clay hand-rolled into balls and dried, known locally as *pele*, and used to supplement the use of domestic coal.

Friday 7 December: Charley Paddison married at St. Mary's Church Swansea to Velindra Mary, daughter of Mr. Walter Jones late Draper of Neath (yesterday).

Tuesday 11 December: Connie Lockyear married today at Caledfwlch to a Mr. Jenkins of Swansea. Very wet.

Wednesday 12 December: Recd. letter from Lizzie saying John Thomas Gwernllwyn, called there yesterday.

Monday 31 December: Paid James Hinkin Garth Poor rate as follows, half year ending March 25th ′95.

		£ .. s .. d
The Garth	£17..10..0 @ 2/8d	2 .. 6 .. 8
Garth Farm	37..15..0 "	5 .. 0 .. 8
3 Cots. Cwm.	7..10..0 "	1 .. 0 .. 0
1 D. Williams	3.. 5..0 "	8 .. 8
1 H. Stephens	3.. 0..0 "	8 .. 0
1 Thos. Jones	3.. 0..0 "	8 .. 0
1 John Jones	2.. 0..0 "	5 .. 4
		£9 ..17 .. 4
Less Commission on Cots		12 .. 6
Total Poor rate		£9 .. 4 ..10

Rate for Special Expenses		£ .. s .. d
The Garth	on £10..15..0 @ 10d	8 ..11½
Garth Farm	" 12.. 5..0 "	10 .. 2½
Cwm Cottages	" 16..15..0 "	13 ..11½
Garth Cot.	2.. 0..0 "	1 .. 8
		£1 ..14 .. 9½
Less Commission on Cots		3 ..10½
Total Special rate		£1 ..10 ..11

Poor rate as above	£ 9 .. 4 ..10
Special " " "	1 ..10 ..11
	£10 ..15 .. 9

Paid by Cash 31st Decr/94

Money Received

1894

1894			£ .. s .. d
Janry.	23rd	Garth ½ year's rent due Sep. 93	28 .. 0 .. 0
"		Cwmllynfell (Wm. Price) ½ a yrs. rent due Sep. 93	22 ..10 .. 0
Feb.	10th	Cottage John Davies 7 wks. to this day	10 .. 6
"	12th	T. Jones Int. on £400 due Octr. 93	12 .. 0 .. 0
"	"	T. Jones " " £100 " Feb. 94	4 . 0 .. 0
Jan.	26th	Grey Cow's Calf 94 lbs. @ 6½d (5 wks. old)	2 .. 11 .. 5½
March	25th	Wm. Rowland 1 yrs. rent due this day	4 .. 0 .. 0
April	7th	Hannah Williams Plas-y-bryn ½ a year's rent due March 25th 94	1 ..10 .. 0
"		Mary Rees Plas-y-bryn " " "	1 ..10 .. 0
"		Dd. Williams Llynfell Cottage " " "	2 .. 0 .. 0
"		John Pugh Llynfell Cottage " " "	1 ..10 .. 0
May	2nd	Gellyluog (Thos. Jones) ½ a yr's rent to Sep. 93	17 ..10 .. 0
"	23rd	Crachllwyn	30 .. 0 .. 0
Augst.	2nd	Cwmllynfell ½ year's rent due March 94 (Wm. Price)	22 ..10 .. 0
Sep.	8th	Gellyluog (Thos. Jones) ½ a year's rent due March 94	17 ..10 .. 0
Oct.	1st	Garth ½ a year's rent due March 94	28 .. 0 .. 0
Novr.	27th	Crachllwyn	20 .. 0 .. 0
May	8th	Julia's Calf 97 lbs @ 7d to Dl. Morgan	2 ..16 .. 7
July	6th	Alice's Calf 88 lbs @ 6d " "	2 .. 4 .. 0
		Fresh Butter sold in lbs. from Jan. to June	4 ..17 .. 4
Nov.	30th	Thos. Jones Colliery House 1 year's rent to Sep. 94	5 .. 0 .. 0
"		1 year's taxes to Sep. 94	15 .. 0
"		Henry Stephens Colliery House 1 year's rent to Sep. 94	5 ..10 .. 0
"		1 year's taxes to Sep. 94	15 .. 0
"		T. Jones Int. on £400 due Octr. 94	12 .. 0 .. 0
			249 .. 9 ..10½

1895

Although there was a slight increase in the number of diary entries from 49 in 1894 to 74, most of the second half of the year was not recorded. During the early months Margaret rarely emerged from her home, noting in March that she "*felt very confused & stupid*" and "*sleepy & stupid*". On 2 May she visited her garden for the first time in three years and on 22 August walked with Lizzie to the adjoining meadow for possibly the first time in four years. Lizzie and T.J., visited her frequently and the children were sent to Garth for days on end, accompanied by Lizzie's young maid Esther, to provide Margaret with the stimulation of their company. Lizzie maintained a regular correspondence during this period and some of her letters are transcribed in the following text. On her sixty-second birthday on 2 September Margaret wrote prophetically in her diary: "*T.J., Lizzie, Douglas, Doddy & Colin here, perhaps we shall never all dine to-gether again*". She left Garth on 15 October to stay with Lizzie's family in Llandeilo and remained there until the following May.

Tuesday 1 January: Douglas here alone with me, his Father, Mother, Doddy & Colin in Llandilo. Ada Davies here sewing.

Saturday 5 January: T.J. walked here last train from Garnant.

Monday 7 January: T.J. measured Wain Vawr hedge, 82 perches 4 yds. Evan took T.J., & Douglas to meet 2 o'clk. train at Garnant. Douglas had been here a fortnight last Saturday & was a very good boy & quite a little companion. Betty and I will miss him very much. He goes to School tomorrow.

Tuesday 8 January: Lizzie took Douglas to School at Mr. James' St. Teilo's College Llandilo. He has been some years with Miss Lewis, Belle Vue & is very forward for his age, 8 yrs. next month.

Wednesday 9 January: Had box of Tea from Llandilo. Load of hard lumps 13 cwt 4..4 paid.

Thursday 10 January: Mr. Williams (PC 46) Swansea died suddenly.

Monday 14 January: PC 46 buried to-day at Llandebie. T.J. to the funeral at the Church, he dined & took tea at Llandebie Vicarage.

Thursday 17 January: Revd. John Jones Ty'n Coedcae buried to-day at Saron Rhydyfro, a very large funeral. W. Price Cwm & his wife came here from the funeral paid ½ year's rent to Sep. 29th 1894.

Thursday 24 January: Had load of small coal 13 cwt, 2..2 paid.

Friday 25 January: Evan took Lizzie to meet 2 o'clk. train to Garnant, <u>very cold</u>. Betty made pancakes to send the Children.

Tuesday 29 January: Conservative meeting at the Drill Hall Llandilo. Lord Halsbury (Sir Hardinge Giffard) spoke. Lord Emlyn in the Chair. T.J., & Lizzie & Douglas there, they enjoyed it.

Wednesday 30 January: Had 10 cwt hard coal (lumps) 3..4 <u>paid</u>.

Thursday 31 January: <u>Deep snow</u>. Evan took M. E. Davies home in D.M.'s Car as she had such a bad cold, said she wd. come back when better.

Tuesday 5 February: Betty went to bed this night <u>seemingly as usual</u>, but to-morrow morning complained of being ill with much pain in her side, & in the White room she has been <u>until March 10th</u>.

Wednesday 6 February: Mary Elizabeth came to my room saying Betty was very ill. Mr. Eben Thomas (Thomas & Sons) Llandilo, died rather suddenly as he was in Church on Sunday as usual. He leaves a Widow & 2 little boys.

Sunday 10 February: Hopkin went for Dr. Rees to Betty. Rees went to Ystalyfera to say Betty was ill. David Phillip & Margaret came down this afternoon. Dr. Rees said Betty had inflammation of the <u>right lung</u>, to have a <u>fire</u> in the room.

Monday 11 February: Lizzie came here <u>quite</u> <u>un</u>expectedly knowing Betty was ill & <u>I</u> not very well. She came by train to Bryn Amman 3.40 p.m. & hired a Car at "The Farmers" to come here. She left the 3 boys at Llandilo. How glad I was to see her.

Tuesday 12 February: Dr. Rees 2nd time to see Betty.

Thursday 14 February: Dr. Rees 3rd time to see Betty. Mary Phillip, Mary & Shonny came in a Car to see Betty.

Saturday 16 February: Adams the man who drove Lizzie here last Monday came to see me, he leaves the Farmers today & wants a situation. I agree with him subject to a month's notice for £20 a year. Washing out.

Sunday 17 February: Dr. Rees 4th time to see Betty, said she was much better & that he wd. not come again unless sent for. Young David Phillip & his wife came to see Betty, also William Troedyrhiw.

Monday 18 February: Lizzie returned to Llandilo. Morgan Harris drove her in his Car to meet 2 p.m. train at Garnant & brought bottle of medicine for Betty. Revd. Evan Thomas, Cwmgorse Curate called here 1st time. Mr. Jones Gellygron called here, told me that if the Railway came this way to be sure to have a Station on Heol Hugh to Stop by Signal. Sent old desk to Douglas. Lizzie took Pan of Butter about 20 lbs.

Tuesday 19 February: In bed all day & unconscious until 9.30 p.m. Margaret wrote to Lizzie. Hopkin D.M. for a load of soft coal, ½ a ton their horse & cart.

Wednesday 20 February: Telegraphed to Lizzie that I was much better this morning. Rees took it in going to School.

Wednesday 27 February: Joseph Adams came here as indoor Servant at the rate of £20 a year washing out, subject to a month's notice.

Friday 1 March: Had new wheelbarrow made by David Jones Nantmelin, 15/- paid.

Sunday 3 March: I was lying on the sofa when Margaret called me to dinner, felt very confused & stupid & could hardly cut or eat anything, went to bed & in a short time felt much better, but did not get up.

Thursday 7 March: Douglas & Doddy had two teeth each out by the Dentist. Dr. Davies gave Doddy a little chloroform, he had much pain poor child. Had Bag of Potatoes & Jar of Oatmeal from Llandilo. Adams fetched them from "Caegurwen Arms".

Monday 11 March: Fanny Gilbertson walked up to see me, she was here 11.5 a.m. & stayed to 12.40. She has been a month at Glanrhyd & leaves to-morrow for Cilybebyll where she stays a few days. She makes her home with Kate at Hanover, the other 3 girls live in London & Mrs. Ford & her daughter still live in Cheltenham. She was 51 this day fortnight Feb. 25th & looks very well & very active.

Thursday 14 March: Lent Morgan Harris Gartheithen £10..0..0 paid.

Friday 15 March: Wrote to Douglas from bed, soon afterwards got sleepy & stupid but not quite unconscious and remained quietly in bed all day & much better about 6 o'clk.

Saturday 16 March: Pontardawe fair. Margaret to the fair, 10.40 when she returned but I did not say a word. Mary Anne who came down about 4 p.m. intended returning to Ystalyfera with Margaret's "company" but I said it was too late & she stayed here & goes tomorrow evening. Adams to the fair.

Sunday 17 March: Mrs. Day & Johnny, & Jinny's little girl Anne Sophia came here in a Car 1 p.m. Mrs. Day will be 56 next May & looks exceedingly well. I am very partial to her for she was so kind & willing. Johnny is 19 next May. He was 9 months old when he left here March 1877.

Monday 18 March: Mr. Jones, Pontardawe Curate called for the first time on the Vicar's horse. He is Noah Jones' son who formerly was my tenant at the Colliery House Cwmllynfell. Evan & Adams to Gellygron for half a Ton of Hay, paid £2..5..0.

Wednesday 20 March: Mary Phillip & her little girl came to see Betty from Ammanford. Had ½ sack of flour, 1 bag oats, 28 lbs sugar & 1 bar of salt from Biddy. Adams for Hard coal 14 cwt lumps 4..6 paid.

Thursday 4 April: Adams drove Lizzie & Colin to meet last train for Llandilo at Garnant. Margaret & Doddy to the Station.

Friday 5 April: Lizzie & Colin returned.

Saturday 6 April: T.J. came here last train.

Sunday 7 April: Douglas & his Father to Llanguicke.

Saturday 18 April: T.J. came here last train.

Easter Sunday 14 April: Lizzie & Douglas to Llanguicke.

Monday 15 April: T.J. to Gellyluog to see what repairs had been done.

Tuesday 16 April: T.J. walked to meet 1st train at Garnant.

Thursday 18 April: Margaret Evans left this evening after been here 10 weeks next Sunday during the time Betty was so ill. Paid her in her aunt's presence, £2..7..0 paid.

Wednesday 24 April: Adams with Gartheithen Car to meet Esther (Lizzie's maid) at Garnant, 2 train from Llandilo. Douglas & Doddy also went. Thos. Thomas, Carpenter, Pontardawe came up this afternoon to see if the Phaeton could be repaired, said it could, & that he would do it for £1..15..0. Adams took it down with Thomas & it is to be ready by Saturday.

Saturday 27 April: Had Phaeton back from Thos. Thomas. Paid him by cheque for repairs £1..15..0 paid. Adams took Douglas & Doddy in the Phaeton to meet their Father at Garnant.

Sunday 28 April: T.J. & Douglas walked to Llanguicke.

Monday 29 April: Adams took Douglas & his Father to meet 11 a.m. train at Garnant.

Tuesday 30 April: Mary Dagmar eldest daughter of Dr. Evan Jones, Aberdare, married to Robert Ajax Lewis of Tycymmer Porth at St. Margaret's Westminster London.

Wednesday 1 May: Mrs. James Tamblyn (M. A. Rees) a son born, her husband died last Feb. 2 Fitzalan Place, Cardiff.

Thursday 2 May: Lizzie to Swansea by 1st train. Paid Messrs Strick & Bellingham as per bill by cheque, £59..15..0 paid. Brought back the Crachllwyn deeds from Strick & Bellingham. Lizzie called at Brynsyfi, she saw poor Miss Jenkins greatly changed & her memory nearly gone. Lizzie returned 4.10 train. Esther took Doddy & Colin in the Phaeton to meet her. I went to the Garden with Adams about the small seeds, told him I thought the Cabbage Plants in a very slovenly, untidy manner & that I was not at all pleased. It is 3 years or more since I was in the Garden.

Tuesday 14 May: Mr. Wm. Jenkins of Conset Hall, Durham died aged 70 years. He was related by marriage to the Kirkhouse's of Pontardawe.

Friday 31 May: Lizzie, Douglas & Doddy came last train.

Whit Sunday 2 June: Lizzie to Church.

Monday 3 June: T.J. went up to Crachllwyn with John Griffiths to see about the repairs required there.

Tuesday 4 June: T.J., Lizzie, Douglas & Doddy to meet 11 train at Garnant, the last time for Adams to drive them as he will be leaving the 14th inst.

Friday 7 June: Mr. Griffiths the Vicar called.

Monday 10 June: Mr. Jevons died at 11 Walmer Road Birkdale, Liverpool aged 75 years.

Tuesday 11 June: Mr. G. H. Strick, Bryn Amman married at Llandilo to Miss Ethel Thomas, Caeglas.

Friday 14 June: Joseph Adams left here 4 p.m. train for his home near Leominster Herefordshire. He had been here 15 weeks last Wednesday. Paid him up to the day at the rate of £20 per year, £5..17..3 paid.

Saturday 15 June: The Vicar & Mrs. Griffiths called, the Warden of Llandovery's Sister is staying with them & was on the road in the Carriage.

Saturday 22 June: Evan drove Esther & Colin in the Phaeton to Garnant to meet 2 p.m. train for Llandilo. Colin looked very pretty in his blue sailor suit.

Tuesday 25 June: Began mowing Cae Barriwns.

Thursday 27 June: David Jones Nantmelyn putting up zinc on Hayhouse pine end. Carried some of Cae Barriwns hay. Andrew, Gartheithen servant helping.

Friday 28 June: Ada put back sofa covering after it had been washed, & swept out Dining room, it looks much better. I put clean blind on the Window yesterday.

Saturday 10 August: Dr. Benjamin Davies M.D. (Froodvale) died at Newport aged 66 years. He is to be buried next Tuesday afternoon at Malpas Church-yard.

Wednesday 14 August: Evan John Harries & his Aunt Gwladys came here about 1 o'clk. They had dinner, & tea at 5 p.m. Evan took them in the Phaeton as far as Gellygron to meet 7.20 train for Swansea. The little boy had been staying there with his Father the last 9 days, he is 13 next Dec. & seems a nice quiet boy. I gave him 5/-. Douglas, Doddy & Colin were here staying. Mrs. Lane & Mrs. Roberts (Mary Carregcegin) came to D.M.'s.

Thursday 15 August: Mary Carregcegin came in to see me about 11 o'clk. She stayed over an hour & took a glass of wine & biscuits. She has been a Widow over 30 yrs. living with her son (her only child & a single man) in Liverpool. She is about 63 & looks a very tidy, respectable woman. Mrs. Lane (her half sister) & herself go this afternoon to see her Brother Thomas who lives near the Trapp. She returns on Monday next to Liverpool. She came to Mrs. Lane to Swansea last Saturday.

Wednesday 21 August: T.J. & Lizzie came here at 8.15 p.m. They had a nice drive over the hill, the children & Esther were here.

Thursday 22 August: T.J. returned to Llandilo leaving here 7 a.m. Hopkin began mowing the meadow, Lizzie & I walked up there. I had not been on the meadow for years 4 I think. The boys & Esther were on the hill. I quite enjoyed the walk, the air was so nice & fresh.

Thursday 29 August: T.J. walked to Crachllwyn after Breakfast to see how the repairs were getting on. It was only to-day John Griffiths men commenced the work. Mr. Griffiths (the Vicar) called on his way to Garnant, his wife is ill at Llanelly & he was going to see her. Asked him if he knew of a tenant for this place, said he wd. enquire.

Monday 2 September: My birthday. I am 62 to-day. T.J., Lizzie, Douglas, Doddy & Colin here, perhaps we shall never all dine to-gether again.

Monday 30 September: Had 4 dozn. beer (Fulton) 10..0 paid.

Thursday 3 October:	Had 12 cwt stone coal	4 .. 0
	" 12 cwt small coal	2 .. 0
	from Cwmgorse by Evan, paid	Paid

Money Received

1895

1895			£ .. s .. d
Jan.	17th	Cwmllynfell (Wm. Price) ½ a yrs. rent due Sep. 94	22 ..10 .. 0
Feb.	2nd	Garth ½ year's rent due Sep. 94	28 .. 0 .. 0
Jan.		Grey Cow's calf 95 lbs. @ 7d. (5 wks. old)	2 ..15 .. 5
March	23rd	T. Jones Int. on £100 due Feb. 95	4 .. 0 .. 0
"	25th	Hannah Williams Plas-y-bryn 1 yrs. rent due March 25th 95	3 .. 0 .. 0
"		Mary Rees Plas-y-bryn	3 .. 0 .. 0
"		Dd. Williams Llynfell Cottage	4 .. 0 .. 0
"	29th	Wm. Rowland 1 yrs. rent due 25th March 95	4 .. 0 .. 0
April	2nd	John Pugh 1 yrs. rent due Mch. 25th/95	4 .. 0 .. 0
"	26th	2½ yrs. Int. on £525 due 31st Dec/94	39 .. 8 .. 4
May	6th	Crachllwyn	25 .. 0 .. 0
"	18th	Cow (Alice) sold to Daniel Pan-y-garn	12 ..12 .. 0
July	17th	Cwmllynfell (Wm. Price) ½ a yrs. rent due March 95	22 ..10 .. 0
Octr.	1st	Bridget Lewis 2 yrs. Int. on £120 due this day	12 .. 0 .. 0
"		Old Newspapers 69 lbs. to Biddy	5 .. 9
"	15th	Garth ½ year's rent due March 95	28 .. 0 .. 0
"	22nd	Gellyluog 1 year's rent due March 95	35 .. 0 .. 0
Novr.	12th	Hannah Williams Plas-y-bryn ½ a year's rent due Sep. 95	1 ..10 .. 0
"		Mary Rees Plas-y-bryn	1 ..10 .. 0
"		Thos. Jones Colliery House 1 year's rent to Sep. 95	4 ..10 .. 0
"		1 year's taxes to Sep. 95	16 .. 6
Decr.	7th	Henry Stephens Colliery House 1 year's rent to Sep. 95	5 .. 5 .. 0
"		1 year's taxes to Sep. 95	16 .. 6
"		Cwmllynfell (Wm. Price) ½ a yr's rent due Sep. 95	22 ..10 .. 0
May	24th	Fresh butter sold 8 lbs. @ 11d.	7 .. 4
March	30th	Julia's Calf to Dl. Morgan 98 lbs. @ 7d.	2 ..17 .. 2
			290 .. 4 .. 0

The Jones boys (clockwise from top left): Alfred Ynyr Douglas (Ducca) Jones (1887-1963); Hubert Wilson Godfrey (Doddy) Jones (1890-1943); Elton Augustus Harold Jones (1896-1967); Colin Jones (1892-1922)

(All photos courtesy of Mrs J. Morris)

1896

Margaret's long absence from Garth had been noted by her friends. Ernest and Jane Benthall of Glan Twrch had sent their 1895 Christmas card to her in Llandeilo and both Arthur and Colin Gilbertson wrote on 26 January to express their concern, the former asking her to "*let me know when you come home*". Margaret's physical condition was undoubtedly at a low ebb and she devoted little of her energy to her diary, although her comments on the first two days of the year might suggest a willingness to begin but an inability to continue. She failed to record the birth of Lizzie's son Harold on 23 March but did later refer to "*the 4 boys*". Margaret returned to Garth in late May and two references to her health in November and December show her continuing deterioration.

Wednesday 1 January: Douglas & Doddy to a Children's Party at the Drill Hall given by Mrs. George Williams, they went 4.30 & returned 7.30 after enjoying themselves.

Thursday 2 January: Lizzie & Douglas went to Garth by the 2 o'clk. train. Dadda, Doddy, Colin & Jane saw them off. Evan to meet them at Garnant.

Tuesday 7 January: Archdeacon James Vicar of Abergwili died this morning after a few days illness aged 65 years.

Tuesday 21 January: The Grey Cow a she-calf which we rear.

Tuesday 28 January: Lizzie, the children & I went to the field garden after dinner, the first time I have been out since I came here (Oct. 15th) ex[cept] twice to call at Mrs. Evans, No. 1. It was a nice afternoon & I enjoyed the air. Put hen to sit in Summer house on 11 eggs. Mrs. Roberts 2 Dirleton Terrace called when I was out.

Monday 24 February: T.J. went to Garth by 2 train. Evan met him at Garnant. Sent ½ cheese by him 25 lbs.

Saturday 16 May: Esther went home for the day to help her Mother, they remove from the College to Dr. Southern's to keep his farm. T.J., Lizzie, the 4 boys, I & Jane the Servant went for a drive as far as Llwynmendy in Castle Wagonette.

Sunday 17 May: In bed all the afternoon.

Tuesday 26 May: Lizzie & Colin called on Mrs. Edwin Hopkin, Mrs. Humphreys, Mrs. Roberts & at Canton [*Stores, Bridge St.*] & bought me large Tin Jug & small tin saucepan.

Wednesday 27 May: Lizzie scraped the Ink off the Drawing room paper that I upset last Sunday. Mrs. Roberts, 2 Dirleton Terrace called to wish me Good bye.

Tuesday 9 June: Wm. Price Cwm. brought me one of his pigs. Paid him £1..10..0.

Saturday 28 November: Colin 4 years old to-day. In bed all day & unconscious from 7.30 a.m. to 6 p.m. Betty sent for Ada, she came down & stayed the night. I was much better when she came.

Saturday 5 December: T.J. & Douglas came to see me 3.30 train. Evan met them, brought beef, night lights, &c. Very poorly for a little time after they came in. Paid David Nantmelyn all I owe him up to this day, £5..0..0.

Friday 11 December: Fanny Gilbertson called to see me, she is now staying at Glanrhyd & leaves there to-morrow for her Cousin's (Mr. Richard) near Bridgend. She came to A.G.'s Nov. 28th from Brecon where she had been staying with Mrs. John Morgan (late of Bolgoed). She met her & her 2 daughters abroad. Fanny said Kate's 4 eldest daughters were out as Governesses, that Violet had been a short time at the Gulston's in Pembrokeshire. She did not like being there, the children (2) were rude & unkind to her.

Money Received

1896

1896			£ .. s .. d
Jan.	9th	Garth (D. Morgan) ½ a year's rent due Sep. 95	28 .. 0 .. 0
"	15th	Crachllwyn 1 yrs. rent to Sep. 95	50 .. 0 .. 0
Feb.	8th	Gellyluog ½ yrs. rent to Sep. 95	17 ..10 .. 0
"		T. Jones Int. on £700	21 .. 0 .. 0
March		Wm. Rowland 1 year's rent due this month	4 .. 0 .. 0
April	11th	D. Williams Llynfell Cottage 1 year's rent due March 96	4 .. 0 .. 0
"	23rd	The Cwmllynfell Cottage sold to Wm. Rowland for	130 .. 0 .. 0
"	17th	1 year's Int. on £525 due Decr. 95	13 .. 8 .. 1
May	31st	Fresh butter sold in lbs. from Jan to May	3 .. 9 .. 8

June	18th	Julia's Calf to Dl. Morgan 100 lbs. @ 7d.	2 ..18 .. 4
April	11th	Hannah Williams Plas-y-bryn ½ a yr's rent due March 25th 96	1 ..10 .. 0
"		Mary Rees Plas-y-bryn	1 ..10 .. 0
July	16th	Cwmllynfell (Wm. Price) ½ a yr's rent due March 25th 96	22 ..10 .. 0
		Llanddarog Cow's Calf to Dl. Morgan	2 ..10 .. 0
Augst.		Garth (D.M.) ½ yr's. rent to March 96	28 .. 0 .. 0
21st July		½ a yrs. Int. on £525 due June 96	6 ..10 .. 9
Oct.	21st	Gellyluog ½ yr's rent due March 96	17 ..10 .. 0
Novr.	5th	Bridget Lewis 1 year's Int. on £120 due last month	4 ..16 .. 0
"	24th	Hannah Williams Plas-y- bryn ½ a yr's rent due Sep. 96	1 ..10 .. 0
"		Mary Rees Plas-y-bryn	1 ..10 .. 0
"		Thos. Jones Colliery House 1 year's rent to Sep. 29th 96	4 ..10 .. 0
"		1 year's taxes to Sep. 96	15 .. 0
"		Henry Stephens Colliery House 1 yr's rent to Sep. 29th 96	5 .. 5 .. 0
"		1 yr's taxes " "	15 .. 0
Nov.	25th	Cwmllynfell (Wm. Price) ½ a yr's rent due Sep. 96	22 ..10 .. 0
"	30th	Crachllwyn (Mrs. Jones) ½ a yr's rent due March 25th 96	25 .. 0 .. 0
			420 ..17 ..10

1897

This was the last of Margaret's diaries and her comments were largely restricted to February and March. Several referred to the normal domestic chores in Garth but others reflected her graver anxieties for her health and for Lizzie's existing illnesses. She resolved to go to Llandeilo but had to admit that she was "not well" and sent a telegram "for them to come for me". The duration of her stay in Llandeilo was not recorded but her last diary entry on 16 September was probably written in Garth. Her last surviving letter to her beloved Lizzie was dated 30 November and was written with all her former fluency and vigour.

Saturday 30 January: Had 13 cwt hard lumps, 4..4 paid.

Sunday 7 February: In bed all day till 6 p.m. Very poorly. Margaret & Maryanne came to see us. They left here at 8 said they wd. be home at 10.

Tuesday 9 February: Jane (Troed y rhiw) left this evening (her ears are very bad). She had been here 10 weeks @ 2/6d, £1..5..0 paid.

Thursday 11 February: Mr. Edward Nugent Bellingham (Mr. Edward Strick's Partner, Strick & Bellingham) died rather suddenly. He was born 12th Oct. 1832, died 11 Feb. 1897 aged 64 years.

Monday 15 February: Had 4 dozn Beer (18 bot. in house) 10 paid. Fulton says I owe him 7 dozn. empties. I think it is 5½ dozn. I owe him. Mr. E.N. Bellingham buried in the Swansea Cemetery today.

Wednesday 17 February: Recd. a letter from Douglas saying his Mother was not well yesterday, head & ears bad. Ada put clean covering on my bed & the next in size to it, & made an unbleached valance for Whiteroom. Principal Owen of St. David's College Lampeter appointed Bishop of St. David's, successor to Bishop Basil Jones. Alban Saunders married today at St. Gabriel's, Swansea to Amy Biddle.

Thursday 18 February: Evan fetched load coal 12 cwt, 2/- paid. Betty washed sofa covering & Ada swept out Dining room & ironed & mended sofa covering. David Williams (Mrs. Davies' Father) brought 23 moles that he had caught on my fields & in my garden. Paid.

Friday 19 February: Ada put sofa covering on, it looks clean, but rather shabby, & no wonder for it has been in use 13½ years.

Saturday 20 February: Ada swept out the Drawing room. I felt very poorly all day, & became unconscious about 5 p.m. & continued so until 7 (two hours). Ada stayed here the night.

Sunday 21 February: Mr. Jordan's son brought up Douglas' letter, his Mother is very ill in Influenza & Neuralgia of the face.

Tuesday 23 February: Douglas says his Mother was just the same yesterday, not any better. I am very unhappy about her. Had 2 dozn. Handkerchiefs from Belfast. Sent Harold one today.

Friday 26 February: Evan for load of hard coal, 13 cwt lumps. 4..4 paid.

Saturday 27 February: Betty packed small hamper for Douglas, sent him ½ dozn. Handfs. I fell down by Little Kitchen outer door, Betty & Sarah helped me up. I was not unconscious then 11.15 but became so soon after 1 o'clk. &

remained so until near 8 p.m. Mrs. Davies came to see how I was. Sent Douglas a letter & cheque also a Handf. with a border by post.

Sunday 28 February: Dear little Douglas 10 years old to-day. I remained in bed all day not feeling well after my attack yesterday.

Wednesday 3 March: A great leakage on the Stairs from the lead gutter, a very wet & stormy day, some trees blown down in Cae Barriwns wood & also the Hay rick.

Thursday 4 March: Recd. letter from Lizzie today saying she was much better but obliged to keep her ears very warm. Recd. letter from Mr. Branfill asking the price of Cwmllynfell farm. Paid D. Williams for 23 moles @ 3d. 5..9 pd.

Saturday 6 March: Davies (my tenant) brought me one ton of soft coal from Pwll bach in his Gambo & 2 horses. Coal 11/6, haulage 5/6, 17..0 paid. Davies & Evan put it in Coal yard. We were quite out of soft coal excepting a little small.

Monday 8 March: Recd. letter from Lizzie, her ears have been very painful the last two days. Intended going to Llandilo tomorrow but I am not well. Sent tel. for them to come for me on Wednesday.

Wednesday 15 March: Paid Evan for 11 loads of Cwmgorse coal had from 19th March to Sep. 8th in this year, £1..5..6 paid. Douglas saw me pay him.

Thursday 16 March: John Griffiths sent a man up to mend the leakage in the leaden gutter in my room.

Nov. 30th 97
2.30 p.m.

My dear Lizzie,

Only just come down stairs.

The man came here yesterday 2.30 p.m. by train from Swansea & left here 4.30 for Garnant to go home. He is a very active, smart man, quite up to business I should say, said there was room for great improvement on this land, that he thought the place would suit him, but that he would speak to them at home before saying any thing and begged me to give him the first chance. He has a Wife, a daughter aged 18, one son 15 & one son 13 & from there down to 2 yrs. He attends the Swansea Market every Saturday.

He said I am off a good deal & keep people to work. He was very near taking a farm from T. J. Drummond but an old tenant was before him. He begged me to write to Mr. Davies Frood Vale for his character, he rents a few fields from him. I told him to bring his Wife, eldest boy & girl to see the place, he said he would, perhaps next week & for me to have Mr. Davies reply before then.

I really don't think I can write to Mr. Davies. Could you speak to Dr. Davies or you or Datta write to the Frood Vale man. I should like to have a good farmer, one to do up the hedges, ditches & to keep all clean and tidy about the house & on the land.

I can't write more. I am much the same. No letter, only paper today but I am quite satisfied.

Love to all from Nanna. I hope you are all middling.

Money Received

1897

1897		£ .. s .. d
Jan.	Garth (Thos. Davies) ½ a year's rent due Sep. 29th 96	20 .. 0 .. 0
23rd	T. Jones Int. on £700	21 .. 0 .. 0
12th	½ year's Int. on £525 due Decr. 31st 96	6 ..12 .. 3
Feb. 20th	Gellyluog ½ yrs. rent due Sep. 96	17 ..10 .. 0
March 3rd	Crachllwyn (Mrs. Jones) ½ a year's rent due Sep. 96	25 .. 0 .. 0
June 12th	Cwmllynfell (Wm. Price) ½ a yr's rent due March 97	22 ..10 .. 0
"	Hannah Williams Plas-y-bryn ½ a yr's rent due March 25th 97	1 ..10 .. 0
"	Mary Rees Plas-y-bryn	1 ..10 .. 0
"	David Williams Llynfell Cottage 1 yr's rent due March 25th 97	4 .. 0 .. 0
"	Llanddarog Cow & Calf	13 .. 0 .. 0
"	½ a yr's Int. on £525 due 30 June 97	6 ..12 .. 3
June 30th	Fresh butter sold in lbs. from Jan. to June	3 ..10 ..11
July	Julia's Calf to Thos. Davies 1 week old	1 .. 0 .. 0
	Garth (Thos. Davies) ½ a year's rent due March 25th 97	20 .. 0 .. 0

Memorial windows dedicated to the Penderel and Jones families formerly placed in Llangiwg Church
(Photo: courtesy of Huda Awad, Swansea)

POSTSCRIPT

Margaret died on Thursday 16 June 1898 in the White Room of Garth House at the age of 64 and was buried in her parents' grave in Llangiwg Churchyard. The notice of her death in the *Local Intelligence* column of *The Cambrian* gave no details of Margaret's life but did comment on her antecedents, referring to her mother as "a sister of the late Rev. Edward Pendrell" and that "The Pendrells are an old Glamorganshire family, tracing their ancestors back to the time of King Charles, when some members rendered valuable service to the luckless monarch".[1]

Margaret's Will, which had been written in 1888, bequeathed £500 to her cousin Richard Pendrill Llewelyn, Vicar of Llangynwyd, and, as he had predeceased her, to his only daughter Olwen Jane Pendrill Llewelyn. Margaret's "old servant Elizabeth Evans" was left £40 and servant Thomas Lloyd and "old workman" Evan Evans received £5 each "if in my service at the time of my death". A marginal annotation to the Will stated that Thomas Lloyd had left her service "5 or 6 years before Miss Jones died". Lizzie's husband Thomas Jones was given £100 and the residue was left to her beloved Lizzie: *"I give devise and bequeath to my cousin Elizabeth Jones who resided with me many years and who is now the wife of the above named Thomas Jones 2 Glenview Villas Llandilo the whole of my freehold farm of Garth the whole of my copyhold farm of Cwmllynfell both of which are situated in the parish of Llanguicke in the County of Glamorgan and the whole of my freehold farm of Gellyluog situated in the parish of Llangavelach in the County of Glamorgan for ever for her own sole and separate use free from debts control and interference of her Husband and the receipt in writing of the said Elizabeth Jones to be the only and sufficient discharge for all rents royalties and all monies paid to her under this my Will."* Margaret further charged her executors, Richard Pendrill Llewelyn and Elizabeth Jones, to "*pay my just debts and funeral expenses and that the residue of my property of whatever nature it may be and wherever situated be given to my afore named cousin Elizabeth Jones free from the debts control and interference of her Husband"*.

---

1. *The Cambrian,* 24 June 1898.

Family gravestone of Evan, Catherine and Margaret Jones, Llangiwg Churchyard
(Photo: P. W. Jackson)

Grave of Thomas and Lizzie Jones, Llangiwg Churchyard
(Photo: P. W. Jackson)

Wishing to perpetuate Margaret's memory in the church she held so dear, Lizzie and Tom commissioned R. J. Newbery of Fitzroy Square, London, to design a stained glass window which was installed on 12 December 1898. Lizzie and Tom moved their family to Garth and an indication of the worth of Lizzie's inheritance may be gained from her return to the Surveyor of Taxes, dated 13 January 1900,[2] which itemised the portfolio of properties in her name, their gross rental and tenants' names:

Garth House & Land	– gross	rental	£20 – Tom Jones
Garth Farm	"	"	£40 – David Morgan
Cwmllynfell Farm	"	"	£45 – William Price
6 cottages on Cwmllynfell Farm	"	"	£19..10..0, minerals valued at £200 in 1898 for duties on land values
Crachlwyn Farm	"	"	£50 – Esther Jones
Gelliluog Farm	"	"	£35 – Thomas Jones
2 houses in Latimer Street, Llandeilo	"	"	£54

Lizzie and Tom lived at Garth until their deaths, within days of each other, in 1923. Tom Jones died on 16 October, aged 77 years, and was closely followed by Lizzie, aged 72, on 25 October. Both were buried in the family plot in Llangiwg Church alongside their sons David Othniel Hilary, who died on 4 May 1886 aged 10 months, and Colin who died of tuberculosis on 14 May 1922 aged 29 years. A memorial tablet inside the church refers to Tom's contribution as Church warden over 20 years and to Lizzie as a faithful worshipper. Inscribed below their names is the dedication: "*They were lovely and pleasant in their lives/ And in their death they were not divided.*"

At her death the gross value of Lizzie's estate was £9,796. Probate of her Will was granted to her three sons Alfred Ynyr Douglas Jones of 37 Claremont Road, Highgate, a local government officer, Flight Lieutenant Hubert Wilson Godfrey Jones, a serving officer stationed at RAF Northolt, and Elton Augustus Harold Jones, who ran the Garth estate with a bailiff. She left £200 to the Swansea and South Wales Institute for the Blind, and an annual sum of £5..5..0 to be paid on the seventh day of the seventh month in each year for the upkeep of Llangiwg parish churchyard "unless and until the Church of England in Wales is disestablished". The residue of her property, including the silver plate known as the 'Pendrill Plate', was left to her sons.

2. West Glamorgan Archive Service, Ace. 3474, Box 1/8.

During the Great War three of the brothers served with distinction. Douglas served in the Royal Army Medical Corps, evacuating wounded and dying soldiers from the battlefields to casualty field stations. He saw action at Ypres, was mentioned in dispatches and was awarded the Meritorious Service Medal. In 1918 he returned to work for the London County Council, becoming the Chief Administrative and Establishment Officer in its Public Health Department until his retirement in 1947. Godfrey volunteered and was gazetted as a Second Lieutenant in the 4th Battalion of the Welsh Regiment in April 1913, was landed at Suvla Bay, Gallipoli and was wounded in the fighting for Scimitar Hill in August 1915. On his recovery he transferred to the newly-formed Royal Flying Corps and qualified as a pilot in April 1916. He flew combat patrols over the Somme, shot down several enemy aircraft, was himself shot down twice and wounded. He was awarded the Military Cross, the Italian Al Valore Militaire and later the Air Force Cross. He remained in the R.A.F. as an instructor at the Central Flying School. He was later given command of No. 19 Squadron until August 1928 when he was placed on the Retired List. As a senior and much decorated pilot he flew again during the early years of the Second World War until he was killed on a test flight in 1943 when his plane exploded. Harold was commissioned at the age of 19 and posted as a tank commander in the Royal Tank Corps, and fought at the Somme and Cambrai. After the war he returned and helped his parents in running Garth and, after their death, was delegated full control of the estate by his brothers.[3]

To honour their mother's wish to commemorate their lineal connection with the Penderel name, the brothers petitioned by deed poll to replace their surname of 'Jones' with that of 'Penderel', and the change was gazetted to take effect from 1 January 1929. Douglas died in 1963 and Harold in 1967. Margaret's home and her farms passed to Harold's daughter, Jennifer Morris, who continues to live in Garth and currently retains ownership of its farm and of the Cwmllynfell property.

3. There are brief pen-portraits of Godfrey and Harold Penderel in *Around Pontardawe*, Second Selection (1999), 102, 123.

BIOGRAPHICAL NOTES

Margaret's relatives, friends and acquaintances most frequently noted in the Diaries.

Alexander Bain: colliery proprietor and owner of Hendreforgan Farm (125 acres).

Ernest Benthall: former Clerk in the India Office, London, married Jane Rogers Price, daughter of Dr. William & Mary Price of Glan Twrch, on 28/12/1876.

Jenkin Davies Berrington: solicitor and partner in firm of Berrington, Jenkins and Berrington, High Street, Swansea. Born 1801, the eldest son of Arthur Davies of Llandovery (who assumed the surname of Davies-Berrington by Royal Licence in 1798) and Anne Morgan of Cathylyd (Childs, 1994, 71, 86). He married Charlotte Hall and lived in Woodlands Castle (now Clyne Castle) and had three sons. He owned land in various locations including Llangiwg parish and 429 acres in Gower. The Berrington Estate Papers (West Glamorgan Archive Service D/D Xge 32) contain the deeds of Pantyffynon Estate near Ammanford and a number of farms between Penclawdd, Loughor and Dunvant.

Mrs. Henry Bowman: Margaret's "affectionate friend" and correspondent, of 13 Sheffield Gardens, Kensington, sister of William Lord Lytton and sister-in-law of Dowager Lady Bowman.

Emily Budd: née Rawson, "a lady of wealth and beauty . . . the ideal Lady Bountiful", married James Palmer Budd (1803-83), D.L., managing partner of Ystalyfera Iron & Tin Plate Company (Phillips, 1925, 41-3), lived in Ynysydarren House, Ystalyfera, died 14/5/1880, aged 64.

Elizabeth Evans (Betty) (1826-1901): daughter of Thomas Evans of Troedyrhiw, general servant at Garth for 40 years and Margaret's constant support. She died on 23/2/1901 aged 75 and was buried in Llangiwg churchyard near Margaret.

Zephania Evans (1834-): postmaster, grocer, corn and flour merchant, Poor Law Guardian for Pontardawe.

Catherine Anne Gilbertson (1845-1933): daughter of William Gilbertson and generally known as Kate, married William Fisk Richardson on 2/8/1871.

Ellen Gilbertson (1850-94): second daughter of Francis Edwardes Lloyd of Plas Cilybebyll. In 1872 she married Arthur Gilbertson, managing director of W. Gilbertson & Company, and died on 15 March 1894 following the birth of her fourteenth child.

Fanny Gilbertson (1844-1937): spinster daughter of William Gilbertson and a good friend of Lizzie.

Richard Douglas Gough (1800-86): son of Rev. Fleming Gough and Martha Taylor. Owned Ynyscedwyn Iron Works, substantial landowner, Sheriff of Breconshire, J.P. for Breconshire and Glamorgan. Married Constance Elizabeth Dansey in 1840.

Katherine Charlotte Grenfell (1843-1906): daughter of Pascoe St. Leger Grenfell and Catherine Ann du Pre of Maesteg House, Kilvey. Married Edward Henry Thornton, a Nottingham banker, on 15/2/1871.

Elizabeth Griffiths (1841-1915): née Whittington of Neath, married Dr. Griffith Griffiths (1840-1908) in 1865 and lived in Bryncelyn, Pontardawe.

Howel Gwyn (1806-88): landowner, local squire and philanthropist. Born in Neath, the son of William Gwyn (1766-1830) and Mary Anne Roberts. Educated Trinity College Oxford (1825-29), member of Inner Temple 1829, Conservative M.P. for Penryn & Falmouth (1847-57) and for Brecon (1866). Lived in Baglan House until 1835. Inherited much of Alltwen from his father and bought Dyffryn mansion in Bryncoch, Neath. Married Ellen Elizabeth Moore in 1851. High Sheriff of Glamorgan (1837), Carmarthenshire (1838) and Breconshire (1839); J.P. for the three counties; Neath councillor (1838), Alderman (1848) and Mayor (1847-57) (Davies, 1992). Owned 1,428 acres in Llangyfelach parish, which was approx. 20% of his south Wales estate (Griffiths, 1973, 42).

Ernest Hall Hedley: J.P., county councillor and mining engineer who married Mary Ann Lewis on 10/2/1881 and lived in Alltacham House, Pontardawe (*AP2, 67, 102*).

John Borlase Jenkins (1823-80): a fire brick manufacturer at the Dinas Works in Neath, living in Bryn Syfi House, Kilvey. He was the nephew of Elias Jenkins (1777-1850) and the son of John Borlase Jenkins Snr. (1790-1850) who was a copper smelting agent (1823) and later works manager of Grenfell's Whiterock Copper Works, member of the Board of Guardians and a Burgess.

Mary Borlase Jenkins (1811-1900): unmarried sister of J.B. Jenkins Jnr., lived in Bryn Syfi House and was a close friend of Margaret. She died on 13/11/1900 and was buried in the parish church of Llantwit-juxta-Neath.

Rachel Borlase Jenkins (1815-75): unmarried sister of J.B. Jenkins and lived in Bryn Syfi House. Died 23/3/1875 after "many years an invalid" (*The Cambrian*, 2/4/1875).

Richard Borlase Jenkins (1818-77): solicitor based at 18 York Street, Swansea, and brother of J. B. Jenkins Jnr.

Sarah Jenkins (1819-75): unmarried sister of Mary Price, living successively at 1, Kensington Place and Grosvenor Cottage, Clifton, and at 6 Berkeley Square, Bristol, where she died on 8/4/75. Her will, with effects under £8,000, was proved by executors Dr. William Price and John Borlase Jenkins.

Catherine Jones (1793-1857): daughter of Richard Jones and Catherine Pendrill of Ynyscedwyn, married Evan Jones, 1831, and was Margaret's mother.

David Jones (1804-75): Evan Jones's only brother, Lizzie's father and Margaret's uncle. Farmed Llwynyronnen, Betws, Carmarthenshire. Married Susan Jones (1821-) on 4/3/1842 in Ystradgynlais and had 6 children. He died on 1/4/1875 and his will, effects under £200, was proved by son John, the sole executor.

Evan Jones (1801-64): son of Richard (1754-1823) of Cwmllynfell Farm and Margaret Rees (1762-1850). Married Catherine Pendrill (1793-1857) at Llangiwg Church on 22/3/1831. Margaret's father.

Lizzie Jones (1851-1923): daughter of David and Susan Jones of Llwynyronnen Farm (34 acres), Betws. Margaret's cousin and companion, married Tom Jones, 10/1/1884.

Tom Jones (1846-1923): son of Rees and Lettice Jones of Llwyn-cwm Farm (194 acres), Betws, a neighbouring farm to Llwynyronnen where Lizzie's father had lived. He married Lizzie Jones in 1884 when his occupation was registered as a farmer of Llwyn-cwm. In 1891 he was employed by his brother as a Brewery Manager and lived in 2, Glenview Villas, Llandeilo. Member of the Llandeilo Rifle Volunteer Band. He moved with Lizzie to Garth after Margaret's death. Children: David Othniel Hilary (1885-6), Alfred Ynyr Douglas (1887-1963), stillborn daughter (17/2/1889), Hubert Wilson Godfrey (1890-1943), Colin (1892-1922) and Elton Augustus Harold (1896-1967).

Sarah Kirkhouse (1832-): Head of The Ferns, a girls' school in Alltwen. Widow of George Kirkhouse, surgeon, 3 children: George, a medical practitioner who died aged 33 on 21/1/1894, Mary, a governess, and Harriet (Lalla) who married Charles Belcher on 17/11/1871.

Anna Jennet (Netta) Lewis: third child of Griffith and Margaret Lewis of Alltacham, married Robert Thornley, a Birmingham merchant, on 13/7/1871.

Griffith Lewis (1814-87): brother of Jacob Lewis. Coal proprietor who, with his brother-in-law John Morgan (1802-67) of Gelligron, owned several coal-mining concerns including the Primrose Coal Company (*AP 3, 100*). His eldest daughter Mary Ann married Ernest Hall Hedley on 10/2/1881 (*AP 2,* 102).

Jacob Lewis (1803-70): established the Pontardawe Chemical Works in 1851. Lived in Ynysgelynen, married Elizabeth Pollard (1806-83) in 1828 and had 10 children (*AP 2*, 53).

Lewis Griffith Lewis (1830-1920): second son of Jacob and Elizabeth Lewis, manufacturing chemist, married Elizabeth Sarah Fear (1835-1903) of Neath in June 1859 and built Brynheulog (*AP 2*, 54)

Lewis Harry Lewis (1860-1943): eldest son of Lewis Griffith Lewis, born at Brynheulog and with his brother Sidney assumed control of the Chemical Works on the death of his father. Married Victoria Ellen Worthington (1870-1944) on 4/12/1889 (*AP 2,* 55).

Richard Pendrill Llewelyn (1813-1891): son of Thomas Llewelyn who was briefly the tenant of Whitney Farm, Merthyr Mawr, and Jane Pendrill, eldest daughter of Richard Pendrill of Ynyscedwyn and sister of Catherine, Margaret's mother. Thomas Llewelyn abandoned his family in 1814 and reputedly died fighting for Bolivar in Venezuela in 1818. Married Mary Catherine, daughter of Thomas Rhys, owner of the Eagle Academy, Cowbridge. He was the Vicar of Llangynwyd for 50 years and a close confidant of Margaret who invariably referred to him as R.P.L.

Frances Harictte Lloyd (1838-1929): formerly Purdon of County Clare, wife of Herbert Lloyd (1838-1914) of Plâs Cilybcbyll, in 1864, and a major landowner in the area, J.P., High Sheriff and several public offices. Eleven children (*AP 1,* 63-4).

Mary Mackenzie: unmarried niece of Miss Pendrill of Bath.

Mary Marryat (1795-1882): formerly Lindsay, married Joseph Marryat the Younger (1791-1876) in St. George's Church, Hanover Square, on 19/10/1819. He was a London banker and proprietor of Ystradgynlais Iron Works, living in Maesydderwen House in 1861 with five servants. A close friend of Margaret to whom she wrote on 9/9/1866 thanking her for her "*kind thought of us, in sending the Partridges*" and warning her: "*Don't think of coming to us if you have <u>any fear</u>. Cholera is <u>here</u> as well as in Ystalyfera.*" She continued to correspond with Margaret after leaving Ystradgynlais in 1866.

Georgina Nancarrow (1839-): born in Gwennap, Cornwall, and married to Henry Nancarrow, manager of the Landore copper works. In 1871 they lived near Bryn Syfi in 1, Mackworth Villas, St. Thomas, Swansea, with their son and daughter and Henry's parents. By 1881 Georgina was widowed and lived at the same address with her stepson George (aged 22), copper works agent, and her unmarried younger sister Selina Michel. By 1891 both Georgina and Selina were living together in Cornwall.

Edward Pendrill: son of Richard and Catherine Pendrill of Pentwrch, Ynyscedwyn, and the Rector of Cilybebyll 1823-37. He officiated at the marriage of his sister

Catherine to Evan Jones in Llangiwg Church on 22/3/1831. He was unmarried and in his will (dated 12/3/1839) bequeathed all his household and personal estate to his three sisters, Jane Llewelyn, Elizabeth Jones and Catherine Jones, with Catherine named as sole executrix. He was not highly regarded by Bishop Copplestone (Brown, 2003, *Letters 194, 198, 203).*

Richard Pendrill (1760-1814): Margaret's maternal grandfather, lived in Twrch Lodge, Ystradgynlais and was buried in the family tomb in St. Cadog's Churchyard, Ystradgynlais, with his wife Catherine, née Hopkins (1762-1838), surgeon sons Thomas (1790-1817) and Richard (1795-1831), and Edward (1799-1839), perpetual curate of Llangiwg.

Gwenllian Price (1806-73): daughter of Rev. Watkin Price, Rector of Cilybebyll, and Dorothy Penderel, and a sister of Dr. William Price of Glan Twrch. Lived in Tretower, Pembrokeshire.

Mary Price (1811-92): daughter of Elias Jenkins (1777-1850), partner and manager for nearly 50 years of the White Rock Copper Works, Swansea, and Jane Rogers. Cousin of John Borlase Jenkins Jnr. She lived at Kilvey House with sisters Rebecca, Elizabeth and Sarah before marrying Dr. William Price of Glan Twrch in 1845. Two daughters: Jane Rogers (1846-) who married Ernest Benthall in 1876, and Dora Penderel (1847-75).

William Price (1802-78): son of Rev. Watkin Price, Rector of Cilybebyll, and Dorothy Penderel (1769-1843). Medical practitioner, married Mary Jenkins on 15/7/1845.

Mary Shenton (1836-): lived with her sister Mrs. Theophila Thomas in 17, Garnant Villas, Betws. Both born in Wolverhampton.

David Bevan Turberville: solicitor, partner in firm of Cuthbertson & Turberville, Neath, Clerk to Llangiwg School Board.

Mary Prescott Whittington (1814-80): widowed *c.*1848 with four dependent children, listed as a postmistress in the Neath censuses of 1851 and 1861. Her daughter Elizabeth married Dr. Griffith Griffiths in 1865. She died at their Bryncelyn home on 24/8/1880.

Amelia Elizabeth Williams (Minnie): married John Morgan, owner of Wauncoed colliery and brother-in-law of Griffith Lewis. Lived in Gelligron House.

Sarah Fox Williams (Dotty): daughter of Rev. Charles Williams, Vicar of Llangiwg, married Stephen George of Bristol on 13/4/1871 at St. Peter's Church, Pontardawe.

Note: *AP 1, AP 2 & AP 3* refer to *Around Pontardawe*, Selections 1, 2 & 3.

APPENDIX 1

THE PENDEREL/PENDRILL LINEAGE

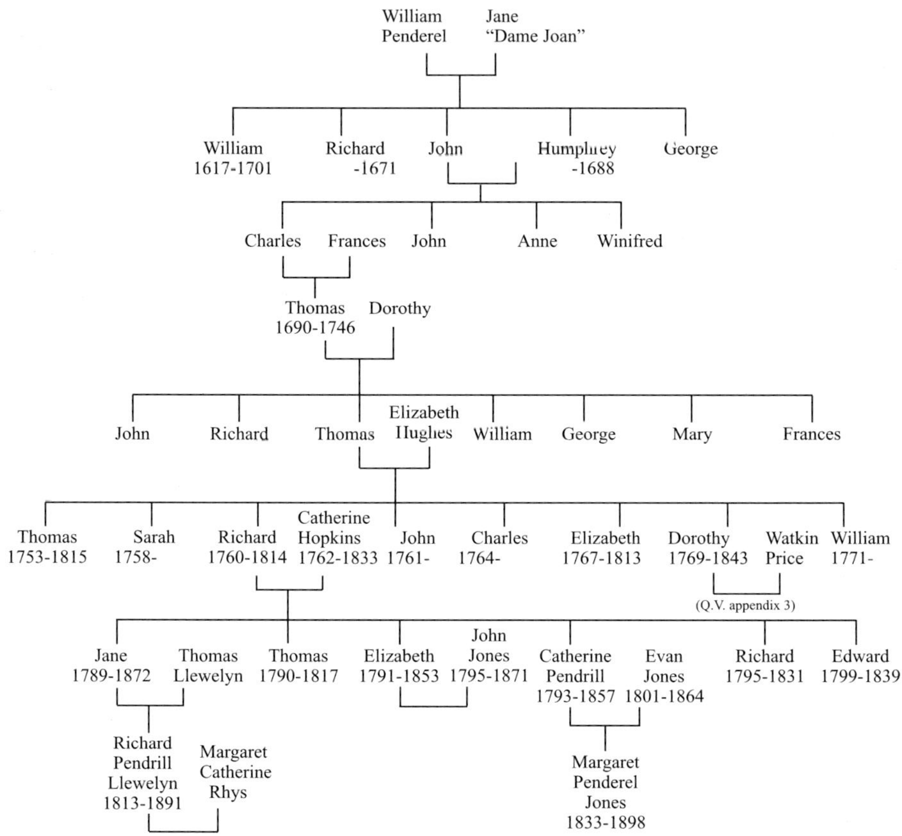

Note: The data for the early generations are based on Whittington 1993 table 4, 24

APPENDIX 2

THE DECENDANTS OF RICHARD AND MARGARET JONES

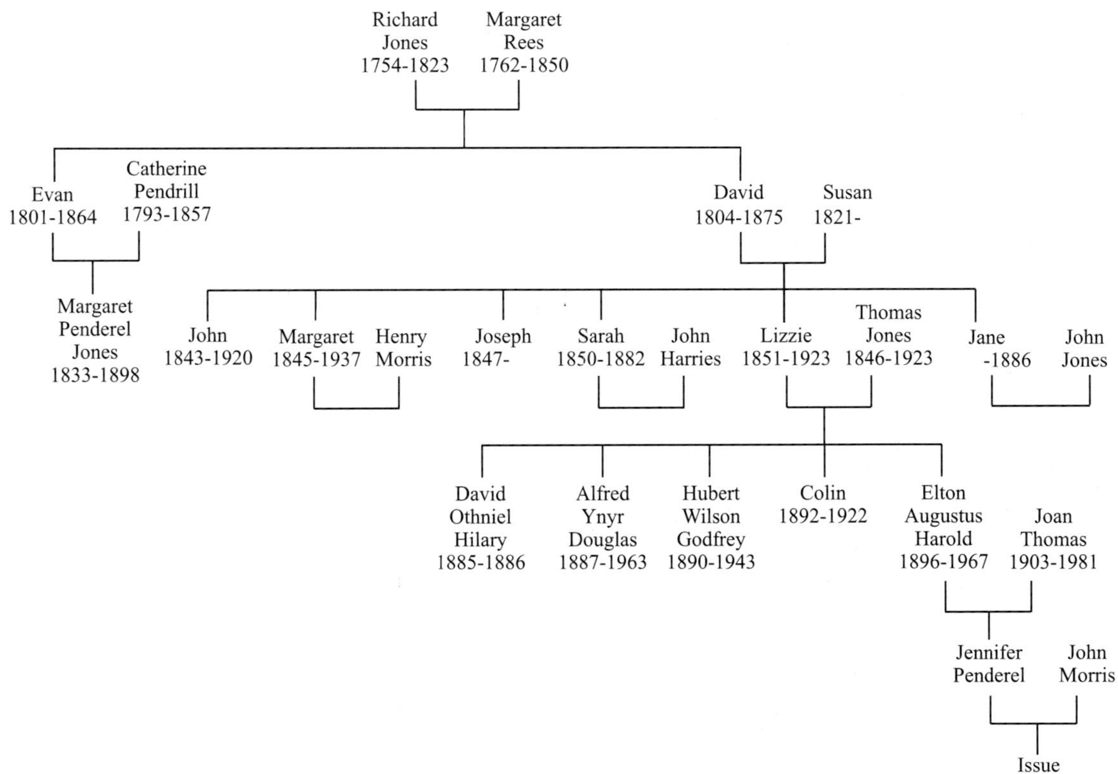

APPENDIX 3

THE PRICE FAMILY OF GLAN TWRCH

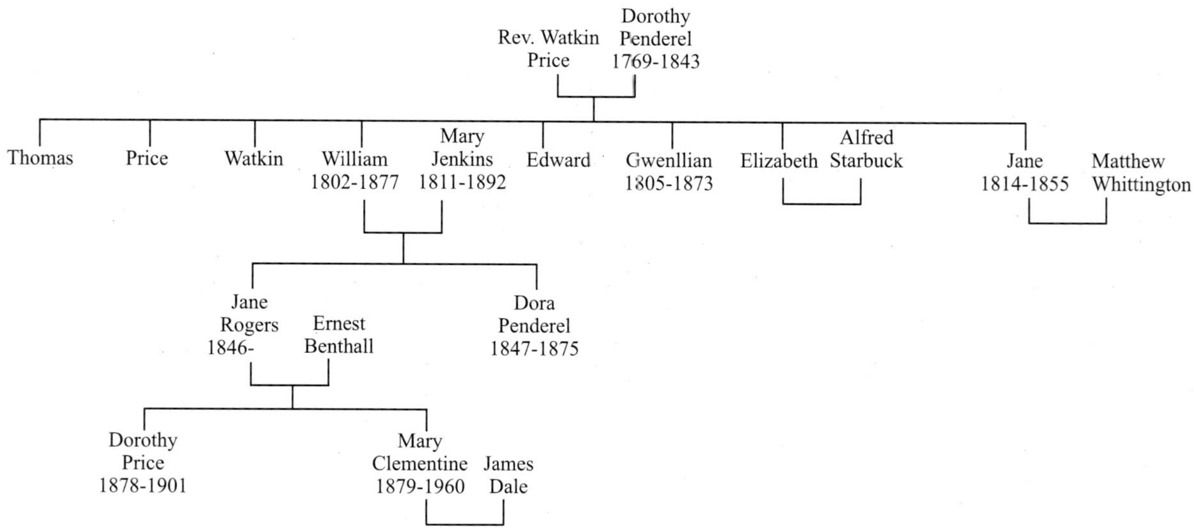

APPENDIX 4

THE JENKINS FAMILIES OF KILVEY

(a) Kilvey House

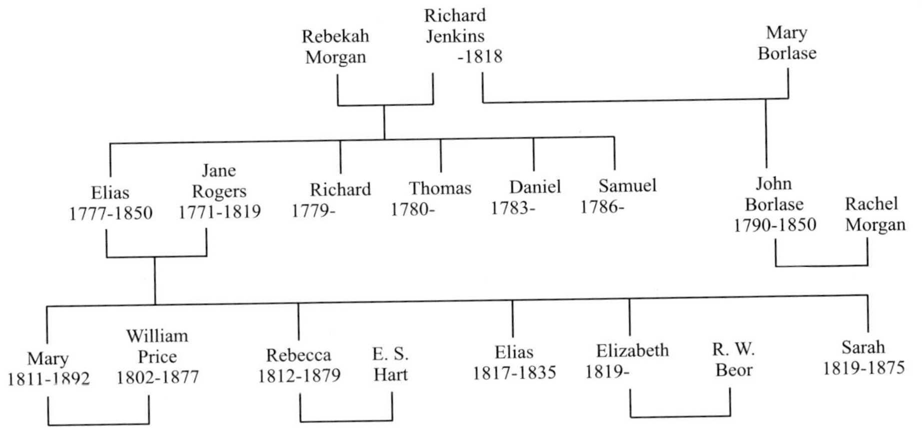

(b) Bay View and Bryn Syfi

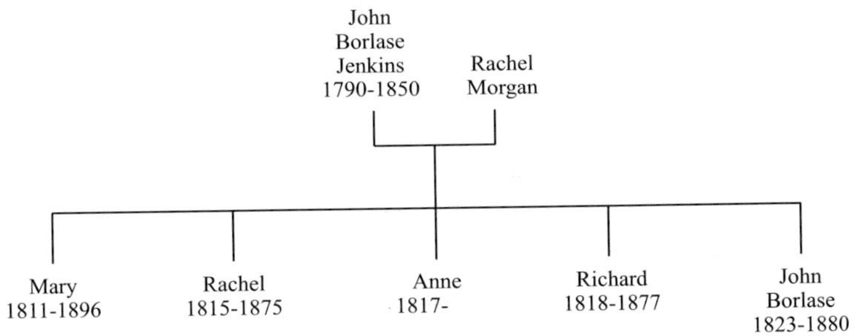

APPENDIX 5

SEMPER EADEM

Fidelity and Fortitude fear no Danger.

For Loyalty is still the same,
Whether it win or lose ye Game;

True as the Dial to the Sun,
Altho' it be not shined upon

Richard Penderel, of Hobball Grange, near Brewood in Staffordshire, generally known at Court in the Reign of King Charles the Second, by the name of **Trusty Dick,** having happily preserved His Majesty from the Fury of those keen hunters after Royal Blood the Soldiers of **Cromwell,** with his five Brothers conduct and guard their unfortunate Sovereign from his Asylum the famous Royal Oak in Roscobel Wood, to **Mr. Whitgreaves,** of Mosely, from whence, disguised like a Farmer's Son, his hair cut short to his ears like the **Roundheads or Puritans** of those times, through innumerable dangers and fatigues, He safely arrived in France; and after the Restoration, that the Fidelity and eminent Services of **Trusty Dick** might be transmitted to Posterity, his Majesty settled an Annuity of one hundred Pounds on Him and his Heirs for ever, and gave him a Coat of Arms apertinently exhibiting his own Troubles and the Bearers Merit.

Mr. Penderel for his unbiassed honesty and Integrity, lived and died in honourable Esteem of all that were friends to the Royal Cause and Regal Government, and lies buried in St. Giles's Church in the Fields, where a small Monument bears this Inscription.

Here lieth

Richard Penderel,

Preserver and Conductor to his Sacred Majesty King Charles the Second of Great Britain, after his Escape from Worcester Fight in the Year 1651, who died February 8th, 1671.

Hold Passenger, here is shrouded in this Hearse,
Unparrallel'd Penderel through the Universe;
Like when the Eastern Star from Heaven gave light
To three lost Kings, so he in such dark Night,
To Britain's Monarch lost by adverse War,
On Earth appeared a second Eastern Star,

A Pole Astern in her Rebellious Main,
A Pilot to his Royal Sovereign;
Now to triumph in Heaven's Eternal Sphere,
He's hence advanced for his just Sovereign here.
Whilst Albion's Chronicle with matchless fame,
Embalms the Story of Great Penderel's Name.

His present Majesty, in Memory of such exemplary Merit in low Life, ordered Mr. Penderel's Monument to be Cleaned up and beautified in the year 1739.

Thus do the virtues of the Brave and Just,
O'er Death triumph and flourish in the Dust.

The Arms appertaining to the Penderel Family, Beareth Argent, an Oak growing out of a Mount proper, On a Chief Azure, three Imperial Crowns proper; The Crest, a Sword and Scepter in Saltire, an Imperial Crown proper.

BIBLIOGRAPHY

Primary sources

Diaries of Margaret Penderel Jones for 1871, 1873 to 1876, 1880 to 1882, 1888 to 1897.

Garth archive of correspondence, notebooks, exercise books, maps and miscellaneous papers.

Manuscripts: West Glamorgan Archive Service: *Price Family Papers c.1790-1890 D/D Z 277, 725; Price, Jenkins and Benthall families of Glantwrch D/D Je 78-122; Indentures, Conveyance, deeds etc. to Crachllwynucha and Crachllwynfach farms; Berrington estate D/D Xge 32; Jones family of Brynbrain Farm D/D Z 620/1.*

Secondary sources

PUBLISHED BOOKS AND PAMPHLETS

R. L. Brown, *The Copplestone Letters*, South Wales Record Society, 2003.

M. J. Daunton, *Progress and Poverty: An Economic and Social History of Britain 1700-1850*, OUP, 1995.

J. H. Davies, *History of Pontardawe and District*, Christopher Davies, Llandybie, 1967.

T. G. Davies, *Howel Gwyn of Dyffryn and Neath (1806-1888)*, Glamorgan Press, Neath, 1992.

Jane Eastoe, *Victorian Pharmacy*, Pavilion, 2010.

D. Gareth Evans, *A History of Wales, 1815-1906*, UWP Cardiff, 1989.

Angela Holdsworth, *Out of the Doll's House*, BBC Books, 1988.

David W. Howell, *Land and People in Nineteenth-Century Wales*, Routledge & Kegan Paul, 1997.

Stephen Hughes, *Copperopolis: Landscapes of the Early Period in Swansea*, Royal Commission on the Ancient and Historical Monuments of Wales, Cambrian Printers Ltd., Aberystwyth, 2008.

S. Hughes & P. Reynolds, *A Guide to the Industrial Archaeology of the Swansea Region*, 1992.

P. W. Jackson, *The Letter-Books of W. Gilbertson & Co. Ltd., Pontardawe, 1890-1929*, Dinefwr Press Ltd., Llandybie, 2001.

Phillip Jenkins, *A History of Modern Wales, 1536-1990*, Longman, 1992.

D. R. & G. A. Jones, *The Mist of Time*, Down to Business, Skewen, 2005.
D. R. L. Jones, *Richard and Mary Pendrill Llewelyn*, Gibbs Maesteg, 1991.
Ieuan Gwynedd Jones, *Health, Wealth and Politics in Victorian Wales*, Gower Press for U.C. Swansea, 1979.
Ieuan Gwynedd Jones, *Essays in the Social History of Victorian Wales*, Llandysul, 1987.
Ray Lawrence, *The South Wales Coalfield Directory*, Vol. 2, 1998.
John Lewis, *The Swansea Guide*, Brewster, 1851, reprinted WGCC, 1989.
Joshua Lewis, *Hanes y Gwrhyd*, Rees, Ystalyfera, 1897.
C. Lloyd, *Rhyd-y-Fro Primary School Centenary 1877-1977*, May 1977.
John Lloyd, *The Lloyds of Plâs Cilybebyll*, Andreas Haaf, Port Talbot, 1990.
Kenneth O. Morgan, *Rebirth of a Nation Wales 1880-1980*, OUP/UWP, 1982.
J. H. Morris & L. J. Williams, *The South Wales Coal Industry 1841-75*, UWP Cardiff, 1958.
G. Parry & M. A. Williams, *The Welsh Language and the 1891 Census*, UWP, 1999.
D. R. Phillips, *The History of the Vale of Neath*, Dinefwr Press, 1994.
Elizabeth Phillips, *A History of the Pioneers of the Welsh Coalfield, Western Mail*, Cardiff, 1925.
Gwynedd O. Pierce, *The Place-names of Dinas Powys Hundred*, UWP Cardiff, 1968.
Matilda Marion Pullan, *Maternal Counsels to a Daughter*, 1855.
The Pontardawe Historians, *Around Pontardawe*, Chalford Publishing Company, 1996; *Around Pontardawe, The Second Selection*, Tempus Publishing Limited, 1999; *Around Pontardawe, The Third Selection*, The History Press, 2013.
G. Penderel Whittington, *Streets Paved with Gold*, GC Book Pub., Wigtown, 1993.
C. H. Williams (ed), *Language in Geographic Context*, Clevedon, 1988.
E. I. Williams, *St. Peter's Church*, Origin, Swansea, 1996.

JOURNAL ARTICLES

Malcolm Barton, 'Pascoe St. Leger Grenfell and his Daughters through the eyes of *The Cambrian*', *Minerva*, No. 17, 2009/10, 22-39.
Muriel E. Chamberlain, 'The Grenfells of Kilvey', *Glamorgan Historian*, Vol. 9, Stewart Williams Pubs., 1973, 123-142.
Jeff Childs, 'Landownership Changes in a Glamorgan Parish, 1750-1850', *Morgannwg*, XVIII, 1994, XX-86.
Abraham Evans, 'Cwmgors Colliery', *Ein Cyngor*, Spring 1964, 40-1.
G. E. Fussell, 'Glamorgan Farming: An Outline of its Modern History', *Morgannwg*, 1957, 31-4.
M. Alan Griffiths, 'Agricultural Developments in South Wales 1830-1875: the case of some Glamorgan parishes', *Morgannwg*, XVII, 1973, 25-50.
D. R. L. Jones, 'Sins of the Father: A Georgian Story of Misfortune', *Morgannwg*, Vol. 38, 1994, 88-100.

R. J. Moore-Colyer, 'Farmers and Fields in Nineteenth-century Wales: the case of Llanrhystud, Cardiganshire', *National Library of Wales Journal*, 1989, Vol. XXVI/1.
Richard Peake, 'The Pendrell Family', *Archaeologia Cambrensis*, 1859, 114.
Hugh Thomas, 'The Industrialization of a Glamorgan Parish Llangiwg', *National Library of Wales Journal*, Vol. XIX.

DIRECTORIES

Slater's Commercial Directory 1871; Post Office Directory of Monmouthshire and South Wales 1871; Swansea Commercial Directory 1873-74; Kelly's Directory of Monmouthshire and South Wales 1895.

UNPUBLISHED DISSERTATIONS

C. P. Bateson, Population Change in a Nineteenth Century Industrial Community: a study of the Census Records of Pontardawe 1851-91, UWE MA, January 2001.

NEWSPAPERS

The Cambrian; The Cambria Daily Leader; South Wales Daily Post.

INDEX

Omitted from the Index are the names of individuals whose diary references were incomplete or obscured by the attribution of nicknames often based on occupational or locational characteristics, e.g. Daniel Saer, Margaret Thomas y Gove, Jacky y Nailer, Mary Tom y Crydd, John Derrybach and Jonah Pistyll Llwyd. This rich diversity of people, familiar to their local contemporaries, must unfortunately remain anonymous for the present.

Previous publications by the South Wales Record Society

1. Rice Merrick, *Morganiae Archaiographia* (1578), ed. Brian James, 1983.
2. George Yates, *Map of Glamorgan* (1799), introduction by Gwyn Walters & Brian James, 1984.
3. C. & J. Greenwood, *Map of Monmouthshire* (1830), introduction by Philip Riden, 1985.
4. *The Diaries of John Bird of Cardiff, 1790-1803*, ed. Hilary M. Thomas, 1987.
5. *Llandaff Episcopal Acta, 1140-1287*, ed. David Crouch, 1989.
6. *The Letterbook of Richard Crawshay, 1788-97*, eds C. Evans & G. G. L. Hayes, 1990.
7. *The Diocese of Llandaff in 1763*, ed. John R. Guy, 1991.
8. Sir J. A. Bradney, *A History of Monmouthshire*, vol. 5, ed. Madeleine Gray, 1993.
9. *The Penrice Letters, 1768-95*, ed. Joanna Martin, 1993.
10. *The Glamorgan Hearth Tax Assessment of 1670*, ed. Elizabeth Parkinson, 1994.
11. *The Diary of William Thomas of Michaelston-super-Ely, 1762-1795*, ed. R. T. W. Denning, 1995.
12. *Monmouthshire Wills, 1560-1601*, ed. Judith M. Jones, 1997.
13. *St Davids Episcopal Acta, 1185-1280*, ed. Julia Barrow, 1998.
14. *The Letter Book of John Byrd, 1648-1680*, ed. Stephen K. Roberts, 1999.
15. *The Pennard Manor Court Book, 1673-1701*, eds Michael J. Edmunds & Joanna Martin, 2000.
16. *The Letter-Books of W. Gilbertson & Co. Ltd., Pontardawe, 1890-1929*, ed. P. W. Jackson, 2001.
17. *The Letters of Edward Copleston, Bishop of Llandaff, 1828-1849*, ed. Roger Lee Brown, 2003.
18. *'Women's Rights and Womanly Duties': The Aberdare Women's Liberal Association, 1891-1910*, ed. Ursula Masson, 2005.
19. *Family and Society in Early Stuart Glamorgan: The Household Accounts of Sir Thomas Aubrey of Llantrithyd, c.1565-1641*, ed. Lloyd Bowen, 2006.
20. *In Conversation with Napoleon Bonaparte: J. H. Vivian's Visit to the Island of Elba*, ed. Ralph A. Griffiths, 2008.
21. *Men At Arms: Musters in Monmouthshire, 1539 and 1601-2*, ed. Tony Hopkins, 2009.
22. *The Swansea Wartime Diary of Laurie Latchford, 1940-41*, eds Kate Elliott Jones and Wendy Cope, 2010.
23. *The Origins of an Industrial Region: Robert Morris and the First Swansea Copper Works, c.1727-1730*, ed. Louise Miskell, 2011.
24. *William Downing Evans: Poetry and Poverty in Nineteenth-Century Newport*, eds. Ian and Wendy Dear, 2011.
25. *The Correspondence of Thomas Henry Thomas, 'Arlunydd Penygarn'*, ed. Christabel Hutchings, 2012.
26. *War Underground: Memoirs of a Bevin Boy in the South Wales Coalfield,* Michael Edmonds; ed. Peter Wakelin, 2013.